AUTHENTIC

SHAWN BOONSTRA

To: Jim Evenhouse
From: Anne Nelson
Hope you enjoy This book
shawn is a great Speaker!

Pacific Press®
Publishing Association
Nampa, Idaho | Oshawa, Ontario, Canada
www.pacificpress.com

Cover design by Gerald Lee Monks
Cover design resources from iStockphoto.com/wingmar
Inside design by Kristin Hansen-Mellish

The author assumes full responsibility for the accuracy of all facts and quotations as cited in this book.

Additional copies of this book may be purchased by calling toll-free 1-800-765-6955 or by visiting
http://www.adventistbookcenter.com.

Library of Congress Cataloging-in-Publication Data
Names: Boonstra, Shawn, author.
Title: Authentic : daily devotional / Shawn Boonstra.
Description: Nampa : Pacific Press Publishing Association, 2018.
Identifiers: LCCN 2018018298 | ISBN 9780816363568 (hardcover : alk. paper)
Subjects: LCSH: Devotional calendars—General Conference of Seventh-day
    Adventists.
Classification: LCC BV4811 .B5925 2018 | DDC 242/.2—dc23 LC record available at https://lccn.
loc.gov/2018018298

May 2018

I Believe

The following pages are meant to be devotional in nature. They are not a full doctrinal exposition of our beliefs; that has been done elsewhere many times. Nor is this an apologetic work, designed to offer a defense of our faith. It is assumed that the reader has already come to understand and believe the essential doctrines that inform our last-day movement. Each entry is simply a moment of reflection, a brief peek at one small facet of the stunning picture of Jesus provided to us through the three angels' messages.

There are currently thirteen vows, summaries of biblical beliefs, that candidates claim as their own upon becoming a part of this movement. There are only twelve months to the year, so I have been left with no choice but to spend less than thirty days on some of them. The space devoted to a single subject is not to be understood as a statement of how much—or little—I might value each topic. I value them all immensely—the doctrines of the Adventist Church are the reason I am here today. In writing this book, I have simply prayed about the topic I should explore each day, and then by faith, I have followed the prompting of the Spirit.

I grew up around Christians. I even had the benefit of a Christian education in my early childhood. I have never seen such a complete and magnificent revelation of Christ as I have found in the Seventh-day Adventist message. To understand our doctrines—from the sanctuary and the Sabbath to the health message and the state of the dead—is to better understand the mind of God and to know Jesus more intimately.

That is my prayer for you this year, that you will find yourself drawn ever nearer to the One who stepped down from glory to be closer to you.

January

I believe there is one God: Father, Son, and Holy Spirit,
a unity of three coeternal Persons.

The Good News About Who You Are

In the beginning God created the heavens and the earth.
—Genesis 1:1

Like many adopted children, Matthew Roberts set out later in life to find his biological parents, and the search led him in a direction he could not possibly have predicted. After some legwork, he managed to find his birth mother, but she proved to be hesitant to reveal his father's identity. When she finally divulged it, Roberts was horrified: his biological father was Charles Manson, the notorious sixties cult leader and serial killer.

The news was unsettling, to say the least. Would Matthew inherit his father's tendencies? Would he turn out to be as psychotic as his father?

"I didn't want to believe it," Matthew said. "It's like finding out that Adolf Hitler is your father. I'm a peaceful person—trapped in the face of a monster."★

Most of us instinctively sense that origins matter. Where we come from plays a role in determining who we are, the tendencies we have, and the direction we are headed. Across cultures and around the globe, the search for our human origin is one of humanity's most basic instincts—and our deepest needs.

Matthew Roberts's search led to a troubling conclusion, but our search need not. The Bible offers good news with the first four words on the very first page: "In the beginning *God*." He is the origin of everything that exists, and He is the reason that you have life. Much of the twenty-first-century world has tried to portray God as untrustworthy: a cruel dictator, a malevolent deity not unlike the capricious gods of pagan mythology. And if all we read were the first few words of the book of Genesis, we might be tempted to draw a similar conclusion: if God gave birth to all that is, then perhaps God is not good.

Fortunately, the Bible contains many more words—astonishing words that paint a picture of hope. God is anxious to have us rediscover Him and find the truth about ourselves. You and I are but a mere shadow of what God intended the human race to be; but in finding the truth about God, we will have a better sense of who we are—or who we are *supposed* to be.

★ Mail Foreign Service, " 'It's Like Finding Out Hitler Is Your Dad': DJ Matthew Roberts Tracks Down Long-Lost Father ... But Discovers He's Charles Manson," *Daily Mail*, November 24, 2009, http://www.dailymail.co.uk/news/article-1230439/.

Your Deepest Need

Thus says the LORD: "Let not the wise man glory in his wisdom,
let not the mighty man glory in his might, nor let the rich man glory in his riches;
but let him who glories glory in this, that he understands and knows Me,
that I am the LORD, exercising lovingkindness, judgment, and righteousness in the earth.
For in these I delight," says the LORD.
—Jeremiah 9:23, 24

Ask a group of people what a human being's greatest need is, and you are likely to hear the word *love*. It is a natural assumption, given the way that popular culture has become saturated with the concept. From the Beatles' "All You Need Is Love" to nearly every pop song written since, we have been told, millions of times over, that love is the most important need we have.

There is little doubt that human beings have a profound need for genuine love and affection. For example, studies have repeatedly shown that in orphanages, neglected babies fare more poorly than those who receive personal attention. We *need* personal relationships with people who care.

But is love our *most* profound need? Probably not. It would seem that our search for *meaning* runs far deeper than our search for love. We want to know that our lives have purpose. To that end, many pursue power and wealth, as Jeremiah points out. The problem with such pursuits, however, is that they rarely satisfy our search for significance: the wealthy and powerful have also been known to suffer from depression and have feelings of hopelessness and suicidal thoughts.

The Creator offers a much surer path to meaning. God says, "Let him who glories glory in this, that he understands and knows Me" (Jeremiah 9:24).

Not only does this passage offer purpose and hope, but it also reveals something profound about the nature of God: He is *knowable*. Even though God is infinite and we are emphatically finite; even though God is vast and we are small; even though our capacity to grasp things outside of our own experience is deficient, God tells us that we can know and understand Him. Not only is He discoverable, He also is understandable.

And what we find as we get to know Him will not only give us purpose, it will offer us incredible hope: God is both loving and just. His character inspires hope. He can be trusted.

The wise understand that human achievement passes away and that might or riches are always fleeting. But those who anchor their existence in the One who gave it, those who long to understand God, will find cause to glory.

He's Waiting—Outside

For since the creation of the world His invisible attributes are clearly seen,
being understood by the things that are made, even His eternal power
and Godhead, so that they are without excuse.

—Romans 1:20

The English clergyman William Paley is probably best remembered today for his watchmaker analogy. "Let's say you're walking around," he argued, "and you find a watch on the ground. As you examine it, you marvel at the intricately complex interweaving of its parts . . . surely you wouldn't think this marvel would have come about by itself." So it is with nature, he explained: something as complex as the universe could not possibly have come into being on its own.

The medieval theologian Thomas Aquinas, building on the work of Greek philosophers, argued that since everything has a cause, the universe must have been brought into existence by something without a cause—in other words, the Creator.

The current wave of neo-atheists is unhappy with such thinking. For example, the late Christopher Hitchens, in his (tragically) best-selling book *God Is Not Great,* stated that "the postulate of a designer or creator only raises the unanswerable question of who designed the designer or created the creator."[*] Sam Harris, another of the so-called four horsemen of atheism, agrees: "The notion of a creator poses an immediate problem of an infinite regress. If God created the universe, what created God?"[†]

For many nonbelievers, this rebuttal of Paul's defense seems unanswerable: If complex things demand a creator, and God is infinitely complex, who created *Him?*

It is a flawed premise because, by definition, God is not a *creation,* He is a *creator.* "What a beautiful work of art!" someone exclaims when presented with a Rembrandt painting. "It's so detailed—so complex! I wonder who painted *Rembrandt?*"

It is silly: Rembrandt is a painter, not a painting. God is an eternal Creator, not a creation. While His work clearly reveals His existence and reflects His mind, He is not identical with His work. He is above it and differs from it. Atheists have unwittingly fallen into the same trap as ancient pagans: "We ought not to think that the Divine Nature is like gold or silver or stone, something shaped by art and man's devising," Paul reminded his audience in Athens (Acts 17:29).

Tragically, human civilization has largely moved indoors. We find ourselves glued to screens for hours each day, separated from the stunning evidence of a loving and purposeful God, all the while wondering if He really exists.

---

[*] Christopher Hitchens, *God Is Not Great: How Religion Poisons Everything* (New York: Grand Central Publishing, 2007), 120, Kindle.

[†] Sam Harris, *Letter to a Christian Nation* (New York: Knopf Doubleday, 2006), 651, 652, Kindle.

Above It All

Before the mountains were brought forth,
or ever You had formed the earth and the world,
even from everlasting to everlasting, You are God.
—Psalm 90:2

There is an old story about a shepherd boy so wise that the king had him brought to the palace. "How many seconds are there in eternity?" the king asked him.

"A long way from here," the boy replied, "there is a mountain made of diamond. It is one-hour high, one-hour wide, one-hour deep, and it reaches one-hour down into the earth. Once every one hundred years, a little bird comes to sharpen its beak on the mountain, and eventually, when it has worn away the whole thing, the first second of eternity will have passed."

"Everlasting" is a very long time. It is hard for those of us with a defined beginning and end to imagine what the Bible means by "everlasting." We are born, we live a few short years (hopefully happy ones), and then we die. Not so with God. The Bible says that He has no beginning and no end.

Dorion Sagan said of his famous scientist father, Carl Sagan, "My father believed in the God of Spinoza and Einstein, God not behind nature but as nature, equivalent to it."* Theologians and philosophers would label that view *pantheism*: the belief that God is not a personal Being who exists apart from creation; instead, He is said to be identical with His creation. Pantheism, in part, was the downfall of Dr. John Harvey Kellogg, who, in an 1897 talk titled "God in Nature," exclaimed, "What a wonderful thought, that this mighty God that keeps the whole universe in order, is in us!"† In 1899, he said, "[Food] is a sacred thing to eat. This grows out of the fact that God is in everything."‡

The psalmist was clearly not a pantheist. God existed before Creation, from everlasting, and He will continue to exist after this creation passes away, to everlasting. He has always been there, and He always will be.

There is no question that God's fingerprints are to be found all over this planet. Creation is a stunning revelation of His character; the human race is made in His image. But the Creator God is distinct from creation and above it—an understanding that counters the rather human temptation to think of *ourselves* as God.

---

* Lynn Margulis, and Dorion Sagan, *Dazzle Gradually: Reflections on the Nature of Nature* (White River Junction, VT: Chelsea Green Publishing, 2007), 415, 416, Kindle.

† Arthur White, *Ellen G. White*, vol. 5, *The Early Elmshaven Years: 1900-1905* (Washington, DC: Review and Herald®, 1981), 282.

‡ White, *Ellen G. White*, 5:285.

Why We Worship

Whenever the living creatures give glory and honor and thanks to Him who sits on the throne, who lives forever and ever, the twenty-four elders fall down before Him who sits on the throne and worship Him who lives forever and ever, and cast their crowns before the throne, saying: "You are worthy, O Lord, to receive glory and honor and power; for You created all things, and by Your will they exist and were created."

—Revelation 4:9–11

"Let's face it," controversial comedian Bill Maher reportedly once said, "God has a big ego problem. Why do we always have to worship him?"[*] If you know anything about Mr. Maher, you know that he is a rather poor authority on religious matters; he is cynical, sarcastic, and downright hostile to believers.

But he does raise an important question: Why worship God?

"For You created all things," heavenly beings declare, "and by Your will they exist and were created" (Revelation 4:11). The living creatures and the twenty-four elders understand something very important: God alone is worthy of worship because God alone is the source of life. If God did not exist, *we* would not exist.

A connection to the Living God, an understanding of who He is, and a recognition of our utter dependence on Him is vital to our well-being. We cannot function properly while separated from God; we cannot be truly *human* apart from Him; and, perhaps most important, we cannot continue to exist without Him.

The act of worship maintains our perspective and reminds us of who God is and who we are. Worship is an invitation. It is not a matter, in the words of the skeptic philosopher David Hume, of God having "a restless appetite for applause."[†] The ability to worship—to have a living connection and relationship with the Creator—is a gift from God. We *need* to worship Him to be spiritually and emotionally healthy, just as we need proper nutrition to be physically healthy.

It is no more ego that drives God to delight in worship than it is for a shepherd to delight in caring and providing for his sheep. "Oh come, let us worship and bow down," the psalmist writes. "Let us kneel before the Lord our Maker. For He is our God, and we are the people of His pasture, and the sheep of His hand" (Psalm 95:6, 7).

The claim that ego drives God to desire worship is but a faint echo of a fallen angel's accusation that something is essentially wrong with the divine government. There is a direct path from that accusation to the misery we find in a fallen world. Worship is a path to restoration. "In Your presence is fullness of joy," David writes, "at Your right hand are pleasures forevermore" (Psalm 16:11).

---

[*] "Bill Maher Quotes," BrainyQuote.com, https://www.brainyquote.com/quotes/bill_maher_384911.

[†] David Hume, *Dialogues Concerning Natural Religion* (Indianapolis, IN: Hackett Publishing, 2012), 107, Kindle.

No, Not Aliens

And the LORD God formed man of the dust of the ground,
and breathed into his nostrils the breath of life; and man became a living being.
—Genesis 2:7

Aliens. That is what they came up with: *aliens.*

Some time ago, I had the TV on in my hotel room as I was ironing shirts. The host was talking about the appearance of human life on this planet. He was at a loss to explain it.

"If we evolved," he said, "then how did we become so hairless? Did women prefer less hairy men, and over time, the hairier men were bred out of the population? It doesn't make sense: we need hair to stay warm."

That is not an exact quote, but that was the gist of it. He was wrestling with the fact that human beings are highly advanced compared to the other inhabitants of our planet. Darwinian evolution did not explain it.

So he hit upon another solution: aliens. He suggested that in the distant past, aliens must have visited this planet to give the human race the extra boost it needed to sprint ahead of the other animals. Aliens, he said, must have tampered with our genetics, changing us from primates into *Homo sapiens.*

He must be kidding, I thought. He was not.

Never mind that the closest star system is impossibly far away—if you traveled 150,000 miles per hour, it would take nearly eighteen thousand years to reach the nearest star. On top of that, the radiation found in space would destroy your reproductive system, meaning that long-distance alien migrants would likely die off quickly.

It is, to say the least, highly unlikely. Yet some people prefer the alien theory to the God of Creation. Why? It does not come with any moral accountability. We would not owe an alien race such things as loyalty or obedience. We have no obligation to listen to the aliens or develop a relationship with them, and there would not be a Judgment Day.

If we came from aliens, our lives mean little, and we can live as we please.

Perhaps that is why so many people work so hard to discount what appears to be the most obvious answer. "Then God said, 'Let Us make man in Our image, according to Our likeness'" (Genesis 1:26).

The real tragedy is the fact that it takes more energy to discount God than it takes to start building a relationship with Him.

Written in the Stars

The heavens declare the glory of God; and the firmament shows His handiwork.
Day unto day utters speech, and night unto night reveals knowledge.
There is no speech nor language where their voice is not heard.

—Psalm 19:1–3

I was born in a place that had cold winters, and I mean *very* cold—the kind where the mercury dips low enough to freeze exposed flesh in mere minutes. That did not stop us from going outside, however, because there was another benefit to living in a remote northern community: the unbelievable night sky. When there is little to no light pollution, you can see *many* stars—enough to stun most city dwellers when they take their first trips into the country. Add to that the staggering beauty of the northern lights, and you find yourself willing to brave just about any temperature to have a look.

I have been known to pull my vehicle over to the side of the highway in minus forty degree temperatures just to lie in the snow and stare at the sky for an hour or more. Why? It is not just the sheer beauty; there is something up there that *speaks* to the human heart, reassuring us that God is indeed there, and He is indeed great. This voice speaks with no need for human language, and it is understandable by all. "There is no speech nor language where their voice is not heard," the psalmist says.

While I am a big fan of the technological advancements of the twentieth century, there has been at least one unfortunate consequence of the electrification of the human race: we have, to a large degree, muted the voice of God. We spend our evenings under artificial lights, in front of unnaturally hued screens, and on city streets awash with dazzling lights. It has made our fallen world seem more comfortable and safe, to be sure, but it has also robbed us of a breathtaking sky experience with the Creator that used to be available nearly every night. In the past, when the sun went down on our struggle to survive a harsh world each evening, the glory of God emerged from the blackness to remind us that we are not alone.

Perhaps, at least once in a while, we ought to consider turning off the TV and the laptop long enough to step outside and see what David was talking about. The good news is that the stars are still there, and so is the voice of God.

The Godhead Needs More Than One

Then God said, "Let Us make man in Our image, according to Our likeness;
let them have dominion over the fish of the sea, over the birds of the air, and over the cattle,
over all the earth and over every creeping thing that creeps on the earth."
—Genesis 1:26

Of all the people who live on planet Earth, a little more than half are mono-theistic; that is, they worship just one God. The vast majority of those are members of the three great Abrahamic faiths: Judaism, Islam, and Christianity. Soon after Moses reminded the children of Israel of the Ten Commandments, he declared the *oneness* of God: "Hear, O Israel: The LORD our God, the LORD is one! You shall love the LORD your God with all your heart, with all your soul, and with all your strength" (Deuteronomy 6:4–6).

It is for this reason that Jews and Muslims often reject the Christian claim to monotheism. "You worship more than one God!" they insist. The confusion is un-derstandable: if there is but one God—and Scripture asserts this is true—then how can we speak of Three Persons: the Father, Son, and Holy Spirit?

The first chapter of the Bible offers a key to understanding. While it seems clear that the one true God created the heavens and the earth, that same God speaks of Himself in the plural: "Let *Us* make man in *Our* image."

You cannot speak of *us* unless you have at least two people!

So how can you have one God but more than one Person? It is a question that Christians have pondered for centuries, but the more you know of God, the more it begins to make sense. The Bible declares that God is love (1 John 4:8) and that He has existed since "everlasting" (Psalm 90:2). God is also unchangeable (Malachi 3:6).

If genuine love is an utterly selfless quality that focuses on the *other*, and love is the essence of who God is, then how could He *be* love before anyone else existed? Jesus explains, "The Father loves the Son" (John 3:35). The love of God is so utter and complete that it demands more than one Person; in fact, it seems to demand *three*. The closest human analogy might be marriage, where the two "shall become one flesh" (Genesis 2:24). One marriage, one indivisible family—but two people.

Consider what this means for us: if we are created in the image of God, we cannot be fully human, we cannot be everything God intended, until *we* also learn to love selflessly.

Lessons From the Master Teacher

God, who at various times and in various ways spoke in time past to the fathers by the prophets, has in these last days spoken to us by His Son, whom He has appointed heir of all things, through whom also He made the worlds.

—Hebrews 1:1, 2

I once had a music teacher who tried to explain how challenging teaching could be. "You need to know how to get your point across," she said, "and if someone doesn't understand what you're saying, you'll have to think of ten more ways to explain the same thing. And if that doesn't work, you'll have to come up with a dozen more."

Fortunately, God is an excellent teacher and communicator. Not only has He revealed Himself through the things He has made (Romans 1:20), He also communicates directly with His people through the words of the prophets. Peter tells us, "For prophecy never came by the will of man, but holy men of God spoke as they were moved by the Holy Spirit" (2 Peter 1:21).

Furthermore, the words of the prophets were directed during more than one generation. They were written down so that successive generations could learn from them. "Now all these things happened to them as examples," Paul writes, "and they were written for our admonition, upon whom the ends of the ages have come" (1 Corinthians 10:11).

God's teaching style, however, is not limited to nature and written revelation. When the moment was right, God the Son took on human flesh and became one of us. God quite literally stepped into our midst. "He who has seen Me," Jesus told Philip, "has seen the Father" (John 14:9). "Believe Me that I am in the Father and the Father in Me" (verse 11).

The One who made us is the One who became one of us. The Son of God, who "made the worlds," became the ultimate lesson in God's character: Jesus, the Son of man, was God in human flesh.

Now that Jesus has physically returned to heaven, He has left behind yet another Teacher. "But the Helper, the Holy Spirit, whom the Father will send in My name, He will teach you all things, and bring to your remembrance all things that I said to you" (verse 26).

When there is a breakdown in communication between God and us, the blame can never be laid at God's feet: He has absolutely spoken, many times. The only real question is how often we choose to respond.

"The Father Himself Loves You"

"For God so loved the world that He gave His only begotten Son, that whoever believes in Him should not perish but have everlasting life. For God did not send His Son into the world to condemn the world, but that the world through Him might be saved."
—John 3:16, 17

Lionel was a cranky, old bachelor who had an equally cranky view of God the Father. One day, after he finished complaining about his neighbor who was "out to kill him," he started to wax eloquent on the nature of the Godhead. "Jesus," he told me, "is a God of love, but the Father is a God of war!" His proof? He associated the violent stories of the Old Testament with the Father; and the healed lepers and accepted outcasts of the New Testament with the Son.

Unfortunately, Lionel is not alone in his assessment. Millions of people love Jesus while they fear God the Father. Some Christian books make it seem as if the Father would gleefully eradicate humanity if it were not for the pleadings of the Son in our behalf. They make Him resemble the Greek god Zeus, eager to throw thunderbolts at us from Olympus.

Yesterday, we read that God has "spoken to us by His Son" (Hebrews 1:2). "For the Father Himself loves you," Jesus told His disciples. How much does He love you? God "so loved the world that He gave His only begotten Son."

There is no divide in the Godhead when it comes to the salvation of the human race. Father, Son, and Holy Spirit were perfectly united in the creation of this world, and They are working together in order to save you as well. Jesus is not trying to save you *from* the Father; He is trying to save you *for* the Father. As John puts it: "In this the love of God was manifested toward us, that God has sent His only begotten Son into the world, that we might live through Him. In this is love, not that we loved God, but that He loved us and sent His Son to be the propitiation for our sins" (1 John 4:9, 10).

Lionel might have been right about his neighbor's desire to kill him (although I personally doubt it). But when it came to God the Father, Lionel was just plain wrong. Jesus *is* the God of the Old Testament, the One whose presence followed Israel across the wilderness (1 Corinthians 10:4), and Jesus says, "He who has seen Me has seen the Father" (John 14:9).

That is remarkably good news.

Understanding God's Name

Now the LORD descended in the cloud and stood with him there, and proclaimed the name of the LORD. And the LORD passed before him and proclaimed, "The LORD, the LORD God, merciful and gracious, longsuffering, and abounding in goodness and truth, keeping mercy for thousands, forgiving iniquity and transgression and sin, by no means clearing the guilty, visiting the iniquity of the fathers upon the children and the children's children to the third and the fourth generation." So Moses made haste and bowed his head toward the earth, and worshiped.
—Exodus 34:5–8

I was finished speaking at a small gathering on the East Coast when a member of the audience approached me, obviously eager to share something. "You *do* realize that we've all been pronouncing God's name wrong?" he said, with a knowing smile. He went on to explain that if we do not get it right, there will be dire spiritual consequences.

Never mind that the pronunciation of the tetragrammaton (*YHWH,* the four letters used to represent the name of God) has been lost in antiquity. Never mind the fact that the Bible uses multiple names for the God of Abraham, each representing a key aspect of God's character. The man had stumbled into that rather small group that *insists* the biblical issue over God's name boils down to how you pronounce it.

To be fair, there *is* an issue surrounding God's name, but it is much, much bigger than the pronunciation of it. Look carefully at Moses' encounter with God. In Exodus 33, he asks to see God's glory, and God promised to make His goodness pass before Moses, at which point He would "proclaim the name of the LORD" (verse 19). In Exodus 34, God keeps that promise.

Does He give Moses a pronunciation guide? Not at all. When God Himself proclaims His own name, He describes His own *character.* He is merciful, gracious, long-suffering, abounding in goodness and truth, and just. Lucifer did not lead the universe to pronounce God's name incorrectly. It is hard to believe such a trivial issue would cause his expulsion from heaven, along with millions of other angels.

No, Lucifer caused us to question the righteous character of God. To this day, we use the word *name* to represent one's character, saying that some people have a "good name," and others have a "bad name." There are more than eight hundred thousand words in the Bible, and yet in all that space, the Bible never gives us a pronunciation guide. Why? It is not the issue.

The issue is whether or not you are going to choose to trust your Creator, to believe that God is everything He has ever claimed to be. That is what makes studying God's Word so vitally important: He is just as willing to proclaim His name today as He was millennia ago on the mountain.

The Mark of God

Then I looked, and behold, a Lamb standing on Mount Zion, and with Him one hundred and forty-four thousand, having His Father's name written on their foreheads.
—Revelation 14:1

As we read yesterday, when Moses asked to see God's glory, God responded by proclaiming His name—which proved to be a description of His character (Exodus 33; 34). As history enters its final phase, John sees a dedicated group of believers standing with the Lamb, Jesus, on Mount Zion. "These are the ones who follow the Lamb wherever He goes," he explains a few verses later. "These were redeemed from among men, being firstfruits to God and to the Lamb" (Revelation 14:4).

You will notice they also have the "Father's name written on their foreheads." In modern Christianity, this is the part of the story that is seldom told. Most people, when commenting on last-day events, are sure to mention the mark of the beast, which Revelation 13:17 describes as "the mark or the name of the beast." This mark is placed on the forehead or the hand.

Few people mention the mark of the beast's counterpart, however: the name of the Father, written on the foreheads of *His* people. As with the mark of the beast, this is not a literal tattoo or microchip implanted under the skin, even though many popular books on the subject insist that it is. If that were the case, a gang of beast worshipers could pin you down, chip you, and you would be lost forever, against your will.

The issue runs much deeper. The forehead is used in Scripture as a symbol for the mind—the place where people make decisions. Those who worship the beast have caved under pressure. They have chosen to believe the beast's claims. On the other hand, those who have the Father's name written on their foreheads have decided that God is trustworthy. They have chosen to believe that the Father is everything He has ever claimed to be. They believe Him. They have allowed Him to write His laws into their hearts and minds (Hebrews 10:16). And because they *believe* God, they "follow the Lamb wherever He goes."

These people stand on Mount Zion by *choice*, which is good news. It is not an elitist group; you, too, can choose to be there.

Nobody Messes With My Kids

*"I taught Ephraim to walk, taking them by their arms; but they did not know
that I healed them. I drew them with gentle cords, with bands of love,
and I was to them as those who take the yoke from their neck. I stooped and fed them."*
—Hosea 11:3, 4

For the parent, there are few moments as rewarding as watching your child take his or her first steps. (Of course, as soon as your child has mastered the art of walking and can explore at a much more vigorous rate, there is the occasional fleeting moment of regret.) I remember how thrilled—no, *moved*—I was when each of my daughters, their faces aglow with both pride and excitement, staggered awkwardly toward me, unassisted by their mother.

To the outsider, it would not mean much. It is just one more baby, walking poorly. But to a *father*, that moment means everything. It is evidence that your child is thriving, heading very slowly but quite surely toward adulthood. There is a reason that first steps are considered a milestone, along with first solid foods, first haircut, first words, and all the other firsts that come along.

Of course, every parent knows there will be some difficult firsts too: first illness, first disappointment, and first heartbreak. But even then, there are moments of unbelievable pride as you watch your children develop the necessary skills to successfully navigate this arduous world we live in.

I can only imagine the thrill our heavenly Father must experience when He watches us stumble our way toward Him, leaving behind the kingdom of darkness to follow His call. The language He uses to describe Israel in the book of Hosea stirs up deep emotions for parents: God the Father loves us like *we* love *our* children; He *loves* to watch us succeed.

It is a feeling that challenges the very limits of human language.

Earlier in Hosea 11, you can *hear* the love in the Father's voice. "When Israel was a child," He says, "I loved him, and out of Egypt, I called My son" (verse 1). When Moses went to Pharaoh to demand the release of God's people, he was told to say, "Thus says the Lord: 'Israel is My son, My firstborn. So I say to you, let My son go that he may serve Me' " (Exodus 4:22, 23).

It is a tone that *this* father understands: Nobody—and I mean *nobody*—messes with *my* kids!

Let it sink in: that is how God the Father feels about *you.*

The Chastening of God

And you have forgotten the exhortation which speaks to you as to sons:
"My son, do not despise the chastening of the LORD, nor be discouraged
when you are rebuked by Him; for whom the LORD loves He chastens, and scourges every son
whom He receives." If you endure chastening, God deals with you as with sons;
for what son is there whom a father does not chasten? But if you are without chastening,
of which all have become partakers, then you are illegitimate and not sons.
—Hebrews 12:5–8

It is a great source of joy to many people to discover that God the Father loves us like a parent loves a child. Yesterday, we read about the tender love of a Father teaching a child to walk, using "gentle cords" to draw us (Hosea 11:4). For some people, it is less exciting to discover that a good Father also disciplines His children.

I have to admit that I have not been the perfect parent. Over the years, I have made the wrong call more than once. I have disciplined the wrong child. I have been both too harsh and too lenient at times. I have done my best, but my best is not perfect. (Fortunately, I am married to an incredible woman who gets it right far more than I do.)

Our heavenly Father *is* the perfect Parent; He never gets it wrong. You and I, however, sometimes misread His motives. Occasionally, we ascribe hardship to God when He was not responsible for it. We point at the trials of others, shake our heads, and assume they must have done *something* wrong for God to bring calamity down on them. It happened in Jesus' day: "Rabbi," asked the disciples, "who sinned, this man or his parents, that he was born blind?" (John 9:2).

We should pay careful attention to the answer: "Jesus answered, 'Neither this man nor his parents sinned, but that the works of God should be revealed in him' " (verse 3).

Sometimes, difficult times are simply the result of living in a fallen world. But the Bible *does* teach that a heavenly Father loves us enough to discipline. If He does not discipline us, the Bible teaches, we are not *truly* His children. In the twentieth century, new approaches to child-rearing convinced some people that making your children feel good and building self-esteem was the essence of good parenting. In hindsight, many of those same people are discovering that it was not such a good idea, after all. Real love disciplines—it instills values, skills, and attitudes for the future.

Our heavenly Father loves us enough to interfere occasionally and pull us off the path to ruin. Do not let it discourage you, the author of Hebrews writes. It simply means He cares enough to be sure you make it to the kingdom.

God Among Us

And being found in appearance as a man, He humbled Himself and became obedient to the point of death, even the death of the cross. Therefore God also has highly exalted Him and given Him the name which is above every name, that at the name of Jesus every knee should bow, of those in heaven, and of those on earth, and of those under the earth, and that every tongue should confess that Jesus Christ is Lord, to the glory of God the Father.
—Philippians 2:8–11

Modern Christianity has become so well-acquainted with the verses above that the impact they must have had on Paul's original audience has, to a certain extent, been lost. In the ancient world, this was an astonishing claim: God had become a human being. The Roman Empire had many qualms with the Christian faith; but among pagan philosophers, one of the key objections was to the Incarnation—the idea that God would humble Himself to become a human being. In the second century A.D., a Roman critic by the name of Celsus ridiculed Christianity: "God is good, and beautiful, and blessed," he writes, "and that in the best and most beautiful degree. But if he come down among men, he must undergo a change, and a change from good to evil, from virtue to vice, from happiness to misery, and from best to worst. Who, then, would make choice of such a change?"★

Celsus could not wrap his mind around the idea that a good and perfect God would condescend to our level. It seemed impossible. Paul's statement to the Colossians would have been difficult for an educated Roman audience.

It would have also been difficult for a first-century Jewish audience because it asserted something about Jesus that might not be immediately obvious to *us* but would have rattled those who were intimately familiar with the Old Testament. Paul is quoting the book of Isaiah: "Look to Me, and be saved, all you ends of the earth! For I am God, and there is no other. I have sworn by Myself; the word has gone out of My mouth in righteousness, and shall not return, that to Me every knee shall bow, every tongue shall take an oath" (Isaiah 45:22, 23).

Isaiah was writing about the one true God, and he is quite clear: there is no other. Paul is telling his audience, in quite decisive terms, that Jesus *is* that one true God. And that is what the philosophers could not understand. Their pagan gods were capricious and cruel, so far removed from humanity that they would never stoop to dirty themselves with our affairs. The God of Abraham, on the other hand, so completely identifies with us that He was willing to set glory aside to come and save us.

★ Origen, *Contra Celsum* 4.14.

The Creator and the Cross

The voice of one crying in the wilderness: "Prepare the way of the LORD;
make straight in the desert a highway for our God."
—Isaiah 40:3

Christians have long recognized that Isaiah's call to action was prophetic. It predicted the ministry of John the Baptist, who was found quite literally crying in the wilderness that the time had come for the appearance of the Messiah. It was also a call to God's people as a whole; they were to expend their time and energy preparing the world for Christ's arrival.

And who would the Messiah be? Read the text carefully. In most English translations of the Bible, the word LORD is presented in all uppercase letters. There is a reason for that: the translators are letting you know that they are offering an English substitute for the name *Yahweh*. (In generations past, we pronounced it *Jehovah*.)

Let that sink in. People usually use words such as "Yahweh" or "Jehovah" to refer to the Father, but the prophecies indicated that the One who would come is *also* Jehovah. Isaiah makes the same point in Isaiah 40, but this time in reference to the second coming of Jesus: "Behold, the Lord GOD shall come with a strong hand, and His arm shall rule for Him; behold, His reward is with Him, and His work before Him" (verse 10).

This time the word GOD is in all uppercase letters, and again, it is *Yahweh* or *Jehovah*. It is no accident that the book of Revelation paraphrases this passage and places it on the lips of Jesus at the Second Coming: "And behold, I am coming quickly, and My reward is with Me, to give to every one according to his work" (Revelation 22:12).

Over the centuries, there have been people—even professing Christians—who have challenged the divinity of Christ, suggesting that Jesus was a mere created being, something less than a coeternal Member of the Godhead. But it becomes exceptionally difficult to maintain such a position after an honest, in-depth reading of the entire Bible. It was not a mere angelic emissary who came to this world, a hired hand assigned to clean up the mess. The One who stepped into our miserable existence was God in human flesh.

It was the Creator who came in person to save His creation.

The Glory of the Temple

" 'The glory of this latter temple shall be greater than the former,' says the LORD of hosts.
'And in this place I will give peace,' says the LORD of hosts."
—Haggai 2:9

When the king's workforce completed construction on the first temple in Jerusalem, Solomon gathered the children of Israel together for prayer. When he was finished, "fire came down from heaven and consumed the burnt offering and the sacrifices; and the glory of the LORD filled the temple. And the priests could not enter the house of the LORD, because the glory of the LORD had filled the LORD's house" (2 Chronicles 7:1, 2).

It was an overwhelming sight. The Bible tells us that the children of Israel "bowed their faces to the ground on the pavement, and worshiped and praised the LORD" (verse 3).

After the Captivity, God's people understandably looked forward to the completion of the second temple. Would the presence of God show up again? Would there be fire from heaven?

It did not happen. And yet Haggai predicted that the glory of the second temple would be greater than that of the first. How could that be possible? Even the ark of the covenant was missing when the second temple opened.

It must have seemed inconceivable that the glory of the second temple would ever *rival* the first, let alone surpass it. Yet Haggai's words proved true. The key to understanding his prediction is found in Haggai 2:7: " 'And I will shake all nations, and they shall come to the Desire of All Nations, and I will fill this temple with glory,' says the LORD of hosts."

As the children of Israel traveled from Egypt to Canaan, the presence of God accompanied them: a pillar of cloud by day and a pillar of fire by night. When they pitched camp, the presence of God would descend on the tabernacle and take up residence in the Most Holy Place, behind the veil. Apart from the high priest who entered once a year, no sinner could enter the inner apartment and stand in God's presence; it would mean certain death.

How was the second temple greater? God the Son—the Desire of all nations—stepped out from behind the veil and appeared in the temple as a living, breathing human being. He taught us, loved us, and saved us, face-to-face. And in God's books, His act of humble condescension was far more glorious than fire from heaven.

God's Thought Made Audible

In the beginning was the Word, and the Word was with God, and the Word was God.
He was in the beginning with God. All things were made through Him,
and without Him nothing was made that was made.

—John 1:1–3

The first few words of John's Gospel stand out as one of the most breathtaking passages describing Jesus: He is the "Word of God," an expression of the Godhead that we can understand. He is the Creator, the One who made this planet, which, in its own right, is a revelation of the character of God.

Sadly, through our rebellion, we have tainted the creation. The world is no longer a perfect expression of God's goodness because we have introduced death and decay. We chose to entertain doubts about God's character when a fallen angel presented us with an alternative. And we disfigured creation, morally blinding ourselves and making God's goodness harder to discern.

With the birth of Christ, the Creator—who had originally walked with us in the perfection of Eden—suddenly stepped into our damaged world as one of us. Where the natural world's ability to reveal God's character had been compromised, an uncompromised expression of God suddenly appeared in our midst. The planet was tainted by sin, but the Son of God was not. As a flesh-and-blood human being, Jesus faced the same moral headwinds as the rest of us, but He never succumbed to temptation. He was "in all points tempted as we are, yet without sin" (Hebrews 4:15).

God can still be seen in the creation He spoke into existence. It was centuries after the Fall that the heart of David was stunned by the magnificence of the heavens (Psalm 8:1). But in Jesus, the human race has a *perfect* declaration of God's character: the Creator who spoke all things into being *is* the perfect Word of God.

Christ's character was never compromised. Near the end of His ministry, He was able to say to His Father, "I have glorified You on the earth. . . . I have manifested Your name to the men whom You have given Me out of the world. . . . For I have given to them the words which you have given Me; and they have received them, and have known surely that I came forth from You; and they have believed that You sent Me" (John 17:4–8).

When the harsh realities of a fallen world begin to discourage you, turn to Jesus, "God's thought made audible."★

★ Ellen G. White, *Humble Hero* (Nampa, ID: Pacific Press®, 2009), 7.

Rejoicing With Angels

No one has seen God at any time. The only begotten Son,
who is in the bosom of the Father, He has declared Him.

—John 1:18

I pulled another question out of the box that had been stationed in the lobby of my public meetings. "How do we know," the question read, "that the remaining heavenly angels won't *also* rebel? Don't they continue to have free will? Isn't it possible that they will do the same thing that Lucifer did?"

It is *possible,* because God *does* permit free will, but the Bible reveals that it is not going to happen. Peter writes that "angels desire to look into" the plan to redeem the human race (1 Peter 1:12). Paul writes that we are "a spectacle to the world, both to angels and to men" (1 Corinthians 4:9). In other words, the drama unfolding on this fallen planet of ours affects more than just the human race. We are not the only ones who have questions. Angels who watched the expulsion of Lucifer from heaven are watching what happens to us with great interest.

In Jesus, the perfect character of God was revealed in no uncertain terms. "Now is the judgment of this world," Jesus said, "now the ruler of this world will be cast out. And I, if I am lifted up from the earth, will draw all peoples to Myself" (John 12:31, 32). It is interesting that in the original language, the word *peoples* does not actually appear in Jesus' statement; He was likely speaking of an audience much broader than the human race.

In the courts of heaven, the cross of Christ forever settled the issue: God's character truly *is* irreproachable, and Satan really is a liar and a murderer (John 8:44). Satanic deception was not broken by force; rather, hearts were awakened by love. If there *was* any doubt, it was eliminated with these words: "Then I heard a loud voice saying in heaven, 'Now salvation, and strength, and the kingdom of our God, and the power of His Christ have come, for the accuser of our brethren, who accused them before our God day and night, has been cast down' " (Revelation 12:10).

It would seem that the ministry of Jesus was on display in front of the whole universe. Angels watched with great interest as Jesus revealed the nature of God more fully, and they rejoiced at what they saw. The same joy is available to us: it only requires that we, too, pay attention.

What It's Like to Be You

*For we do not have a High Priest who cannot sympathize with our weaknesses,
but was in all points tempted as we are, yet without sin. Let us therefore come boldly to the
throne of grace, that we may obtain mercy and find grace to help in time of need.*
—Hebrews 4:15, 16

You have met them: people who love to dole out unsolicited—and frankly, *unwanted*—advice. Some of them watch their fellow believers like birds of prey, waiting for an opportunity to swoop down and explain what is wrong. "I don't want to meddle," they say, but the truth is, they *do*. And it is more than likely that they would love it if people would only consider their more perfect example.

Jesus had some advice for such people. "How can you say to your brother, 'Let me remove the speck from your eye'; and look, a plank is in your own eye? Hypocrite! First remove the plank from your own eye, and then you will see clearly to remove the speck from your brother's eye" (Matthew 7:4, 5).

When someone tells you, "You don't know what it's like to be me!" that person is probably right: you do not. Our ability to assess someone else's life is compromised by our own sinful natures—the plank in our eye. But fortunately, that is not the case with Jesus. He *does* understand.

We might feel tempted, at times, to think that God is like our fellow human beings—that He does not know what it is like. But the Bible assures us that is not the case. Jesus *gets* it, and He gets it from the clear, objective vantage point of Someone who has never caved in to temptation. He has experienced intense physical pain and deep emotional distress. He has been hungry, thirsty, rejected, and lonely.

The God of creation has not isolated Himself in some remote corner of the universe where He does not have to deal with the fallout of our rebellion. He would certainly have that right, but He has chosen to so completely identify with us that He became one of us and joined us here in the most painful location in the cosmos. Jesus *does* understand what it means to be you, and for that reason, you can trust that His offer to help is entirely motivated by love.

With mere people, you will often find critical judgment. With the Eternal Judge, the One who embraced what it means to be human, you can be bold, because you will find "mercy and . . . grace to help in time of need."

The Permanent Incarnation

And the Word became flesh and dwelt among us, and we beheld His glory,
the glory as of the only begotten of the Father, full of grace and truth.
—John 1:14

The astonishing thing about the incarnation of Christ is how *permanent* it is. Jesus' decision to become one of us was not a fleeting moment of curiosity where He wondered what it might be like to be human for a while; it was a lasting decision to become the "last Adam" (1 Corinthians 15:45). The language that John employs is quite specific. When he says that "the Word became flesh and *dwelt* among us," it literally means that Jesus "fixed His tabernacle" among us.

It is no coincidence that, in the Old Testament sanctuary service, the final feast of the year was the Feast of Tabernacles. It was a commemoration of the Exodus, and it celebrated the fact that God had faithfully delivered His people to the Promised Land. The spring feasts—the Passover, the Feast of Unleavened Bread, and the Firstfruits—pointed to the death, burial, and resurrection of Jesus. The Feast of Pentecost foreshadowed the establishment of the New Testament church. The Feast of Trumpets and the Day of Atonement predicted the final judgment, followed by the Feast of Tabernacles, which points to the day when Jesus will dwell in our midst forever.

When Jesus rose from the dead, He was still a human being, albeit in a glorified state. "Behold My hands and My feet, that it is I Myself," He encouraged His disciples. "Handle Me and see, for a spirit does not have flesh and bones as you see I have" (Luke 24:39). "This same Jesus," the angels told the disciples, "will so come in like manner as you saw Him go into heaven" (Acts 1:11).

Once Jesus decided to become one of us, He made that decision for eternity. He may be away for the moment, preparing a place for us (John 14:3), but His ultimate plan is to "tabernacle" among us forever: "And I heard a loud voice from heaven saying, 'Behold, the tabernacle of God is with men, and He will dwell with them, and they shall be His people. God Himself will be with them and be their God. And God will wipe away every tear from their eyes; there shall be no more death, nor sorrow, nor crying. There shall be no more pain, for the former things have passed away' " (Revelation 21:3, 4).

Come quickly, Lord Jesus.

The Person of the Spirit

But Peter said, "Ananias, why has Satan filled your heart to lie to the Holy Spirit and keep back part of the price of the land for yourself? While it remained, was it not your own? And after it was sold, was it not in your own control? Why have you conceived this thing in your heart? You have not lied to men but to God."

—Acts 5:3, 4

Years ago, I heard of a young teacher trying to explain the Holy Spirit to a classroom full of young children. The first *Star Wars* movie had just come out, and struggling to explain something as mysterious as the workings of the Spirit, she made a desperate appeal to George Lucas. "The Holy Spirit is like the Force," she said, and suddenly the eyes of the children started to sparkle with understanding. They knew what the "Force" was.

It was a clever analogy; but unfortunately, it was also wildly—and dangerously—inaccurate. The Force of *Star Wars* fame more closely resembles pantheistic concepts found in Eastern religion than it does the Person of the Holy Spirit. For example, "the Force," to quote the movie script, is an "energy field created by all living things that surrounds us and penetrates us."

You and I do not "create" the Holy Spirit. He is not an impersonal force, an unseen energy current in the universe that is available to all living things regardless of whether they are good or evil. The Bible is clear: the Holy Spirit is a Person and a Member of the Godhead. If He were nothing but a force or an energy field, it would be hard to understand how Ananias could lie to Him.

Lying is an act of personal interaction. You cannot lie to a rock, a stump, or a kitchen table. You can only lie to a thinking, rational being—someone who can assess the truthfulness of your claims. The Holy Spirit "searches all things, yes, the deep things of God." He "knows the things of God" (1 Corinthians 2:10, 11).

When Ananias lied to the Holy Spirit, he was informed by Peter that he had lied to God. While it is true that human beings have an easier time wrapping their minds around Someone who became a human being (like God the Son), or Someone who compares Himself to a father (like God the Father), the Holy Spirit is nonetheless a full Member of the Godhead, and the Bible uses all the language of sentience and personality to describe Him.

It means, in essence, that we do not use the Holy Spirit, but the Holy Spirit uses *us*.

The Sevenfold Lamb

And I looked, and behold, in the midst of the throne and of the four living creatures, and in the midst of the elders, stood a Lamb as though it had been slain, having seven horns and seven eyes, which are the seven Spirits of God sent out into all the earth.

—Revelation 5:6

When John, in vision, sees Jesus enter the throne room of heaven, he sees a slain Lamb, and he describes three sets of seven: seven horns, seven eyes, and seven Spirits. For centuries, theologians have described three key characteristics of God. He is omnipotent, or all-powerful. He is omniscient, or all-knowing. And He is omnipresent, or can be everywhere.

Look carefully at this description of Jesus, because it is clear evidence that Jesus is, indeed, God in human flesh, "the image of the invisible God" (Colossians 1:15). In the language of Bible prophecy, horns are used to depict *power*. You will notice, for example, that the ram used to represent the Medes and the Persians in Daniel 8 has two horns, with one larger than the other. The horns represent a major power (the Persians) and a minor power (the Medes). Likewise, the goat of Daniel 8 has one "notable" horn, representing the power of the "first king," or Alexander the Great (verses 5, 21).

Eyes are used to represent *knowledge* and *wisdom*. "For the eyes of the LORD run to and fro throughout the whole earth," the Bible tells us (2 Chronicles 16:9). When the little-horn power emerges from the divided western Roman Empire, it is said to have "eyes like the eyes of a man" (Daniel 7:8), because it is a kingdom built on human, rather than divine, wisdom.

The Spirit of God, of course, has the quality of *presence*. At Creation, "the Spirit of God was hovering over the face of the waters" (Genesis 1:2). When God drew especially close to His people, the Bible often says that "the Spirit of God" came upon them (see, for example, Judges 6:34).

The number *seven*, of course, is God's number—the number of perfection and completion. This description of Jesus in Revelation 5:6 is profound: not only is He the slain Lamb, the Sacrifice for our sins, He is also perfect in power, perfect in wisdom, and perfectly present in all the earth. He truly *is* God, and even though He is now in heaven, applying the merits of His sacrifice on our behalf, He is still ever present with His church. His perfect power and His perfect wisdom are still available to you for this day.

The Advantage of Absence

"Nevertheless I tell you the truth. It is to your advantage that I go away; for if I do not go away, the Helper will not come to you; but if I depart, I will send Him to you."
—John 16:7

Going away used to be much harder than it is now. In the past, when I was working in another part of the country—or in another part of the world, for that matter—I knew that contact with my wife would be infrequent. Phone calls meant paying long-distance charges, and we did not have a lot of disposable income.

The proliferation of cell phones and the internet changed all of that. Long-distance calling is a thing of the past. Videoconferencing has made calling home a visual experience.

Communication is better than it used to be, but it is still hard to be apart. The heart aches for *togetherness.* I can only imagine the feeling of panic that must have twisted the hearts of the disciples when it started to dawn on them that Jesus really *was* going to leave. It had taken more than three years to come to grips with who He was and why He had come, and now they were convinced that the Messiah was in their midst. God was physically in their midst!

But the fact that Jesus had *permanently* taken on human form meant that He could only be in one place at a time, physically speaking. The church in the Old Testament had been blessed with the pillar of cloud and the pillar of fire that followed them across the wilderness, and (before the Babylonian captivity) the Shekinah glory resided above the ark of the covenant in the Most Holy Place.

Would the New Testament church not also be blessed with the immediate presence of God?

"It is to your advantage that I go away," Jesus explained. That must have been hard to grasp. How could Christ's departure be an *advantage*? The answer? The Holy Spirit, the Third Person of the Godhead. Through the Spirit, Jesus could be anywhere, anytime. The disciples could spread across the face of the earth, each to his own mission field, and *never* be away from Christ.

Christians still have a longing—a heartache—to see Jesus face-to-face. That day is coming soon; in the meantime, the same Spirit is present with the church today. "And lo," said Jesus, "I am with you always, even to the end of the age" (Matthew 28:20).

Tongues of Fire

When the Day of Pentecost had fully come, they were all with one accord in one place.
And suddenly there came a sound from heaven, as of a rushing mighty wind, and it filled the
whole house where they were sitting. Then there appeared to them divided tongues, as of fire,
and one sat upon each of them. And they were all filled with the Holy Spirit and began to
speak with other tongues, as the Spirit gave them utterance.

—Acts 2:1–4

Pentecost, or the Feast of Weeks, was a festival designed to commemorate Israel's arrival at Mount Sinai and the giving of the Ten Commandments at Mount Sinai, which took place forty-nine days after they left Egypt. It was a breathtaking occasion: the presence of God descended on the mountain with fire and smoke, and the "whole mountain quaked greatly" (Exodus 19:18).

There is an old belief, based on Genesis 10, that Noah had seventy grandchildren (although some people have counted seventy-two), and each of them became the progenitor of a nation.* That led to the tradition that the world had seventy languages after the Tower of Babel. There is also an old legend, well established by the time of the New Testament church, that when God spoke the Ten Commandments from Mount Sinai, He spoke it in all seventy of those languages simultaneously.

Imagine the impact that the events of Pentecost must have had on those who witnessed what happened to the disciples of Christ. Not only did tongues of fire fall on the heads of the disciples on the very day when the original fire on Sinai was celebrated, but visitors from other nations were able to hear what the disciples were saying—in their own languages!

"And how is it that we hear, each in our own language in which we were born?" they marveled (Acts 2:8).

The message was strikingly clear: the Power that was present in that assembly was the very same Power who had descended on the mountain so many centuries earlier and spoken to His covenant people. Prior to His crucifixion, Jesus had declared the temple in Jerusalem desolate (Matthew 23:38), and in a few short decades, it would be utterly destroyed by the Romans. The first temple had been visited by the Shekinah glory, and the second temple by the incarnate Jesus Himself. Now the presence of God had fallen on the New Testament church through the power of the Holy Spirit, and He will continue to be with us until Jesus returns.

What happened at Sinai was powerful and life changing. What can happen in our hearts today when we surrender to Christ is no less powerful and certainly just as life changing.

---

* Kaufmann Hohler and Isaac Broydé, "Nations and Languages, the Seventy," in *The Jewish Encyclopedia* (New York: Funk and Wagnall, 1906), http://www.jewishencyclopedia.com/articles/11382-nations-and-languages-the-seventy.

Learning to Listen

"But the Helper, the Holy Spirit, whom the Father will send in My name,
He will teach you all things, and bring to your remembrance all things that I said to you."
—John 14:26

Once upon a time, in the good old days, I kept my schedule organized with a little pocket day planner made of paper. Today, it is all digital, and everybody in the office uses software such as iCal or Outlook to keep themselves organized. The big advantage, of course, is that we can share our calendars with everyone else, and everyone in the office can keep others aware of what they are doing. The downside? Now I see *everybody's* appointments popping up, all day long—and because most of the items do not apply to me, it has actually taught me to ignore most of the notifications.

I have been inadvertently trained to miss almost everything on the calendar. I usually do not even *hear* the little *ping* announcing my next agenda item, and there are days when I miss some really important things. Is it possible that I would have been better off with the careful attention that a paper schedule required?

Jesus spent three and a half years training His disciples, and much of what He taught them is still available to us through the Gospel accounts. "After I go back to heaven," Jesus told them, "My Father will send the Holy Spirit, who will remind you of the things I said when we were together."

Of course, in order for the Spirit to bring to mind the words of Christ, you first have to put them into your memory bank. Some modern Christians treat the Holy Spirit as a miraculous bypass for Bible study, but that is not how Jesus explained His role. You still have to spend time in God's Word, absorbing the information inspired by the Spirit.

The other potential pitfall of skipping Bible study? It is possible to train yourself to ignore the Spirit's prompting. If you do not spend time with God each day, you may fail to recognize the Spirit's voice. He may be nudging you rather strongly in an attempt to remind you that Jesus has already provided an answer to the situation you are facing; but because you have formed the habit of not paying attention to divine notifications, the alarms go unheeded.

For the believer, quiet time with God is not optional; it is essential. It is what we need to develop the all-important skill of paying attention to the voice of the Spirit.

The Eternal Reference Point

"And when He has come, He will convict the world of sin, and of righteousness, and of judgment: of sin, because they do not believe in Me; of righteousness, because I go to My Father and you see Me no more; of judgment, because the ruler of this world is judged."
—John 16:8–11

Years ago, as a little kid, I witnessed a murder. It was on TV, and it was long enough ago that I saw the whole thing in black and white. I watched as a man begged his captors not to hurt him, but they ignored his pleas and tossed him off a high balcony. The scene plagued my conscience so much that I could not sleep that night because even though I *knew* it was playacting, it still bothered me that the writers would conceive of such a horrible thing. Of course, as the years went by, I joined the ranks of those who witness approximately forty thousand murders before their eighteenth birthday, and scenes like that stopped bothering me.

The thing about sin is that the more we immerse ourselves in it, the less sinful it can seem. The mere fact that we were born sinners means that our moral gauges are compromised from the starting line: we are inherently self-centered and selfish; and by ourselves, it is nearly impossible to gauge just how sinful we are. It is like having inaccurate speedometers in our cars: we might think we are driving well within the speed limit when the truth is we are reckless drivers. Or worse yet, it is like having broken engine lights, and we do not realize our engines are overheating until it is too late.

As sinners, we lack moral objectivity. Our own wants and desires are the standard by which we measure our own behavior, which means that we have no idea just how far short of God's glory we fall. That is where the Spirit of God steps in: He convicts the world of sin. The Holy Spirit is an outside reference point that leads us to compare ourselves to God's standards rather than our own. It is a gift of immeasurable value: if God did not point out our sins, we would never see them for ourselves. Left entirely to ourselves, we would be lost.

The gift of the Spirit is clear evidence that God is highly invested in bringing us home. And the good news? It is the opposite of dwelling in sin: the more we dwell in the Spirit, the more we pay attention and respond—the more clearly we begin to discern His voice.

Speaking the Language of Heaven

Likewise the Spirit also helps in our weaknesses. For we do not know what we should pray for as we ought, but the Spirit Himself makes intercession for us with groanings which cannot be uttered. Now He who searches the hearts knows what the mind of the Spirit is, because He makes intercession for the saints according to the will of God.
—Romans 8:26, 27

Imagine, for a moment, that you are a British citizen and the Queen of England gave you her personal cell phone number. "Here," she says, "if you ever need *anything*, give me a call." It would be an astounding level of privilege, but it pales in comparison to God's offer. The Bible invites us to "come boldly to the throne of grace" (Hebrews 4:16). Can mere sinners *really* approach the throne of a holy God? The answer is *yes*; because of the cross, you can!

There is a critical problem, however. The Bible promises that "if we ask anything according to His will, He hears us" (1 John 5:14). That is the good news. The bad news? The human heart is warped by sin, and that means we have an exceptionally limited ability to hold an appropriate conversation with God. Our understanding of God's will is paltry and compromised. We are supposed to pray according to God's will, but as finite, sinful beings, we only have the first inklings of what God's will might be.

God has already anticipated that issue, and He has a solution. The Holy Spirit serves as a Divine Translator. When we do not know what to pray for, He steps in and completes our prayers. When our needs defy mere human utterance and we find it hard to express them, the Spirit understands and intercedes for us "with groanings which cannot be uttered."

We do not even know what our real needs are until the Holy Spirit reveals them to us. He turns our sinful hearts towards Jesus. "When the Helper comes," Jesus explained, "the Spirit of truth who proceeds from the Father, He will testify of Me" (John 15:26). He reveals to us the mind of God, He brings conviction to our hearts, and He transforms our prayer lives so that they *are* in harmony with the will of God.

It would be one thing to have the Queen of England's cell phone number. But now imagine that she invited you to live in the palace, taught you to think and speak as a blue blood, and then adopted you as a member of the royal family. That is a little closer to what God is doing for you this day through His Spirit, if you are willing to let Him.

The Harmony of Word and Spirit

"And we are His witnesses to these things, and so also is the Holy Spirit whom God has given to those who obey Him."

—Acts 5:32

Pastor, the Holy Spirit is telling me to marry that man in order to save him!" The expression on the woman's face made it clear that she was only half convinced of what she was saying, and she was hoping that I might endorse the idea and give her the courage to move ahead. I knew the man in question was not a believer, and I could not do it.

"Why would the Holy Spirit contradict Himself?" I asked gently. "The Spirit inspired the words of Scripture, and the Bible is pretty clear about not marrying unbelievers. I don't believe He's going to give you advice that runs contrary to the advice that He's already given you."

A lot of today's Christians easily confuse impressions with the voice of the Spirit. I remember a rather wild church near the airport in Toronto that emphasized "manifestations" of the Spirit, which included uncontrollable fits of laughter and barking like dogs. Some of the congregants would fall to the ground and act like infants, insisting that the Spirit of God was leading them through another "born-again" experience. Some of the proponents of the movement were knowingly living in open violation of God's moral law, and yet they claimed that they had been handpicked by the Holy Spirit for a special display of His presence.

The Bible, however, is clear. Shortly after the Spirit had fallen on the New Testament church, Peter told his audience that the Holy Spirit had been "given to those who obey Him." The Spirit is not going to tell you to disobey the Word of God, and He is not going to fall on those who refuse to heed His counsel.

Many Christians wonder why they have not felt the presence of the Spirit or heard His voice in a while. Sometimes there is silence simply because it is a season of quiet. But other times we have to consider the possibility that we have silenced the voice of God simply because we have stubbornly refused to heed His counsel in the past—particularly as He speaks through the pages of the Bible.

The Holy Spirit is not merely a religious battery, engineered to motivate and excite us. Like the other Members of the Godhead, He works through a relationship, and that requires our cooperation.

Letting God Lead

Now in the church that was at Antioch there were certain prophets and teachers: Barnabas, Simeon who was called Niger, Lucius of Cyrene, Manaen who had been brought up with Herod the tetrarch, and Saul. As they ministered to the Lord and fasted, the Holy Spirit said, "Now separate to Me Barnabas and Saul for the work to which I have called them." Then, having fasted and prayed, and laid hands on them, they sent them away.
—Acts 13:1–3

When Jesus returned to heaven, He left the church with only one assignment: "Go, therefore and make disciples of all the nations" (Matthew 28:19). There is not a human being alive who could possibly carry out the gospel commission alone. Not only would it prove impossible to execute such a gargantuan task by oneself, sinful human beings simply do not have the capacity to conceive of a workable plan of action that would achieve Christ's objectives.

That is why you and I are not in charge of the work. It is directed from heaven's sanctuary by our great High Priest, Jesus, and He communicates with the church through the voice of the Holy Spirit. If it were left to a church committee to select appropriate workers to carry out the gospel commission, we would likely choose all the wrong people, using the wrong criteria. It is far better to seek God's will. Ask Him to reveal *His* plan for the work, and then join Him where He is working.

That was the approach of the early church. As they performed the work of the kingdom, they were in constant contact with the Savior, seeking His direction. When it came to selecting a missionary team, their hearts were sensitive enough to God's leading that they *heard* God choose Saul and Barnabas. (And you will notice, in Acts 13:9, that God chose people who were "filled with the Holy Spirit"—people who were already in a responsive, obedient relationship with Him.)

The key to working successfully for God is to allow Him to lead. The church is organized, and God requires us to apply our wisdom and talents to its work. We are required to be diligent stewards of God's holy things. But at the same time, we must always remember that the church is not a Fortune 500 company. You and I do *not* elect a chair or choose a president; Christ will always be in charge of the operation. If a group of believers wishes to succeed in the work assigned to the church, there is only one Voice that really matters. If we push self aside and allow the Spirit to lead, we will discover that He still speaks rather clearly.

The Voice of Hope

Now may the God of hope fill you with all joy and peace in believing,
that you may abound in hope by the power of the Holy Spirit.
—Romans 15:13

There is an ancient Greek myth about King Sisyphus, who managed to trick the gods and defeat death. His punishment? He was forced to roll a stone uphill, for all eternity. Each time he managed to push the heavy stone up to the summit, it rolled back to the bottom, and he had to begin again. Fittingly, the twentieth-century philosopher Albert Camus titled his collection of essays on the meaninglessness of life *The Myth of Sisyphus*. He begins with these words: "There is but one truly serious philosophical problem, and that is suicide. Judging whether life is or is not worth living amounts to answering the fundamental question of philosophy. All the rest—whether or not the world has three dimensions, whether the mind has nine or twelve categories—comes afterwards."★

As the discipline of philosophy moved into the twentieth century, the voices of more and more thinkers became despondent. A world that had untethered itself from God—or even declared Him dead—found itself at a loss to explain the meaning of life. Trying to understand human existence in a broken world became an impossible task.

I have often felt sorry for those who have to attend a funeral bereft of hope. If you do not believe that human life has a purpose, if you do not believe that there is hope beyond the grave, how do you console yourself?

Christians live in the same broken world, and we also struggle (as did Job) to understand the challenges of pain and suffering. But we do not struggle without hope. As we push our way through an existence hampered by sin and rebellion against God, there is a gentle Voice that reassures us, each step of the way, that there is hope. We are *not* alone in the universe. Life will not *always* be painful. Our questions *will* eventually be answered. There will be a full restoration of God's original plan for the human family.

Prompted, comforted, and encouraged by the Holy Spirit, we can forge ahead with confidence, knowing that our existence *is* meaningful to the One who created us—meaningful enough that the Son has chosen to become one of us.

★ Albert Camus, *The Myth of Sisyphus, and Other Essays* (New York: Vintage International, 2012), 70–72, Kindle.

February

I accept the death of Jesus Christ on Calvary as the atoning sacrifice for my sins and believe that by God's grace through faith in His shed blood I am saved from sin and its penalty.

A Tomb and a Garden

Then the LORD God said, "Behold, the man has become like one of Us, to know good and evil. And now, lest he put out his hand and take also of the tree of life, and eat, and live forever"— therefore the LORD God sent him out of the garden of Eden to till the ground from which he was taken. So He drove out the man; and He placed cherubim at the east of the garden of Eden, and a flaming sword which turned every way, to guard the way to the tree of life.
—Genesis 3:22–24

It has been called a "teardrop on the cheek of time." Shah Jahan built the Taj Mahal, easily one of the most recognizable architectural marvels in the world, in the seventeenth century after his favorite wife died in childbirth. Eventually, he built a stunning monument to his devastating heartbreak.

As impressive as the domed tomb is, however, there is another marvel at its feet: a square garden based on a very ancient design borrowed from the Persians, who in turn borrowed it from ancient Mesopotamian civilizations. In the center is a fountain, and there are four channels of water that reach out from the fountain toward the four points of the compass. Seen from the sky, the design of the garden is no accident: it is a representation of the Garden of Eden, which was a "paradise" garden, with a source of life in the center and four rivers running from it.

The tomb of the beloved wife is placed right up against the garden. It is a picture of the human race standing outside the gates of Eden, the bride of Christ doomed to die from the wages of sin. It is a portrait of a groom's deep grief, but it is not without hope. You will notice that God did not place cherubim at the gates of Eden to "prevent" the way to the tree of life but to "guard" it.

The path back into the Garden is closed for now, but through the cross of Christ, it will once again be opened. You and I are the beloved bride, the wife who was snatched away by the arch deceiver. But a grieving God has not abandoned us to the grave. He kept us right next to Eden, knowing that our loss will be completely reversed when the Lamb of God claims the kingdom He purchased with His blood.

Owning the Problem

And He said, "Who told you that you were naked? Have you
eaten from the tree of which I commanded you that you should not eat?"
Then the man said, "The woman whom You gave to be with me, she gave me of the tree, and I ate."
—Genesis 3:11, 12

One afternoon, when our youngest daughter was just a toddler, we found her in the bathroom with a mostly empty tube of toothpaste in her hand. The contents were spread all over the room: there was toothpaste on the mirror, on the counter, on the walls, and in the bath mat. "Did you squeeze out all the toothpaste?" we asked incredulously.

"No!" she answered emphatically.

"Do you care to revise your story?" we asked. "You're still holding the tube! If *you* didn't do it, how did this happen?" I must admit I was disappointed in her pint-sized estimate of my intelligence. Her answer? "It happened all by itself!"

Sin has created a stubborn unwillingness to accept responsibility for our actions. Witness the litigious world we live in: it is always someone else's fault when something goes wrong. It is the product of pride, a twisted love of self that is willing to sacrifice others to preserve oneself.

It has been happening since the moment we first rebelled against God. It only took a matter of hours for Adam and Eve's newly acquired sinful natures to manifest themselves. "It wasn't *my* idea to eat from the tree," Adam told God. "It's my *wife's* fault! Moreover, it's *Your* fault for creating her in the first place!"

The sinful human heart has an astonishing capacity for evading responsibility. We seem to be able to justify any behavior and effortlessly deflect blame to others when we are caught. Eve did the same thing: "The *serpent* deceived me, and I ate," she postulated (Genesis 3:13; emphasis added).

Jesus, however, is radically different. The "last Adam," as Paul calls Jesus (1 Corinthians 15:45), handled it much differently. Even though He was without sin, "a lamb without blemish and without spot" (1 Peter 1:19), He became "sin for us" (2 Corinthians 5:21). He emptied Himself of the dignity and majesty He had with the Father, humbly preferring lost sinners to Himself. The love of God stands in stark contrast to the pride of sinners, and it silences all claims that God is arbitrary or that His government is self-serving. The Cross is God's antidote to our pride. When faced with Christ's gift, what choice do we have but to humbly admit that we are, indeed, sinners in need of a Savior?

Disconnected

Then the LORD God took the man and put him in the garden of Eden to tend and keep it. And the LORD God commanded the man, saying, "Of every tree of the garden you may freely eat; but of the tree of the knowledge of good and evil you shall not eat, for in the day that you eat of it you shall surely die."
—Genesis 2:15–17

To many people, the penalty for eating from the tree of the knowledge of good and evil seems rather severe. We live in a world saturated with violent crime, and to our human way of thinking, eating forbidden fruit seems akin to stealing a cookie: naughty, but not evil.

The more you read the Bible, however, the more sense it makes. God is the sole Source of life in the universe. Not only did He create all things, "in Him all things consist" (Colossians 1:17). Paul told his audience in Athens that God "gives to all life, breath, and all things" (Acts 17:25). When Adam and Eve chose to disobey God, they made a conscious choice to stop trusting Him. They rejected His authority and voluntarily stepped outside of His kingdom.

Human beings, unlike God, are not self-existent. We depend on the Source of life for our existence. And what happens when you impair your connection to the Source of life? You die. It is the natural consequence.

"But I've sinned, and I'm not dead!" some will protest. True, you are not dead—not yet. Our situation is not unlike an electric fan that suddenly is unplugged from the wall. The blades may keep spinning for a few minutes, but eventually, they slow down and stop. A car that runs out of gas on the freeway may coast for a quarter of a mile before it stops, but it will stop. Our whole world has been impaired by the choice we made to separate ourselves from God, and the signs of decay are everywhere. The world is still running, but it is running *down*.

When you look at the declining life spans throughout the book of Genesis, you will see that we have gone from living for nearly a millennium to living for nearly a century. When God told our first parents that sin would result in death, it was not a threat. It was a warning—a reminder that we need Him to live. He was pointing to the natural consequence of rebellion.

It is not a hopeless case, however. The Bible reminds us: "In Him was life, and the life was the light of men" (John 1:4). The best way to use this today? Take advantage of the gift: find every opportunity to reconnect with the Creator.

No Rest for the Wicked

For the bed is too short to stretch out on,
and the covering so narrow that one cannot wrap himself in it.
—Isaiah 28:20

I am not the world's tallest man, but I am six feet tall; and in my travels, I have occasionally had to spend the night on a short sofa with a small blanket. My calves are on the armrest on one end, my head is uncomfortably contorted against the armrest at the other, and I wake up in the morning feeling as if I have not slept at all.

The leadership in Jerusalem knew that they had a serious problem. The nation had been disobedient to the covenant, and as a result, they had given up God's protection and were faced with fending off the Assyrians who had already wreaked havoc in the northern kingdom of Israel. Instead of turning back to God, however, they hoped to find a solution by creating a confederacy of nations to fight off the invaders. They dreamed of strength in numbers, but they were underestimating the power of the enemy.

It was a man-made solution to a spiritual problem, and God warned them that they would discover their solution was a tiny bed that offered no rest. Judah was like Adam and Eve in the Garden, desperately stitching together fig leaves in the hopes of covering their nakedness—another man-made solution to a deeply spiritual problem. Even though they had been told that sin would lead to death, they were underestimating the true cost of sin: it is a problem that we cannot fix on our own. Even after they had clothed themselves, Adam and Eve still dove into the bushes to hide when they heard God approaching.

The real solution? "Also for Adam and his wife the Lord God made tunics of skin, and clothed them" (Genesis 3:21). The Bible does not specify that the animal used to provide the skin was a lamb, but the weight of evidence throughout the Bible would certainly suggest it. The message is clear: The wages of sin is death, and the only workable solution, if we want to avoid the prospect of eternal death, is for an innocent Substitute to cover us with His righteousness. Only then will we find a bed big enough to offer rest.

"Come to Me," said Jesus, "all you who labor and are heavy laden, and I will give you rest" (Matthew 11:28).

The Road to Hope

"And I will put enmity between you and the woman, and between your seed and her Seed;
He shall bruise your head, and you shall bruise His heel."

—Genesis 3:15

The moment the human race was escorted out of Eden, God offered incredible hope. "I have a way back in," He told Adam and Eve. Before they had chosen to separate themselves from God's government, God had already established a plan to heal the tragic illness of sin: a "Lamb slain from the foundation of the world" (Revelation 13:8). The Creator's love for His creation had already impelled Him to offer Himself as a sacrifice for sin.

No sooner had God spelled out the consequences of sin—hard labor, pain, and death—than He also spelled out the solution: Someone would come from their line of descendants who would utterly defeat the serpent. God Himself would join the human race, becoming one of us, and through His life, ministry, death, and resurrection, the devil would be crushed.

It would not be easy. Waiting for the Messiah would be a long and difficult process. The book of Revelation pictures God's people as a woman in labor, waiting for a child to be born: "Then being with child, she cried out in labor and in pain to give birth" (Revelation 12:2). Life became much harder outside of Eden. The hosts of fallen angels did what they could to discourage human beings from placing their allegiance with the God of heaven. The world was quickly filled with violence, hate, pain, and suffering—and many people, listening to the serpent, placed the blame on God Himself.

Others patiently placed their hope in the promise of God: the Child would come, and the dragon would be destroyed. And of course, God kept His promise. The Messiah arrived, right on schedule. The hope of the fallen human race was realized the day that the Child was born.

Today, some have given up hope that Jesus will come again; but when we are tempted to doubt the promise of God, we should remind ourselves that only half the time God's people waited for Christ's first coming has passed. We, like our ancestors, are asked to be patient and to believe. The devil has already been defeated at the cross, and Christ *will* come again in glory to seize the throne He has purchased with His own blood.

The Gift of the High Priest

Then Melchizedek king of Salem brought out bread and wine;
he was the priest of God Most High. And he blessed him and said:
"Blessed be Abram of God Most High, Possessor of heaven and earth;
and blessed be God Most High, who has delivered your enemies
into your hand." And he [Abram] gave him a tithe of all.
—Genesis 14:18–20

The encounter between Melchizedek, the king of Salem, and Abraham, the father of the faithful, is one of the briefest stories in the Bible, but it is potent with meaning. Speculation over the identity of Melchizedek has run wild over the centuries because the details are sparse. What we do know is that he was king of Salem, the city that would eventually become God's earthly capital, Jerusalem. He was both a king and a priest, and his name means "King of Righteousness." He is obviously a type, or symbol, that pointed forward to Christ.

The Bible gives the impression that worshipers of the true God were few and far between at this point in history. Even though Abraham and Melchizedek came from far-apart places, they both happened to worship the same Creator God: *El Elyon,* the "Most High God." Their meeting could not have been a coincidence: the king of Salem just "happens" to bump into the father of the nation that would call his city home?

Pay careful attention to the gifts that Melchizedek presented to Abraham on the occasion of his victory over the wicked kings who had kidnapped his nephew. He presented the father of all faithful with bread and wine, the symbols God chose to represent the broken body and shed blood of His Son. The blessing that the king of Salem pronounced on Abraham did not come without a cost, and the blessing that God is able to pronounce on His children today did not come without a cost either. Our salvation cost the Lamb of God His life.

Our path into the heavenly Jerusalem is a gift. We do not earn it. The only way we can have it is to accept it, and the most appropriate response we can offer back is to put our lives in the hands of the Possessor of heaven and earth. Abraham did not purchase the gift, but he *did* respond by offering "a tithe of all." What is a *tithe*? It is a token, a small portion of our possessions that acknowledges that all we have, all we are, and everything we are about to receive is a gift from the Creator—a gift that was purchased at the cross.

The Son and the Altar

Then He said, "Take now your son, your only son Isaac, whom you love,
and go to the land of Moriah, and offer him there as a burnt offering
on one of the mountains of which I shall tell you."

—Genesis 22:2

Isaac was the son of promise, the impossible child born to a couple well past their child-bearing years. In fact, Abraham was so old when Isaac was born that the book of Hebrews describes him as a man who was "as good as dead" (Hebrews 11:12). If something happened to the child of promise, there was little hope that he would ever have another son.

Then God asked the unthinkable. "Abraham," He said, "I want you to take your son and sacrifice him on one of the mountains of which I shall tell you." Of course, we already know the end of the story: Isaac was ultimately spared and went on to become a father to a mighty nation that would bear the name of *his* son Israel. But at the outset of the story, Abraham did not know his boy would survive. The Hebrew retelling of the story informs us that Abraham was willing to go through with the sacrifice, "concluding that God was able to raise him up, even from the dead" (Hebrews 11:19).

Christians have debated the significance of the story for centuries, and there are many shades of meaning to be found. One theme, however, quickly rises to the surface: the agony of a father faced with the prospect of giving up his only son. Abraham and Isaac point forward to the awful moment when God the Father would hear the cry of His own Son from Calvary: "My God, My God, why have You forsaken Me?" (Matthew 27:46).

The details of the story leave little doubt that God is showing us the unspeakable agony that the Father and the Son endured at the cross. An only son makes a journey to a mountain in Moriah—the very location, outside the city of Jerusalem, where Jesus was sacrificed on a cross. Like Jesus carrying His own cross to Golgotha, "Abraham took the wood of the burnt offering and laid it on Isaac his son" (Genesis 22:6).

Perhaps the most incredible part of the story? The Bible offers no record of Isaac resisting when the awful moment of sacrifice came. The Father and the Son were *willing* to go through with the cross if it meant our salvation.

"Behold the Lamb"

But Isaac spoke to Abraham his father and said, "My father!"
And he said, "Here I am, my son."
Then he said, "Look, the fire and the wood, but where is the lamb for a burnt offering?"
And Abraham said, "My son, God will provide for Himself the lamb for a burnt offering."
So the two of them went together.
—Genesis 22:7, 8

Sometimes serious students of the Bible refer to something called "the law [or rule] of first mention." It is a general principle that suggests it is always a good idea to look for the first time a principle or doctrine is mentioned in the Bible because that first mention often sets the stage for understanding that same principle or doctrine throughout the rest of the Bible.

Today's reading is a case in point: This is the first time a "lamb" is mentioned in the Old Testament. That comes as a surprise to many Bible students because there is an unspoken assumption that lambs made their first appearance outside the gates of Eden, when God clothed Adam and Eve with "tunics of skin" (Genesis 3:21). The context of the rest of the Bible would suggest that the skins were *probably* made from lambs, but the Genesis account does not state it explicitly. Likewise, given the frequency with which Jesus is compared to a lamb (more than twenty times in the book of Revelation alone!), we know that Abel *likely* offered a lamb in obedience to God's request for a sacrifice, but we infer that from our knowledge of Bible types and from the statement, "Abel was a keeper of sheep" (Genesis 4:2).

The first time a *lamb* is specifically mentioned in the Bible, it comes from the lips of the promised son who is also a symbol of Christ: "Where is the lamb for a burnt offering?" Abraham's response? "God will provide for Himself the lamb." It foreshadows Jesus' statement to Nicodemus, where He identifies God the Father as the Provider of the gift: "For God so loved the world that He gave His only begotten Son" (John 3:16).

Interestingly, the earliest mention of a lamb in the New Testament story is found in John's Gospel. (There is an incidental mention of the Passover lamb in Mark 14, but chronologically, it comes at a much later point in Christ's ministry.) It comes from the lips of John the Baptist, and it just so happens that it is a direct answer to both Isaac's query and our deepest need as sinners: "Behold! The Lamb of God who takes away the sin of the world!" (John 1:29).

Exposed!

For He made Him who knew no sin to be sin for us,
that we might become the righteousness of God in Him.
—2 Corinthians 5:21

Back in 2015, security at the adultery website AshleyMadison.com was compromised by hackers, who then began to release names to the world when the owners of the website refused to meet their demand to shut it down. Imagine the panic that users must have felt as they waited to see whether or not *their* misdeeds would become public knowledge.

There is a passage in Luke's Gospel that used to terrify me as a child: "Therefore whatever you have spoken in the dark will be heard in the light, and what you have spoken in the ear in inner rooms will be proclaimed on the housetops" (Luke 12:3). Really? *Everything*? I imagined a humiliating public experience where angels would literally stand on rooftops, reciting my darkest secrets, to the amusement of just about everybody I knew.

It would be humiliating, not Ashley Madison humiliating, but humiliating nonetheless.

But consider this, poor sinner: Christ was publicly humiliated so that you will not be. He hung naked on a cross, condemned as a criminal, and your sins were placed on His shoulders. He was made "sin for us," Paul writes. "Christ has redeemed us from the curse of the law, having become a curse for us," he told the Galatians (Galatians 3:13).

Christians have become so used to the idea of the cross that we forget how scandalous it was: the innocent Son of God dying a shameful public death. "Who for the joy that was set before Him," the book of Hebrews says, "endured the cross, despising the shame" (Hebrews 12:2).

Imagine (God forbid) that your name was among those leaked to the public in the data dump. With fear and trembling, you search through the information, knowing your shame. But instead of finding *your* name, you find *Christ's*. He is innocent, but He has stepped in and agreed to wear your shame because He cannot imagine eternity without you. The world ridicules Him—and you are free.

You and I are still guilty of the sins that cost Jesus so much. Sin is spiritual infidelity, and it disqualifies us from God's kingdom. That should have been the end of the story, but "where sin abounded, grace abounded much more" (Romans 5:20).

That ought to profoundly change how you live.

Back Home

Grace to you and peace from God the Father and our Lord Jesus Christ,
who gave Himself for our sins, that He might deliver us from this present evil age,
according to the will of our God and Father, to whom be glory forever and ever. Amen.
—Galatians 1:3–5

All of creation was deeply affected by our choice to rebel against the Creator. Sin was not merely a legal transaction that incurred a spiritual debt; it profoundly altered who we are and the way the planet worked. Today, what we call "real life" was not part of our original existence. Death and decay were caused by *us*, and we found ourselves powerless to reverse what we had done.

When Paul speaks of "this present evil age," he is referring to the world we re-created in our own sinful image. In the world of biblical thought, there were two distinct periods of time, or ages. The "present age" is the one we find ourselves living in now—a time when God's creation has been seriously compromised by sin. The "age to come" will arrive when all of the effects of sin have been reversed and God's original order in creation is restored.

"And God shall wipe away every tear from their eyes," a voice from heaven told John after he was shown the age to come—new heavens and a new earth. "There shall be no more death, nor sorrow, nor crying. There shall be no more pain, for the former things have passed away" (Revelation 21:4).

Modern Christianity tends to point to the cross of Christ as a mere legal transaction that gives us a ticket to heaven, but what happened at Golgotha runs much deeper than that. In giving His life, Jesus secured the whole planet. You and I will not be spending eternity in an ethereal existence, strumming harps on fluffy clouds. We will be living in a restored creation, the home originally created for the human race.

Notice that Paul does not say Jesus plans to deliver us from this earth, even though this planet in its current form will be "burned up" (2 Peter 3:10). He says that Jesus will "deliver us from this present evil age." Yes, we will spend time in heaven, perusing the books (Revelation 20:4, 12) and reigning with Christ. But then we will return to our proper sphere: planet Earth, with the "last Adam" claiming dominion as our King.

Yes, the Cross purchased your salvation. But it also purchased the whole world, and through Calvary, you are warmly invited back home.

The Price of a Scam

For thus says the LORD: *"You have sold yourselves for nothing,*
and you shall be redeemed without money."

—Isaiah 52:3

You can make up to twenty dollars an hour stuffing envelopes!" Back in the pre-internet days, when Tim found the ad in the classified section of the newspaper, twenty dollars an hour was an inordinate hourly wage. He chose to ignore the pleadings of common sense and sent away for the offered kit. When it arrived, he was excited. It told him there were two available options: an entry-level position and a high-level position. The materials for one cost twenty dollars; the other cost forty. He was in no doubt about which one he wanted, so he put forty dollars in the enclosed envelope and sent it away.

What he got in return was, to say the least, a bitter disappointment. It was a single sheet of paper that read, "Nobody is going to pay you twenty dollars an hour to stuff envelopes. That job does not exist. But you *can* potentially make that much if you put an ad in the classifieds offering people an envelope-stuffing opportunity."

The return on his "investment" was ridiculous. Today, there are more sophisticated versions of the scam that pop up in your email inbox—some of which offer millions of dollars if you would only help fund the release of the money from a foreign country. The people who fall for such things often find themselves out of thousands of dollars, and unfortunately, it is often the people who can least afford it who fall for such things.

The same is true of the human predicament. In spite of God's clear warning, we chose to believe that disobedience would bring special wisdom, even godhood. The price for believing lies was incalculable. It was the spiritual equivalent of an email scam: like Israel in Isaiah's day, we sold everything we have in return for nothing—and there is nothing we can do, no sum we can pay, to rectify the situation.

Fortunately, God is willing to redeem us "without money." That does not mean our redemption is cheap, however: It is not inexpensive to redeem an entire planet. It cannot be done with money, and it cannot be done with our efforts, no matter how noble. It could only be accomplished with the sacrifice of God's only begotten Son.

Extravagant Abundance

"Why do you spend money for what is not bread, and your wages for what does not satisfy? Listen carefully to Me, and eat what is good, and let your soul delight itself in abundance."
—Isaiah 55:2

One summer, when I was about six, my family went camping. While my parents were busy with pitching camp, I walked into the woods to explore. About forty feet into the trees, I suddenly felt a blinding pain above my left eye, and I ran, crying, back to the campsite. When the pain eventually subsided, my spirit of adventure returned, and I walked back into the woods. Again, about forty feet into the forest, I suddenly felt more pain above my eye and then a sharp pain on the side of my neck.

It was caused by a hornets' nest, hanging at face level. The nest was green, like the foliage around it, so it was nearly invisible. I had bumped it with my head while ducking under the branch—twice!

One would think that the intense pain of a venomous sting would keep a small child from returning to the same location, or at least cause him to investigate the scene carefully before proceeding, but human beings do not always act rationally. Sometimes, we have to be stung several times before we figure out that walking the same path will always hurt.

In Isaiah 52:3, God told Israel that they had "sold" themselves for "nothing." Now in Isaiah 55:2, He points out a secondary, but equally serious problem. Once we have bartered away our eternal life with God for an empty lie, we seem to feel that we can find our own solutions to the problem. It hurts to discover that we are lost sinners with an empty existence, and yet we persist in making the problem worse by seeking our own resolutions. Some turn to religious systems based on human merit. Others turn to money, power, sex, fame, or just about anything that promises to replace what has been lost.

What we invariably discover is that our man-made solutions are just other lies. We sold ourselves for nothing, and then we spend our lives chasing very expensive, but utterly empty promises that leave us just as hungry as before. God reminds us that there is only one solution to our sin problem: to listen to Him carefully and delight ourselves in His extravagant abundance, which, of course, was on full display at the cross of Christ.

The Inspectable God

"Speak to all the congregation of Israel, saying: 'On the tenth of this month every man shall take for himself a lamb, according to the house of his father, a lamb for a household.' "
—Exodus 12:3

On the day that most of the world now calls Palm Sunday, Jesus rode into the city of Jerusalem to the delight of adoring crowds who wanted to crown Him as King. The tragic irony, of course, is that just a few days later, the adulation of the masses would turn to mockery. But for one day, they could not get enough.

It was the Passover season, and the city was packed with observant pilgrims who would sacrifice a spotless lamb on the fourteenth day of the month to commemorate the night that the league of death passed over homes where the blood of an innocent lamb was smeared above the doorpost (see Exodus 12:6–14). Each family chose the lamb several days in advance and tied it to a stake, putting it on display for their neighbors to inspect. Was it *really* the best they had? Was it *really* free of blemish?

The lambs were chosen on the tenth day of the month and kept on display until the fourteenth. It just so happens that Jesus—"the Lamb of God who takes away the sin of the world" (John 1:29)—rode into the city on the very day when families were busy with the business of selecting a lamb to put on display. The whole process had been anticipating this very moment. Heaven was putting its Lamb on display for the nation to inspect, and for the moment, they deemed Him worthy with loud Hosannas.

After His arrest, when the high priest asked Jesus about His doctrine, Jesus was able to say, "I spoke openly to the world. I always taught in synagogues and in the temple, where the Jews always meet, and in secret I have said nothing. Why do you ask Me? Ask those who have heard Me what I said to them. Indeed they know what I said" (John 18:20, 21).

It had been true throughout Jesus' ministry: God had put Himself on full display for our inspection. It was especially true of His last week. Even though twenty centuries have passed since that triumphant ride towards the cross, Jesus, your Passover, remains on full display for you in the pages of the Bible. The decision left to you is whether you will deem Him worthy and crown Him as your King.

Heaven's Valentine

"This is My commandment, that you love one another as I have loved you.
Greater love has no one than this, than to lay down one's life for his friends."
—John 15:12, 13

In much of the Western world, today's date has been marked as Valentine's Day, a day of love. For most people, it means flowers, chocolates, cards, and maybe dinner. (For the people in Loveland, Colorado, it means taking people's Valentine's Day cards and remailing them, so they can bear the Loveland postmark.) But the man behind the day has been obscured by hundreds of years of tradition.

Valentine was a clergyman who, in the third century A.D., defied the orders of Claudius II, the Roman emperor, who apparently forbid monogamous marriage to many on the grounds that unmarried men fought more bravely because they had no outside considerations. Valentine secretly conducted marriages until he was caught, at which point he was beaten, then stoned, and finally beheaded.

Or so the story goes. As with many of the hagiographies written about Christian martyrs long after their deaths, the story has probably been embellished to the point of distortion, and you will find multiple versions of his biography online as people continue to pad the story. Did he truly die for marrying people? We do not know. But he *did* apparently die for his faith in the year A.D. 269, as did many Christians who lived before Constantine's conversion in the fourth century.

His most likely "crime" was not matrimony but a refusal to quit preaching the gospel. And so it goes with many Christians: once we see the lengths to which Jesus was willing to go to secure our salvation, we begin to mirror that same kind of selfless love, to the point where we do not love our lives to the death (Revelation 12:11).

When someone is willing to die to save us, there is little room to question the depth of that person's love and commitment. As we see Jesus writhing in agony on a rough Roman cross, it begins to dawn on us that He values mere sinners more than He values His own life. Real love—the kind that God exhibits and longs to have reproduced in His children—runs much deeper than cards and flowers. Real love lays "down one's life for his friends." Perhaps today, you can find an opportunity to express real, selfless love that asks for nothing in return so that someone can see Jesus in you.

FEBRUARY 15

Once and for All

*And every priest stands ministering daily and offering repeatedly the same sacrifices,
which can never take away sins. But this Man, after He had offered one sacrifice for sins forever,
sat down at the right hand of God, from that time waiting till His enemies are made His
footstool. For by one offering He has perfected forever those who are being sanctified.*
—Hebrews 10:11–14

Read the language of today's passage carefully, and you will notice something interesting. The author mentions that "every priest stands" but then goes on to say that Jesus *sits*. That is because the business of running the sanctuary was never finished. Every sacrifice offered was symbolic, which meant that it could not actually serve to cleanse the sinner of guilt. A few verses earlier we are told that "it is not possible that the blood of bulls and goats could take away sins" (Hebrews 10:4).

The lambs and bulls offered at the altar were *types*, or symbols, of a greater reality that was still to come: the Lamb of God who would come to take away the sin of the world. Once the yearly cycle of sacrifices had been complete, the children of Israel had to start it all over again, because the reality had not yet come. That meant that the priests were very busy with the business of sin, day in and day out. But when Jesus gave His life at Calvary, He cried out, "It is finished!" The cross is *enough*. The sacrifice of God's Son is sufficient for all time and will provide for your needs *forever*.

Jesus did not continue to offer Himself daily, although He continues to represent us before the throne in order to apply the merits of His sacrifice to us. One of the great misunderstandings that arose in Christianity as it pushed into the medieval period was the notion that Christ had to be "sacrificed" by ordained clergy every day for sinners to find forgiveness through His blood. The emblems of the Communion service—the bread and the wine—were said to become the *actual* body and blood of Christ, and the Communion table was described as an "altar."

When studied through the lens of Hebrews 10, we know that what Christ did at the cross was enough. Read it again, and have faith in what He has accomplished for you. When He gave His life for you, He was able to *sit* because the work of sacrifice was utterly complete. Today, you can rest in the knowledge that the Cross is indeed enough for you and that there is nothing you can add to Christ's sacrifice that will make it any more efficacious.

The Anonymous Roman

There were also two others, criminals, led with Him to be put to death.
And when they had come to the place called Calvary, there they crucified Him,
and the criminals, one on the right hand and the other on the left. Then Jesus said,
"Father, forgive them, for they do not know what they do."
—Luke 23:32–34

The Bible never names the Roman soldier who picked up the hammer and pounded the spikes through Jesus' hands and feet. To be sure, the Bible writers had no trouble implicating the other individuals who helped orchestrate His execution. Annas, Caiaphas, and Judas, for example, have been memorialized forever. But the actual executioners remain anonymous; the Bible simply says "they" crucified Him.

Was it the soldier's first crucifixion or his hundredth? Did he wince or recoil as he brought the hammer down on Jesus' hand? Did he feel remorse or reticence? Was he a hard man who felt little compassion, or a feeling man compelled by Roman society to carry out something he personally found repulsive? We do not know; we know nothing about the individual because the Bible chooses to be silent about his identity.

I am convinced that the omission is deliberate. Perhaps, if the soldiers had been named, the Crucifixion would become too impersonal, looking too much like someone else's fault. Without names, however, the blame falls exactly where it belongs: We are *all* guilty at the foot of the cross. "*All* have sinned and fall short of the glory of God," Paul wrote to the Christians in Rome (Romans 3:23; emphasis added). "But He was wounded for *our* transgressions," Isaiah reminds us. "He was bruised for *our* iniquities. The chastisement for *our* peace was upon Him, and by His stripes *we* are healed" (Isaiah 53:5; emphasis added).

Isaiah's language is generic and universal, and because of that, the implications are deeply personal. Somebody *else* did not do it; *we* did. The sinful human race must accept responsibility. Those who want the peace Christ offers and who wish to be healed by His stripes must also own responsibility for what happened to Him. Read that passage from Isaiah one more time, out loud, but place your name in the blanks: He was bruised for _____'s iniquities. The chastisement for _____'s peace was upon Him, and by His stripes _____ is healed.

Now go back and look at the incredible mercy of Jesus as He suffers at our hands; His prayer of forgiveness can also be claimed by all: "Father, forgive them, for they do not know what they do." Unbelievably, if you are willing to claim your sins, you can also claim your forgiveness.

A Talent for Love

And those who passed by blasphemed Him, wagging their heads and saying,
"You who destroy the temple and build it in three days, save Yourself!
If You are the Son of God, come down from the cross."
—Matthew 27:39, 40

One of the most disturbing things about human nature is how capable we are of ignoring even the most basic instinct for compassion. A Man is writhing in agony on the cruelest instrument ever devised, and the passersby cannot help but mock Him. He has already been crucified for His supposed crimes, but that is not sufficient. The crowd is not satisfied. The hatred of Jesus' enemies runs deep. It is not enough to see Him permanently removed from public ministry; they must let Him *know* how much they hate Him, rubbing salt in His wounds until He draws His final breath.

It is an awful moment for the human race; our faces ought to burn with shame as we watch our behavior. Instinctively, we know it is true: in our lifetime, we have seen enough of our own species' behavior that we recognize in the words of Christ's enemies our own penchant for cruelty.

How can we explain it? Most people generally consider themselves to be good until the very worst products of our sinful hearts begin to surface; and we find ourselves at a loss to explain how we still have not solved the problems that plague us most. People lie, steal, and murder. We riot in the streets, and we commit unspeakable crimes against our own kind.

Listen carefully to the words of those who mock Jesus; you will find an important clue to the source of our wickedness: "*If* You are the Son of God, come down from the cross!" These words bear the unmistakable signature of their author. In the wilderness, Satan approached Jesus with the same question: "*If* you are the Son of God, command that these stones become bread." "*If* You are the Son of God, throw Yourself down" (Matthew 4:3, 6; emphasis added).

The original author of doubt, the devil himself, inspired our hatred for God. By sinning, we have thrown ourselves so completely into his camp that we find ourselves capable of killing the innocent Son of God. And make no mistake: He *could* have come down from the cross. He did not owe us salvation. But His love for us runs deeper than our talent for wickedness, and He knew He needed to stay there if we were ever going to be re-created in His image.

"He Saved Others"

Likewise the chief priests also, mocking with the scribes and elders, said,
"He saved others; Himself He cannot save. If He is the King of Israel,
let Him now come down from the cross, and we will believe Him."
—Matthew 27:41, 42

I will confess that ever since I was a very young man, I have been a political enthusiast. In fact, before I became a professing Christian, my life's ambition was to run for political office. Those dreams have now been pushed aside for a life of full-time ministry; but I must admit that every election season, I am still somewhat drawn to the spectacle of candidates seeking public office.

When I listen to the words of politicians, however, and then I hear how the news media portrays what was said, I sometimes wonder if we were listening to the same speech. Sometimes, the portrayal of a candidate's position—the caricature painted by a string of disjointed but well-parsed sound bites—is so inaccurate that I am tempted to believe that the reporter is running against the candidate. Small statements are wrenched from their context and made to look as if the person who originally stated them is naive, foolish, or downright evil.

It is a practice that is as old as the human race, and it was on full display the day we crucified Jesus. "He saved others," the religious leaders mocked, "Himself He cannot save." The public conduct of Jesus was widely known and reported. People knew that He had miraculously touched countless lives—that He had gone about "doing good and healing all who were oppressed by the devil" (Acts 10:38).

There was simply no denying the power of Jesus' ministry and the beauty of His flawless character. It would be hard to explain why they crucified Him; the only choice they had was to diminish and ridicule what He had done. "If this Man is *truly* a Savior," they mocked, "then why can't He save Himself?"

It was the same thing Satan had done in the Garden of Eden: cast doubt by raising questions about God's right to occupy the throne. As with most spin doctors, the sad tragedy is that the chief priests, the scribes, and the elders were *almost* right. They would have been absolutely correct had they changed but one word: "Himself He *will* not save." Jesus could have saved Himself, but that is not the nature of God's love. He *would* not save Himself if it meant that He could not save *you*.

Where He Is When It Hurts

Now from the sixth hour until the ninth hour there was darkness over all the land.
And about the ninth hour Jesus cried out with a loud voice, saying,
"Eli, Eli, lama sabachthani?" that is, "My God, My God, why have You forsaken Me?"
—Matthew 27:45, 46

Karen was understandably angry. When she was a small girl, someone had hurt her very badly. "Where was God when that man did that awful thing to me?" she demanded as we sat together in the sanctuary. "I was just a little girl!" The tears started to stream down her cheeks.

There are times in life where silence is better than trying to cobble together a hasty answer; to me, it felt like one of those moments. Sometimes, it is just appropriate to weep and tell God how much things hurt and how confused you are by the way things played out. Even the Son of God cried out in His humanity when it felt like His Father was not there. Of course, there is a profound difference between my experience and His: He was utterly innocent. He did not *have* to live in this world and subject Himself to the ravages of a human race detached from God; He *chose* to.

The hard reality of living in a fallen world is that sin has a harsh—and unavoidable—price. Our sins do not only affect *us*, but they negatively impact our environment as well: the people we meet, the relationships we build, and the homes we live in. If God were to start eliminating *all* evil, preventing all consequences, on this side of the Second Coming, where would we like Him to stop? Before He comes to the way *we* hurt people?

And sometimes, it is best to remember that there *is no good* explanation for sin. In the words of Ellen White, "It is mysterious, unaccountable; to excuse it is to defend it. Could excuse for it be found, or cause be shown for its existence, it would cease to be sin."★

One thing is certain: God Himself is not responsible for sin and suffering, and yet He willingly and fully bore the consequences of our sin. The sins that separate us from God were placed on Jesus; He bore them so fully that He felt complete absence from His Father.

Where was God that time you felt hurt and alone? On a cross, feeling the pain and separation of sin more fully than any of us ever will—and that cross is His pledge to one day wipe away every tear in a world free from separation.

★ Ellen G. White, *The Great Controversy* (Nampa, ID: Pacific Press®, 2002), 492.

To Have a King

When they had twisted a crown of thorns, they put it on His head,
and a reed in His right hand. And they bowed the knee before Him
and mocked Him, saying, "Hail, King of the Jews!"
—Matthew 27:29

The original Old Testament, which ended with the book of 2 Chronicles before we changed the order, leaves off with an incredible sense of anticipation.
It is obvious to the reader that the story is not finished; the kingdom of God has
not yet been realized. The story ends with Nebuchadnezzar sacking the temple in
Jerusalem, suddenly followed by Cyrus pledging to restore the temple.

It is obviously incomplete. To its earliest readers, the Old Testament was a story
that begged for a conclusion. To the careful modern reader, it is obvious that the
authors of the New Testament were deliberately picking up where 2 Chronicles left
off: Jesus *was* the King they were waiting for.

It makes the mockery that took place in the Praetorium that much worse. To be
sure, it was not an Israelite who pushed the crown of thorns onto Jesus' head; it was a
Roman soldier. Romans would not tolerate anybody perceived to be a threat to the
empire. But the reason Jesus was in the Praetorium, suffering such incomprehensible
indignities, was because the rulers among God's own people *also* perceived Him as a
threat. They had rejected the long-awaited King.

It is easy to look back in history and stand aghast at the behavior of God's supposed covenant people, but what is not so immediately obvious is our own tendency
to reject the kingship of Christ. We often beg God for solutions to our problems,
insisting that He intervene to make things right. We demand that the Author complete the story, solving our own incompleteness, but often we reject the answer
when He does.

To be sure, we go through the motions. We bow the knee to Scripture and pay
lip service to the inspired Word when in the company of other Christians. But in
private, we push God's solution to one side, making a mockery of it by our neglect.
Like Naaman, we refuse to wash in the humble, muddy Jordan, choosing instead to
repair our problems in our own way.

Yes, it is easy to feel disgusted as we watch ancient Roman soldiers mock the
King of heaven, certain that we would never do it. But in truth, we often do the
same thing. Is Jesus really our King, and if He is, do our lives reflect that we truly
believe it?

The Indictment

And they put up over His head the accusation written against Him:
THIS IS JESUS THE KING OF THE JEWS.
—Matthew 27:37

It is not a light matter to condemn a prisoner to death. In our own world, a death sentence can take many years to implement. Appeals are filed, evidence is reexamined, and every stone is turned over to be *sure* that the person convicted of a capital crime is actually guilty. In Jesus' day, if the court landed on a guilty verdict in a capital case, they had to take a full day off and then come back and vote again. If you had previously voted for acquittal, you could not change your mind; you could only change if you had previously voted *guilty.*

Every precaution was taken to be sure that severe penalties were not imposed accidentally—or maliciously. If you had a personal stake in the case, you were not allowed to join the proceedings, and the purpose of the court was *not* to convict. The court was required to find, if possible, a reason for acquittal. Even voluntary confession by the accused was not enough to convict; they had to have the testimony of at least two independent witnesses to the same act. A false witness, when discovered, would suffer the fate he was trying to impose on the accused.

The court was stacked in your favor. If you were found guilty of a capital crime and sentenced to die, the odds were exceptionally good that you were, indeed, blameworthy.

Of course, in the case of Jesus, the trial was a sham, and they broke nearly every rule in the book: The witnesses were false, the evidence was rigged, and the proceedings were illegal! Even before the arrest, they knew they would find Jesus guilty.

That is why the sign above Jesus' head is so telling: He was supposedly guilty of a capital crime, but the sign was noticeably devoid of any substance. All they could say was "King of the Jews," and ironically, *that* happened to be true. Even the sign, intended to mock Christ, was an unwitting declaration that He really is "a lamb without blemish and without spot" (1 Peter 1:19).

What was intended as an indictment of Jesus proved to be an indictment of *us*: it was not God's crimes that led to His execution; it was exclusively our sin. Oh, what wondrous love is this!

King of the Jews

Then many of the Jews read this title, for the place where Jesus was crucified was near the city; and it was written in Hebrew, Greek, and Latin. Therefore the chief priests of the Jews said to Pilate, "Do not write, 'The King of the Jews,' but, 'He said, "I am the King of the Jews."' " Pilate answered, "What I have written, I have written."

—John 19:20–22

When the angry crowd brought Jesus to Pilate, he asked them, "What accusation do you bring against this Man?" (John 18:29). The original charge, the one brought by the high priest himself, was blasphemy. They did not have the political authority, however, to impose the death penalty. They knew that the Romans would find the charge of blasphemy insignificant; the Romans simply did not care about the religious regulations of the Jews. When the crowd told Pilate that Jesus was an "evildoer" (verse 30), he dismissed the charge as trivial. "You take Him and judge Him according to your law," he declared (verse 31).

That is when they changed tactics and made an appeal to the political stability of the Roman Empire. "We found this fellow perverting the nation," they told Pilate, "and forbidding to pay taxes to Caesar, saying that He Himself is Christ, a King" (Luke 23:2). For the Romans, building a kingdom, challenging the authority of Caesar, was a crime worthy of death.

Thus the irony of the sign over Jesus' head. Some of the religious authorities had been worried that Jesus' preaching would bring the wrath of the Romans on the Israelite nation. To be sure, they were eager to overthrow the Roman Empire and be ruled by the One who would come to sit on David's throne; but they would not concede that Jesus was the Messiah, the King they had been anticipating.

In bringing the charge of sedition against Jesus, they were actually cooperating with the Roman Empire, acknowledging its authority and claiming Caesar as their king. In fact, when Pilate asked them, " 'Shall I crucify your King?' the chief priests answered," unbelievably, " 'We have no king but Caesar!' " (John 19:15).

So the question comes to us today: Is Jesus truly our King, or do we only acknowledge Him when it suits our own ambition? In our personal, unspoken protests against the revealed will of God, are we willing to hang a sign over the head of Jesus that pays higher tribute to the god of this world than it does to Him? Like the crowds that clamored for an addition to the sign, do we say that Jesus *says* He is King, or do *we* say He is King?

There is a world of difference.

Seizing Christ's Garment

Then the soldiers, when they had crucified Jesus, took His garments and made four parts, to each soldier a part, and also the tunic. Now the tunic was without seam, woven from the top in one piece. They said therefore among themselves, "Let us not tear it, but cast lots for it, whose it shall be," that the Scripture might be fulfilled which says: "They divided My garments among them, and for My clothing they cast lots." Therefore the soldiers did these things.

—John 19:23, 24

One of the more uncomfortable truths about the cross is just how complete the humiliation of the victim was. Medieval painters are careful to protect the dignity of crucified victims, but the Roman historians assure us of the hard truth: any semblance of dignity was stripped away. Jesus was treated as worthless, and His executioners did not hesitate to refrain from heaping as much humiliation on Him as possible.

His garments were divided among the soldiers, five items in total. The Bible does not tell us what the first four items were, but commentators have made an educated guess: headgear, belt, sandals, and the *tallith,* a fringed shawl used for prayer. The Bible is more specific about the fifth item of clothing: the tunic, which was essentially an undergarment worn like a long shirt. It was the most intimate of the items given to the soldiers, made of one piece. Instead of ripping it apart and sharing the material, they gambled and gave the garment to the winner.

The Roman soldiers could not have possibly understood that they were fulfilling prophecy at that moment, but students of the Psalms should have seen it. In their attempt to humiliate Jesus, the Romans were inadvertently advertising Him as the long-awaited Messiah.

Imagine, for a moment, the coldness of watching grown men seize your possessions, more concerned about personal gain than the fact they have just subjected you to the cruelest form of torture ever conceived. Your *garment* is more important than you are, and their absolute apathy toward your suffering would suggest they do not *deserve* it.

The irony? Jesus would have given it to them had they asked. "If anyone wants to sue you and take away your tunic, let him have your cloak also," He once taught (Matthew 5:40). The bigger irony? His death on the cross meant that you and I could be clothed with the garment of His righteousness, which is also complete and indivisible in its own right. Without that garment, we *cannot* be admitted to the great wedding feast that awaits the saved (Matthew 22:11).

Without the death of Christ, there would be no garment for the Romans to seize. And without the death of Christ, there would be no garment for *us* to seize either.

The Plight of the Immigrant

Therefore remember that you, once Gentiles in the flesh—who are called Uncircumcision by what is called the Circumcision made in the flesh by hands—that at that time you were without Christ, being aliens from the commonwealth of Israel and strangers from the covenants of promise, having no hope and without God in the world. But now in Christ Jesus you who once were far off have been brought near by the blood of Christ.
—Ephesians 2:11–13

Moving to America as an immigrant was not an easy process. Every day there were constant reminders that I was *not* American; I was "other." My credit was suddenly nonexistent. Even though I held a license that validated me as a driver if I happened to be a *tourist*, I was required to pass a road test if I wanted a California license—like a sixteen-year-old novice. Admittedly, my immigration experience was not as difficult as it could have been: except for a handful of words and a few silent *u*'s I had to drop from my spelling, I already spoke the language.

I came on a work visa that was constantly being questioned by immigration authorities, and more than once, I was detained at the border for questioning. The process of acquiring permanent resident status was long, difficult, and often involved humiliation at the hands of government employees who seemed to care very little for my well-being. Ultimately, it took several years, many dollars, much frustration, and the help of a good lawyer to become a fully integrated member of society.

It would do us well to understand that in the kingdom of heaven, you and I are "other." As sinners, we have a value system that is utterly at odds with the will of God. We have different priorities, and we speak a different language. And while people wonder aloud whether or not certain groups of immigrants might pose a danger to their way of life, we should probably understand that sinners *do* pose a threat to the peace and happiness of God's universe. If you happened to be of first-century Gentile extraction, you were not even party to the covenant God made with Israel.

Is it difficult to become a citizen of God's kingdom? It is *unbelievably* hard. In fact, you and I do not have what it takes; our sins utterly disqualify us forever. We have "no hope" and are "without God in the world." The good news? Jesus handled the immigration process. He has done all the hard work, and now "you who once were far off have been brought near by the blood of Christ."

Immigration means starting all over. It also means a lot of blood, sweat, and tears; but the blood, fortunately, belongs to Jesus.

The Ministry of Reconciliation

*For it pleased the Father that in Him all the fullness should dwell, and by Him to reconcile
all things to Himself, by Him, whether things on earth or things in heaven,
having made peace through the blood of His cross. And you, who once were alienated
and enemies in your mind by wicked works, yet now He has reconciled in the body of His flesh
through death, to present you holy, and blameless, and above reproach in His sight.*
—Colossians 1:19–22

The actor Morgan Wallace is usually given credit for a now-famous saying about disputes. "There are three sides to an argument," he said, "your side, my side, and the right side." Anybody who has been involved in a long-standing argument knows that he was right. Over time, tempers grow hotter, small issues and off-the-cuff statements swell to disproportionate dimensions, and the guiltier each party becomes.

Seldom is one party completely innocent. Everyone is in need of reconciliation. But unwittingly, many of us carry the same assumption into our dispute with God: If there is a gulf between humanity and the Creator, there must be blame on both sides! We look at the pain and suffering caused by our own rebellion, and then we tend to hang the blame on God. Over the centuries, He has quietly endured the unjust shaking of many fists in His direction.

But you will notice that when the Bible speaks of reconciliation, it *never* says that God must be reconciled to man. God is an innocent party; we have no legitimate claims against Him. You and I are "alienated and enemies," the only guilty parties in a contest against a blameless Creator.

We are in need of reconciliation to God, not the other way around. It ought to be up to us—entirely—to heal the gulf that exists between us and our heavenly Father. But God knows that we are incapable of bridging the chasm. Our hearts are so corrupted by sin that we *cannot* make things right. So what does He do? He takes the initiative where we could not and reconciles *us* to *Him*.

How did He accomplish that? He came over to our side of the controversy and bore our guilt, even though He is perfectly innocent. He became one of us—a human being—and He lived a perfect life. He satisfied the claims of the law and now offers to be your Substitute, to stand in your place. "Through the righteousness of Christ," Ellen White explains, "we shall stand before God pardoned, and as though we had never sinned."★

Could it be any clearer that we are defenseless and hopeless without Jesus? "Nothing in my hand I bring," says the old hymn, "simply to Thy cross I cling."†

★ Ellen G. White, *Selected Messages*, bk. 3 (Hagerstown, MD: Review and Herald®, 2007), 140.
† Augustus Toplady, "Rock of Ages," 1763.

The Sacrifice of Faith

By faith Abel offered to God a more excellent sacrifice than Cain, through which he obtained witness that he was righteous, God testifying of his gifts; and through it he being dead still speaks.
—Hebrews 11:4

When I was a little boy, the story of Cain and Abel used to bother me. It just seemed so arbitrary: God accepted Abel's sacrifice but refused Cain's. They both just brought what they had. The shepherd brought a sheep, and the farmer brought vegetables. Was God being unreasonable?

It was not until later in life, when I studied the book of Hebrews, that I finally got it. Neither offering intrinsically did *anything* for either of them. You cannot ask a vegetable *or* a sheep to stand in as your substitute; they are not sinful human beings faced with the wages of sin. The reason Abel's sacrifice was accepted is because he offered it by *faith*. He understood that the lamb on the altar was only a symbol pointing forward to the Lamb of God who would come to take away the sin of the world (John 1:29). He was not placing his faith in the lamb; he was placing his faith in the Seed of the woman, who would come to crush the serpent's head (Genesis 3:15). His faith was in the merits of Jesus.

The wages of sin is death, the Bible assures us (Romans 6:23). God told our first parents that if they chose to rebel against His government, they would "surely die" (Genesis 2:17). The penalty for transgression is death. Not the death of an animal, "for it is not possible that the blood of bulls and goats could take away sins" (Hebrews 10:4). The lamb on Abel's altar could not possibly solve his problem; his sins required his *own* death.

But Abel had faith that God's promise would be realized and God's solution would work. He understood that we are saved through Christ's death. Jesus' innocent blood was shed for us, and the demands of the law have been met. Jesus stands in our place. Our guilt is placed on Him. Paul says that Jesus was made "to be sin for us, that we might become the righteousness of God in Him" (2 Corinthians 5:21).

Try as you might, like Cain, to correct your own guilt, but the only thing that will meet the demand of sin is your life. You have nothing of value to throw at the problem unless you have the blood of Jesus, which God declares to be enough.

The Anxious Father

Being justified freely by His grace through the redemption that is in Christ Jesus, whom God set forth as a propitiation by His blood, through faith, to demonstrate His righteousness, because in His forbearance God had passed over the sins that were previously committed.
—Romans 3:24, 25

When our daughter was scheduled for surgery, I could see her anxiety growing as the circled date on the calendar grew near. She is a brave kid, and it is enviably hard to dampen her spirits. But I did notice her growing grimmer by the day. "Nobody looks forward to surgery," I assured her, "including me." I have had a number of procedures myself, so she was constantly asking what it would be like. I knew the road to the operating room.

But what I did not know was the road a parent must travel. I found myself even more anxious than her. I knew the pain she would suffer, and I knew the risks of surgery. Submitting your child to a general anesthetic is never 100 percent risk free.

When the day came, I was nearly sick to my stomach with worry—but I did not let her see it.

As the human race walked out of Eden, the waiting began. We were sick and in need of a radical solution. The promised solution was the Seed of the woman who would come to crush the serpent's head. As each new child was born into the world, God's people wondered, "Could *this* be the Messiah?" Humanity was anxious, and justifiably so—the wages of sin, after all, is death.

We understand our part of the equation well. What we do not understand is the anxiety felt in the courts of heaven. Each sin, each violation of God's moral law, demanded the life of the sinner. The accuser could point to each violation and insist that God was being unfair: Satan had been removed from heaven for sin, and the human race appeared to be freely perpetuating it.

Was God merely passing over human sin? According to Paul, the astonishing answer is *yes*. He was not excusing sin—that would be impossible, a violation of His own just character—but He *was* passing over it, waiting for the day when Jesus would stand in our place and justice could be satisfied. Some people suggest that Jesus is shielding us from a Father who wishes to destroy us. On the contrary, Paul shows us that the Father was waiting anxiously for the whole ordeal to be over, passing over our sins so that He could save us.

God, it seems, is more anxious than we are.

I Am a Worm

But I am a worm, and no man; a reproach of men, and despised by the people.
—Psalm 22:6

I once read the description of an audience reacting to the great nineteenth-century preacher Charles Spurgeon, who was describing the crucifixion of Christ. There were audible gasps, people who sobbed openly, and some who were not able to sleep for days afterward.

It made me question whether or not a modern audience would ever react the same way. Please do not misunderstand what I am saying: I have met many good Christians who are profoundly moved by the events at Calvary. I have seen many sinners shed tears. But what Spurgeon's audience was reacting so viscerally to was the mere description of the Crucifixion.

The cruelty was enough to make them feel sick.

You know this statistic well: today, the average Western child has witnessed more than two hundred thousand violent acts and sixteen thousand murders by the age of eighteen, thanks to popular media. Why so much violence? Is the devil simply trying to make us bad people? Or is it possible that all that violence might be designed to *numb us to the violent reality of what we did to Jesus*?

I do not know of many Western audiences who would be moved by simply reading the account of the Crucifixion anymore. Perhaps the closest we have come is Mel Gibson's movie *The Passion of the Christ*, which many audiences, when confronted with a visual representation of what Jesus endured, found *too* violent. (I do not recommend the movie; it is not a faithful biblical account. I am only pointing out how high our tolerance for violence against others has become. Our tolerance for violence against ourselves? That has dropped significantly.)

What is widely regarded as a Messianic prophecy shockingly describes Jesus as a "worm." I used to wonder why, until a wise scholar pointed out that the original word describes a "crimson grub." It was a small worm used to dye clothing; it had to be *crushed* to obtain the dye. Only then could a bolt of fabric be altered into something beautiful.

It is almost impossible to comprehend what Jesus suffered in order to cover our sins. Perhaps it is time to silence the media in our lives and "spend a thoughtful hour each day in contemplation of the life of Christ."★ Dwell on it; marvel at the infinite price paid by God's Son. It cannot help but change you.

★ Ellen G. White, *The Desire of Ages* (Nampa, ID: Pacific Press®, 2002), 83.

March

I renounce the world and its sinful ways, and have accepted Jesus Christ as my personal Savior, believing that God, for Christ's sake, has forgiven my sins and given me a new heart.

Set Free

Then I heard a loud voice saying in heaven, "Now salvation, and strength, and the kingdom of our God, and the power of His Christ have come, for the accuser of our brethren, who accused them before our God day and night, has been cast down."
—Revelation 12:10

I was finished speaking, and the usual line of visitors gathered by the side of the platform: a few to express appreciation for the meeting, some to correct what they perceived to be errors, and others to ask questions. After a quarter century of presenting the Bible, I had come to expect the group and settled in for a few hours of visiting. Near the front of the line was a man who looked deeply concerned. "I'd like to follow Jesus," he said, "but there's something in my life I need to stop doing."

"So stop doing it," I said. A look of genuine surprise washed across his face. I suppose he had been used to having preachers listen to him describe his problems for hours on end, but nobody had ever thought to tell him he could simply *quit*. "Look," I continued, "I'm sure you're frustrated because whatever it is, you probably did it today—or yesterday. But tomorrow, you don't have to do it, because you have been freed by the cross of Jesus."

Millions are slaves to sinful habits because they do not understand that one simple concept: The devil was utterly defeated at the cross of Calvary. He only has power over your life if you grant it to him.

No, you cannot just stop a long-ingrained habit by exerting more willpower. Your own initiative is not enough to break the bonds of sin. But you *can* stand on the fact that the accuser of the brethren has been cast down, and Jesus offers you a new life. You *can* claim the victory that God wants to give you over a destructive lifestyle. By God's grace, you can accept His gift and declare yourself free.

There is a timeworn tale about a massive elephant being held in place by a small stake and a rope that was obviously too thin to hold him. A tourist marveled at the fact that the elephant felt trapped, until the trainer explained, "I started with that stake when he was just a calf, and it held him. He became so used to it that he still thinks it will hold him. He doesn't even try."

It is time to try the rope. It has already been broken by the same force that broke the bonds of death for Jesus.

"All That I Have"

"And he said to him, 'Son, you are always with me, and all that I have is yours.'"
—Luke 15:31

By the time most people come to the last few verses of the parable of the prodigal son, they are skimming past the details. It is, after all, a rebuke aimed at the bitter son who could not understand why his wayward brother would be celebrated when he was the one who had faithfully served his father.

There is, however, a key detail in the rebuke that we should not overlook. "All that I have is yours," the father told the angry sibling. Allow your heart to bathe itself in those words today: *All that I have is yours*. When Jesus purchased your salvation at Calvary, He did not merely obtain a "get out of jail free" card for you; He gave you a share in His kingdom. You will sit on a throne. You will live and reign with Him (Revelation 20:4). All that the Father has is yours.

It is a thought that not only boggles the imagination, it also changes how you choose to live. What is there to worry about when Christ's kingdom is yours? Anything that happens to you during the course of your life—no matter how challenging, no matter how painful—is fleeting. It will pass. The moment is coming when you will hear Christ's voice inviting you into the kingdom He secured through His faithfulness: "Well done, good and faithful servant; you have been faithful over a few things, I will make you ruler over many things. Enter into the joy of your lord" (Matthew 25:23).

It is a gift that defies human comprehension. How can we afford to waste time comparing ourselves to others when the reward we have been granted through the Cross is already inconceivably larger than we deserve? How is it that we allow the faults of others to irritate us when we do not deserve the gift *we* have been given?

Through the cross of Christ, you will not slide into heaven by the skin of your teeth. You will enter heaven with the applause that only Jesus deserves. You will be given a victor's crown to wear, knowing that the only One who truly deserves such recognition is Jesus (Revelation 4:10, 11).

"All that I have is yours," the Father says. Knowing *that* ought to profoundly influence how you live.

To Forgive Like God

"For if you forgive men their trespasses, your heavenly Father will also forgive you. But if you do not forgive men their trespasses, neither will your Father forgive your trespasses."
—Matthew 6:14, 15

Deborah eyed me suspiciously. "What do you mean *forgive him*? Do you have any idea how badly he hurt me?"

"No, I don't," I answered softly. "But I do know that he's *still* hurting you, because you haven't let go of it. You're living with that pain every single day. Forgiveness doesn't mean you have to like what he did or say that it's acceptable. It *isn't* acceptable, which is precisely why it requires forgiveness. Why not let him go?"

Forgiveness can be a really tall order. As I was dispensing advice, I knew full well that I struggle with the same problem: some hurts seem too big to release. But the only person being destroyed by allowing yourself to marinate in the pain is *you*. It is far better to let go.

After all, God has let go of what *you* did through Christ.

The gist of what Jesus is saying appears to be, "I want you to be as generous and patient with others as I have been with you!"

"Forgive us our debts," Jesus taught us to pray, "as we forgive our debtors" (Matthew 6:12). "But if you do not forgive men their trespasses," He explained further, "neither will your Father forgive your trespasses" (verse 15).

When you begin to grasp the magnitude of Christ's gift on the cross—when you hear Him cry out for a Father who doesn't appear to be there at that moment, when you begin to realize what a high price He paid to secure your place in His kingdom—it becomes obvious that God's generosity is boundless. His capacity to forgive is incomprehensible.

"A new commandment I give to you, that you love one another," Jesus told His disciples, "as I have loved you, that you also love one another" (John 13:34).

Left to our own devices, it is hard to love, and it is especially hard to forgive. Grudges often run deeper than the pain actually caused by the offense committed against you. But as you witness Jesus taking your bill of debt and nailing it to His cross (Colossians 2:14), it becomes very difficult to hang on to bitterness.

Once you begin to realize how completely you have been forgiven, it changes how you live with those around you.

Rewriting the Bible

If we confess our sins, He is faithful and just to forgive us our sins
and to cleanse us from all unrighteousness.

—1 John 1:9

It was a cold night in northern Europe. I had finished preaching, and just outside the door to the auditorium, a young woman was waiting to talk to me. She could barely start speaking before the tears welled up in her eyes, and her voice cracked. "I get what you've been saying in there," she said, gesturing toward the stage where I had been speaking for several days, "and it sounds so wonderful, but I don't think it's for me."

I asked her why not. "You don't know what I've done," she said in a hoarse whisper, not daring to make eye contact.

"That's true," I responded. "I don't. But God does, and I can tell you right now that if you feel remorse for it—if it bothers you *this* much—that's an indication that the Spirit of God is trying to bring you home. Otherwise, you wouldn't even care. I promise: You're being called by God, and He will forgive you. He's not just teasing you; this is for real."

She could not accept it. I opened my Bible and handed it to her, pointing to a verse. "Read this for me," I said. "Out loud."

She read the words. "If we confess our sins, He is faithful and just to forgive us our sins and to cleanse us from all unrighteousness." She was quiet for a moment and then looked up at me.

"Here," I said, handing her a pen from my coat pocket. "I want you to take this pen and write something in my Bible, right behind that verse." She hesitatingly took the pen. "I want you to write the word *except* at the end of that verse, and then write in whatever it is that you've done."

She handed the pen back in horror. "I can't do *that!*" she said. "I can't change what the Bible says!"

"You might as well," I said, "because you're already changing what God says by the way you refuse to believe that He means *you.*"

She blinked and then smiled—she got it. She was finally free. There are no ifs, ands, or buts: there are no exceptions in the verse. If you confess your sin, He is willing to cleanse you from *all* unrighteousness.

Not Good Enough

For scarcely for a righteous man will one die; yet perhaps for a good man someone would even dare to die. But God demonstrates His own love toward us, in that while we were still sinners, Christ died for us.
—Romans 5:7, 8

"Can I talk to you for a moment?" I had never seen him before, but the first impression he gave was that of a defeated man.

"Sure," I said. "Just let me finish what I'm doing, and I'll be with you in a couple of minutes." I quickly wrapped up the task at hand and followed him into the hall. We sat next to each other on a bench, where he let out a deep sigh, almost as if the impact of sitting had forced the air out of his lungs. He was quiet for a moment, and then turned his head toward me, revealing tears piling up on his lower eyelids.

"I just don't know that I'm going to make it," he said. "You don't know what I've done, and there's no way for me to make things right with God. I'll never be good enough."

"You're right on a number of counts," I responded. "I *don't* know what you've done. But God does—and you're right, you're never going to be good enough."

He looked surprised. I suppose some people had tried to make him believe that he *was* good enough in order to cheer him up. But long after empty platitudes evaporate into the air, a sinner's heart has a way of reminding him how impossible it is to fix what ails him most and just how far short of God's glory he falls. No pep talks and positive thinking in the world can convince a sinful heart that it can redeem itself. A heart gripped by conviction knows better.

"That's the whole point," I explained, pointing him to today's text. "Paul tells us that Jesus didn't wait for you to become good enough to give His life for you. He did it while you were still a sinner, and that's because He knows you can't make the first move. He gave His life not because you were good enough, but because you *weren't*, and you *couldn't be*. It's the whole point: We're not good enough, but He is. And if there's one thing I know you can count on, it's that His love will overcome every deficiency you have. Listen to me carefully: God *wants* you."

Let it sink in today: God wants you.

The Real Prize

Again, the devil took Him up on an exceedingly high mountain,
and showed Him all the kingdoms of the world and their glory. And he said to Him,
"All these things I will give You if You will fall down and worship me."
Then Jesus said to him, "Away with you, Satan! For it is written, 'You shall
worship the Lord your God, and Him only you shall serve.' "
—Matthew 4:8–10

For most people, the devil's offer would be irresistible. Just one quick bow, one quick act of obeisance, and he gives you the whole world. I do not know of many people who could resist—even if they suspected there might be a catch.

Fortunately, Jesus is not most people. The devil knew that He had come to reclaim the planet that we had recklessly handed to Lucifer the moment we rebelled against God. Since the Fall, Satan has been claiming this world as his own, even making an appearance in the heavenly council to mention that he had been "walking back and forth on it." The fact that he considered himself able to offer it to God's Son is further proof that he believes he owns the earth.

He does not; that was clearly proven at the cross. But before Christ finally takes it back and establishes His kingdom, our world will undergo an exhaustive renovation, because Jesus did not come to retake the world the way it *is*; He came to restore it to what it *was*.

This is the reason that Christians "renounce" the world. We understand that this planet is only a shadow of what it once was, so we reject the philosophy and government of fallen angels—a dispensation that led to our present misery. If Jesus had bowed the knee to Satan, all would have been lost. He would have been in violation of His own moral law, and He would not have been fit to stand in as our perfect Substitute. And, even if the devil *had* made good on his promise and given this planet to Jesus, it would not have been the prize He was seeking.

We reject the world the same way Jesus did: He loved the people who lived here and gave His life for them. He walked with them, befriended them, and worked for their good. But then He pointed them forward to something better: the kingdom of Christ, Paradise restored.

Those who love this world the way it is should understand that it is destined for the trash heap of history—because God did not create us to suffer, weep, and die. And even though Jesus has not yet come, we can already start living as if we were in the world made new.

To Renounce the World

*Do not love the world or the things in the world. If anyone loves the world, the love
of the Father is not in him. For all that is in the world—the lust of the flesh,
the lust of the eyes, and the pride of life—is not of the Father but is of the world.*
—1 John 2:15, 16

Martin had been coming to evangelistic meetings for several weeks. Ron, the evangelist, was delighted to discover a request for baptism on one of the decision cards that had been turned in over the weekend. By Monday night, he was at Martin's house.

Like any good evangelist, he began to lead Martin through the baptismal vows to be sure that he understood what joining the church means. When they came to the third vow, which states, "I renounce the world and its sinful ways," Martin hesitated. *Oh no*, Ron thought. *There's some obstacle in his life that he's not willing to deal with.*

"I'm not sure I can say this," Martin protested. Ron flinched, fearing the worst. "Because how can I renounce the world when Jesus died for it?"

It was an excellent point. When Christians say that they "renounce" the world, they do not mean the people who live on planet Earth. The Bible is referring to the worldly mind-set that has kept human beings in rebellion against their Creator and the painful results of sin that have plagued us ever since our fall from grace. There is little question that the pain and suffering Jesus witnessed broke His heart during His years of public ministry. How could a loving Creator possibly feel any love for the devastating results of sin? And who could possibly love the mind-set that nailed God's Son to a cross?

Hating the *world* is not the same as hating the *worldly*. In Gethsemane, Jesus did not relish the thought of bearing the consequences of our sin. "If it is possible, let this cup pass from Me," He prayed (Matthew 26:39). Mere hours later, He was overwhelmed with compassion for those who had crucified Him: "Father, forgive them, for they do not know what they do" (Luke 23:34).

It is nearly impossible to stand at the foot of the cross, witness such amazing love, and not begin to hate the things that caused the awful moment when we cried for the death of Christ. That is hating the world. Then, as we begin to love the God who gave His life for us and our hearts become more like His, we will find ourselves irresistibly drawn to other sinners who have yet to see the Jesus we know.

Finding True North

"The heart is deceitful above all things, and desperately wicked; who can know it?"
—Jeremiah 17:9

I am not sure if kids still do it, but most kids of my generation had to make a compass with a sewing needle and a tiny bit of cork. If you rubbed the needle with a magnet a few times, the needle would become magnetized. Then when you pushed it through a tiny piece of cork and floated it in a dish of water, the needle would spin until it was aligned with the North Pole. (Or the South Pole, if you lived in the Southern Hemisphere.)

It was a handy bit of information, especially if you happened to find yourself lost in the woods with a magnet, a needle, and a bit of cork. The problem with a compass, however, is that while it *approximates* the direction of north, it does not lead to the North Pole. It points to a sort of "magnetic island" (as the early explorers called it) that lies at a considerable distance from the actual North Pole. If you are far enough south, the difference is somewhat negligible; your compass is roughly accurate. If you are in the high Arctic, the disparity becomes more dramatic—and far more problematic. You can actually be north of magnetic north.

Another problem? The magnetic north *moves*. During the twentieth century, it moved almost seven hundred miles to the northwest; and presently, it continues to move about thirty miles each year.

The sinful human heart is like a compass that only approximates true north. We have retained some capacity for judging the difference between right and wrong (thanks to the prompting of the Holy Spirit), but our hearts have been so deeply affected by sin that we tend to follow the drifting moral standards of sin and selfishness. Sin is not merely a list of wrong actions; it is a deep-rooted problem that has affected our moral instrumentation. Our actions may be sinful, but that is because our *hearts* have become sinful.

Jeremiah points out that our hearts have been corrupted to the extent that, much of the time, we cannot even determine how far we have strayed from God's will. That is why we need new hearts; the old ones will never find true north. Fortunately, Jesus knows exactly where true moral north is, and He has offered to give us brand-new compasses.

Only Human

*For I delight in the law of God according to the inward man. But I see another law
in my members, warring against the law of my mind, and bringing me into captivity
to the law of sin which is in my members. O wretched man that I am! Who will deliver me
from this body of death? I thank God—through Jesus Christ our Lord! So then,
with the mind I myself serve the law of God, but with the flesh the law of sin.*
—Romans 7:22–25

It was late on a Friday afternoon, and I was at the Greyhound station, eagerly waiting for the bus to arrive. I was planning a number of baptisms for the next morning in a church that did not own any baptismal robes. It was not an insurmountable problem: I knew of a church that had plenty, so I phoned and asked if I could borrow some. They promised to put them on the next bus.

When the bus arrived, the package was *not* on it. The clerk behind the counter did not care. "I'm sure it will show up one of these days," he told me.

"Can't we trace it?" I asked. He shrugged. "Listen, I don't need them 'one of these days,'" I assured him a little more forcibly, "I need them *now!*" His indifference was pushing my buttons, and I lost my temper.

The exchange grew testier by the moment, and eventually, I stormed out. A few hours later I got a phone call: they had found the package. When I walked back into the bus station, the box was on the counter—with the name of my church written on the side in big, unmistakable letters.

I felt deeply ashamed. I had been a terrible witness and was horrified to discover just how close to the surface some of my old, pre-Jesus nature still lurked. But then I remembered Paul's words. He wrestled with the same thing. He loved the Lord, and he *wanted* to live as a new creature. But in this world, immersed in a sinful atmosphere and confronted daily with temptations, he discovered that the old nature still pushes back sometimes.

There is a reason the Bible teaches that we are to live by faith: we must consciously *choose* to believe that we are new creatures. The devil will present many opportunities for us to doubt that the new birth is real; and when we slip, he will be quick to make us question everything. We must refuse to listen.

I apologized to the bus station clerk. It was the least I could do. I even told him that I had behaved poorly for a man who professes to be a Christian. He smiled. "I get it," he said, "you're just a human being."

Smart guy. We should all be so smart.

It's Just a Furnace

"If that is the case, our God whom we serve is able to deliver us from the burning fiery furnace, and He will deliver us from your hand, O king. But if not, let it be known to you, O king, that we do not serve your gods, nor will we worship the gold image which you have set up."
—Daniel 3:17, 18

The response of Daniel's friends to Nebuchadnezzar can be a tough pill for twenty-first-century Christians to swallow. Throughout the latter part of the twentieth century, a lot of Western Christian preaching has emphasized the temporal rewards for choosing Christianity. We have been assured that following Jesus probably means success and wealth. Those who do *not* realize such "benefits" can find themselves wondering if God has overlooked them.

The prosperity gospel, as it has come to be known, is not an accurate biblical picture of what it means to live in a covenant relationship with God. While there are moments when God underlines His plan for prospering the nation of Israel, overlooking the point of this story is to miss something very important: when we choose to follow Christ, we are deciding that we are willing to forgo the comforts of this world to have Him forever.

Sometimes, there are *no* rewards to be realized in this life. Hebrews 11 provides a long list of people who did not see the reality of the rewards of God in this life: "All these," the author reminds us, "having obtained a good testimony through faith, did not receive the promise" (Hebrews 11:39).

Jesus once told the story of a man who discovered a pearl that was so valuable, he was willing to sell everything he had—absolutely everything—to be able to buy it (Matthew 13:45, 46). That is the essence of choosing Christ: once you realize who He really is, the value of everything else pales by comparison, even your life itself.

"For what profit is it to a man if he gains the whole world, and loses his own soul?" Jesus taught us (Matthew 16:26).

Sometimes, forsaking the world comes with a price. That is the reason Jesus told us to count the cost of discipleship carefully (Luke 14:28). "Even if we *knew* that God wouldn't rescue us from the furnace," the young Hebrews explained to the king of Babylon, "that wouldn't change our minds. We won't give up Jesus in order to pledge allegiance to you."

Perhaps you know all too well that discipleship comes with a cost. Remind yourself that it is just a furnace; and when you reckon accounts a million years from now in the presence of Jesus, you will see that He was all the reward you ever needed.

Jumping a Rope

Let no one deceive you by any means; for that Day will not come
unless the falling away comes first, and the man of sin is revealed, the son of perdition,
who opposes and exalts himself above all that is called God or that is worshiped,
so that he sits as God in the temple of God, showing himself that he is God.
—2 Thessalonians 2:3, 4

In the tenth grade, I paid a visit to the Parliament buildings in Ottawa. A Canadian senator had invited our class to visit the Senate chamber, where we were allowed to sit behind the senators' desks. But the big chair at the front of the room caught my attention—the seat reserved for the queen. It was roped off to keep visitors from accessing it.

I could not help myself. Just as the visit came to an end, I hopped over the rope and sat in the queen's place. I do not know how many visitors have done the same thing over the years, but I do know this: it is a stunt the entire human race has pulled with God.

In his second letter to the Thessalonians, Paul predicted the rise of the "son of perdition," who would attempt to lay claim to God's throne. In doing so, the man of sin would be following in the footsteps of Lucifer himself, who wanted to sit on the throne of the universe (Isaiah 14:13, 14).

The man of sin, however, is not alone in this act of defiance. He is merely standing at the head of the entire human race, which first rejected God's rule in Eden and has been trying to usurp God's authority ever since. Apart from Christ, we are all guilty of the same thing: we attempt to sit on God's throne, second-guess His counsel, and call the shots ourselves. The result, tragically, is nearly always the same—it ends in heartbreak or even outright disaster.

It is one thing to point fingers at large institutions that obviously fit Paul's description; it is quite another to understand our own complicity in the rebellion. The man of sin and the "prince of the power of the air" (Ephesians 2:2) would not have empires to rule if it were not for the millions of self-interested subjects willing to follow their lead. Evil reigns because human beings are willing to entertain it or, at the very least, are unwilling to embrace Christ's offer to free them from its grip.

When Christians pledge to renounce the world, they admit that it is time to quit jumping over the rope to sit in a seat that clearly does not belong to them.

Sharing a Throne

But God, who is rich in mercy, because of His great love with which He loved us,
even when we were dead in trespasses, made us alive together with Christ
(by grace you have been saved), and raised us up together, and made us sit together
in the heavenly places in Christ Jesus, that in the ages to come He might show
the exceeding riches of His grace in His kindness toward us in Christ Jesus.
—Ephesians 2:4–7

Back in college, I used to hang out a lot at the legislative buildings in Victoria, British Columbia, because I enjoyed watching members of the assembly duke it out during the question period, which is a time set aside in the afternoon for the opposition party to question the government. One day, after leaving the visitors' gallery, I stumbled into the premier of the province in the rotunda; he was trapped in a crowd of hostile journalists.

He had no idea who I was, but when he saw me across the rotunda, he jumped at the chance to end his torment and break free from the reporters. "Hey!" he called out, as if I was a long-lost friend. "It's good to see you!" He walked over, put his arm around my shoulder, and said, "Let's take a walk." We walked down the hall to his office complex. When we stepped into the lobby, there were some highly influential people waiting to see him; I recognized them from the news.

"I'll be with you in a moment," he said and then walked me past them into his office. He closed the door, invited me to sit, and spent the next ten minutes asking me about my life before he stood up and wished me well. Even though I was dressed in a ratty, old sweater and ripped jeans, the most powerful man in the province had just treated me like I belonged in his office.

Most human beings spend their lives tragically trying to seize God's throne or trying to play God's role in their own lives. Ultimately, it is a losing battle: nobody but God will ever occupy that throne because God alone is the Creator. There is a sad irony in fighting God's rule, however: In the end, Jesus actually wants to share His throne with those who are willing to follow Him. He wants to seat you in heavenly places with Him. "To him who overcomes I will grant to sit with Me on My throne," Jesus promises, "as I also overcame and sat down with My Father on His throne" (Revelation 3:21).

The key to peace of mind in this world is to trust the generosity of God; He is not ruling this universe for His sake but for ours.

Name-Dropping

*"Therefore whoever confesses Me before men,
him I will also confess before My Father who is in heaven."*
—Matthew 10:32

There is no more sure way to reveal your personal insecurities than to become a name-dropper. Name-dropping is the art of deliberately mentioning the names of famous and influential people you have (hopefully) encountered to persuade others that you move in much higher circles than you believe you do.

Those who are truly connected or influential, however, seldom feel the need to impress others by mentioning the people they know.

The beautiful thing about forsaking the world is the way it puts the powerful, the influential, and the wealthy people of this planet back in their proper perspective: they are just other human beings who happen to have more. And sometimes, that "more" can serve as a tether to this world, making it harder to forsake everything in order to pursue Jesus.

Once you have seen Jesus through the light of Calvary, and you have grasped His magnificent gift—forgiveness and redemption through the cross—mere human beings cease to impress you unless you happen to catch a glimpse of the character of Christ in them. It can be one of the most liberating moments in a person's life to realize that the crowned heads of Europe, the members of Congress and Parliament, and the captains of industry all stand on an equal footing at the foot of the cross. No human law could ever hope to achieve the kind of human equity that Jesus provides.

Once you begin to grasp that God is offering direct access to His throne through Jesus, it is not hard to forsake the power structures of this world or to walk away from the demands the priorities of a sinful world place on you. While the Bible requires believers to respect the governments they find themselves subject to—as far as is possible without violating the will of God—forgiven sinners can delight in the fact that we are not merely forgiven but truly free to start living as if the kingdom of God has already arrived.

As it turns out, Jesus is also a name-dropper, but He drops names quite unlike the way we do it. There is no human being more influential than Jesus; ultimately, the name He most loves to drop in heaven is *yours*.

Digging Up the Dead

"Therefore if the Son makes you free, you shall be free indeed."
—John 8:36

Consider the old story of a motorist who accidentally ran over a cat while speeding down a country road. The driver pulled over, got out of the car, and discovered that the animal had not survived. Racked with guilt, he looked up and down the road, trying to figure out who might have owned the cat. Spotting a farmhouse in the distance, he picked up the deceased pet and carried it to the front door.

When the homeowner answered his timid knocks, he broke into tears. "I don't know how to tell you this, but I'm afraid I have killed your pet," he said, presenting the body.

The cat's owner was visibly shaken but spoke softly. "Listen," she said, "I know that accidents happen, and this could have happened to anybody. So I forgive you. Why don't we go out back and bury this cat together?"

Together, they walked over to the garage to retrieve a shovel, and then they went behind the house for a quick, impromptu funeral service. Afterward, the homeowner tried to reassure the still-shaken driver: "Now remember, this is over, and I forgive you. I want you to put this out of your mind."

A week later the same motorist was driving down the same country road, when he suddenly saw the farmhouse where he had been the week before. The same feeling of guilt suddenly overwhelmed him, so he stopped the car, walked around to the back of the house, and *dug up the cat.* Then he rang the doorbell again, and when the surprised homeowner answered, he said, "I don't know how to tell you this, but I'm afraid I have killed your pet." He broke into tears again.

"You fool!" said the lady of the house. "I forgave you for this a week ago! I told you to leave it behind! What are you doing digging up the body?"

Admittedly, the story is a little macabre, but it makes a powerful point. The Bible teaches complete and utter forgiveness for sin. "If the Son makes you free," Jesus told His disciples, "you shall be free indeed." When God offers forgiveness, the matter is closed. So ask yourself, Why do you continue to go back and dig up that which God has already buried?

Probing Your Wounds

*Who is a God like You, pardoning iniquity and passing over the transgression
of the remnant of His heritage? He does not retain His anger forever,
because He delights in mercy. He will again have compassion on us,
and will subdue our iniquities. You will cast all our sins into the depths of the sea.*
—Micah 7:18, 19

James Garfield is not among the best-remembered American presidents, in spite of the fact that he is one of only four who were assassinated. On July 2, 1881, Charles Giteau—an eccentric and delusional man who had believed Garfield would give him a diplomatic position in France—took revenge for his disappointment by shooting the president in the back at the train station in Washington, DC.

Garfield probably should have survived the wound. The bullet did not hit any vital organs and became lodged behind his pancreas. Most modern experts agree that it was not the bullet that killed him; it was the *doctors.* Why? Because within minutes of the assassination attempt, they began to probe the wound with their unwashed fingers, attempting to find and extract the projectile. Twelve different physicians examined his back with various instruments in vain while on the floor of a less-than-sterile train station.

The medical community had not yet accepted Joseph Lister's germ theory. For eighty days, the president slowly grew weaker as infection ravaged his body. He began to shed pounds, dropping from 210 pounds to 130 in a matter of weeks. Desperate to remove the bullet, the president's doctor summoned Alexander Graham Bell, who he hoped would be able to find the bullet with a metal detector. The instrument was useless; the metal springs in the president's bed gave false readings all the way through the examination.

Finally, on September 9, Garfield succumbed to his wounds. He had not died from the assassin's bullet, however, but from the repeated probing of his wound.

For many of us, it is not the individual sins we commit that destroy our Christian experience. It is our refusal to believe that we are truly forgiven. Instead of leaving things with Jesus, we insist on probing old wounds again and again, to the point where our failure to believe leaves us spiritually sick. The practice of faith means choosing to believe that when God says He is finished with your guilt and sin, He means it. Continually retrieving your confessed and forgiven past will rob you of the joy Jesus intends for you to have. It is time to quit probing your old wounds and believe what God says: old guilt lies far too deep to be retrieved.

The Patience of God

Then Peter came to Him and said, "Lord, how often shall my
brother sin against me, and I forgive him? Up to seven times?"
Jesus said to him, "I do not say to you,
up to seven times, but up to seventy times seven."
—Matthew 18:21, 22

For years, I read the above story as if Jesus had simply pulled a massive number out of His head to emphasize to Peter that forgiveness should know no bounds. Of course, the prominence of the number seven in Jesus' formula also underscores the concepts of completion and perfection. So, on the one hand, Jesus is telling Peter to go above and beyond any human understanding of forgiveness to something much bigger and far more generous—the love and forgiveness that God offers.

Those ideas are certainly present in Jesus' formula, but I cannot help but notice that the total in Jesus' example comes to 490. To Peter's Hebrew mind, that would have been a significant total. Remember that the Jews were exiled to Babylon for seventy years—one year for every sabbatical year they had failed to observe (2 Chronicles 36:20, 21; Jeremiah 25:11). Since the sabbatical year fell every seventh year, the total period of apostasy would be 490 years.

Was Jesus perhaps suggesting that we should be as forgiving and tolerant with others as God is with us? Nearly half a millennium is a very long time for God to wait for Israel to make things right; you and I are clearly not that patient with each other.

When God's people returned from Babylonian captivity, they were given another 490-year opportunity to reestablish the covenant and prepare for the Messiah to come, "to make reconciliation for iniquity, to bring in everlasting righteousness, to seal up vision and prophecy, and to anoint the Most Holy" (Daniel 9:24). In other words, God waited patiently for the same period of time *twice*.

Those who are convinced that God is an angry, vindictive deity have likely failed to notice just how much patience God exercises throughout the Bible. He is incredibly reluctant to lose even one sinner. If you are ever tempted to doubt God's capacity and willingness to forgive, remember Jesus' words to Peter: God is far more patient and forgiving than we are. Try to imagine the extent of God's willingness to forgive, His willingness to save you and bring you into His kingdom, and you will likely be wrong. He loves you even more than *that*. Your job is to believe that He forgives and live as if it is true.

Upside Down

But when they did not find them, they dragged Jason and some brethren to the rulers of the city, crying out, "These who have turned the world upside down have come here too."
—Acts 17:6

March 17 is the day much of the world has set aside to remember Saint Patrick, the missionary who brought Christianity to a decidedly pagan Ireland. At the age of sixteen, he was kidnapped by Irish pirates, who were among the most feared slave traders in northern Europe. They were so skilled at stealing children that they were able to sneak into homes undetected, and the parents only found out what had happened when the sun came up in the morning.

At the time of his abduction in the early fourth century, Patrick was not a Christian, even though he had been exposed to the faith at home. Forced to work as a shepherd for an Irish chieftain, he was often hungry and miserably cold. He found himself with little to no human company, and with no place to turn but the God his father had served. Through much prayer, he became a devout believer.

After six years, he suddenly heard a voice in his sleep, telling him that he was about to go home. *"Look, your ship is ready,"* the voice said. He chose to believe what he had heard and walked about two hundred miles to the coast, where he discovered the ship he had been promised. After trekking the European mainland for a few years, he eventually found his way back to Britain.

Then he suddenly had another profound dream, in which the voices of the Irish were imploring him to come and share the gospel. How could he possibly return to his tormentors? At first, he resisted, but when the dream repeated itself, he became convinced that Jesus was sending him.

At a time when the rest of Europe was descending into the ignorance of the Dark Ages, the Celts in Ireland suddenly accepted Christ and became the most literate and dedicated missionaries the world has ever seen. Before long, they had established centers of learning from one end of Europe to the other and kept the light of the gospel alive when it was in danger of extinction just about everywhere else. That is the power of a life changed by Christ. If we could only accept that He is able to give us new hearts and clean slates, we would become unstoppable. Like Patrick, we could turn the whole world upside down.

It's a Gift

For in it the righteousness of God is revealed from faith to faith;
as it is written, "The just shall live by faith."

—Romans 1:17

Before Martin Luther truly grasped the terms on which God forgives and accepts us, he lived a tortured existence as a monk. Believing that right living and self-denial would somehow expunge his record of sin and guilt, he punished himself repeatedly in an attempt to bring his sinful nature under control.

"I was a good monk," he writes, "and I kept the rule of my order so strictly that I may say that if ever a monk got to heaven by his monkery it was I. All my brothers in the monastery who knew me will bear me out. If I had kept on any longer, I should have killed myself with vigils, prayers, reading, and other work."★

Of course, all of his efforts failed because the problem of sin is too serious and our guilt far too deep to be overcome by our own efforts. Luther's attempts at self-cleansing—the fasting, the self-deprivation, the punishment—failed him so miserably that even the Sermon on the Mount began to torment him. "This word is too high and too hard that anyone should fulfill it," he said of Jesus' words, "flesh and blood cannot rise above it."†

It was in the city of Rome, where sinners climbed Pilate's staircase in an attempt to expunge their sins that Luther finally struck upon the all-important truth of the gospel: we do not *earn* forgiveness; we accept it by faith. According to some versions of the old story, as he was climbing the staircase, our text for today suddenly flashed into his mind: "*The just shall live by faith.*"

The moment changed Western Christianity forever. There is nothing you and I can do to *earn* forgiveness. Yet the Bible promises that we *can* be forgiven, which leads to the astonishing conclusion that we can only obtain forgiveness as a gift. But for some reason, to the sinful human mind, that seems harder than working off a debt. Our pride can stand in the way of receiving large gifts because we believe that we have to return the favor or earn the gift. Not so with Jesus: our job is to believe that when He says we are forgiven, His word is absolutely true—and live as if it is so.

★ Martin Luther, quoted in Roland Bainton, *Here I Stand: A Life of Martin Luther* (New York: Abingdon Press, 1950), 45.

† Luther, quoted in Bainton, *Here I Stand*, 46.

"Remember the Duck!"

Do you not know that to whom you present yourselves slaves to obey,
you are that one's slaves whom you obey, whether of sin leading to death,
or of obedience leading to righteousness? But God be thanked that though you were slaves
of sin, yet you obeyed from the heart that form of doctrine to which you were delivered.
And having been set free from sin, you became slaves of righteousness.
—Romans 6:16–18

Brian was beyond excited; his grandfather had given him a slingshot for his birthday. He ran out into the backyard and started launching stones against everything: trees, fence posts, and firewood. It did not take long for Brian to realize, however, that he was a terrible shot. He missed everything. Disgusted with himself, he returned to the house, and that is when he saw Grandma's pet duck walking past the firewood pile.

I'll probably miss anyway, he thought to himself and quickly fired a stone in the duck's direction. To his horror, the stone found its mark, and the duck dropped dead. Panicking, Brian grabbed the dead bird and stuffed it into the woodpile. When he had disposed of the evidence, he turned to find his sister Marilyn smirking. She did not say a word; she simply turned around and went inside.

After lunch, Grandma asked Marilyn to help her with the dishes. "But Brian said *he'd* like to do the dishes today, didn't you, Brian?" Under her breath, she whispered, "Remember the duck!" Brian did the dishes. That evening Grandpa asked Marilyn to clean up the toys in the basement. "But Brian said he would do it!" she protested, giving Brian a knowing look.

For two weeks, Brian did all of Marilyn's chores, terrified that she would expose his crime. After a while, he could not take it anymore. Choking back the tears, he went into the living room and confessed. "Grandma," he said, "I need to tell you something. A couple of weeks ago I was out in the yard with my slingshot, and I killed your duck!"

Grandma put down the book she was reading and signaled for Brian to sit next to her on the couch. "Come here," she said softly. Brian climbed up next to her, and she put her arm around him. "I know what you did," she told him, "because I saw the whole thing through the kitchen window. And I forgive you because I love you. But I *was* wondering how long you were going to let your sister make a slave out of you!"

The devil would love to hold you in bondage to sins that God is willing to forgive. He knows what you did, and He is eager for you to simply come clean.★

★ This is not an original story, and it may well be apocryphal. It is, however, a personal favorite that powerfully illustrates slavery to sin. I have used it many times.

The Paradox

Jesus answered and said to them, "Those who are well have no need of a physician, but those who are sick. I have not come to call the righteous, but sinners, to repentance."
—Luke 5:31, 32

Tragically, there are some people who are simply too good to be saved. Some people barge their way through life with a growing list of personal accomplishments on a clipboard attached to their belts, ready for the moment when God (or whatever they happen to believe in) asks them to give an account. "Just look: I have always been a good person. To the best of my knowledge, I have never cheated, lied, or stolen. I have always tried to live by the golden rule, and I believe I'm the perfect candidate for heaven."

There is nothing God can do for such people; those who are blind to the serious flaw of sin will never ask the Great Physician for help, and God will not force Himself on people who do not ask. In the minds of some of Jesus' contemporaries, the Messiah would naturally want to devote much—or most—of His time to the moral luminaries who were keeping Israel on the straight and narrow during the years of Roman occupation. Desperate to keep the nation from falling into the same sins that had led to the Babylonian exile, many of the scribes and Pharisees had fallen into the opposite ditch and had become fastidious about rules, rites, and regulations.

It was still the sin of pride and self-sufficiency, however. Before the Babylonian exile, God's people had chosen self-determination by creating a homemade, pagan-hybrid religion to suit their own taste. Now they were clearly rejecting the paganism of the Romans, but they were still relying entirely on self and, in trying to remain pure, had ironically become blind to their true condition.

Those who were painfully aware of their sins found little hope in such a religious atmosphere. Surrounded by people who continually underscored their personal moral achievements, they became even more despondent, certain that heaven was not for them.

Jesus came to set despondent people free. "I know you're not well," He says to broken sinners. "That's why I came: because you needed Me."

Approaching Jesus is paradoxical: The closer you get, the less righteous *you* seem. That is not a problem. Comprehending your brokenness is the path to the solution. The real problem? When you are so far from the Light that you become blind to your true nature.

Renovate or Rebuild?

Then He spoke a parable to them: "No one puts a piece from a new garment
on an old one; otherwise the new makes a tear,
and also the piece that was taken out of the new does not match the old."
—Luke 5:36

Years ago in college, I used to do disaster restoration. One afternoon the phone rang, and a woman's voice informed me that some of her friends had noticed a slight odor in her home, and she was wondering if I could fix it.

A few days later I knocked on her door, and when she answered, the "slight" odor spilled out of the open doorway and nearly made my eyes water. I stepped inside and immediately spotted the problem: the bottom of the living room walls were stained all the way around. Her cat had been spraying, and the damage was extensive and horrific. I was about to tell her, in very plain terms, what the problem was when I spotted a large oil painting of a cat above the fireplace—*her* cat.

I knew it was not going to be easy for her to hear the truth. "Is it possible," I asked gently, "that your cat has had a little accident at some point?" Honestly, I have no idea how she could have missed it!

I will never forget her response. She immediately grew tense and retorted hotly: "My cat doesn't do that!" There was no convincing her.

I gave her an estimate for fixing the problem, which amounted to thousands of dollars. She was incensed. "Just spray a little deodorizer in here!" she demanded. She wanted a twenty-dollar solution to a two-thousand-dollar problem.

Far too many people, sensing their sin and guilt, attempt to cover them up. We dust off our spiritual résumés and put our best foot forward, convinced that all we really need to be right with God is a little deodorant. While our friends will occasionally be fooled by the masking effects of deodorizing spray, God is not fooled. We cannot throw twenty dollars at a billion-dollar problem. The solution is not a new patch on an old garment or a little paint on a sin-stained heart. The only solution is a *new* heart. A renovation will not do it; only a rebuild will make you spotless and odor free. You must get out of the way and turn it over to a professional—and the only One with the resources you need is Jesus Christ, the sinless Lamb of God.

My *Im*perfect Feet

But we are all like an unclean thing, and all our righteousnesses are like filthy rags;
we all fade as a leaf, and our iniquities, like the wind, have taken us away.
—Isaiah 64:6

I cannot, for the life of me, remember what started the conversation, and I will readily admit that it seems very strange to write it down for your consideration. For some reason or another, I was looking at my feet, and knowing that there is little about my physical presence that a sculptor would find inspiring, I wondered aloud if perhaps my feet were not nice looking—you know, for *feet*.

I know; it is not the kind of thing most people contemplate. In reality, my feet are exceptionally asymmetrical, one being a full size and a half larger than the other. But apart from that, I had never considered the possibility that they were unattractive until my wife actually *laughed*.

"What?" I asked, a little confused.

"Really? Your *feet*?" She laughed again. Apparently, my feet are not among the things that first attracted my wife to me. But how could I possibly be so blind and not see them as they really were?

So it is with sinners. Before we are faced with the incarnate truth of God in Jesus, we tend to believe that we are somehow morally attractive. On most days, we have no problem looking in the mirror and seeing people whose accomplishments have more than paid any moral debt we might owe. Sin so warps the human heart and mind that, without an outside opinion, we can scarcely see the problem.

But then it happens: at some point in your life, the carefully crafted persona your mind has convinced you is authentic is suddenly ripped away and you can suddenly see yourself as God does. In the light of His glory, any supposed good a human being has done is suddenly revealed as being thoroughly tainted by sinful motives. You will hear a sudden voice from heaven, letting you know that even your best has not redeemed you—and *cannot* redeem you—from sin.

The longer you stand in God's presence, the worse it seems. You have a choice: You can ignore it and try to return to a state of ignorance, but that will solve nothing. On the other hand, you can admit your guilt and accept forgiveness, at which point God considers the matter closed, because you now appear to look very much like His Son.

New Heart, New Eyes

For I consider that the sufferings of this present time are not worthy to be compared with the glory which shall be revealed in us. For the earnest expectation of the creation eagerly waits for the revealing of the sons of God. For the creation was subjected to futility, not willingly, but because of Him who subjected it in hope; because the creation itself also will be delivered from the bondage of corruption into the glorious liberty of the children of God.
—Romans 8:18–21

We appear to be born with the expectation that life will be beautiful, that people will be good, and that the world will cooperate with us. The painful realization that our natural expectations will not be met is one of the greatest wounds our hearts receive. At some point, we all realize that our fellow human beings prefer themselves above all else and that they are willing to squash our hopes and dreams if it means advancing theirs. We become aware that the natural world fights against us too. In addition to natural disasters, the planet will always push against the things we build: foundations and roofs leak; lawns and trees become sick and die; our bodies begin to disintegrate with age.

Unless we come to grips with reality and both identify the cause of it and begin to understand that we are unable to fix the problem ourselves, we are destined for a life of disappointment. One of the most important gifts God grants us in giving us new hearts is the capacity to recognize that something has gone devastatingly wrong with this world, along with a stubborn defiance that rejects the way things *are* and hungers for the way things *were* before we derailed God's original plan with our rebellion.

Many of the nineteenth-century nihilist philosophers who rejected God's existence were left psychologically defenseless against the harsh reality of a world that seems brutally pitted against life. They had nowhere to turn and nothing to hope for. With the gift of new hearts, however, you and I have been given the liberty to lift our eyes above the fray and fix our hopes on what God has promised for the future.

A new heart gives us the gift of a prayer life, allowing our own hopes and dreams to become more completely aligned with God's. It grants us the ability to speak directly to Someone whose heart also aches over this world and longs for complete restoration. It dares us to hope, to start once again to notice the fingerprints of God in creation, and to begin to sense that God has not abandoned the planet but has a profound plan to restore what we have ruined.

Consider your new heart a down payment on a brand-new world.

MARCH 24

What Jill Got Wrong

For we know that the whole creation groans and labors with birth pangs together until now. Not only that, but we also who have the firstfruits of the Spirit, even we ourselves groan within ourselves, eagerly waiting for the adoption, the redemption of our body. For we were saved in this hope, but hope that is seen is not hope; for why does one still hope for what he sees?
—Romans 8:22–24

Taking my cue from the popular evangelist Dan Bentzinger, I named my first-ever global positioning system (GPS) unit. The fact that she *talked* to me as she gave me directions seemed to demand that she have a name. Not having much of a gift for naming things, I simply stole the one he used for his GPS: Jill. I confess to having discussions—even disagreements—with Jill. "Why didn't you tell me to start moving over to the right lane sooner, Jill?" I readily admit that I have spoken to her so frequently that today, every computerized voice in the world is her. You might call the voice in your iPhone "Siri," but to me, she is Jill.

I remember distinctly the first time Jill let me down. Our family is wildly fond of Thai food, and I heard rumors of a new restaurant. I punched the name into my GPS unit, and Jill started guiding me toward what I hoped would be a culinary adventure. When Jill finally said, "Arriving at destination on the right," I found myself in the middle of an empty field, perched on a set of railway tracks.

A few weeks later, when I was trying to find a church, Jill tried to steer me into the heart of a private country club. I tried to assure the man at the guardhouse that there *must* be a church beyond his gates because Jill had told me so. He assured me, with language suggesting he should *also* find his way to church, that there was no house of worship, and would I be so kind as to turn my vehicle around.

There was something wrong with Jill. Over the next few weeks, she consistently took me in the wrong direction, and I eventually had to replace her. That, in short, is the story of our sinful hearts. They have aligned our interests with those of fallen angels, and they continually steer us in the wrong direction. The only hope we have is to allow God to replace our guidance units with ones that pull us in His direction instead. It does not mean we will never make another mistake or suffer disappointment on this side of heaven; it simply means that we now have hearts that continually pull us in the right direction.

Eternity in Your Heart

He has made everything beautiful in its time. Also He has put eternity in their hearts,
except that no one can find out the work that God does from beginning to end.
—Ecclesiastes 3:11

I do not have too many digital addictions, although I do find myself especially fond of Twitter. My other digital habit—do not laugh—is *Minecraft*. I was first introduced to the game when my children were *Minecraft* age. They lost their interest years ago, but their dad is still fascinated by it.

No, it is not because of the assorted cartoon monsters that make life difficult for players. (A note to parents: You can turn those off.) What do I find so captivating? In part, it is the game's ability to manufacture random landscapes that have no limit, complete with oceans, rivers, mountains, and forests. No two worlds are alike; you can explore them for hours on end and never see the same thing twice.

But the bigger attraction is the ability to tame the landscape and build things. It is, in essence, the world's biggest Lego set. On long nights when my lifelong case of insomnia is getting the upper hand, I occasionally find myself building large virtual houses and tidy little villages. And there is no need to clean up afterward, as with *real* building blocks; you just snap your laptop shut.

A while ago I was trying to put my finger on what was so deeply compelling about a game that lets you explore and build, and I settled on it: It mimics the original instructions God gave to the human race. "Fill the earth and subdue it," God said (Genesis 1:28). We are *supposed* to enjoy exploring and creating.

Of course, sin has turned that original impulse inside out; we no longer instinctively create for the sake of God's glory but rather build for the sake of self. Yet we cannot deny that the original impulse is still there. And that is because, in spite of our rebellion, God has kept something of our original hearts alive. We may live lives of sin, but there is still eternity in our hearts—impulses that pull us in His direction, even before we receive forgiveness and the gift of new hearts. God grants to every human being the first spark of interest, and then He leaves it to us to accept His offer and allow Him to fan that spark into the flames of a brand-new heart more closely aligned with His.

The Confidence of God

By faith Abraham, when he was tested, offered up Isaac,
and he who had received the promises offered up his only begotten son.
—Hebrews 11:17

Betrayal is among the worst things that can happen to a person, psychologically speaking. The damage runs much deeper than the first shock of discovering that your spouse has been unfaithful, your friends have been using you to further their own interests, or your coworkers have been whispering behind your back. The initial anger, pain, and humiliation are bad enough, but the first sting is eventually replaced with a potentially lifelong problem—the inability to trust people.

If you have not experienced it, you have probably seen it: that person who is always suspicious of other peoples' motives, always assuming that he or she is about to be cheated or hurt. It can carry over into future relationships and wreak untold havoc. The act of betrayal always has countless victims.

In human relationships, the betrayer destroys someone else's ability to trust. The paradox of our broken relationship with God is that our original betrayal has broken *our* trust in *Him*: the perpetrator is also the victim. That is not to say that God does not feel the painful impact of our betrayal; He repeatedly refers us to marital infidelity as an illustration of what we have done to Him.

But you will notice that in spite of our betrayal, God has not lost confidence in us. The story of the Bible tells us that God believes that we can be restored. The biggest obstacle to restoration is our reluctance, ever since we chose to value the word of a fallen angel over God's—that God can be trusted and that we are safe in doing so.

It seems to be a key reason that God requires faith. If He simply did everything for us, and the path forward always seemed logical and clear, we would learn little in the way of trusting God completely. Along with Abraham, God asks us to do the impossible: to trust Him completely. He asks us to put what we value most on the altar, trusting that He knows what He is doing.

On our own, we will never come to that point. But by choosing to live as if God's promises are trustworthy, even when the evidence of our senses suggests otherwise, He is surely giving us new hearts so that we will once again learn to trust Him.

First Steps

Therefore, if anyone is in Christ, he is a new creation;
old things have passed away; behold, all things have become new.
—2 Corinthians 5:17

Consider the length of a human being's childhood compared to God's other creatures. A newborn calf is pushed up on its wobbly feet and standing on its own within thirty minutes or, at most, a few hours. A bear cub typically stays with its mother for about two years before striking out on its own. Newborn salmon reach maturity in about four years—but all without having ever met their parents, who died weeks before they were born.

Then consider the one creature made in God's image, the human being. Most of us live with our parents until our late teens or early twenties before finally striking out on our own. We are among the most dependent creatures in the world. (Elephant calves come close, staying by their mothers' side for about sixteen years.)

Humanly speaking, a new life is not an independent or fully matured life. We need many years of support and instruction before we are ready to assume full responsibility for ourselves. In a way, the same applies to the new-birth experience we have in Christ. Paul tells us that in Jesus, we have become new creations. When our sins are forgiven and we have turned away from sin and toward God, it is as if we have just been reborn. You will remember that is precisely the way Jesus described it to Nicodemus: "You must be born again" (John 3:7).

The new birth is not an arrival; it is the beginning point. We have been given new hearts, but we will be training those hearts in the school of Christ for the rest of our lives. In fact, given the infinite nature of God, we will likely be in training for all eternity. Malachi points to the period after the final destruction of sin and wickedness as a time when we "shall go out and grow fat like stall-fed calves" (Malachi 4:2). In other words, we continue to grow even *after* Jesus returns.

Remember: Your heart may be new in Jesus, but that does not mean there is not room to grow. The exciting part, however, is getting to start all over. Today, you have just been pushed up on your wobbly legs, and God Himself is cheering as you grow stronger and take your first steps toward the rest of forever.

Marriage Changes You

Your glorying is not good. Do you not know that a little leaven leavens the whole lump?
Therefore purge out the old leaven, that you may be a new lump,
since you truly are unleavened. For indeed Christ, our Passover, was sacrificed for us.
—1 Corinthians 5:6, 7

If I had a dollar for every time I have had to explain to a young person that he or she will not be able to change or "train" a spouse after marriage, I would be rich. When it comes to a lifelong commitment, it is important to assume that your spouse-to-be is WYSIWYG—what you see is what you get. If anything, many young people (men in particular) bring their A game to the dating process, and then it goes somewhat downhill after that. If you see something you do not like before marriage, assuming that you are going to change it after marriage is a recipe for disaster.

It is not that marriage does not change you; it really does. Anybody who has known me over the years could tell you that I am not the same person I was the day I walked down the aisle. My wife has been a refining influence on me. But did it happen by design? No. It happened organically. The more time I spend with her, the more my interests merge with hers.

Marriage is a brand-new start—an almost entirely new set of circumstances. It is a chance to redefine yourself and become a better you. The same is true of the new birth: you are given a new heart and a new relationship with Christ; and from that point forward, change begins to happen naturally, if you spend time with Christ.

Trying to force it does not work. Making a long list of dos and don'ts and then gritting your teeth, determining to live right no matter how hard it is, does not work—not in the long run. It is behavior-based Christianity that usually leads to disappointment and disillusionment. And if you are always focused on behavior, it still means that your focus is on *you.*

Behavior does matter; it clearly does. There will be tough decisions to make and a Christian lifestyle to pursue. But if your primary focus remains your relationship with Christ, and you make it a priority to spend meaningful time in His presence, He will change you just as surely as spending time with the leaven of sin changes you. Focus on Christ, and self is out of the way. And the more you bask in His presence, the more your interests begin to align with His.

Why You're Interested

*These things we also speak, not in words which man's wisdom teaches
but which the Holy Spirit teaches, comparing spiritual things with spiritual.
But the natural man does not receive the things of the Spirit of God,
for they are foolishness to him; nor can he know them, because they are spiritually discerned.*
—1 Corinthians 2:13, 14

I have often marveled at how Richard Dawkins—or any of the other "new" atheists—can read the same passages of Scripture that Christians read and come to such wildly different conclusions. Where believers see a God of love, justice, and mercy, he sees a capricious and vindictive God. Where we see the unfortunate tragedy of a broken world untethered from its Creator, many people see an angry deity, not unlike the pagan gods of Olympus, who plays cruel games with the human race.

How do two people come to such radically different conclusions? How can a college professor present the Bible as merely a work of literature and utterly fail to see its beauty? Paul provides the answer in his first letter to the Corinthian church: spiritual things are spiritually discerned. When we are armed with only our natural intellect, much of the Bible remains a mystery. To truly comprehend its message, we must be willing to submit to the guidance of the Holy Spirit. Apart from willing submission, it is not going to make sense.

That, in part, is the gift of a new heart in the believer: the God-given ability to see things you have never noticed before; the ability to shake off the thick layer of dust that has formed over your mind and dulled your senses because of sin. Instead of a heart that constantly seeks its own pleasure and selfish desires, you are suddenly infused with a desire to pursue the heart and mind of God.

John Wesley might have called this gift "prevenient grace." When he spoke of this concept, he was referring to the fact that human beings are so tainted by sin and selfishness that we cannot come to Christ unless God first draws us. "No one can come to Me unless the Father who sent Me draws him," Jesus once explained (John 6:44). What does that mean for you? If you have ever been worried that perhaps you *do not* have a new heart, that your struggles perhaps disqualify you, you can rest in the fact that you would not even consider such questions if God was not already working on you. The process is already well under way. Trust that God is deeply interested in getting you home; if that were not true, *you* would not be interested.

MARCH 30

How Tastes Change

"Then I will give them one heart, and I will put a new spirit within them, and take the stony heart out of their flesh, and give them a heart of flesh, that they may walk in My statutes and keep My judgments and do them; and they shall be My people, and I will be their God."
—Ezekiel 11:19, 20

Near the end of our lunch together, a good friend of mine was slowly pulling grapes from a stem and popping them in his mouth. "Imagine this," he said, "this isn't meaty, or fatty, or starchy, and I'm actually enjoying it!" My friend's doctor had recently suggested reining in some of his meal choices in order to deal with some symptoms he had been experiencing.

I thought about his comment carefully because, for most of the men I know, it really is a surprising statement. Many reluctantly concede the fact that we should make healthier meal choices but grumble all the way through, longing for the meals of the past. I suppose we could blame it on our youth or our culture; we seem to be wired very early on to enjoy all the wrong things. Most of us dread the day that the medical establishment suggests we switch to salad and stir-fries. Personally, I know that if someone had suggested to my twenty-year-old self that one day I would be a vegan, I would have laughed.

I eyed my friend suspiciously. Was he *truly* enjoying his new diet, or was he simply trying to *convince* himself that he was? After watching him for a few minutes, I decided that he actually *meant* it.

A sudden change in circumstances can bring about a sudden change in tastes, and the same holds true for the spiritual life. Regardless of how our early circumstances shaped our preferences and perceptions, an encounter with Christ can radically change how we view the world and create a distinctly new disposition. The more you are exposed to the character of Jesus, the faster you start to hate the things you used to love and love the things you used to hate.

On your own, you simply cannot change the essence of who you are. You can try to artificially change your tastes, but you will be the person who begrudgingly suffers through a healthy meal instead of genuinely enjoying it. Notice how God explains it to Ezekiel: "I will *give* them . . . [a new] heart." Our hearts are changed by God, not by our level of stubborn determination. Spend time with God, and as you grow to love Him, He gives you a heart to love the things that He loves.

Careful Where You Park!

*And do not be conformed to this world, but be transformed by the renewing of your mind,
that you may prove what is that good and acceptable and perfect will of God.*
—Romans 12:2

The first dent or scratch on a new vehicle is the hardest one. Most of the cars I have purchased over the years have been used and therefore prescratched. But even then, the first dent I put in a car that is new to me is still a disappointment. To avoid it, I will usually park in the farthest corner of a grocery store parking lot, as far as I can get from other vehicles and their treacherous dent-inducing doors.

A new heart, of course, is of far greater value than any car. No matter how wonderful a new car is, it is still going to decay and fall prey to mechanical problems. A new heart is quite different: under the influence and guidance of an infinite God, your new heart has infinite potential to grow and actually get better with age. Eternity in the presence of God is a very long time; given the fact that God is a Creator who loves beauty, I cannot imagine that He will ever be done with putting the "finishing" touches on you.

Perhaps—especially in the beginning—it is a good idea to keep your heart in as safe a place as possible, away from the doors of careless drivers and the perils of stray shopping carts being pushed by the wind. Your new heart was purchased at an infinitely high price: the sacrifice of God's own Son on Calvary. There is no shortage of harmful influence and perilous contact in a world that has become untethered from its Maker. With the sharp moral decline of Western civilization and our high levels of media saturation, our generation may face more threats to the new heart than any that has gone before.

Of course, you cannot simply avoid all contact with the world, and neither should you. Our commission, after all, is to engage the world and make disciples for Christ. But on a daily basis, we should be taking stock of the influences we allow ourselves to be exposed to and ask ourselves which ones are causing damage to the new heart Christ has given us. We must live in the world, but as Paul recommends, we cannot afford to be conformed to it. You have been given an incredibly precious gift; be careful where you park it.

April

I accept by faith the righteousness of Christ, my Intercessor in the heavenly sanctuary, and accept His promise of transforming grace and power to live a loving, Christ-centered life in my home and before the world.

The First Sanctuary

So He drove out the man; and He placed cherubim at the east of the garden of Eden,
and a flaming sword which turned every way, to guard the way to the tree of life.
—Genesis 3:24

Let us revisit the Taj Mahal—one of the few tourist destinations on this planet that will exceed your expectations. You know how it is: Most of the time, the photos in the travel brochure exaggerate and oversell the attraction, resulting in an anticlimactic experience when you finally lay eyes on it. But not so with the Taj Mahal.

Shah Jahan built it in the seventeenth century after the death of his favorite wife. History records that he was so distraught initially that he contemplated suicide, but his friends managed to talk him back down and encouraged him to build a monument to his wife instead. The structure is magnificent but so is the garden in front of the building. If you look at the Taj Mahal on Google Earth, you will see it has a "fountain of life" in the middle of the garden, with four waterways that run to the edges of the garden. It is known as a "walled garden" or, in the original language, a *pairidaeza*, from which we get the word *paradise*.

When you look at the whole arrangement, it is striking: just outside of the garden is the beloved bride, who is a victim of death. The hope, of course, is that she will one day be readmitted to the garden. It is a vivid picture of Genesis 3; God's people, condemned to death, are outside the Garden.

But not all hope is lost. Notice the powerful sanctuary imagery at the gates of Eden: two cherubim with a fiery presence between them. The original language describes a brilliance "like the glint off of a sword," not an actual physical sword; and when it says that God "placed" the cherubim there, the word is *shaken,* which is the root word for Shekinah: the presence of God Himself.

It was, like the tabernacle Moses built, a depiction of God's throne and a powerful reminder that God wasted no time in providing hope. "I've got a plan"—He reminds Adam and Eve—"and one day, thanks to the Seed of the woman, you will return to the Garden."

Investigating God

*"Suppose there were fifty righteous within the city; would You also destroy the place
and not spare it for the fifty righteous that were in it? Far be it from You to do such a thing as
this, to slay the righteous with the wicked, so that the righteous should be as the wicked;
far be it from You! Shall not the Judge of all the earth do right?"*
—Genesis 18:24, 25

When the sanctuary was eventually built, it was a place where God displayed His plans to deal with sin and redeem the world. But you will find hints of the sanctuary message woven into the stories that happened earlier too.

When God paid Abraham a visit at Mamre, He shared with Abraham His plans to destroy Sodom and Gomorrah. "Shall I hide from Abraham what I am doing, since Abraham shall surely become a great and mighty nation?" (Genesis 18:17, 18). The story offers insight into how God intended to carry forward the plan of salvation: He wanted to keep His people informed. This story is in perfect keeping with Amos's assertion that "the Lord GOD does nothing, unless He reveals His secret to His servants the prophets" (Amos 3:7).

The God of Abraham is a God of revelation. Not only does He provide a way to save the sinful human race, but He also keeps us informed at every significant turn in salvation history. If it is important to our salvation, He is going to share it.

But there is another important detail in this story. When salvation history draws to a close, the book of Revelation indicates that the universe will have an opportunity to examine the books of heaven (see, for example, Daniel 7:10; Revelation 20:12). Before God executes final judgment, He will open His plans to our scrutiny, because He has nothing to hide.

Many people refer to this moment as the "investigative judgment," and we can see it already prefigured at Mamre. God is about to destroy the wicked cities; but before He makes a move, He discloses His plans to Abraham and opens the floor for questions: "Shall not the Judge of all the earth do right?"

Abraham is not alone with his question. If you are human, you have had moments when you questioned the way God has dealt with you or the world. You will have your chance to ask those questions. We may not understand everything now, but we *will* be satisfied with God's answer, just as Abraham was by the time the discussion was over. What is the ultimate conclusion, according to Revelation? "Great and marvelous are Your works, Lord God Almighty! Just and true are Your ways, O King of the saints!" (Revelation 15:3).

The Anointing

"This Jesus God has raised up, of which we are all witnesses. Therefore being exalted
to the right hand of God, and having received from the Father the promise
of the Holy Spirit, He poured out this which you now see and hear."
—Acts 2:32, 33

It took a few moments for people to absorb what they were witnessing: The disciples of Jesus, men who had been afraid for their lives only weeks earlier, were telling the story of a resurrected Jesus, now unafraid of whatever consequences might befall them. But more than that, they were somehow communicating in the languages of those present. How was that possible?

Peter, who had publicly denied knowing Jesus of Nazareth mere days ago, explained it to the mystified crowd. "What you're witnessing here," he told them, "is happening because Jesus has just received the gift of the Spirit, and He has poured it out on His church." We often say the disciples received the Spirit at Pentecost, which is a mostly accurate statement, but it is not quite the way the Bible explains it—Jesus was the primary recipient.

Now compare that story to the language of Psalm 133, and you will see a remarkable parallel: "Behold, how good and how pleasant it is for brethren to dwell together in unity! It is like the precious oil upon the head, running down on the beard, the beard of Aaron, running down on the edge of his garments" (verses 1, 2).

This remarkable psalm predicts the Day of Pentecost. The believers were dwelling together in unity, or as the book of Acts puts it, "with one accord" (Acts 2:1). The psalmist tells us the reason for the occasion: the high priest is about to be anointed with oil. Of course, oil is a symbol of the Holy Spirit, and the real High Priest is Jesus Christ Himself. It would seem that the Day of Pentecost was the very day that Jesus was anointed as our High Priest in heaven's sanctuary.

Note also that even though Jesus had already told the church to spread the gospel to the world, the disciples were not permitted to start until the Spirit fell on them (Acts 1:4). Put all the pieces together, and a beautiful picture emerges. When Jesus returned to heaven, He did not leave us to fulfill the gospel commission on our own. He is not gone, and we are not alone. Through the presence of the Holy Spirit, heaven's High Priest is busy directing the work of His church, and He has guaranteed its ultimate triumph.

Seeing Jesus

Then Abraham lifted his eyes and looked, and there behind him
was a ram caught in a thicket by its horns. So Abraham went and took the ram,
and offered it up for a burnt offering instead of his son.
—Genesis 22:13

The famous artist William Holman Hunt once told his friends that he was planning to paint a picture of Jesus. His friends protested, insisting that such a task was utterly impossible. "A real artist can only paint something he can see," they said, "so obviously you can't paint a portrait of Christ because you have never actually seen Him!"

"You don't understand," Hunt reportedly replied. "I *am* going to see Him. I will work by His side in the carpenter's shop. I will walk with Him over the hills of Galilee. I will go with Him among the poor, the blind, the naked, the lepers. I will travel with Him to Calvary and climb the cross with Him, until I see Him and know Him, and then I will paint Him."

Hunt found a way to see Jesus when Jesus was not physically present, by studying His life in the words of Scripture. Today, millions continue to see Jesus in the words of the Gospels. But what of the people who lived thousands of years *before* the life and ministry of Christ? How would someone like Abraham see Jesus?

Modern Christians look back to what Christ accomplished at the cross, accepting by faith that His sacrifice at Calvary is sufficient to pay their debt and secure their salvation. Old Testament believers were also "Christians," even though the term was coined in the city of Antioch many years later (Acts 11:26). Even though he could not read the historical story of the Cross, because it was still in the future, Abraham had access to the story anyway: God provides a Substitute who takes our place on the altar.

From the moment God covered our first parents' nakedness with animal skins (Genesis 3:21), it was understood that Someone would have to solve our sin problem for us. Before the construction of the tabernacle and the later temple, animal sacrifices were instituted to tell the story of the Cross ahead of time. When the tabernacle was built, the imagery grew even more detailed; even today, when we look back to the sacrificial system and the incredible details of the temple, we can find nuances in the plan of salvation that make the story of the Cross all the more profound.

Old Testament Faith

*Not with the blood of goats and calves, but with His own blood He entered the Most Holy
Place once for all, having obtained eternal redemption. For if the blood of bulls and goats
and the ashes of a heifer, sprinkling the unclean, sanctifies for the purifying of the flesh, how
much more shall the blood of Christ, who through the eternal Spirit offered Himself without
spot to God, cleanse your conscience from dead works to serve the living God?*
—Hebrews 9:12–14

"Old Testament believers were saved by keeping the law and performing animal sacrifices, but you and I are under the blood of Christ," the exasperated man told me. We were sitting in the kitchen, studying the Bible together.

"I agree with you one hundred percent," I answered, "that you and I are saved under the blood of Christ. But so were the Old Testament believers." I opened my Bible to the tenth chapter of Hebrews. "Listen to this," I explained. "For it is not possible that the blood of bulls and goats could take away sins" (Hebrews 10:4).

He had never noticed the verse before, and he grew quiet. In his defense, his understanding of the Old Testament is a very common one. Millions seem to believe that animal sacrifices were actually a way of dealing with sin. The author of Hebrews makes it abundantly clear, however, that the animal sacrifices themselves could do nothing to save lost sinners. The blood that was spilled in the courtyard of the tabernacle was symbolic; it was a tangible object lesson that allowed sinners to look forward by faith to the cross of Christ.

It was faith that saved Old Testament sinners, not works. Genesis 15:6 (and Romans 4:3) makes it abundantly clear that it was Abraham's *faith* that "accounted it to him for righteousness." The author of Hebrews is speaking to an audience that knew the rites and rituals of the temple well, and he underscores how valuable the imagery of sacrifice had been to help them understand what Jesus was now doing in heaven's sanctuary. Today's passage, in essence, is telling us that if the symbolic rituals that pointed forward by faith to Jesus were so effective in securing forgiveness, just imagine how solid the plan of salvation is, now that you can see the *real* High Priest applying His own blood to you in *heaven's* sanctuary.

The Old Testament believers had the security of watching the blood of animals carried into the sanctuary, knowing that if they were repentant, they would be declared forgiven and innocent and would be permitted to remain in the presence of God. You and I need be no less certain or secure; the Bible reminds us that heaven's sanctuary and High Priest are not mere shadows but are an even greater reality.

The Light of the World

Then I turned to see the voice that spoke with me. And having turned I saw seven golden
lampstands, and in the midst of the seven lampstands One like the Son of Man,
clothed with a garment down to the feet and girded about the chest with a golden band.
—Revelation 1:12, 13

The seven-branched candlestick was the only source of light in the Most Holy Place, and like everything else in the sanctuary, it was a powerful symbol of the Messiah. In a dramatic vision, the prophet Zechariah was shown a candlestick being continuously supplied with olive oil to keep it burning day and night. When he asked the angel what it meant, he was told, " 'Not by might nor by power, but by My spirit,' says the LORD of hosts" (Zechariah 4:6).

Notice that Jesus did not begin His public ministry until after the Holy Spirit visibly descended on Him at the Jordan River. After that moment, it was as if someone had suddenly thrown on the lights in a dark room; the character of God was on full display through the words and deeds of His Son. People could now see, by watching Jesus, what God was really like.

"I am the light of the world," Jesus explained. "He who follows Me shall not walk in darkness, but have the light of life" (John 8:12).

After three and a half years, Jesus physically returned to heaven to serve as our great High Priest, representing the human race before God's throne. But that does not mean that light has gone out of the world; on the contrary, Jesus promised, "I will never leave you nor forsake you" (Hebrews 13:5). Additionally, He told His disciples that it was to their *advantage* if He left for heaven (John 16:7). How could that be?

Jesus continues to be present with His church through the Holy Spirit. The oil continues to flow from heaven's sanctuary, and now it is up to us to exhibit the loving character of God to the world. "You are the light of the world," Jesus explained. "A city that is set on a hill cannot be hidden. Nor do they light a lamp and put it under a basket, but on a lampstand, and it gives light to all who are in the house" (Matthew 5:14, 15).

Jesus first appears in the book of Revelation dressed as a High Priest, standing in the midst of seven lampstands, which represent the church of all ages (Revelation 1:20). The challenge for us today is to let Jesus continue to shine—through us.

The Living Bread

"I am the living bread which came down from heaven. If anyone eats of this bread, he will live forever; and the bread that I shall give is My flesh, which I shall give for the life of the world."
—John 6:51

When God chose bread as a symbol for the body of Christ, He chose something that virtually everyone on the planet can relate to. It is a near-universal staple in that almost every culture on the planet has some version of it. Bread is so ubiquitous that it has come to symbolize essential nutrition, that which we cannot live without. In Western culture, for example, we call the primary wage earner in a home the "breadwinner." Close friends are said to be "companions"; the term is derived from a compound Latin word that describes people who share bread together (from *com*, "with," and *panis*, "bread.")

When Jesus compared His broken body to bread, He was trying to underscore how desperately we need Him. The Cross is not a frivolous extra, a decorative garnish on Christ's earthly ministry. Without the Cross, humankind could not heal the massive rift between the human race and the One who gives us the gift of life; we would have only the wages of sin—death—to look forward to.

Every week when the priests in the sanctuary replaced the twelve loaves of bread on the table in the Holy Place, they encountered a vivid reminder that our very lives depend on the presence of the Creator. God is the ultimate staple without which the human race would die.

Notice the condition for life: You have to *eat* the bread. It is not enough to know that God exists or that He is the only true Source of life in this universe. The Christian faith is not simply a set of beliefs to which we assent; it is a living relationship with the Creator. Buying bread and keeping it on the shelf is not what keeps you alive; you need to consume it.

And so the powerful symbol of the Bread of Life found in the sanctuary also appears in the New Testament Communion service. It is not enough to know who Jesus is. It is not even enough to know that the Bible is true. You have to *accept* the gift and allow Christ to transform your life radically. Christianity is surrender; a process by which the believer pushes aside selfish desires and allows the Spirit of Christ to enter the heart and mind to nourish the whole being.

The Maestro's Touch

Then another angel, having a golden censer, came and stood at the altar.
He was given much incense, that he should offer it with the prayers of all the saints
upon the golden altar which was before the throne. And the smoke of the incense,
with the prayers of the saints, ascended before God from the angel's hand.
—Revelation 8:3, 4

In the Holy Place, right up against the veil that separated it from the Most Holy Place, stood a small altar of incense where the priest would burn a special blend of aromatic spices, producing a sweet-smelling smoke that would waft up over the veil into the presence of the ark of the covenant, which represented the throne of God. The smoke, the book of Revelation tells us, represented the prayers of God's people.

The veil hid the Most Holy Place because sinners cannot enter into the presence of a holy God. Likewise, our prayers are also tainted by sin and selfishness and by themselves are not fit to be presented before God's throne. That is why they are blended with incense and introduced into the Most Holy Place: Jesus adds His own righteousness to our prayers, making them acceptable for presentation in the courts of heaven.

Years ago a little girl begged her parents for piano lessons, because she wanted to become a concert pianist. All she could manage to bang out on the keys was "Chopsticks," but she longed to be able to play more. Her parents sought a teacher, and to their delight, they managed to book a session with a famous concert pianist.

When they arrived, they were shown to the studio, but the great teacher had not yet arrived. Too excited to sit still, the little girl raced over to the piano and started to hammer out the same obnoxious tune that had driven her parents nearly mad. To the parents' embarrassment, the great virtuoso suddenly walked into the room as their daughter was indelicately assaulting the keyboard. They moved to stop her, but the teacher motioned for them to stay put.

Quietly, he slipped onto the bench next to her and began to add a delicate accompaniment to her coarse hammering, and before long, "Chopsticks" started to sound like a stunning duet. To be sure, the original tune was still there, as plain as day, but with the maestro's touch, it had become beautiful.

Nothing about sin is beautiful. But never forget that our heavenly High Priest is one of us: fully human, even though He is fully God. When He adds His beauty to your life, it becomes a sweet-smelling incense that fills the courts of heaven.

No Room for Creativity

*"And let them make Me a sanctuary, that I may dwell among them.
According to all that I show you, that is, the pattern of the tabernacle
and the pattern of all its furnishings, just so you shall make it."*
—Exodus 25:8, 9

To be created in the image of a Creator God is to resemble Him and exhibit His attributes, which no doubt includes the nearly limitless capacity human beings have for creativity. Sadly, since the Fall, we have applied our creative minds to ungodly pursuits, tragically underscored by the fact that some of our most useful inventions—such as canned food and the internet—have been the by-products of warfare.

Nevertheless, our original propensity for creativity still has its beautiful moments, and the beauty of art has often relieved some of the pain that sin brought to our world.

There is one place, however, where human creativity will never contribute to God's plan to restore us. Notice that Moses was not permitted to improvise or add little expressive touches to the design of the tabernacle. He was to build it "just so." That is because the sanctuary was designed to reveal Jesus and His atoning work for us. There is nothing we can add to the Cross and no price we can pay to secure our own salvation. Try as you might to cure the sin that resides in your heart, it will be a futile exercise.

The Israelites were not permitted to add any details to the plan of salvation on display in the temple. There was but one way back to the throne of God, to the Most Holy Place: through the work of the high priest who carried the blood of sacrifice into the presence of God. Cain's offering attempted to alter this God-given plan; he offered the fruits of his own labor, as opposed to Abel's simple faith in the Lamb of God (Hebrews 11:4). When Naaman realized that he was being asked to humble himself in the muddy waters of the Jordan River, he nearly succumbed to the temptation to find another, less humiliating way. Had he failed, he would have died of his leprosy instead of experiencing the healing touch of God.

The world tells us there are many paths to God, but it simply is not true. Even those who have never heard the name of Christ but still wake up in the resurrection of the righteous will be there because of the one path God has provided—Jesus (Zechariah 13:6).

The Mercy Seat

"And there I will meet with you, and I will speak with you from above the mercy seat,
from between the two cherubim which are on the ark of the Testimony,
about everything which I will give you in commandment to the children of Israel."
—Exodus 25:22

When I was sixteen years old, I managed to drive my father's new car into a deep ravine. It was completely destroyed. The half hour I spent waiting for my father to pick me up from the scene was probably the longest moment of my life.

Early the next morning he was at my bedroom door. "Get up," he said quietly. I was afraid of what was going to transpire next. Was he finally going to yell at me? Would I be taken to the army recruitment office?

We got in his old rusty van, the only vehicle he had left, and drove out to the sharp corner I had so poorly navigated the night before. "Get behind the wheel," he said, slipping out of the driver's seat. I did not want to do it, but he insisted. With my hands shaking, he made me navigate the corner. When it was over, he made me turn around and do it again—and again. My father made me negotiate that miserable corner until I could do it with confidence.

The original Hebrew word translated "mercy seat" is *kapporeth*, and it is something of a mystery. It is a legal term that implies canceling of debt and covering of error. Translators have struggled to transport it into other languages. Martin Luther rendered it *gnadenstuhl*, which means "seat of grace." When Hebrew scholars produced the Septuagint and tried to translate the term into Greek, they had to invent a new word: *hilasterion*, which (based on its etymological roots) appears to mean "a thing for propitiation."

It is a difficult concept to translate because the lid of the ark represents a massive, hard-to-grasp concept. When the human race disobeyed God, we violated His moral law that was placed inside the ark, which represents the throne of God. "Meet Me here," God says, "at the very scene of the crime, because I want to show you something. I can cover your sins. I can extend you mercy through the blood of the Lamb." He meets us precisely where the transgression took place and shows us His solution. God could have justifiably called that covering "the justice seat," but He did not.

No wonder the author of Hebrews urges us to "come boldly to the throne of grace" (Hebrews 4:16).

Where Mercy and Truth Meet

"And they shall make an ark of acacia wood; two and a half cubits shall be its length, a cubit and a half its width, and a cubit and a half its height. And you shall overlay it with pure gold, inside and out you shall overlay it, and shall make on it a molding of gold all around."
—Exodus 25:10, 11

A leper throws himself on the ground in front of Jesus, begging for healing. "If You are willing," he pleads with Jesus, "You can make me clean" (Mark 1:40). What happens next is stunning: "Then Jesus, moved with compassion, stretched out His hand and touched him, and said to him, 'I am willing; be cleansed' " (verse 41).

I often wonder how long it had been since the leper had experienced human touch. How long since someone had hugged him? Leprosy was untouchable. To contract leprosy was not only to die, it also was to spend the rest of your days as one of society's most despised people. Jesus not only healed the man physically, but He did also the unthinkable: He touched him, healing him emotionally at the same time.

Read the Bible carefully, and you will notice that the ark had two natures combined into one. The surface was of pure gold, which many scholars consider to be a symbol of divinity. The gold was an overlay; the rest of the ark was made of acacia wood, a virtually indestructible organic material.

Is it possible that the ark foreshadowed the nature of Christ? Jesus did have two natures blended into one: He was both fully human and fully divine. Perhaps the hardy nature of the wood foreshadowed the fact that Jesus would experience death, a distinctly human experience, but also that He would not be defeated. "Nor will You allow Your Holy One to see corruption," the psalmist predicted (Psalm 16:10).

The dual nature of the ark's construction may also point us to another stunning picture of Christ. It was where God's justice met God's mercy, the moral law covered by the mercy seat. Your salvation is purchased by the blood sprinkled over it. In Jesus, we see God's justice and His mercy on full display: "Mercy and truth have met together," the psalmist predicted of Jesus, "righteousness and peace have kissed" (Psalm 85:10). Just like the leper who approached Jesus and found healing, the sinner may also approach God's mercy seat and receive forgiveness.

In Jesus, the true nature of God was on full display. We are told in 1 Chronicles 13:6 that the ark is "where His name is proclaimed." The best light through which to understand the nature and government of God is Jesus. After all, Jesus Himself said of His ministry, "I have manifested Your name" (John 17:6).

No End of Detail

Now this is the main point of the things we are saying: We have such a High Priest,
who is seated at the right hand of the throne of the Majesty in the heavens,
a Minister of the sanctuary and of the true tabernacle which the Lord erected, and not man.
—Hebrews 8:1, 2

If you were in God's place, how would you communicate incredibly large ideas to a race of beings that (a) has an inferior capacity for understanding compared with your own, and (b) has compromised their ability to understand by corrupting their minds with sin? At the gates of Eden, the Master Teacher started simply. He told Adam and Eve that the Seed of the woman would come and, while suffering a blow Himself, would ultimately bruise the head of the serpent (Genesis 3:15). Then God replaced our first parents' attempts to clothe themselves with a covering of skin, pointing forward to the day when the Lamb of God would give His life to cover our transgressions (verse 21). Finally, He placed two cherubim at the gates of Eden (verse 24), providing the Bible's first glimpse at the sanctuary.

Over time, the symbolism grew more and more complex, moving from regular animal sacrifices to the construction of the temple. The details of the sanctuary and its rituals fill hundreds of pages in the Bible.

Why would God make it so complex? It is because the tabernacle points us to Jesus, a subject so powerful, detailed, and intricate that we will continue to study Him throughout the eternal ages to come, never arriving at the end of His beauty. In Peter's first letter, he speaks about "the manifold grace of God" (1 Peter 4:10). The Greek word he uses is *poikilos*, which means "many colored."

Just when you think you understand who Jesus is, the Holy Spirit suddenly opens new vistas of understanding, showing you a dimension of Jesus you had never considered before.

I once heard a student in a religion class complain, "Why should we study all the details in the sanctuary when what we should *really* be studying is Jesus?" Talk about missing the point! To study the sanctuary *is* to see Jesus more clearly. That is the key point the author of Hebrews is making: to study the earthly copies is to suddenly see the High Priest of the *true* sanctuary and to understand what He is now doing in the presence of God. Every detail, every action, every nuance is meant as a careful and deliberate setting for the most beautiful jewel in Scripture, Jesus.

Someone Who Knows

For Christ has not entered the holy places made with hands, which are copies of the true,
but into heaven itself, now to appear in the presence of God for us.
—Hebrews 9:24

One of the issues that helped to spark the American Revolution was the matter of representation. The British Parliament, removed from the thirteen colonies by a vast ocean, was passing laws that affected life in the colonies. Most of the people making the decisions, of course, did not know what life in America was like, and most did not care, viewing the colonies as a mere accoutrement and supply line for the empire.

In the middle of the eighteenth century, the colonists were becoming deeply disgruntled about the burdensome taxes being levied on them, insisting there would be "no taxation without representation."

It was an understandable complaint. Today, people often have to live with the decisions made by government bureaucrats—people who have little idea of how the unintended consequences of their policy decisions are going to affect the day-to-day lives of real people. "We can't trust what they decide," someone will mutter, "they have a government pension, they have a good health plan, and they just don't get what my life is like."

Some people have grumbled that God could not possibly understand what they are living with. "God doesn't have to live in this place. How can He judge someone like me?" Not only does the Incarnation turn such a complaint on its back, because Jesus really *has* lived here, but the Bible also reveals that we have human representation in the courts of heaven. Jesus does not stand before the throne of God to simply represent the interests of the Godhead; He is there "to appear in the presence of God for us." Not just *for* us, mind you, but *as* one of us. He is the "last Adam" (1 Corinthians 15:45), the new Head of the human race.

You can forge ahead in a relationship with God with confidence, knowing that one of our own stands in heaven's sanctuary. You are well represented by Someone who knows. It was a position that Adam once held, but when we stopped living for God's glory, God replaced him with One who would live perfectly for both God's glory and your good. You can face this day knowing that the Firstfruits of humanity has already arrived in glory and that He is securing a path for you to do the same.

Stand Under the Light

In Him was life, and the life was the light of men.
And the light shines in the darkness, and the darkness did not comprehend it.
—John 1:4, 5

Perhaps you remember those three-dimensional posters from the 1990s that to the untrained eye simply appeared to be a page full of colorful dots. If you could teach yourself to relax your eyes and look past the surface of the poster, a three-dimensional image would suddenly rise out of the chaos. Some people could look at the image and instantaneously see it; others (like me) usually had to work on it for a few minutes. And then there were those unfortunate few who, no matter how hard they tried, could never seem to find the prize.

There is a similar phenomenon in the world of religion. I often marvel at the deeply sarcastic and spiteful anti-Christian memes some people post on social media sites; many of them amount to outright mockery of both Christ and Christians. Sometimes, they quote Bible passages out of context in order to make the notion of God seem hateful or foolish. I frequently wonder how they can look at the same Bible and *not* see the beautiful image of Christ that I see.

It is a problem as old as the Christian faith itself. John explains that Jesus ultimately came to reveal the beauty of God's character (John 17:1–6). Some people saw Jesus for who He was and rejoiced in the light. Others looked at the same Man and perceived a threat; they wanted Him dead.

How can two people look at the same Jesus and see such radically different things? Perhaps there is a clue in the sanctuary. The candlestick was the only source of light, representing Jesus, the Light of the world. "I am the light of the world," Jesus said. "He who follows Me shall not walk in darkness, but have the light of life" (John 8:12).

To see the light of the candlestick, you had to enter the sanctuary. You had to cooperate with the plan of salvation and, under the blood of Christ, choose to approach the throne of God. To resist the wooing of the Holy Spirit is to fail to see the light. But to take a step toward Jesus is to begin seeing more clearly than you ever have. The light of Christ never stops shining, but you have to follow Him in order to see it.

The Table of Demons

You cannot drink the cup of the Lord and the cup of demons;
you cannot partake of the Lord's table and of the table of demons.
—1 Corinthians 10:21

Rising obesity rates have long been considered a Western problem and an affliction that falls mainly on the wealthy. But according to a 2018 report from the World Health Organization, global obesity rates have tripled since 1975. In 2016, roughly 39 percent of the world's population was overweight, and 13 percent was clinically obese.★

There are any number of factors that have contributed to the rise of global obesity, but prominent among them is poor nutrition. It is easy to find enough calories in modern processed foods; in fact, it is easy to find *too many* calories. But those same fast foods are often nutritionally poor and do little to satisfy the human body's actual needs.

The same is true of our spiritual needs; the wrong spiritual diet invariably leads to a diseased heart and mind. It leaves us unsatisfied, sickens our spiritual senses, and compromises our ability to hear God's voice and discern truth.

While dealing with the issue of false worship, Paul points out that there are but two diets available: the Lord's table and the "table of demons." Feed at the wrong table, fill your heart with the lies and suggestions of the enemy, and you will never find true satisfaction. You will also eventually corrupt your spiritual appetite to the point where, as with junk food, you will begin to crave all the wrong things. You will notice that those who turn to entertainment, sex, substance abuse, or other forms of carnal stimulation to silence the spiritual hunger pains in their souls never seem to get enough because they are feeding on a nutritionally deficient spiritual diet. Eventually, the wrong diet will even kill them, because the wages of sin is death.

There is but one menu that will truly satisfy your deepest needs and quiet the most profound cravings of your heart. The wrong food will leave you perpetually hungry for something better, but the right food will leave you forever satiated. In the tabernacle, God displayed a table laden with bread so that we would grasp that there is only one place for the heart to go for sustenance. "I am the bread of life," Jesus told His audience in John 6:35. "He who comes to Me shall never hunger, and he who believes in Me shall never thirst."

★ World Health Organization, "Obesity and Overweight," Fact Sheet, updated February 2018, http://www.who.int/mediacentre/factsheets/fs311/en/.

Trusting the Priest

" 'If his offering is a burnt sacrifice of the herd, let him offer a male without blemish;
he shall offer it of his own free will at the door of the tabernacle of meeting
before the LORD. Then he shall put his hand on the head of the burnt offering,
and it will be accepted on his behalf to make atonement for him.' "
—Leviticus 1:3, 4

The altar of burnt offering in the courtyard of the tabernacle pointed forward to the cross of Christ. The sanctuary itself represented a greater reality in the heavens, and the act of sacrifice took place outside—just as Jesus was sacrificed outside of heaven's sanctuary, on earth. Before the sacrificial victim, a symbol of Christ, was put to death in the courtyard, the penitent sinner "put his hand on the head." The original language is a little stronger; it says that the sinner *leaned* on the animal.

It gives us some idea of how much sinners must rely on the sacrifice of Christ. In order to claim the blood of Christ as our own, we must lean entirely on Jesus, placing every hope we have in Him. Our role in the plan of salvation is to act by faith, confessing our sins, throwing ourselves entirely on the mercy of God, and trusting in Christ's merits completely. We believe that the Cross settles the matter, and the blood of Christ saves us.

It is interesting to note that just as the act of sacrifice took place in the courtyard, outside of the tabernacle itself, the role the sinner plays in the drama of salvation also takes place entirely outside of the tabernacle. From that point forward, the priest takes over, carrying the blood inside the tabernacle to symbolically present it before the throne of God.

The sinner did not enter the tabernacle but had to trust the act of reconciliation to the priest, who ministered in his or her behalf out of sight. It points to our role in the plan of salvation: we are to confess our sins and repent of them here in the outer courtyard of the world, throwing our weight fully upon Jesus. Sinners are not saved by their own works but by grace through faith (Ephesians 2:8). After our confession and repentance, we are to trust completely in the ministry of Jesus as our High Priest in heaven's sanctuary, where out of our sight, He handles the matter of our salvation. We can return to daily life, trusting that God knows what He is doing, and the matter really is safely in His hands.

"For we walk by faith," Paul wrote to the Corinthians, "not by sight" (2 Corinthians 5:7).

The Price of Sin

" 'He shall kill the bull before the LORD; and the priests, Aaron's sons, shall bring the blood and sprinkle the blood all around on the altar that is by the door of the tabernacle of meeting.' "
—Leviticus 1:5

In 2008, the Vatican suddenly updated an ancient list of sins it had compiled in the seventh century when Gregory I was the bishop of Rome. The original list of seven deadly sins was expanded to include new offenses such as pollution, drug dealing, and abortion. According to medieval tradition, a deadly sin leads to the eternal loss of your soul.

The ancient tradition of categorizing sins persists in some corners of Christianity, where a distinction is made between "mortal" and "venial" sins. A mortal sin has grave consequences. If you do not repent, it is said, the end will be the loss of your salvation. This would include any transgression of the Ten Commandments. A venial sin, on the other hand, is considered less serious and has far less severe consequences.

It is understandable that human beings would want to categorize sins in order to make some of them seem less serious; many of us do the same thing. For example, we differentiate between lying on the witness stand and telling a "little white lie." But contrary to ancient tradition and our desire to minimize some sins, the Bible teaches that *all* sin is serious and *all* sin leads to death. Today, most people would consider eating from the forbidden tree in Eden as an insignificant offense, about as serious as a child sneaking a cookie from the kitchen. But God was abundantly clear that it carried the death penalty, just like every other sin.

Nothing could make the seriousness of sin more painfully obvious to the ancient Israelites than the act of sacrifice in the courtyard of the sanctuary. The sinner did not merely surrender an animal; he had to take the animal's life himself. It was obvious that it was his own actions that had cost the innocent animal its life.

"The exceeding sinfulness of sin can be estimated only in the light of the cross," Ellen White reminds us.* As we see the Son of God on His altar of sacrifice, we know that our sins placed Him there, and there is no question that sin is serious and deadly. There is also no question, as you contemplate the magnitude of His gift, that His love for you is also serious and knows no limit.

---

* Ellen G. White, *Steps to Christ* (Nampa, ID: Pacific Press®, 1999), 31.

"You Can't Come In Like That!"

*Then the L*ORD *spoke to Moses, saying: "You shall also make a laver of bronze, with its base*
also of bronze, for washing. You shall put it between the tabernacle of meeting and the altar.
And you shall put water in it, for Aaron and his sons shall wash their hands and their feet
in water from it. When they go into the tabernacle of meeting, or when they come near the altar
*to minister, to burn an offering made by fire to the L*ORD*,*
they shall wash with water, lest they die."

—Exodus 30:17–20

When I was just seven years old, I was playing at the neighbor's dairy farm when the gate I was climbing on suddenly swung open out over the manure pit, depositing me unceremoniously into a chest-deep pile of filth. With great difficulty, I waded up out of the pit and walked an undignified half mile down a hot country road to my own house.

I was embarrassed, miserable, and very uncomfortable. I wanted nothing more than to be safe at home, but I soon discovered that going home was not going to be as easy as I thought. My mother was in the front yard when I approached and immediately cut off access to the house. "You can't come in like that!" she exclaimed, probably picturing the horrible mess I would leave between the front door and the bathroom. "You're going to have to clean up before I can let you in!" And with that, she turned the garden hose on me, rinsing off the results of my unhygienic misadventure.

Before the priests were permitted to participate in the rituals associated with the sanctuary, they were required to wash in the laver, which was a large bronze basin filled with water. They were, after all, still sinful human beings tainted with the awful effects of sin, and the sanctuary was a symbol of God's throne room in heaven. There is no question that God loves us and that His kingdom is our original home; but before He simply allows us back into His presence, He has to deal with the filth of sin that has infected our lives. Our sin and deeply entrenched rebellious attitude will not be allowed to corrupt the kingdom and must be cleansed away before we can be readmitted.

The good news is that God did not push us away. Instead, He made provision for our cleansing, and everything we need can be found in Christ. If we are willing, He can help us leave behind the filth of sin and find a place at home with Him. "The unrighteous will not inherit the kingdom of God," Paul warns the Corinthians. "But you were washed, but you were sanctified, but you were justified in the name of the Lord Jesus Christ and by the Spirit of our God" (1 Corinthians 6:9, 11).

A Royal Priesthood

But you are a chosen generation, a royal priesthood, a holy nation, His own special people, that you may proclaim the praises of Him who called you out of darkness into His marvelous light.
—1 Peter 2:9

The disciples were not to be idle while Jesus went back to heaven to begin His high-priestly ministry in heaven's sanctuary; they were to carry the gospel "to the end of the earth" (Acts 1:8). Just as Jesus used His ministry to reveal the name—the character—of His Father to the world, we are to use our time to reveal Jesus to the world. As the Holy Spirit guides, instructs, and inspires us, we become the face of Christ to the world.

Just as Christ is the Light that came into this world, Jesus has told us that we, too, are the light of the world (Matthew 5:14), and we are to find every opportunity to let our light shine. Just as Jesus is the Bread of Life, He told the redeemed and restored Peter to "feed My sheep" (John 21:17). Just as Jesus humbled Himself and laid down His own life to save us, we have been instructed to follow in His footsteps and "let this mind be in you which was also in Christ Jesus" (Philippians 2:5). As Jesus works on our behalf as our great High Priest, we have been told that we, too, are a "royal priesthood" and that we have been given the ministry of reconciliation (2 Corinthians 5:18, 19). As Jesus washes us, justifies us, and sanctifies us (1 Corinthians 6:11), we have been told to go and make disciples of all nations and baptize them (Matthew 28:19).

The path through the sanctuary, from the atoning sacrifice in the courtyard to the ultimate cleansing of the Most Holy Place, is an object lesson that reveals the details of Christ's work to save us. But in some ways, it also shows us the path *we* are to take in carrying out the work that Christ gave to the church. Our path, too, is through the sanctuary because we have the privilege of mirroring Christ to the world. Of course, we cannot save anybody, for we have no merits of our own, but we can reflect the ministry of Christ so that other people can see Him in us. First John 2:6 reminds us that "he who says he abides in Him ought himself also to walk just as He walked."

The Only Way to Grow

"And the King will answer and say to them, 'Assuredly, I say to you,
inasmuch as you did it to one of the least of these My brethren, you did it to Me.' "
—Matthew 25:40

I'll try harder" is a useful statement when it comes to learning a new skill or attempting to conquer a problem at work. But it is a useless statement when it comes to being more Christlike because more effort will not make it happen. The Christian walk is the one time that trying harder simply does not work; if it did, then we would be able to boast that we had contributed something to our own sanctification.

The issue with trying harder to be more like Jesus is that your primary focus is still on self, and a preoccupation with self is the problem that led to sin in the first place. The very act of gritting your teeth and applying more effort to cleaning yourself up keeps your eyes on yourself!

Perhaps that is a key reason that the tasks Jesus left to the church focus on others. Jesus' parting instruction to the disciples was not to buckle down and clean themselves up; it was to carry the gospel to the world. And Jesus makes it clear, when speaking about the sheep and the goats, that He takes the matter of caring for others very seriously. He considers working for others as working for Him.

By allowing ourselves to become absorbed in the work of the gospel, we have little time to obsess about ourselves. Ego is pushed aside, and suddenly the time we spend with Jesus in study and prayer becomes powerfully transformative. We do not change by working on ourselves; we change by getting out of the way and letting Christ change us. "The only way to grow in grace," Ellen White writes, "is to be disinterestedly doing the very work which Christ has enjoined upon us—to engage, to the extent of our ability, in helping and blessing those who need the help we can give them. Strength comes by exercise; activity is the very condition of life. Those who endeavor to maintain Christian life by passively accepting the blessings that come through the means of grace, and doing nothing for Christ, are simply trying to live by eating without working. And in the spiritual as in the natural world, this always results in degeneration and decay. A man who would refuse to exercise his limbs would soon lose all power to use them. Thus the Christian who will not exercise his God-given powers not only fails to grow up into Christ, but he loses the strength that he already had."★

★ Ellen G. White, *Steps to Christ* (Nampa, ID: Pacific Press®, 1999), 80, 81.

The Day of Atonement

And as it is appointed for men to die once, but after this the judgment,
so Christ was offered once to bear the sins of many. To those who eagerly wait
for Him He will appear a second time, apart from sin, for salvation.
—Hebrews 9:27, 28

In the Old Testament sanctuary services, a repentant sinner's guilt was symbolically transferred to the sacrificial animal and then symbolically carried into the temple by the priest. It pointed forward to the work of Christ on our behalf. At the cross, He fully satisfied the requirement of salvation in giving His life. Our sins were heaped on His shoulders, or as Paul puts it, Jesus was "made . . . to be sin for us" (2 Corinthians 5:21).

After the Cross, Jesus appeared in the courts of heaven to present His sacrifice as the atonement for human sin. In the great throne room scene in the book of Revelation, as John wept over the fact that no one worthy could be found to open the scroll in God's hand, he suddenly saw Jesus as a slain Lamb (Revelation 5:2–6). Just as the priest presented the blood of the sinner's substitute inside the sanctuary, Jesus presented His own sacrifice in the heavenly sanctuary. The twenty-four elders declared Jesus to be worthy: "For You were slain, and have redeemed us to God by Your blood" (verse 9).

In the camp of Israel, the blood of sacrifice, along with the guilt of God's people was carried into His presence in the tabernacle all year long. Then on the Day of Atonement, all of the "uncleanness" (Leviticus 16:16) that had accumulated in the sanctuary was completely cleansed away.

Notice the order of events portrayed in the book of Hebrews. First, Jesus was offered "to bear the sins of many." Our sin and guilt have fallen on Jesus, and He has borne them away. Then, at the Second Coming, Jesus appears "apart from sin, for salvation." The sin is completely and finally eradicated. The salvation that He secured for us, which we can confidently claim by faith, will be fully and finally realized when He comes for us. Sin and suffering will be finished, and God will finally be able to "wipe away every tear" for good (Revelation 21:4).

In the meantime, the Holy Spirit serves as a "guarantee of our inheritance" (Ephesians 1:14) and allows us to start living as if we were already there. As you live this day, let someone else catch a glimpse of what the Lamb of God could do for him or her.

The Throne Above the Storm

And above the firmament over their heads was the likeness of a throne,
in appearance like a sapphire stone; on the likeness of the throne was a likeness
with the appearance of a man high above it.

—Ezekiel 1:26

When the *Project UFO* TV series rolled out in the late 1970s, it opened with a narrator making reference to the book of Ezekiel as pictures of flying saucers scrolled across the screen: "Ezekiel saw the wheel. This is the wheel he said he saw. These are unidentified flying objects that people say they are seeing now."

The book of Ezekiel, of course, has nothing to do with flying saucers. The imagery used in the opening chapter corresponds to other passages in the Bible that describe the throne room of God, such as those found in Isaiah and Revelation. It is a vision Ezekiel receives as a Babylonian captive, at one of the lowest points of Israel's existence. There was great discouragement among God's people, and many were wondering if God had abandoned them forever. It is not unlike the situation in which John the revelator receives his vision: he, too, was an exile, alone on Patmos.

As the vision opens, Ezekiel witnesses a tumultuous, confusing scene: a fiery whirlwind approaches from the north, representing the descent of Nebuchadnez-zar's armies on the city of Jerusalem. It was an event that was hard for Israel to understand; but as Ezekiel looks more closely, he sees the symbols of the sanctuary and the divine presence—cherubim and a glorious brilliance radiating from a cloud. The seemingly strange movements were directed by "the spirit" (Ezekiel 1:12). Finally, above it all, he sees the throne of God.

The message? Even when life serves up its hardest moments, God is still in control, working out His plans from heaven's sanctuary. There will be times when the evidence of our senses will tell us that all is lost and that God has abandoned us. You will face days when you are tempted to despair and to give up hope. Those are the moments when you will most need to cling to your faith, to look up above the chaos to heaven's sanctuary, believing that above all the chaos God is still on His throne, Christ is still your High Priest, and He will keep His promise to replace the kingdoms of this world with His own everlasting kingdom.

"Let not your heart be troubled," Jesus said, "if I go . . . I will come again and receive you to Myself" (John 14:1, 3).

Get Off the Throne

Let no one deceive you by any means; for that Day will not come
unless the falling away comes first, and the man of sin is revealed, the son of perdition,
who opposes and exalts himself above all that is called God or that is worshiped,
so that he sits as God in the temple of God, showing himself that he is God.
—2 Thessalonians 2:3, 4

In Paul's second letter to the Thessalonians, he identifies one of the biggest challenges Christians will face before the second coming of Christ: the man of sin will lay claim to the throne of God. The developments within Christianity during the Dark Ages prove that Paul was absolutely right, and Revelation 13 indicates that the issue is not yet closed.

But it is not the man of sin alone who is guilty of laying claim to God's throne. He is, after all, following in the footsteps of the arch rebel Lucifer, whose pride led him to covet God's position and authority. "I will ascend above the heights of the clouds," he told himself, "I will be like the Most High" (Isaiah 14:14).

When you consider that the dragon gives the beast his authority (Revelation 13:2) and that all the world wonders after the beast (verse 3), we should be conscious of the fact that fallen angels are pouring effort into having human beings follow in their footsteps. To that end, we should not only be vigilant when it comes to the aspirations of the son of perdition but also be aware of our own tendency to do the same thing. There are moments when we are tempted to second-guess God's authority and claim His rightful place as our own.

Pay attention to the Bible's most memorable characters: The biggest mistakes take place when they claim God's throne—even for just a few moments—and make some of God's decisions for Him. Cain second-guessed the sacrificial system. Abraham tried to fulfill God's promise in his own way with Hagar. Jacob attempted to force the matter of his inheritance. Eve second-guessed God's authority by accepting the serpent's proposal.

We do it too. We try to force God's hand, praying for things that are not His will and making them happen as if He had answered. We make decisions for God, ignoring counsel and doing things our own way, telling ourselves that we are clever enough to rethink what God has made clear.

Part of understanding that Christ is leading His church from heaven's sanctuary is to start living now as if the kingdom has already come, with God restored to His rightful place on the throne of our hearts.

The Medicine of Hope

Be of good courage, and He shall strengthen your heart, all you who hope in the LORD.
—Psalm 31:24

Shakespeare's play *Measure for Measure* is an examination of ethics and corruption. The Duke of Vienna sends his deputy Angelo into the community to investigate the degree of moral decay among his subjects. Angelo catches a young man by the name of Claudio in a moral indiscretion and condemns him to death. As the young man appeals in the hopes of a pardon, he states one of the most famous lines in Shakespeare's work: "The miserable have no other medicine but only hope."

There comes a point in every life when you will run out of solutions: there will be no money to pay your debt, no cure for your illness, and no taking back what the grave has stolen from you. Human beings will have nothing to offer; in fact, many of the things people will say at your worst hour may hurt more than they help.

Christians are not exempt from suffering; the idea that Christianity provides a prosperous, easy path is a modern distortion of the gospel that is not supported by Scripture. Jesus was not exempt from suffering and grief, and on this side of eternity, His followers will not be exempt either. Consider Elijah, whose discouragement was deep enough after the showdown on Carmel to make him question whether he wanted to live.

Part of living in a fallen world is wrestling, at least occasionally, with misery. But for the Christian, there is time-tested Shakespearean medicine: hope. When nothing in this world offers a way out, when human solutions fail to bring relief, we still know that our great High Priest is victorious over the grave. We know that He represents us, personally, in the courts of heaven and that He holds the future securely in His hands. With the risen Jesus in the heavenly sanctuary, we have hope. To study the Bible is to realize that God has not missed a beat in executing His plan to save us and that our redemption is not only secure but also near.

The miserable may have no other medicine but hope, but what powerful medicine hope in Jesus has proven to be for the wounded and the brokenhearted.

Nothing to Chance

He indeed was foreordained before the foundation of the world, but was manifest
in these last times for you who through Him believe in God, who raised Him
from the dead and gave Him glory, so that your faith and hope are in God.
—1 Peter 2:20, 21

Even though, at the time of this writing, I have not yet achieved the age of fifty, I have moved more than twenty times, and I have accumulated a wide variety of experiences with movers. Of those, one of the most memorable is the time we called Mickey's Movers★ to help us move across town. They were an utter disaster: they arrived hours late, *and* they were as careless with our possessions as the worst pessimist might fear. The truck was packed carelessly, multiple items were broken, and at one point, they even broke a water line in the kitchen and did not tell us. I discovered the disaster when I walked into the lake forming on the kitchen floor.

Never again. I can accept that mishaps occasionally happen, but when it is obvious that the damage occurred through carelessness and an obvious lack of planning, I have trouble labeling what happened as an "accident."

When you study the plan of salvation through the lens of the sanctuary, it becomes abundantly clear that God leaves nothing to chance. His strategy to save you is carefully planned; in fact, the Bible tells us that Jesus is the "Lamb slain from the foundation of the world" (Revelation 13:8). Peter underscores the same point: Jesus was "foreordained before the foundation of the world." Before you needed Jesus, He was ready for you.

As you walk through the sanctuary with Jesus, from the altar of sacrifice in the courtyard to the mercy seat in the Most Holy Place, you cannot help but notice the incredible level of detail: practically every little element and every little ritual *means something*. The furniture points to Jesus. So do the priest and the ceremonies involved in the sacrifice. It should be abundantly clear to all honest seekers that the plan to save sinners is not a haphazard afterthought or a hastily constructed damage control plan designed to mitigate destruction that caught God off guard.

No, it is careful and deliberate, and the only real variable in the equation is your choice to cooperate. Apart from that, everything else is completely guaranteed. Once you have decided to "follow the Lamb wherever He goes" (Revelation 14:4), you can rest in the knowledge that your move to God's kingdom will be executed flawlessly.

★ The company's name has been changed.

APRIL 26

Better on a Piano

For now we see in a mirror, dimly, but then face to face.
Now I know in part, but then I shall know just as I also am known.
—1 Corinthians 13:12

It is a five-mile walk to the office in the morning, which means there is a little over an hour in which to immerse myself in the classical music that streams from my smart phone. One morning, just as I rounded the final bend in the road, someone was playing Bach on the piano. It was breathtaking—so much so that I wanted to sit on the side of the road for a few minutes and just listen. It was gorgeous but inauthentic. Why? Bach did not write the piece for piano. In fact, he wrote almost nothing for piano, because the piano did not come into its own until the century after his death.

Bach wrote for clavichord (an instrument so quiet and timid that it cannot be heard in a concert hall) and harpsichord (an instrument that plucks the strings rather than strikes them with a hammer, which severely limits the dynamic range available to the performer).

See? Bach on a piano is inauthentic. Unlike some purists, it does not bother me, because the piano is far and away my favorite keyboard instrument. Its full name? The *pianoforte*, which means "soft-loud," because, unlike the harpsichord, it allows the performer almost limitless control over the volume of each note. In my humble opinion, Bach sounds *better* on a piano.

Think of your first day—your first year—in heaven. God has granted you a single brief moment on this planet in which to compose something beautiful. Your life is a remarkable instrument, capable of producing melodies that prove God's existence and demonstrate His goodness. But your capacity has been severely limited by sin. As attractive as a human life might become through the sanctifying grace of our heavenly High Priest, it is still just like a harpsichord. The dynamic range has been crippled.

But when you finally stand in glory, after a lifetime in the transforming hands of the Savior, completely restored to what God originally intended, when the barriers imposed by sin have at long last been lifted, your character will suddenly become a magnificent instrument. The melody God composed with your broken, limited life will then be played on a new instrument with a far broader dynamic range, and it will be stunning. In fact, angels might stop what they are doing just to listen.

The Real You

I have been crucified with Christ; it is no longer I who live,
but Christ lives in me; and the life which I now live in the flesh I live
by faith in the Son of God, who loved me and gave Himself for me.
—Galatians 2:20

The tree was twisted, gnarled, and rough. Someone had ruthlessly pruned back about half the branches, and it was ugly. It probably did not help that spring had not yet arrived. I tried to picture the tree with a full head of green leaves, but it did not help. I was about to move on when I suddenly noticed that the side of the trunk had split open, exposing evidence of a much younger tree that had been encased deep inside the coarse exterior over time. Was it an absorbed twin, or the younger heart of the same tree?

That's a lot like me, I thought. *I have been forced to confront my sinful self enough times to know the truth: there is little about my fallen nature that would recommend me to God.* But somewhere deep under my weathered exterior lies a remnant of what the human race used to be. No matter how many times we have been pruned, no matter how scaly and heavy our outward bark has become through sin, the innocence and wonder of God's original design have not been completely lost. The real you is still in there, encased in the scar tissue of a hard life.

Nearly every man or woman with a rough exterior was once a starry-eyed idealistic child, convinced that life would be generous and kind. As the years progress, layer after crusty layer builds up over our dreams, snuffing them out slowly. Eventually, our shells become twisted, gnarled, and rough. That is what sin does to us.

But every so often—during those moments when we remember the freedom of childhood or we think about the promise of heaven—our rough exterior cracks just a little and we catch a glimpse of what we soon shall be. The real you, the one God hopes for, is still there, and the more you place yourselves in the hands of the High Priest, the more you will see that person begin to emerge. Each day a little more of the bark is peeled away, until the day when Jesus returns and all of it will be removed forever. At that moment, you will resume the dreams God planted in your heart when He first designed the human race.

Truth be told, you have not yet truly begun to live.

The Remains of the Mouse

But Christ came as High Priest of the good things to come, with the greater and more perfect tabernacle not made with hands, that is, not of this creation. Not with the blood of goats and calves, but with His own blood He entered the Most Holy Place once for all, having obtained eternal redemption.

—Hebrews 9:11, 12

Early one morning, as I walked to work, I nearly stepped on the remains of a mouse. Or, to be more precise, *half* a mouse; its back half was completely gone. I found myself trying to imagine what had led to such a horrible fate. Had the mouse been attacked by a neighborhood cat? Maybe. But it seemed very strange to me that the cat would leave half a mouse behind.

I can only guess what might have occurred, because I wasn't actually there. I have nothing but an overactive imagination to help me reconstruct the unfortunate incident, but I will never truly know.

It's not unlike the way some people approach the inevitable discovery that our world can be a horrible place, complete with pain, suffering, and untimely deaths. All that we can see is the way the world is now, because we weren't actually present when things went awry.

Some people try to explain it in evolutionary terms: this is simply the way it is in a world that is clawing its way toward a better existence. The weak among us suffer and die; the genetically advantaged do a little better: survival of the fittest. And of course, the assumption is that evolution is (somehow) moving *forward*—so eventually it will solve most of our problems.

Others become despondent nihilists, telling themselves that life doesn't mean anything: we hurt, and that's just the way it is. But don't worry, when you die, it will all be over—forever.

It is all imagination: theories concocted by people who weren't there when the original tragedy took place, when we traded paradise for a horror show. How much better to consult Someone who *was* there: He knows the tragedy of sin intimately, because He watched it happen. Not only that, He stepped into this world and took the price on Himself. Now He ministers His own blood—a potent symbol of His intimate knowledge of our painful situation. I have read the philosophers and the poets extensively, and not one of them has ever produced an explanation that resonates as perfectly as the one presented by our heavenly High Priest.

There is a reason our world is broken, and there is a definite solution on display in the sanctuary. Take it from Someone who was there.

That First Class in Heaven

For we know in part and we prophesy in part. But when that which is perfect has come,
then that which is in part will be done away. When I was a child, I spoke as a child,
I understood as a child, I thought as a child; but when I became a man,
I put away childish things. For now we see in a mirror, dimly, but then face to face.
Now I know in part, but then I shall know just as I also am known.
—1 Corinthians 13:9–12

When Isaac Newton gave us a formula to explain how gravity works, he was giving us a mathematical model that appeared to accurately predict how bodies reacted with each other. His model was excellent and served us well until the twentieth century when Einstein gave us something *more* accurate—the theory of relativity. Relativity gave way to quantum mechanics and string theory as we struggled to explain why physical laws appeared to work differently in the world of subatomic particles.

Those physics formulas you scribbled in your notebook as a student were *all* models: reasonable mathematical explanations for phenomena found in nature. If any of them should prove to be slightly inaccurate, adjustments will have to be made.

In the sanctuary, we have a tangible model to help us understand some of the loftiest concepts in the universe. How does the cross of Calvary save us? Why does the incarnation of Christ matter? How deep is God's love for us? How will God finally judge the human race and settle the matter of our sinfulness without compromising His moral law? How can God bring sinners into His kingdom without risking a second rebellion?

These are the kinds of questions that will keep us busy for all eternity. "The knowledge of God's works and ways we can only begin to obtain in this world," Ellen White explains, "the study will be continued throughout eternity."[*] God opened the discussion with the model of His sanctuary that He presented at the gates of Eden, where the shining cherubim and brilliant presence were found. It continued in the tabernacle and then in the temple.

All of these were models of God's plan, crafted out of physical materials and arranged to give us understanding. Today, we continue our study of the plan of salvation through the heavenly sanctuary as it is described in the pages of Scripture. It is a course of study that will last a lifetime; it is so profound that we will never finish plumbing its depths. Then to know, as Paul points out when describing God's love, that we have only just *begun* to understand—well, it is breathtaking.

Time to crack the books and glean all you can from Scripture; you will want to be prepared for that first class in heaven.

---

[*] Ellen G. White, *Child Guidance* (Hagerstown, MD: Review and Herald®, 2002), 50.

Twenty-Four Seven

Therefore He is also able to save to the uttermost those who come to God through Him,
since He always lives to make intercession for them.
—Hebrews 7:25

It was early in the morning, just as the sun was cresting the horizon, when I suddenly felt a sharp pain on my left side. *Oh no,* I thought to myself. *A kidney stone!* Experience had taught me what to expect next: brutal, stabbing pain that would quickly become disabling. I have been able to pass a few stones at home, unassisted, but I could tell that this was going to be a doozy. Not wanting to wake my wife, I hopped in the car and searched for the closest urgent care clinic on Google maps. To my dismay, I discovered that the closest one would not be open for another hour!

Not content to wait that long, I opted instead to drive to the emergency room at a local hospital, which of course was more expensive. The pain was so bad that I did not care.

How often have you needed some essential service at an inconvenient hour? The furnace runs perfectly fine until it is a holiday, and you cannot get someone to come and fix it. A pipe bursts outside of business hours when the plumber is going to charge a premium to come. Your internet connection goes down when you have an important videoconference scheduled, and a call to the service provider lands at an answering service. The world around us does not run 24/7—a fact that can be terribly frustrating at times.

But look at the heavenly sanctuary for a moment. The author of Hebrews tells us that Jesus "always lives to make intercession" for us. In other words, He is available around the clock, whenever you need Him most. You do not have to wait for heaven to open tomorrow morning when you need an Advocate (1 John 2:1), because He is available right now.

Not only that, but He also does the job perfectly the first time; there are no callbacks. The Bible says that Jesus is "able to save to the *uttermost* those who come to God through Him." In some modern translations, it says "completely." Some scholars believe it means that Jesus saves us *fully,* and others believe it means *forever.* Either way, it is incredibly good news: your broken, sinful heart will be forgiven without any reservation, and your stay in the kingdom will last for all eternity.

May

I believe that the Bible is God's inspired Word, the only rule of faith and practice for the Christian. I covenant to spend time regularly in prayer and Bible study.

What God Is Thinking

"As He spoke by the mouth of His holy prophets, who have been since the world began."
—Luke 1:70

God has always been interested in communicating with us. Prior to our expulsion from the Garden, God visited with us in the cool of the evening (Genesis 3:8). He also made a distinct effort to communicate His plans to reverse what we had done and redeem us from sin (verse 15).

After our removal from Eden, God never quit communicating with us. He has been utterly open and honest about our condition, the consequences of rebellion, His profound love for us, and His ability to save us through Christ. More than that, He has openly offered us invaluable advice for daily life on a fallen planet, including matters such as personal finances, interpersonal relationships, and health.

At the beginning of Luke's Gospel, God sends another message through the father of John the Baptist, reminding us that He has always been in communication with us. "The prophets have told us that the Messiah is coming right from the very beginning," Zacharias prophesies. We may have severed our connection with God, but He has never completely let go of us. As Paul explained to the citizens of Lystra, since the Fall, God has allowed us to determine our own path through life, refusing to use coercion to force us to come back. But all throughout the rebellion, God "did not leave Himself without witness" (Acts 14:16, 17).

There is a startling contrast between the government of God and human government. God uses persuasion, reason, and love to win us back; human beings frequently resort to force of some sort to strengthen laws and ideological agendas. On the campaign trail, politicians promise they will establish open and transparent governments, but they almost invariably fall far short of their promises. God, on the other hand, tells us exactly what He is up to. "Surely the Lord GOD does nothing," Amos tells us, "unless He reveals His secret to His servants the prophets" (Amos 3:7).

Short of email leaks and whistle-blowers, we may never know what human governments are actually up to. But with God, you only need to spend prayerful time in His Word to know what He is thinking. Surely, there is no privilege greater than to be on the inside track with the only government that will never need to be replaced.

Unquestionable Authority

All Scripture is given by inspiration of God, and is profitable for doctrine,
for reproof, for correction, for instruction in righteousness.
—2 Timothy 3:16

The incarnation of Christ is one of those mysteries that theologians have wrestled with for millennia, and every generation has come to the same conclusion: The Bible plainly reveals that Jesus is God in human flesh. The Gospel of John states it point blank: "And the Word became flesh and dwelt among us" (John 1:14). That much is clear. What is not so apparent is how it works. How can someone be fully God and fully human at the same time?

Sure, there are aspects of the Incarnation that we can wrap our minds around, and occasionally, we will catch glimpses of God's glory by studying the subject, but the *how* always seems to lie just beyond our grasp. Through the ages, people who wrestle with the topic have occasionally ventured onto dangerous ground, either robbing Christ of His divinity or His humanity. "Be careful," Ellen White once counseled a preacher who was tackling the topic, "exceedingly careful as to how you dwell upon the human nature of Christ." She noted, "The incarnation of Christ has ever been, and will ever remain a mystery."★

The Bible itself has something in common with Jesus. Not only are the written Scriptures and Christ Himself referred to as the "Word," but both are also a blend of the divine and human. The Bible is God's Word, revealed through human authors. It is the infinite mind of God, presented in finite human language. For the last two hundred years, scholars have spent many hours trying to dissect exactly what that means. Some of their conclusions have been disastrous, stripping the Bible of its divine authority.

Paul tells us the Scriptures are "God-breathed" (2 Timothy 3:16, ESV). It is God's word, delivered through human authors. And of course, Jesus is *the* Word, revealed in human flesh. In both cases, God has stooped down to reveal Himself because we were incapable of rising to His level. As with the Incarnation, we would be wise to exercise the utmost caution in trying to define precisely how that works. Ellen White's advice? Jesus "pointed to the Scriptures as of unquestionable authority, and we should do the same. The Bible is to be presented as the word of the infinite God, as the end of all controversy and the foundation of all faith."†

★ Ellen G. White, *Manuscript Releases*, vol. 13 (Silver Spring, MD: Ellen G. White Estate, 1990), 18, 19.
† Ellen G. White, *Christ's Object Lessons* (Hagerstown, MD: Review and Herald®, 2003), 39.

Jumping on Glass

As for God, His way is perfect; the word of the LORD is proven; He is a shield to all who trust in Him.

—2 Samuel 22:31

Spoiler alert: if you've never been to the CN Tower in Toronto, I'm about to ruin your first visit. On the observation deck, near the top of the tower and more than 1,100 feet above the sidewalk below, there's a section of the floor made of glass. On any given day, you'll find nervous tourists gathered around it, scared to set foot on what looks like a long fall in the making. You actually have to fight your *brain*—every basic human instinct—to walk out on the glass. As you plant your foot on something you've been *told* will hold you, your mind is screaming *No!*

Of course, once you've gingerly stepped onto the glass a few times, you experience a rising sense of boldness. Before long, you're taking pictures of yourself with the sidewalk far beneath you. And then, as your confidence continues to build, you might even take a running start at the window and *jump* on it.

It's all good fun, until you tire of it and decide to take the elevator back to terra firma. When you board the elevator, the guide who runs it has one final surprise for you. "What we didn't tell you on the way up is that the *whole floor is made of glass,* and because people found it nerve-wracking, we decided to carpet everything except for a small observation window."

Imagine that: the whole time you had been working up the courage to stand on the glass, you were actually already standing on it.

And so it goes with the Word of God. Many people approach its pages with a sense of fear, wondering what it would be like to actually trust God with everything— to step out by faith and actually *do* what the Bible says and live like you *know* that the promises God makes are all true. In time, you work up the courage to take your first steps, and when you discover the path is perfect, you dare to do it again. God really *is* a shield to all who trust Him.

Of course, when we all finally step into glory, and the books are opened so that we can have the eyesight of heaven, we're going to discover that there never *was* a time when God wasn't holding us up.

A Truthful Guide

Then He turned to His disciples and said privately, "Blessed are the eyes
which see the things you see; for I tell you that many prophets and kings have desired to see
what you see, and have not seen it, and to hear what you hear, and have not heard it."
—Luke 10:23, 24

When you know you are about to travel somewhere, it is only natural to buy a travel guide or hop online and look for pictures of your destination. You want to have an idea of what to expect. But no matter how many pictures you look at, you will almost inevitably discover when you arrive that it looks different than you expected. It is not that the picture is inaccurate; it is that your imagination filled in all the wrong details. Perhaps you expected a certain building to face the ocean, and it does not. Or perhaps you thought that some object in the photo would be larger than it really is.

The Old Testament Scriptures are a powerful description of the Messiah, which is a fact that Jesus had to remind two discouraged followers about while on the road to Emmaus (Luke 24:27). Nathanael also had his understanding challenged when he discovered that the Messiah lived in Nazareth; it simply did not match what he had always believed. "Can anything good come out of Nazareth?" he asked (John 1:46). When Jesus entered this world, the reality of who He was continually challenged the understanding of people who had built wrong expectations. Sometimes, as with much of the religious leadership of the day, pride stood in the way of an accurate understanding; other times, it was simply ignorance.

Shortly after sending out the Seventy, Jesus turned to His disciples and told them of their good fortune. "The things you're seeing," He explained, "are the very things the kings and prophets of old wished they could see." They were standing in fuller light, blessed with far more vivid detail than previous believers because they were in the presence of Jesus Himself.

This is a critical key to getting the most out of Bible study. Think of the Old Testament as a travel brochure, full of gorgeous photos of your destination. The photos are completely accurate because photos simply portray what the camera sees. But to be certain that your imagination is not reading into the picture what may or may not be there, always compare what you read to the message and the person of Jesus Himself. Apart from Christ, the Bible is just another ancient document; with Christ, it has the power to open your eyes and change your life.

The Power of Bible Study

*And beginning at Moses and all the Prophets, He expounded to them
in all the Scriptures the things concerning Himself.*
—Luke 24:27

Shortly after the Resurrection—before many people realized that Jesus had come back from the dead—there was a lot of confusion among His followers. Near the end of Luke's Gospel, we meet two discouraged people who are struggling to understand what has transpired during the past three days. The religious authorities took the Man they had hoped would be the Messiah and put Him to death on a Roman cross, and now the two Marys have come back from the tomb, insisting that Jesus was once again alive. It was all very confusing.

In some ways, these two frustrated disciples are not unlike the postmodern generation of today who have all but given up on certainty. After rationalism and mechanization failed to deliver their utopian promises and instead produced the most violent century in world history, many people have philosophically given up on the idea that life has any objective direction or purpose or that truth can be objectively known.

What we all *thought* was going to solve our human problems did not turn out to be what we hoped. That is the language of these two disciples: "But we were hoping that it was He who was going to redeem Israel" (Luke 24:21). Now they were not sure what to think.

Pay careful attention to Jesus' response, because it speaks powerfully to the Bible's potential to breathe hope into our lives. He is with these two people, in person. He *could* have simply revealed Himself to them, saying in effect, "Here I am!" Surely, that would have solved their problem. Notice the course Jesus chooses to pursue: "Beginning at Moses and all the Prophets, He expounded to them in all the Scriptures the things concerning Himself."

He could have provided a miraculous epiphany, but instead, the Son of God gave these two troubled people a Bible study—and a prophecy study at that. Since the Fall, the Bible has been the primary means by which God communicates His plan for hope to the human race. The message between its covers is so powerful that even a resurrected Jesus continued to use it when one might be tempted to think He did not have to. And today would be a magnificent day to start leaning on God's Word, the source of *your* hope too.

Of Absolutes and Madness

The entirety of Your word is truth, and every one of Your righteous judgments endures forever.
—Psalm 119:160

One of the things that makes some modern audiences terribly uncomfortable with the message of Scripture is the Bible's insistence that it is not merely *telling* the truth—it *is* the truth. "I, the LORD, speak righteousness," God tells us through the prophet Isaiah, "I declare things that are right" (Isaiah 45:19).

To the postmodern mind, this is nonsense. There is no objective truth, some insist, and what you define as right and wrong is shaped by your own personal preference, context, and situation. The notion of objective truth is something invented by people trying to control others.

This kind of thinking boggles the minds of older generations, who were not exposed to that relativistic thinking in college. But it was the philosophical framework for most people educated in the 1960s onward, and it has led to some astonishing conclusions. A college professor in New York, curious to see how pervasive relativistic thinking had become, surveyed his students and made a horrific discovery: as many as 20 percent of them "could not bring themselves to criticize the Nazi extermination of Europe's Jews. Some students expressed personal distaste for what the Nazis did. But they were not willing to say that the Nazis were wrong, since no culture can be judged from the outside and no individual can challenge the moral worldview of another."[*]

It is a distinctly twentieth-century mind-set, brought on by the philosophers of the nineteenth century. But Shakespeare had already described this philosophy four hundred years earlier when he wrote *Hamlet*. "There is nothing either good or bad," Hamlet states at one point, "but thinking makes it so."[†] In other words, everybody gets to define his or her own morality. Things are only evil if you *think* they are.

The thing to remember, as author Andrew Klavan points out in *The Great Good Thing*, is that Hamlet was pretending to be crazy—and in the four hundred years since Shakespeare penned his play, a mind-set that was considered utterly insane has now suddenly been deemed sane.[‡]

I have discovered, after working with tens of thousands of people, that this mind-set has left many people miserably despondent. After all, the idea that nothing is true is horrible news, which may be why so many are starting to find the beautiful certainty of Scripture as deeply refreshing.

---

[*] John Leo, "At Postmodern U., Professors Who See No Evil," *Jewish World Review*, July 16, 2002, http://www.jewishworldreview.com/cols/leo071602.asp.

[†] William Shakespeare, *Hamlet*, ed. Barbara A. Mowat and Paul Werstine, New Folger ed., act 2, scene 2, lines 268–270, http://www.folgerdigitaltexts.org/download/pdf/Ham.pdf.

[‡] Andrew Klavan, *The Great Good Thing* (Nashville: Nelson Books, 2016), 136, 137.

Creative Power

By the word of the LORD the heavens were made,
and all the host of them by the breath of His mouth.

—Psalm 33:6

I remember a weekend when I was feeling particularly overwhelmed and anxious about everything I had on my to-do list. There were problems that did not seem to have solutions, and they were keeping me up at night. So even though I was very busy, I dropped everything for a few hours. I grabbed two essential items—my red portable hammock and my small blue pocket Bible—and then I drove ninety minutes up into the mountains to be alone, or to be more precise, to be alone with God.

It took a while to find the perfect spot. I wanted to be somewhere where I could not be found because it was essential that I would not be disturbed. I finally discovered the perfect spot on the edge of a river, behind a large rock that concealed me from view. (I will keep that wonderful spot a secret until the day I die!) I strung my hammock between two trees, and with nothing but the wind in the treetops and the river bubbling two feet beneath me, I opened my Bible and began to listen for God's voice.

It never fails: if you approach the Scriptures with an open and willing heart, God will make Himself heard. Within a few hours of listening to the One who repeatedly told His disciples, "Fear not," my anxiety started to subside, my confidence was restored, and I had utter peace of mind about the decisions I faced in the week ahead.

I suppose someone might be tempted to assume that all I needed was a little space to gather my thoughts. But the healing did not come from the solitude, as useful as solitude can be. The healing happened when God's voice massaged my wounded heart from the pages of the Bible.

The Bible is not like other books. It is the voice of God to the human race, and when God speaks, it is powerful enough to breathe the universe into existence with just a few phrases. Notice that God also breathed His Written Word into existence; it is what "inspiration" literally means. Scripture has the creative power to heal a broken heart and remake it in the image of Christ.

What a shame that more people do not take advantage daily of what the Bible has to offer.

The Truth About You

For the word of God is living and powerful, and sharper than any two-edged sword,
piercing even to the division of soul and spirit, and of joints and marrow,
and is a discerner of the thoughts and intents of the heart.
—Hebrews 4:12

During my freshman year of college, there was a guy in my dorm who had a remarkable talent for drawing caricatures—those cartoon drawings that highly exaggerate your best (or worst) features. Most of us could not *wait* to return to the dorm at the end of the day to see who his latest victim was, and he never disappointed us. There were nearly eighteen thousand potential victims on campus, so he never ran out of material.

Some days it would be a professor that nobody liked; other days it would be someone from a rival dormitory. And then one day, he produced a drawing that made absolutely no sense; every other drawing had been a work of evident genius, but now he had drawn something that did not resemble anybody I knew.

That is when I noticed that the other guys in the room were laughing. Finally, someone said, "You don't see it, do you?" And then he delivered the deathblow: "It's *you.*"

And then, suddenly, I *did* see it, and I must confess, I did not like it. If it was not funny before I understood, it was doubly unfunny now because it revealed some painful truths. The fact that absolutely everyone else saw it made it even more painful, because obviously, the drawing was telling the truth. There was no escaping it.

It is not unlike that awful moment when you hear your voice on a recording. Most people do not think it sounds anything like them. But consider this awful fact: Everyone else in the room thinks it sounds *exactly* like you, because the recording is the truth. That is how you sound without the distorting influence of the skull that separates your mouth from your ears.

The author of Hebrews warns us that studying the Bible can be a painful experience sometimes. God loves you too much not to show you the truth about yourself—the way that He sees it. God's perspective is the unvarnished, unspun truth. But take heart; He is only doing this because you must see how desperately you need Jesus before He can remake you into the child of God you were supposed to be. Before you can move forward with Jesus, God needs you to leave some things behind; and if you are willing, He will show you exactly what those are.

Sharing the Word

Blessed is he who reads and those who hear the words of this prophecy,
and keep those things which are written in it; for the time is near.
—Revelation 1:3

The last five hours of the day, from seven o'clock onward, are usually the most productive for me. I relish the quiet that falls over the house when everyone else goes to bed, and I am alone with my books and my thoughts. The stories of the Bible become most vibrant under the glow of a solitary desk lamp in my study, and at times, the presence of Christ is palpable—almost as if Jesus Himself has walked into my study, placed His hand on my shoulder, and whispered into my ear.

Of all the books in my library, the Bible has provided me with countless thousands of hours of joy. But I must confess I have learned that the greatest joy the Bible has to offer does not present itself in the privacy of my study, or even from those incredible *eureka* moments when the answer to a biblical question that has evaded me for years suddenly presents itself.

No, the greatest fulfillment comes from sharing the Bible with someone else. As I look back over the decades, I can see in hindsight that it is the moments when I opened the Bible with an audience of seekers that rewarded me most richly. To watch the light of recognition go on in someone's eyes, to watch stubborn resistance to Christ melt in the presence of His Word—that has been the most rewarding. The questions that others ask have caused me to spend countless hours on my knees and combing the Scriptures for answers.

Most students of Bible prophecy recognize the triple blessing found in the opening verses of John's final work. We are promised that if we read the book of Revelation, we will be blessed, and I can testify that the promise is true: I *have* been blessed every time I have returned to Revelation to read it again. But the blessing is not just for those who spend quiet hours privately contemplating God's Word; the original language implies that the blessing falls on those who read it aloud so that others can hear it. The language is a reflection of Old Testament times when the Scriptures were read aloud to God's people.

To read God's Word is a blessing. To share it with someone else? Even better.

God's Measuring Tape

And when they say to you, "Seek those who are mediums and wizards,
who whisper and mutter," should not a people seek their God?
Should they seek the dead on behalf of the living? To the law and to the testimony!
If they do not speak according to this word, it is because there is no light in them.
—Isaiah 8:19, 20

When my grandfather died—a man who loved carpentry as much as he loved life—I drove a long way to attend the funeral service. The pastor who conducted the graveside ceremony was a man I instinctively liked, and at one point during the committal service, he suddenly reached into his pocket and pulled out a tape measure. "Let me talk to all of the grandchildren here for a moment," he said.

"When Joe was alive, he used a tape measure like this every day, to make sure that every cut was exactly right. This is the tool he relied on for his *trade*. But he relied on something else for his *life*: the Bible. That is what he used to make sure that every decision in his life was always aligned with the will of God. There is no question he led a godly and successful life, and that is because he always measured twice and cut once. So my challenge to you is to do the same: make the Word of God the infallible guide for the rest of your life."

If you walk into any bookstore, you will see an ever-expanding self-help section loaded with the works of authors who promise to make your life a little bit easier. I have no doubt that you will find some very useful titles among the books. But you will also find the works of uninformed authors who offer counterfeits; poor substitutes for an actual relationship with God. There is some horrific spiritual advice awaiting the unwary, ranging from non-Christian spiritual practices to outright spiritualism.

In other words, not much has changed in the thousands of years since Isaiah wrote the passage you just read. The specific case in his day was channelers: people who offered, for a fee, to obtain advice from the dead. Today, it might not be as overtly spiritualistic, but the world of self-help can still be a minefield of very bad ideas.

Let me pass on the challenge that pastor gave us: never fail to have the Word of God handy, so you can accurately measure every idea you read by God's standard. It is so much better to measure twice and cut once than the other way around. It will hurt a lot less in the long run.

Still the First Edition

"The grass withers, the flower fades, because the breath of the LORD blows upon it; surely the people are grass. The grass withers, the flower fades, but the word of our God stands forever."
—Isaiah 40:7, 8

If you still happen to have any of your textbooks around the house, grab one and look at the cover. Chances are, it will not be a first edition, since textbooks are forever being rewritten and re-released. I have one biology textbook that was in its sixty-seventh edition when I bought it many years ago. I recently went online to see what edition was being sold to this year's biology majors, and it seems that in the decades since I took the class, the book has been scrapped altogether in favor of a new book—which is already in its eighth edition.

Why do textbooks go through so many revisions? My inner cynic has always suspected that it keeps sales brisk since few students would dare risk using an older edition and miss a vital point that might appear on an exam. The more likely scenario, however, is that the nature of human knowledge is such that we often have to change our minds as new information is uncovered. What was rock-solid science in the 1950s might not appear quite as solid to a freshman class in the twenty-first century.

Human knowledge changes. God's knowledge does not. You will notice that while we are forever tweaking our imperfect *translations* of the Bible, the message of the Bible itself has stood unchanged for thousands of years. The discovery of the Dead Sea Scrolls confirmed what Christians have claimed for generations: the content of the Scriptures has remained unaltered since the very beginning.

That is not to say that people will not challenge the content; they will. The Word of God stands in stark opposition to the values of the world. It is distinctly countercultural. But you can bank on its veracity; even the concepts we find hard to understand today will one day be vindicated in the light of Christ's presence. Christians may have to apologize for their behavior, and we may have to apologize for the way we misapply the Word of God, but we can rest assured that we will never have to apologize for what God said. Human opinions will continue to go through endless revisions, but the Word of our God stands forever.

"That Book Changed My Life!"

*Since you have purified your souls in obeying the truth through the Spirit in sincere love
of the brethren, love one another fervently with a pure heart, having been born again, not of
corruptible seed but incorruptible, through the word of God which lives and abides forever.*
—1 Peter 1:22, 23

That book changed my life!" The man was speaking about Dostoevsky's *Crime
and Punishment*, the story of a man who undergoes mental anguish after
committing a heinous crime. I immediately knew he was right; many people can
point to a powerful novel or philosophical work as a watershed in their lives. Looking back, I can point to a number of occasions when a powerfully argued book
has shifted my perspective on the world. There are a number of such books on my
library shelf, and I find myself referencing them often.

While human authors can sometimes change your mind, none of them can actually alter the core essence of who you are. It is true that you can, by all outward
appearances, seem to be a different person if someone convincingly changes your
mind. But at your core, you are still a sinner. You are still driven by things such as
pride, ambition, and selfishness.

The Bible stands completely apart from other books in its ability to remake *you*.
Peter writes that we have been "born again . . . through the word of God." Of
course, it is Jesus, the "Word [who] became flesh" (John 1:14) who changes us, but
the Bible is a primary method by which He accomplishes the change. It is the voice
of the Creator to your heart, the voice that spoke the world into existence, and the
voice that commanded demons to release their victims and made the sick well when
He walked the earth. The Bible was inspired by the Holy Spirit and has the potential
to utterly change your life.

After we broke communion with God in Eden, His Word became the primary
method by which He ushers us into His presence. It is how we can spend time in
the presence of Jesus, and that time is radically transformative. "But we all," Paul
writes, "with unveiled face, beholding as in a mirror the glory of the Lord, are being
transformed in the same image from glory to glory, just as by the Spirit of the Lord"
(2 Corinthians 3:18).

The Bible does more than change your mind or give you a new way to see things;
the Bible, if you will allow it, can actually alter who you *are* and re-create you in the
image of Christ.

You Must Continue

But you must continue in the things which you have learned and been assured of, knowing from whom you have learned them, and that from childhood you have known the Holy Scriptures, which are able to make you wise for salvation through faith which is in Christ Jesus.
—2 Timothy 3:14, 15

A prison guard once told me of an inmate who had recently escaped. The prison was on a rocky peninsula, jutting out into the icy waters of the ocean. There was no fence around the waterfront because it was presumed that anybody trying to escape by swimming away from the penitentiary would succumb to hypothermia long before he would manage to reach land. Someone had just proven them wrong.

"Do you think they'll find him?" I asked. And that is when he dropped the bombshell: "Oh, they already think they know where he is; they are just waiting for him to commit another crime so they can give him a much longer sentence."

Wow. I still have my doubts as to the truth of the story, but it started me thinking about the Christian experience. In the penal system, if you commit a crime, you pay society by spending a defined period of time in jail. After that, when the matter is settled, you are expected to go and live a model life—and not commit another crime. You are supposed to continue in your new lifestyle. At least, that is the theory.

Many people approach forgiveness with a legal mind-set; once you have taken care of the legal proceedings, you can go back to life as it was. It is an attitude that treats baptism like a final destination: you are good with God, so you can forget about the whole matter, because you now have what you need. It is as if you just paid a parking ticket; once it is paid, it is over. You do not need to remember the city clerk's name. You will (hopefully) never see the clerk again.

But notice Paul's advice to Timothy: "You must *continue* in the things which you have learned." Forgiveness is not an arrival point; it is the beginning. God is not a heavenly clerk who simply collects fees and marks you "reconciled." He wants a relationship, and the only real future is wrapped up in Him. Yes, God forgives, but that is just the beginning. It is not merely your legal security He craves; it is an eternity with a brand-new *you*. And on this side of the Second Coming, He has given you the "Holy Scriptures, which are able to make you wise for salvation through faith," as a reliable way to continue the relationship every single day.

A Tale of Two Revolutions

Now after the three-and-a-half days the breath of life from God entered them,
and they stood on their feet, and great fear fell on those who saw them.
And they heard a loud voice from heaven saying to them, "Come up here."
And they ascended to heaven in a cloud, and their enemies saw them.
—Revelation 11:11, 12

Seventh-day Adventists understand the two witnesses of Revelation 11 to be the Old and New Testaments, which were treated with contempt and trampled underfoot during the time of the French Revolution, when reason was exalted as a new god. The Scriptures, however, experienced an incredible global revival with the birth of Bible and missionary societies during the very next century, and even the house of Voltaire—one of the great skeptics of the day who predicted the end of Christianity—ended up becoming a Bible depository.

There were two key revolutionary movements in the late eighteenth century in the Western world: the French and American Revolutions. One of those revolutions, the French, ultimately failed in its desire to produce a free republic. Napoleon Bonaparte, in fact, proved to be another despot with kingly ambitions. The other revolution, the American, produced a free republic with guaranteed religious liberty that extends to this day.

While there are many factors that can explain the different outcomes, there is one that should be of interest to Christians—the Bible. During the seventeenth century, some of the English Protestants who were dissatisfied by the lack of genuine liberty in England began to flee the country and, in particular, study the Scriptures closely. They soon realized that the Israelites' request for a king had disappointed God (1 Samuel 8). They began to wonder if their problems with human kings might not be dispensed with if they tried to return to a society where people could serve God as they see fit, without a middleman trying to interfere in matters of conscience.

That led to an examination of Deuteronomy 17, where God predicted the Israelites would ask for a king and established safeguards to prevent trouble: the king must not be a foreigner, and he must write himself a copy of the law and abide by it. It was, in the minds of seventeenth-century reformers such as John Locke, a description of a *republic*.

In the eighteenth century, the Protestants' ideas were incorporated into the American Constitution—a nation that was lamblike, or Christlike, at its birth (Revelation 13:11). The difference between America and France was striking; and the difference will be striking if you, too, lean on the Word for solutions to the problems that plague *you*.

The Monuments of God's People

"O Jerusalem, Jerusalem, the one who kills the prophets and stones those who are sent to her! How often I wanted to gather your children together, as a hen gathers her chicks under her wings, but you were not willing! See! Your house is left to you desolate."
—Matthew 23:37, 38

The magnificent ruins of ancient civilizations have, in many cases, become the only remnants of the cultures that built them. From the astonishing beauty of Machu Picchu to the quiet, crumbling majesty of the Roman Forum, the builders of yesterday have left an impressive record of past glory for those of us who now live in fleeting wood-frame houses. While most people, outside of required college reading, have never taken the time to wade through Homer's *Iliad* or Plato's *Republic*, many of us immediately recognize pictures of the Acropolis, the Great Pyramid, or the Colosseum.

In some ways, however, the finely chiseled monuments of ancient civilizations have proven to be less enduring than the nonphysical legacies of another important ancient culture. The crumbling ruins are little more than tombstones on the cultures that did not survive.

By contrast, the ancient Hebrew civilization has left us very few physical monuments. Its crowning achievement, the temple in Jerusalem, has been destroyed twice, and all that remains of it today is the Wailing Wall. There are notable tourist sites, to be sure, such as the Cave of the Patriarchs or Jacob's Well, but the architectural marvel of Abraham's tribe has been obliterated.

But it would be hard to argue that the Hebrew civilization has not had a lasting impact on the world. While other ancient civilizations have faded from memory, the impact of Abraham's children is still clearly felt around the world. Not only did the most recognizable figure in human history emerge from Hebrew culture—Jesus of Nazareth—but so did the best-selling book of all time, the Bible.

Shortly before His arrest and crucifixion, Jesus wept over the city of Jerusalem, lamenting the fact that He had repeatedly sent messengers to warn His people. Instead of heeding the Word of God delivered through prophets, they had pointed to the glory of the temple as evidence that no harm could ever befall them (Jeremiah 7:4). The temple is now gone, but the living Word of God, the greatest gift bequeathed to the world by the Hebrews, remains.

What monuments are you building with your brief time in this world? Would there be any greater than the Christlike character God longs to chisel from your life through the power of His Word?

Free for the Taking

Wisdom calls aloud outside; she raises her voice in the open squares. She cries out in the chief concourses, at the openings of the gates in the city she speaks her words: "How long, you simple ones, will you love simplicity? For scorners delight in their scorning, and fools hate knowledge."
—Proverbs 1:20–22

You have to wonder, sometimes, how much time and effort are wasted by people who search for solutions to problems that have already been solved. One of the reasons I love YouTube is because it offers me a free home-renovation education. If I am about to pull my furnace apart, chances are someone with exactly the same model has already done it, and they have recorded the whole procedure for my benefit. If I am trying to figure out what is wrong with my car, chances are someone else with the same car has already had exactly the same problem.

The days of heading to the library, desperately hoping for a book that deals with my situation, are long over, because the internet instantaneously connects me with someone who can help.

The book of Proverbs opens with a plea to pay attention to the fact that nothing we experience in this world is brand new or unique to us. Someone, somewhere, has already passed through what we are experiencing, and that person has something important to say about it. It is an almost heartbreaking scene: this ancient wisdom is free for the taking, but nobody seems to want it. Wisdom is portrayed as a woman standing in the town square, begging to help people who desperately need her—and the pleas fall on deaf ears.

The Bible is an astonishing book, in that it deals openly and frankly with the entire range of human experience, from sexuality and finances to discouragement and despondency. It is the cumulative record of people who have experienced God firsthand and found incredible hope and courage by entering into a covenant relationship with Him.

Yet in most homes, the Bible sits on the shelf, unopened, as the occupants of the house struggle with issues that drive them to the brink of despair. A source of wisdom greater than the cumulative efforts of the world's great philosophers—the wisdom of God Himself—is available to sinful mortals. It lies just within reach, and yet most of the time, its pages never see the light of day. "If you seek her as silver," the author of Proverbs continues, "and search for her as for hidden treasures; then you will understand the fear of the LORD, and find the knowledge of God" (Proverbs 2:4, 5).

An Easy Read

"Your words were found, and I ate them, and Your word was to me the joy and rejoicing of my heart; for I am called by Your name, O LORD God of hosts."
—Jeremiah 15:16

When I was a boy, there was a popular new paraphrase of the Bible in circulation. Its publishers boasted that it read "as easily as a novel," which was true. For a few years, it produced the desired effect; people were reading the Bible copiously because it was easy. And then, for the same reason, they suddenly stopped, and sales plummeted. It turns out that people *quit* reading the paraphrase for the same reason they *started*—it was too easy.

There are a number of occasions in the Bible, such as Ezekiel 3, Revelation 10, and today's passage from Jeremiah, where the prophets are said to "eat" the Word of the Lord. When you eat something, it becomes a part of who you are. The digestive system extracts vital nutrients from your food and uses them to repair and build your body. Today, we live in a world of fast food, which is highly processed, calorie dense, and tragically low in nutritional value. The more fast food we eat, the less healthy we become.

The information in the Bible is best consumed deliberately. It is far better to read a few lines and ponder them carefully than it is to plow quickly through vast swaths of Scripture, reading much but comprehending little.

Henry David Thoreau once bemoaned the fact that modern readers (he was writing in the 1800s) had become careless and shallow in their reading choices. He was speaking of the classics rather than the Bible, but consider his point: "We must laboriously seek the meaning of each word and line, conjecturing a larger sense than common use permits out of what wisdom and valor and generosity we have. The modern cheap and fertile press, with all its translations, has done little to bring us nearer to the heroic writers of antiquity."★

What was his point? It is worth it to read carefully and deliberately. No, the Bible is not always easy reading, but it is not supposed to be. It is, after all, the mind of God portrayed in human language, and that fact alone should compel us to relish every word carefully. In a world used to two-minute online videos, we would do well to slow down and take much time to ruminate on the great thoughts God longs to speak to our hearts.

★ Henry David Thoreau, *Walden* (New York: Barnes and Noble Classics, 2003), 82.

It Lasts Forever

"Most assuredly, I say to you, he who hears My word and believes in Him who sent Me has everlasting life, and shall not come into judgment, but has passed from death into life."
—John 5:24

The hard truth of human life is that, unless you were particularly famous, within a generation or two of your death, nobody will remember any of your accomplishments. You can become a successful legislator who passes impressive bills; but unless your legal efforts produce some kind of calamity, nobody will remember your accomplishments a generation after you are dead. You can erect massive skyscrapers that bear your name; but within a few generations, your name will become as impersonal and meaningless to most people as the names of the ancient Egyptian pharaohs who constructed massive tombs for themselves.

When you use this one precious life God has granted you to accumulate property or pursue worldly fame, you remain decidedly mortal, which is, of course, the fate of all sinners. There is a prescribed sunset over your notoriety and a moment after which nobody remembers you or cares. I know it sounds harsh, but it is true. How fond are you of your great-great-grandparents, after all? You never knew them, except through the handful of stories that may have trickled down to your generation and the sepia-tinged photo or two that may have survived to this day.

To be sure, there is nothing wrong with accomplishment, and the Bible counsels us not to be idle while we wait for Jesus to come (Luke 19:13). If you are going to work—and you should—work hard and produce great things. But remember that human accomplishments are fleeting; if you stake the meaning of your life on such things, you will ultimately become meaningless.

You do have an opportunity, however, to spend your days tapping into something much larger than yourself, something that will outlive this lifetime and last forever. In the pages of the Bible, we meet people who encountered the eternal and living God. They lived unusual lives—the kind that are not only remembered but left a lasting imprint on thousands of generations that followed them. They are resting now, waiting for Jesus to come, but they have built something that continues to change *our* lives today. And the words they recorded through Inspiration show us a better way. They help us discard all that is meaningless and use our brief lives to invest in something that *will* last forever: the kingdom of Christ.

The Size of the Future

For all the promises of God in Him are Yes, and in Him Amen, to the glory of God through us.
—2 Corinthians 1:20

In the spring of 2016, gas prices in the state of Michigan suddenly plummeted to forty-seven cents a gallon (a little over twelve cents a liter!), prompting nationwide headlines that asked, "How Low Can Gas Go?" While the rest of the country did not reach the same lows, gas prices were still historically economical. Filling the car's gas tank had not felt that good since the 1990s, when I remember complaining that the price of gas had crept up over the dollar mark.

Something curious often happens when gas prices start dropping. Some people feel so liberated by the new freedom in their budgets that they start buying larger cars. When the price of petroleum was double—or even triple—what it currently has been, the sales of high-consumption vehicles stagnated, because people did not consider them affordable. They opted for tiny budget cars. When gas prices dropped, however, trucks and SUVs began to seem like reasonable choices.

It demonstrates just how shortsighted we can be, because (of course) what goes down, must come up. Gas prices inevitably rebounded.

The future always looks smaller and further away than reality might suggest. Remember the last time you promised to watch your neighbor's kids at some distant future date? It was an easy promise to make when the date was still six months away. When it is happening *tomorrow*, you often find yourself regretting the decision because it is suddenly more real and seems like a far bigger imposition.

The same holds true for the promises of God in the Bible. Even though the prophetic forecasts of Daniel and Revelation have been completely accurate to date—not one of them has been wrong—some will still turn to a passage such as Revelation 13, which predicts the loss of religious liberty. "This will never happen in my lifetime!" some will say. "I just can't see it. We have so many different religious groups out there, so much diversity, that I can't see how someone would ever force religious homogeneity."

Some say the same of the Second Coming: "Not in my lifetime!" It seems so distant and so hypothetical. Remember the sudden collapse of the Soviet Union in 1989? That caught most of us by surprise; nobody saw it coming. God's promises? You will be amazed how quickly they come to pass.

The Great Parenthesis

Your throne is established from of old; You are from everlasting.
—Psalm 93:2

Fred bought a real lemon of a house. He was in love with the property until the first rains of winter revealed why the house had been so affordable. It leaked—badly. He tried to repair it, but it continued to leak. Eventually, he gave up and sold it at a rather large loss. It was a dark parenthesis in his life, but he managed to move on.

The Bible is the great parenthesis in the story of the universe. The events portrayed in the Bible take place in a few thousand years; a mere eyeblink compared to the vast eternity of God. He has always been there, and He always will be. Compare the scope of God's existence to the short story of humanity portrayed in the Bible, and suddenly human history—all of it—seems like a brief parenthetical thought in the unfolding of God's greater purposes.

If we had never sinned, human history would have been part of a much larger, much longer, uninterrupted story. When we rebelled, the story was interrupted. Our planet was no longer part of God's overall purpose because our hearts had turned against Him. "The carnal mind," Paul reminds us, "is enmity against God" (Romans 8:7).

God could have justly wiped us out of existence, but He did not. Instead, He decided to push the pause button and take the time necessary to sort out the mess we created. This is the story that is told between Genesis and Revelation, and it is a great parenthesis in the universe.

But oh, what a parenthesis! When we sinned, God the Son became one of us in order to save us. He continues to exist in human form, for all eternity, as our personal Representative in front of the throne. And, unbelievably, this world will become the new headquarters for His kingdom. "Behold, the tabernacle of God is with men," John heard Heaven declare, "and He will dwell with them . . . and be their God" (Revelation 21:3).

God did not bulldoze our planet, as one might expect; instead, He kept it. While our story is the dark parenthesis in the history of the universe, God has managed to turn it into a brilliant declaration of His glory—and *that* story will be told throughout the ceaseless ages of eternity.

Paid to Pray

Therefore, brethren, having boldness to enter the Holiest by the blood of Jesus, by a new and living way which He consecrated for us, through the veil, that is, His flesh, and having a High Priest over the house of God, let us draw near with a true heart in full assurance of faith, having our hearts sprinkled from an evil conscience and our bodies washed with pure water.
—Hebrews 10:19–22

In a recent election season, much was said about government officials engaging in a practice known as "pay to play," in which politicians grant access to important government employees and programs in exchange for large campaign contributions. The practice is, of course, highly unethical (and often illegal), but it does give some indication what people will pay to have direct access to the halls of power. The bribes are almost always enormous.

The book of Acts tells the story of a former sorcerer by the name of Simon, who, shortly after his baptism, saw people receive the gift of the Holy Spirit when the disciples prayed for them. Accustomed to performing tricks for money, Simon begged the disciples to share their secret. Offering them what one can only assume was a considerable sum of money, he said, "Give me this power also, that anyone on whom I lay hands may receive the Holy Spirit" (Acts 8:19).

It would seem that "pay to play" is a very ancient practice indeed.

Peter, of course, rebuked him, explaining that the gift of God cannot be purchased with money. The kingdom of God operates in a mode completely foreign to the ways of fallen human beings. You cannot buy access to God; you could not possibly produce a sum large enough to secure admission to the throne room. The depth of our sin is simply too profound.

Fortunately, there is a way. The author of Hebrews explains that through the blood of Christ, there is a "new and living way" to enter into the Most Holy Place, right into the presence of God. Our path through the veil is Christ's "flesh"; He is not only God but also fully human and utterly sinless. We do not have to slink in quietly and cower in the corner; we can approach the throne with "boldness" and in "full assurance of faith."

In this world, people pay for favors. In the kingdom of God, Jesus showers you with favor and pays a steep price to give you incredible access to the most powerful Being in the universe. Instead of "pay to play," Jesus *paid* so you can *pray* and have your words fall on the ears of God Himself.

Who would not want to take advantage of that?

In the Name of Jesus

"And whatever you ask in My name, that I will do, that the Father may be glorified in the Son. If you ask anything in My name, I will do it."
—John 14:13, 14

One of the distinguishing marks of a Christian prayer—as opposed to the prayers of other faiths—is the mention of Jesus' name as the prayer comes to a close. When public officials ask officiating clergy to "broaden the appeal" of their public prayers, what they are usually asking is that the one praying omit the mention of Jesus' name in order to make the prayer generic.

Praying in Jesus' name is not optional for the Christian, however, because Jesus Himself told us to do it. But to truly pray in Jesus' name is not to merely mention Him; it implies something much more profound.

There is an old story that has been handed down to us from the days of Alexander the Great. One night, as most of the camp was sleeping, someone noticed a guard had fallen asleep at his post. Sleeping on duty meant compromising the safety of one's fellow soldiers, which made it a very serious crime.

The soldier was dragged into the presence of Alexander himself and thrown on the ground, knowing full well that his negligence was going to cost him his life. "What is your name, young man?" the great conqueror demanded.

There was suddenly a glimmer of hope in the guilty man's eyes. "My name is Alexander, sir; just like yours."

The general grew quiet for a moment before softening his demeanor and clearing his throat. "Well then, soldier, I suggest you either change your name or you change your conduct."

In the Bible, the word *name* is virtually synonymous with one's character. To take on the name of Jesus means more than to mention it aloud; it means to become like the One whose name you have claimed. To pray in the name of Jesus implies more than merely uttering it; it also means that you are ordering your life in such a way as to pattern it after His. To pray in the name of Jesus is to consider what He would want from your life before you ask; it is to come in such close communion with Him that when you are finished praying, your character has been honed, chiseled, and sanctified. It is a meeting of the minds, a harmonizing of purpose, and the blending of hearts. Such prayers, Jesus assures us, are always answered.

According to His Will

Now this is the confidence that we have in Him,
that if we ask anything according to His will, He hears us.
—1 John 5:14

Notice that the model prayer Jesus gave His disciples—the one we usually refer to as the "Lord's Prayer"—begins with an appeal to God's will. "In this manner, therefore, pray," Jesus explained. "Our Father in heaven, hallowed be Your name. Your kingdom come. Your will be done on earth as it is in heaven" (Matthew 6:9, 10).

The first order of business in any prayer is to address God's agenda, rather than our own, trusting God to take us in the right direction. In the original order of things, God lived for our good, and we lived for His glory. That arrangement was broken by our failure to trust Him, and now we find ourselves enrolled in the school of faith. Before we speak about our wishes and wants, which are always tainted by selfishness and shortsightedness, we place ourselves in a position of trust, asking for the will of God to be done first.

Not only is it an act of deference, but it is also wise. We are learning to trust that God knows us better than we know ourselves and that He will always do what is best for us. We are waiting for the kingdom of God to be restored on this planet, waiting for the moment when the Stone finally comes to replace the kingdoms of this earth. We long to be a part of Christ's kingdom, but while we wait, we are already learning how to live there.

When we finally step into glory, we will still have to exercise faith. Before his expulsion from heaven, Lucifer was not permitted to join the counsels of the Godhead; he was expected to live by faith and trust that God knew what He was doing. The same will be expected of us when we finally reach home: We will not suddenly become omniscient, knowing everything that God knows. We will still have to trust and live by faith.

That is why we pray according to God's will now, before we arrive. Once we have established that God's agenda is the most important thing He must accomplish, then we examine our own wants and wishes, checking that they are in harmony with the direction God is taking the whole world. That is the prayer that always makes it to God's ears.

The Speed of Prayer

Yes, while I was speaking in prayer, the man Gabriel, whom I had seen in the vision at the beginning, being caused to fly swiftly, reached me about the time of the evening offering. And he informed me, and talked with me, and said, "O Daniel, I have now come forth to give you skill to understand. At the beginning of your supplications the command went out, and I have come to tell you, for you are greatly beloved; therefore consider the matter, and understand the vision."
—Daniel 9:21–23

We are only beginning to comprehend how vast the universe is. Before we developed the ability to see deep into space, our ancestors were able to conceive of a universe that was relatively close and familiar. Now that we have been able to determine that the universe we can *see* is something like 93 billion light-years across (a single light-year is about 5.9 trillion miles), our perspective has changed dramatically. There is nothing cozy about the observable universe.

People wonder whether there is life out in one of the other star systems. If there is, would we ever be able to make contact? The closest star system to ours is about 25 trillion miles away; nobody could ever make the journey in a single lifetime. Even if we planned to have a colony make the trip, with future descendants arriving at the destination, the intense radiation of space would likely destroy our ability to procreate long before we arrived.

So scientists and theoreticians dream of developing warp drives that could propel a spacecraft faster than the speed of light. They talk about wormholes—shortcuts through space, if you will, that bend the space-time continuum so that two distant points are suddenly pushed much closer together, as if a sheet of paper with two dots on separate ends had been folded in half to make the dots touch.

Here is something worth pondering: when Jesus returned to heaven, He went with a physical, human body. We do not know where heaven is; but the distance between here and there must be incredibly vast. And yet, when you utter a prayer, it reaches the ears of God immediately.

The ninth chapter of Daniel begins with the prophet praying for understanding. If you read the whole prayer out loud, it only takes a couple of moments to recite. When Gabriel arrives, he explains that he was sent at the beginning of Daniel's prayer, and he arrives before Daniel is finished. Angels appear to be able to cross the vastness of space in mere minutes, and apparently, your prayers can do the same.

Scientists will continue to dream of ways to cross the vastness of space. God's people have already discovered it: the quickest path across the cosmos is on your knees.

Determined to Pray

Now when Daniel knew that the writing was signed, he went home. And in his upper room,
with his windows open toward Jerusalem, he knelt down on his knees three times that day,
and prayed and gave thanks before his God, as was his custom since early days.
—Daniel 6:10

A sk yourself how many things you might be willing to die for. Some would be willing to place themselves in harm's way to save a family member or even a friend. Countless people have placed their lives on the line for the sake of king or country, believing that the nation at large is of more value than their personal well-being. But how many people would be willing to die for the sake of prayer?

Daniel is one of those few Bible characters who does not seem to have any flaws. Abraham lied about Sarah to save himself. Noah got drunk. Moses murdered an Egyptian and occasionally lost his temper. David committed adultery and contrived the death of his mistress's husband. But all through the telling of Daniel's story, we find no obvious faults. As the book of Daniel opens, he is declared to be "ten times better" than the wisest men in Babylon (Daniel 1:20). In the story that provides today's Bible reading, we are told that "the governors and satraps sought to find some charge against Daniel concerning the kingdom; but they could find no charge or fault, because he was faithful; nor was there any error or fault found in him" (Daniel 6:4).

Daniel, of course, was just a fallen human being like the rest of us. His sterling, Christlike disposition was the result of a deep, submissive connection with God. He derived the strength of his character and his steely resolve from a supernatural Source.

Part of his secret, obviously, was his determination to pray. Daniel believed prayer was so important to his spiritual well-being that even in the face of the death penalty, he refused to give it up. Just as he did the day before the new law took effect, he opened his window three times a day and communed with the Living God.

How often do modern Christians prize prayer like Daniel did? How much richer, how much deeper, would our own spiritual experience be if we valued our private time with Christ more than we valued life itself? "As the deer pants for the water brooks," the psalmist writes, "so pants my soul for You, O God" (Psalm 42:1).

What is more valuable than daily lingering in the presence of God?

Pray for Who?

*"But I say to you, love your enemies, bless those who curse you, do good
to those who hate you, and pray for those who spitefully use you and persecute you,
that you may be sons of your Father in heaven; for He makes His sun rise on the evil
and on the good, and sends rain on the just and on the unjust."*
—Matthew 5:44, 45

I find it remarkably easy to pray for my wife and children. They are, from my perspective, the most valuable people on the planet. I also find it easy to pray for my friends and coworkers—people whose company I enjoy. But the path of Christ is not the easy path; He makes demands of His followers that are not as easy as the modern-day prosperity gospel would have you believe.

Jesus asks us to forsake self and pick up a cross. He asks us to value others more than we value ourselves. And then He asks us to pray, not just for family, friends, and strangers but "for those who spitefully use you and persecute you."

That is a pretty tall order. How do you pray for someone you do not even like? Someone who stirs up deeply negative emotions when you think about him or her? Someone who delights in causing you anxiety or pain? Why would God ask for such a thing?

The answer is found in the next words that Jesus spoke: "That you may be sons of your Father in heaven." Prayer is something deeper than simply communicating your thoughts to God: it is one of the key methods by which God actually changes who you are. Perhaps you have noticed that the more time you spend with someone, the more you begin to mirror his or her personality traits. Move someone to another part of the country, and before long, that person starts to speak with an accent, however slight. The mere act of spending time with someone changes you.

To pray is to enter into the presence of God, to step boldly into His throne room (Hebrews 4:16). To linger deliberately in His presence is to allow God to transform your character into something more Christlike. And you will notice that Christ gave His life for the human race, not after we corrected our sinful path but "while we were still sinners" (Romans 5:8). On the cross, He prayed for His persecutors, "Father, forgive them, for they do not know what they do" (Luke 23:34).

When you pray for those who wrong you, you are learning to think like Jesus and see the world the same way He does. That, in the kingdom of heaven, will prove to be an invaluable skill.

You Have Membership!

Elijah was a man with a nature like ours, and he prayed earnestly that it would not rain;
and it did not rain on the land for three years and six months. And he prayed again,
and the heaven gave rain, and the earth produced its fruit.

—James 5:17, 18

I was walking through the airport with a friend when he suddenly pulled out his wallet and produced a card. "Here," he said, "this card will allow us to go in *there!*" He gestured over his shoulder at a swank-looking private airport lounge that was completely unaffiliated with the airline we were traveling on. Sure enough, the card *did* get us in. I must admit it was a wonderful place: comfortable chairs, amazing food choices, and access to the internet and newspapers from all over the world.

"How did you get that card?" I asked my friend as I sat back with a fancy vegetable platter. "Did you have to buy it?"

"No, it came with my credit card," he said. He pulled out the credit card and showed it to me. I was stunned: I carried the same card! "All you have to do is ask them for a pass to this lounge, and they'll send it to you."

I had no idea. I had been traveling the world for years, never realizing that I had free access to a series of upscale lounges that span the globe.

The same holds true for the privilege of prayer. Often, we look at the great heroes of faith and wish that we could be like them: If only we had *that* kind of access to God! If only God heard our prayers the way He heard theirs!

The point that James is making in today's Bible reading should never be underestimated: You carry the same access card in your wallet that Elijah did. He was not a superhero. The Bible reveals that he, like you, got tired and discouraged, even wishing on one occasion that he could die! "It is enough! Now, LORD, take my life, for I am no better than my fathers" (1 Kings 19:4).

It was true: he was not better than his fathers, but it is also true that he was not better than *you*. James points out that Elijah "was a man with a nature like ours," and God answered his prayers in miraculous ways. The Bible is the story of ordinary people who are given extraordinary access to God. The key point is that you have the same privilege: heaven is no further away today than it was on the day Elijah prayed for rain.

Relief From Anxiety

Be anxious for nothing, but in everything by prayer and supplication, with thanksgiving,
let your requests be made known to God; and the peace of God, which surpasses
all understanding, will guard your hearts and minds through Christ Jesus.
—Philippians 4:6, 7

Anxiety is fast becoming one of the most common afflictions in the Western world, with something like one in four adults experiencing an anxiety disorder in his or her lifetime. Some people have observed that it seemed to become worse when the bulk of society moved from an agrarian lifestyle to the sedentary pursuits that came with urban living. Our bodies produce a natural fight-or-flight response to immediate danger, enabling us to flee a vicious animal or jump out of harm's way at a moment's notice. Unfortunately, the same mechanism kicks in when we face nonphysical sources of stress: a huge load of paperwork, imminent deadlines, or perhaps the fear of a presentation. Because the stressors are ever present and we do not respond physically, the mechanism never seems to shut off.

When stressed-out people read a Bible verse that says, "Be anxious for nothing," a natural human reaction is to say, "Yeah, right. How am I supposed to do that?" The answer is found in the rest of the verse—through intimate contact with God. Notice the remedial elements in the verse: bring your problems to God, and do it with an attitude of thanksgiving.

Just knowing that the One who set the universe in motion hears you—and cares about your life—can relieve a great deal of stress. You are not alone. You can figuratively climb up on your heavenly Father's lap, just like you climbed up on your parents' laps when you were little, and tell God what is bothering you.

But do it with gratitude. Do not treat prayer as a gripe-and-whine session. Spend time being thankful for the ways God has provided for you in the past, and be grateful for what you have in the present. Then, by faith, be grateful for the future, trusting that God will provide, even on the days when your senses tell you He will not.

Being thankful is a remarkable stress reliever, and it is a phenomenal way to come back down out of orbit and ground yourself in your present reality. Start making lists of what you are happy about, and then set aside time each day to thank God for those things. Over time, you will notice, "the peace of God . . . will guard your hearts and minds through Christ Jesus."

Praying, or Preaching?

*"And when you pray, you shall not be like the hypocrites. For they love to pray standing
in the synagogues and on the corners of the streets, that they may be seen by men. Assuredly,
I say to you, they have their reward. But you, when you pray, go into your room,
and when you have shut your door, pray to your Father who is in the secret place;
and your Father who sees in secret will reward you openly."*
—Matthew 6:5, 6

When I was a little boy, my family went to a church where the pastor always seemed angry. It may have just been high blood pressure, but it seemed to me that his face was always red, as if he was fuming about something. When his sermon was finished, he always closed the service with a prayer—a very *long* prayer. I remember peeking at my little Timex watch on more than one occasion to see how long he had been praying; it once exceeded twenty-five minutes!

The reason the prayer was long is that just in case the congregation did not get the point—or *points*—during the sermon, he repeated them all in the closing prayer. In later years, when I reflected on what he had done, it occurred to me that he was not really praying at all. God had already heard the content of the sermon, so He certainly did not need an encore performance. It was not communication with God; it was a message to the congregation.

Over the years, I have heard others do the same thing, albeit a little differently. Sometimes after a lively discussion in a Bible study or church business meeting, someone will pray in a way that makes it obvious he or she is not speaking to God. The person is simply trying to use prayer to get a point across to the rest of the room and make it seem as though disagreeing would be irreligious.

Jesus advises us that prayer is intimate time with God. If you are truly praying, it is just you and God—or perhaps your family. If you are trying to impress God, forget it; it is impossible to impress Him with your so-called human wisdom. He already knows far more than we will ever know.

What He craves from you is the same thing you crave from your loved ones: meaningful time. What He wants is sincerity, openness, and transparency. He wants from you what you would want from your own children.

It is one thing for a child to loudly proclaim that he loves his parents. It is quite another for that same child to snuggle up to Mom or Dad on the couch and just *be* with his parents. If you give it a try, you will find that the secret places with God are indeed exceptionally rewarding.

The First Hour

Now in the morning, having risen a long while before daylight,
He went out and departed to a solitary place; and there He prayed.
—Mark 1:35

I must confess that I am not a morning person. For years, I have tried to approach the first hours of the day with enthusiasm, rising earlier and earlier in an attempt to make early morning seem natural and pleasant. For a while, I forced myself out of bed at four thirty in the morning, hoping that beginning the day earlier would make the blessings of full alertness arrive sooner. All the bright, cheerful Christians I met at the early morning service at church inspired me.

My efforts proved to be in vain. Today, I rise earlier than ever, often at three thirty in the morning, but this is due more to advancing age and insomnia than any attempt to claim the morning as my best hours. Everything is still too bright and too loud before eight or nine o'clock.

I have tried preaching in the early morning hours, but I find myself tongue-tied, stumbling over words that would flow easily in the evening. Early morning meetings are useless to me; my body's refusal to cooperate with the morning makes the agenda move either too slowly or too quickly.

No, morning is not my time—with one exception.

In those early hours, there is Someone I can dialogue with who is quite happy to carry the conversation at my hindered pace. Even when I cannot find adequate words to share my deepest feelings and concerns, the Spirit translates what my heart feels into the language of heaven and delivers it directly to my heavenly Father's throne (Romans 8:26). In the earliest moments of the day, phone calls and emails do little to stimulate my interest; but amazingly, the Word of God speaks in ways that arrest my attention and change who I am.

From a worldly perspective, there is little I can find to redeem from the morning. But perhaps that is because the first hours of the day belong to God, and the most productive thing I can do as the sun begins to crest over the horizon is ask my heavenly Father how He would have me structure the rest of my day. If I begin the day in the presence of God, even the more alert moments later in the day will be far more productive for His kingdom.

Practical Atheism

The fool has said in his heart, "There is no God." They are corrupt,
they have done abominable works, there is none who does good. The LORD *looks down*
from heaven upon the children of men, to see if there are any who understand, who seek God.
—Psalm 14:1, 2

We often say that it is a foolish man or woman who refuses to believe in God, often quoting the fourteenth psalm in support of our position. But read the passage carefully, because the psalmist goes beyond mere mental assent when he discusses belief. From God's perspective, the atheist is not only the one who *decides* that God does not exist, but he is also the one who does not seek Him and the one who *lives* as if God does not exist.

Writing in 1885, D. W. Whittle (a soldier who was inspired by Dwight L. Moody to become an evangelist and hymn writer) made this important observation about prayer: "It would be horrible to admit the existence of a Supreme Being, with power and wisdom to create, and believe that the creatures he thought of consequence and importance enough to bring into existence, are not of enough consequence for him to pay any attention to in the troubles and trials consequent upon that existence."★

In other words, to *not* pray is a form of atheism, or at least a form of deism, which teaches that God may have started the world in motion but has had little to do with it since. For the deist to pray would make little sense, since he believes that God does not intervene in the affairs of the human race.

It is impossible, however, to read the Bible and come away convinced that God does not interact with us. The crowning act of His intervention is the incarnation of Christ, which is His decision to assume our form forever and live as one of us. To know that Jesus walked this earth is to believe in prayer: if "God so loved the world that He gave His only begotten Son" (John 3:16), then we can live with confidence, knowing that "if we ask anything according to His will, He hears us" (1 John 5:14).

Your prayers do not stop when they hit the ceiling; the God who gave you life and perpetuates that life each day is obviously interested. While He may occasionally delay or deny your requests because He knows they would harm you, you can know for certain that He hears you.

To fail to pray is to live as if God does not exist. It is practical atheism.

★ Daniel Webster Whittle, *The Wonders of Prayer*, rev. ed. (New York: Fleming H. Revell, 1885), 5.

June

I accept the Ten Commandments as a transcript of the character of God and a revelation of His will. It is my purpose by the power of the indwelling Christ to keep this law, including the fourth commandment, which requires the observance of the seventh day of the week as the Sabbath of the Lord and the memorial of Creation.

JUNE 1

Self-Guided Blindness

Your throne, O God, is forever and ever; a scepter of righteousness is the scepter of Your kingdom. You love righteousness and hate wickedness; therefore God, Your God, has anointed You with the oil of gladness more than Your companions.

—Psalm 45:6, 7

"That might be *your* truth," the young protestor explained in an email after hearing a presentation I had made on TV, "but it certainly isn't mine!"

"I can understand that you don't see things the way I do, but maybe, between us both, we can figure out what's actually true."

"No," she said, "there *is* no such thing as true. There's what's right for me, and what's right for you, and we all have to live our own narrative, the truth that we make for ourselves."

If only that was an isolated point of view in the twenty-first century. But we now find ourselves living in a world where clear-cut moral standards are viewed as a relic of the past. "You can't judge me!" is not just a plea for kindness; it's a declaration that nobody can discern what is right or wrong except for what they deem to be right for self.

Admittedly, it is an improvement over the Dark Ages, when the official state church acted as conscience for all. People were told what was right and wrong and had no liberty to dispute it. It is far better to live freely, with the right to answer to God individually.

But that is not to suggest that objective standards of morality do not exist. We may live as we please, but we do not have the ability to redefine sin. We may wish to live by the dictates of our conscience, but we should understand that eventually, our gut instinct will lead us astray if it is not informed by an authoritative outside source. "If one listens to the faintest but constant suggestions of his genius," Thoreau once wrote, "he sees not to what extremes, or even insanity, it may lead him."★

Self-guided people are blinded by the selfishness of sin. Eventually, our self-guided instincts will lead us astray. God may have designed us as free moral agents, but the wise will always look to God's righteous throne to determine if their instincts are correct. They will recognize that the example of Jesus, as the psalmist points out, is considered praiseworthy because He loves "righteousness and hate[s] wickedness." We may not believe in a moral standard, but God does—and His perfect Example, Jesus, is on full display for our consideration.

★ Henry David Thoreau, *Walden* (Princeton, NJ: Princeton Univeristy Press, 2016), 216.

Inscribed in Our Hearts

Now the LORD descended in the cloud and stood with him there,
and proclaimed the name of the LORD. And the LORD passed before him and proclaimed,
"The LORD, the LORD God, merciful and gracious, longsuffering, and abounding in goodness
and truth, keeping mercy for thousands, forgiving iniquity and transgression and sin,
by no means clearing the guilty, visiting the iniquity of the fathers upon the children
and the children's children to the third and the fourth generation."
—Exodus 34:5–7

At the heart of the book of Revelation, we find a powerful description of God's last-day people: They are "the ones who follow the Lamb wherever He goes" (Revelation 14:4). They are also the ones who have the "Father's name written on their foreheads" (verse 1). What, exactly, is the Father's name? When Moses asked to see God's glory, God offered to show Moses His "name" (Exodus 33:18, 19). He hid Moses in the cleft of a rock and "proclaim[ed] the name of the LORD" by giving the patriarch a powerful description of His character.

Another powerful description of God's character? The moral laws that form the foundation of His government. The Ten Commandments reveal who God is. They tell us what God loves: things such as respect for life and for others, honesty, justice, and love. These, the Bible tells us, are the things God wishes to inscribe in our hearts (Hebrews 8:10).

Bible prophecy indicates that at the very end, the human race will polarize into two distinct camps: those who accept the beast power's authority and receive his mark on their foreheads (Revelation 13:16), and those who, instead, have the Father's name on their foreheads. The forehead, of course, represents the mind—the place where we make moral judgments. To say that God's name is written on our foreheads is a symbolic way to say that God's character has been written in our hearts. Not only do we accept *who* God is, but we also allow Him to rework our own sinful, selfish characters so that they become more like His. It comes to the point where our overwhelming impulse is to go where Jesus goes and do what Jesus does. We have been so captivated by the loving, merciful character of God that we have completely bought into His kingdom.

You Already Have a Copy

"This is the covenant that I will make with them after those days, says the LORD:
I will put My laws into their hearts, and in their minds I will write them,"
then He adds, "Their sins and their lawless deeds I will remember no more."
—Hebrews 10:16, 17

In the year 2016, lovers of Christian history and antiquity were excited by the announcement that the earliest known copy of the Ten Commandments was about to hit the auction block. The opening bid? A cool quarter of a million dollars. The engraved stone may date as far back as A.D. 300, possibly predating the conquest of Rome by Constantine.

It was discovered during excavations for a new railway station in the early twentieth century, and it is especially rare because it comes from the Samaritans, one of history's most oppressed religious groups. You will remember that in New Testament times the Samaritans, as Mesopotamian transplants to Israel, were not particularly welcome in most Jewish circles. They worshiped at Mount Gerizim rather than in Jerusalem.

The Samaritan version of the Ten Commandments reflects their unique beliefs, compressing the first four commandments into two, splitting the tenth commandment (as the Catholic Church does), and adding a final commandment instructing them to keep the commandments on Mount Gerizim.

I must admit that it was tempting to *break* a commandment and covet the artifact. What Bible scholar would not love to have such a fascinating part of history? But alas, I do not have the kind of money that lets me collect things of value, so I posted the news on Twitter instead: "If you have an extra $300K, you could own the oldest known copy of the 10 Commandments."

I was, of course, just having fun, but someone thoughtfully replied, "I have a copy in my Bible." She was right: nobody needs an expensive copy because we all have access. But we should also notice where God really wants us to keep a copy: not on Mount Gerizim or the temple mount, nor on a bookshelf. God wants His moral code, His character, to be unmistakably chiseled into our hearts and minds so that our lives become vivid reflections of His perfect, loving character.

Christ offers us the opportunity to know that God has forgotten our sins and "lawless deeds." But then He takes it even further: He offers to re-create us in His image. Not only can we know and claim His name, but we can also demonstrate it so that the rest of the world can meet Him through us.

The Forehead and Hand

*"And these words which I command you today shall be in your heart. You shall teach them
diligently to your children, and shall talk of them when you sit in your house,
when you walk by the way, when you lie down, and when you rise up. You shall bind them
as a sign on your hand, and they shall be as frontlets between your eyes."*
—Deuteronomy 6:6–8

Modern books on Bible prophecy suggest that the mark of the beast could be a microchip inserted into the hand that would replace credit cards as a means of making purchases. Others have suggested that it would be some kind of visible tattoo that makes one's allegiance to the beast power obvious to the authorities. Both of these suggestions, however, were invented by people who made a critical error in reading the book of Revelation: they failed to put it in the context of the entire Bible.

The language of Revelation is largely borrowed from the Old Testament. When John prophesied that the beast's followers would have his mark on their foreheads or their hands, it was a direct allusion to the instruction God gave the children of Israel on at least four occasions: they were to bind His *law* on their foreheads and hands as a sign. Some observant Jews take this command quite literally by using *tefillin* or phylacteries; these are little leather boxes containing passages of Scripture that are tied to their foreheads and hands with leather straps.

Modern expositors of Bible prophecy also fail to notice that there is an analogous sign among God's people: the Father's *name* is written on their foreheads (Revelation 14:1). God's "name," of course, is a reference to His character, as Jesus explained: "I have manifested Your name to the men whom You have given Me out of the world" (John 17:6).

When you put all the pieces together, the contrast is striking. There are only two groups in this world: those who adopt the character of fallen angels—who have determined that they will decide for themselves what is right—and those who have submitted to the will of God, realizing that His government is both just and merciful and that God can be trusted. As world history draws to a close, the polarization between these two groups will be abundantly evident. Given the late hour in which we live, the choice facing us today is clear: Will we choose to believe, in our thoughts (represented by the forehead) and actions (represented by the hand), that God can be trusted? Will we use our lives to acknowledge, privately and publicly, that God truly does belong on the throne of this universe?

The Missing Color

"Speak to the children of Israel: Tell them to make tassels on the corners of their garments
throughout their generations, and to put a blue thread in the tassels of the corners.
And you shall have the tassel, that you may look upon it and remember
all the commandments of the LORD and do them, and that you may not
follow the harlotry to which your own heart and your own eyes are inclined,
and that you may remember and do all My commandments, and be holy for your God."
—Numbers 15:38–40

There is a narrative of divine heartbreak running throughout the pages of the Bible. In Ezekiel 16, God describes His people as an unwanted baby girl he found cast aside in the wilderness. He takes her home, washes her off, raises her, and she is destined to be the bride of Christ. The same story emerges in the New Testament, as Paul reminds the church in Corinth: "For I have betrothed you to one husband, that I may present you as a chaste virgin to Christ" (2 Corinthians 11:2).

In both the Old and New Testaments, the bride is found unfaithful. "But you trusted in your own beauty, played the harlot because of your fame," God tells Israel (Ezekiel 16:15). The New Testament church followed the same path as she moved past the era of Constantine, eventually departing from the faith so widely that she is depicted as a prostitute in the book of Revelation: "The woman was arrayed in purple and scarlet, and adorned with gold and precious stones and pearls, having in her hand a golden cup full of abominations and the filthiness of her fornication" (Revelation 17:4).

There is a fascinating detail in the description of the Revelation 17 woman (or church) that is easy to miss if you do not look closely. She is described wearing two colors—purple and scarlet—both of which make appearances in the threads used to create the Old Testament sanctuary (Exodus 25:4). To many, the woman has the appearance of being God's people; she expects and demands worship. But there was a third color in the threads that is noticeably absent in this unfaithful woman's garments: blue.

Why would the color blue be left out of the unfaithful woman's clothing? It represents the law of God, the essential foundation of God's throne and the covenant with His people. The Israelites were told to place a "blue thread in the tassels of the corners" of their garments to remind them to keep God's commandments. There are voices today that suggest God is not interested in a commandment-keeping people, but those voices are coming from the wrong woman, the one presented as a stark contrast to the people "who keep the commandments of God and the faith of Jesus" (Revelation 14:12).

Crime Park

But know this, that in the last days perilous times will come: For men will be lovers
of themselves, lovers of money, boasters, proud, blasphemers, disobedient to parents,
unthankful, unholy, unloving, unforgiving, slanderers, without self-control, brutal,
despisers of good, traitors, headstrong, haughty, lovers of pleasure rather than lovers of God,
having a form of godliness but denying its power. And from such people turn away!
—2 Timothy 3:1–5

I once heard a political theoretician describe a place he called a "crime park"; a place where those who liked to break the law could voluntarily go and do whatever they wished. It would be acceptable, he suggested, because everybody inside the park would be there voluntarily, knowing the risks involved. Outside of the park, they would have to refrain from violating other people's person and property. But inside the park? Anything goes.

I suppose there might be a few people on this planet whose consciences have been sufficiently seared that they might find the "crime park" appealing; after all, the occasional psychotic criminal does emerge among us from time to time. But for most people, the thought of a murder park is abhorrent. We would not want to live there.

Some well-meaning Christians suggest that God's moral law places an unnecessary burden on us. They speak of it as a roadblock in the way of fun. "We don't *have* to keep the commandments," more than one person has told me, "because we live under grace!"

Usually, they are picking and choosing *which* commandments they would like to exempt themselves from, and then they insist that the rest are still binding. They would like to have their fun, but keep *your* activities from impinging on *their* lives. In the end, Paul predicts, the world will drift toward a global crime park, where everybody decides their own moral code. When you line up all of the moral standards that the collective human race would like to disregard, you would virtually have no moral standards at all. It is the kind of place you might wish to visit in order to do what you want for a few minutes, but you would not want to live there!

God's law is not designed to restrict your life or rob you of fun; it is designed to enhance it. Who would not want to live in a place where nobody steals from you, kills your loved ones, or defames your character? We are assured there will be no tears or suffering (Revelation 21:4). Today, before Jesus arrives, you already have the privilege of making your sphere of influence a "peace park"—the kind of place where people can experience what God's kingdom is like and where they might just decide it is the kind of place they would like to be forever.

Certainly Not!

For sin shall not have dominion over you, for you are not under law but under grace.
—Romans 6:14

"The Sabbath doesn't apply to Christians," Steve told me as he thumbed his way through his Bible and finally landed in the book of Romans, "because we are specifically told that we are not under the law, but under grace." When I asked a few questions, it became apparent that Steve did not think that *all* of the moral law had become irrelevant; he still believed that murder, theft, adultery, and taking God's name in vain were still wrong.

"It's interesting," I told him, "that it doesn't just say the Sabbath is no longer applicable. It mentions the whole law."

What should we make of the statement that we no longer live under the law? It is really pretty simple. A while ago my wife and I were in a hurry to drive down from the mountains on our way to Utah, and my impatience with a slow driver in front of me got me in trouble. I sped up to pass her the moment an opportunity presented itself. What I did not count on was the state trooper on the side of the road, who pulled me over.

"I don't have a problem with you passing another driver," he told me. "I have a problem with you doing seventy in a forty-five-mile-per-hour zone."

He took my paperwork back to his car, and I knew I was done for. There was little doubt I was going to face a stiff penalty for having violated the law. When he came back, however, I was pleasantly surprised. "It doesn't look like you have any other infractions or warrants, so I'm going to let you go with a warning," he said. I was, needless to say, delighted. I had been under the *penalty* of the law, forced to face the consequences of breaking it, but I had just received grace in the form of a pardon I did not deserve. I did not receive a permanent exemption from keeping the law, however.

That is precisely what Paul is describing in Romans 6:14, as his next words make abundantly clear: "What then? Shall we sin because we are not under law but under grace? Certainly not!" (verse 15). Christians are immensely grateful that Christ has secured a pardon for us; our love and appreciation for Jesus makes us *want* to live within His moral boundaries.

Unchangeable

Jesus Christ is the same yesterday, today, and forever.
—Hebrews 13:8

Growing up, you expect a doctor to be older and wiser than you. The first time you encounter a physician who appears to be younger than you, it comes as a bit of a surprise. I remember the first time it happened to me. I was in an emergency room, and the doctor treating my injury seemed so new that I thought I could almost see him mentally flipping through his textbooks to see what he should do next.

Of course, in my own youthful past, there were times when people expressed surprise when I told them I was a pastor. In their minds, pastors were gray haired and wise, not in their twenties. "Where do you think the old pastors come from?" I would sometimes playfully reply.

In most occupations, we become wiser and more capable with experience. We grow into the role. Not so with God: He is the same yesterday, today, and forever. That is why His moral law, which is a reflection of His character, can be safely engraved in stone: It is not going to change. What was sin in the past is still sin today, and what is sin today will still be sin tomorrow.

In a world of rapidly changing moral standards, where the moral values of your childhood are dismissed as irrelevant in adulthood, it comes as a relief to discover that God's standards do not change. Even though the world around us might suggest that morality is relative and changing (which ultimately suggests there *is* no morality), we can find the stability our hearts crave in an unchanging God. He does not have to grow into the God we want and need; nor will He drift away from the God He presently is. He is unchanging.

That also means that His promises, which are rooted in His very nature, will never change. When God says that He can save us to the uttermost (see Hebrews 7:25), that is not going to change. When God says that the essence of His character is love (1 John 4:16), that is also never going to change. And when Jesus tells us that He will come again, that promise is also not going to be amended or rewritten to suit the times.

They Even Dress Alike

Here is the patience of the saints;
here are those who keep the commandments
of God and the faith of Jesus.

—Revelation 14:12

Most thoughtful readers of the Bible recognize that God asks obedience of His people, but that recognition sometimes leads to distorted thinking about the nature of obedience. It is easy to read a passage from the Bible like today's verse and come to the conclusion that God guards the gates of heaven with a checklist and a clipboard, only admitting people who earn enough obedience points to warrant admission. Anything less, and you are out.

The first problem with this point of view is its misunderstanding of the character of God. It is nearly impossible to study the cross of Christ and come to the conclusion that God is in the business of trying to keep people out of His kingdom. Why would He give a gift of such magnitude—the life of His Son—only to subsequently try and find ways to bar you from His kingdom?

The second problem has to do with motivation. God's people do not keep His commandments merely out of obligation. To be sure, there are days when you do what you know to be right, even if you do not feel like it. After all, the practice of love is a decision, not an emotion, and true love for Christ is guided by principle rather than mere feeling. But we do not obey God to earn merit points on God's checklist.

The real motivation is found earlier in Revelation 14. We have the Father's name written on our foreheads (verse 1); our interests have become so wrapped up in His that His character becomes a part of who we are, and we naturally begin to reflect His will in our lives. Our longing to be with Him is so profound that we "follow the Lamb wherever He goes" (verse 4).

Pay attention to older couples, and you will notice something interesting: they have spent so much time in each other's presence that they may even begin to *dress* alike. That is why God's people keep His commandments—they have basked in His presence so long that His moral law becomes a part of who they are. Spend time with Jesus, a preacher friend of mine used to say, and you will begin to love the things you used to hate and hate the things you used to love.

Your Life, a Billboard

And the dragon was enraged with the woman, and he went to make war with the rest of her offspring, who keep the commandments of God and have the testimony of Jesus Christ.
—Revelation 12:17

The devil seems to have two key weapons in his arsenal: deception and force. If his lies fail to woo you away from God, then he resorts to fear and coercion, hoping that you will not have the courage to remain faithful in the face of imminent threat. Ever since the Fall, the human race has been following in his footsteps, using precisely the same weapons.

Consider the case of oppressive totalitarian regimes. Most of them rise to power on a wave of propaganda, crafting the national narrative in such a way that they begin to appear as the only hope of a bright future. Both Joseph Stalin and Adolf Hitler used propaganda effectively to construct new national myths—ideological frameworks in which people could rationalize supporting their respective governments. Those who disagreed with them would face punitive measures: social isolation, torture, and ultimately, death.

Underneath the strong-arm tactics of totalitarians lies a deep-seated sense of fear. The truth does not need to resort to coercion because it can bear careful scrutiny. But a lie? It quickly falls apart. Even if nobody says anything, the simple life of someone who bucks the system can speak volumes against the regime.

The devil does not persecute those who keep God's commandments simply because they are on the other side. He tries to eliminate them because their lives highlight the truth of God's kingdom and prove him a liar. Satan has expended considerable energy trying to make God appear malevolent. In some circles, God is even made to bear the lion's share of the blame for human crimes.

Unfortunately, to an extent, the devil has a point: Christianity *is* to blame for the atrocities of the Dark Ages. But that happened because we failed to keep God's commandments and demonstrate His character. The impact was profound; we still find it difficult to explain away the dark past. But imagine the impact of living *rightly* in the last days. Keeping God's commandments shows the world what God is really like, and that is why the devil hates it. It exposes him for who he is. The lives of commandment-keeping people prove that Satan is the real liar and murderer who cannot be trusted.

Today, you can make sure your life is a billboard for the truth about God.

Obsessed With Youth

"Honor your father and your mother, that your days may be long upon the land which the LORD your God is giving you."

—Exodus 20:12

We live in a culture obsessed with youth. To some extent, it is understandable. Few people enjoy the twin prospects of aging and death, and once you have passed a certain boundary on the chronological scale, you naturally pine for the days when your body did not hurt and malfunctioned less frequently. The kingdom of God becomes more and more desirable.

But it is not merely the vitality of youth that our culture worships; it also frequently appears that we have told ourselves that the locus of wisdom resides among the young. The older generation is dismissed as irrelevant and out of touch while the opinions of the young are splashed across the media.

To be sure, you do not have to be old in order to be wise. "Let no one despise your youth," Paul wrote to Timothy, encouraging him to exercise his pastoral office (1 Timothy 4:12). Yet I cannot help but notice that it is the elder Paul—a man who was approaching seventy years of age—who is dispensing counsel to the younger Timothy.

It might be true that your parents (and grandparents) do not understand social media or do not keep up with the latest trends. But pop culture is not wisdom, and young people are missing out on an incredible resource when they ignore those who went before them. Considered carefully, it seems foolish because someone close to you has already successfully navigated the stage of life you are currently facing, and you choose to approach the path blindly in spite of that. It is akin to driving across the country without a map, which is the record of someone who has already made the trip.

It can lead to devastating consequences for society as a whole. A case in point: the philosophy of the late nineteenth century led to the atrocities of the twentieth, the most blood-soaked century in history. Yet we still hear members of the next generation toying with the same morally bankrupt ideologies that produced such untold misery.

We ignore our elders at our own peril, dooming ourselves to repeat their mistakes. How much better to tap into the resource God placed in our lives right from the start, so that we, too, may live long in the land, which the Lord has given us.

The Fear of the Lord

The fear of the LORD is the beginning of knowledge, but fools despise wisdom and instruction.
My son, hear the instruction of your father, and do not forsake the law of your mother;
for they will be a graceful ornament on your head, and chains about your neck.
—Proverbs 1:7–9

"The nuclear family is a thing of the past according to new research," declared Leah Flynn in a 2016 news article from New Zealand. The research "found that only a quarter of 15-year-olds live with both their biological parents."* Sadly, researchers have found the same news across most of the Western world: the traditional family has been in rapid decline since the 1960s.

Is it a coincidence that the decline of the family seems to follow in the wake of the sexual revolution? Probably not, and the impact on children has been considerable. When we tear apart families, we often disconnect our children from the conduit of heavenly values God means to expose them to through the family. When we treat our spouses as disposable, we rob our offspring of an important God-given resource: parental guidance.

God expects parents to pass on *His* values to their children, who are only on loan so that we can "train up a child in the way he should go, and when he is old he will not depart from it" (Proverbs 22:6).

There is little question that sometimes the breakdown of a marriage is inevitable. Sometimes a parent is left with little choice but to separate, so we must always be diligent not to demean or criticize single parents who are doing their best to raise godly children. Criticism only adds to their already difficult load. Part of living in a broken world is an understanding that life is not always ideal, but adverse circumstances should be understood as exceptions and not stop us from striving for God's best plan.

There is also the question of parents who do *not* exhibit godly values. How do children honor parents who are selfish, abusive, or negligent? You will notice that the wise man's counsel in our Bible passage today is framed in the context of the "fear of the LORD." It is understood that parental instruction is a graceful ornament only as far as that instruction is godly. At one point, God commended the Israelites for *ignoring* their parents' counsel when it was based in sinful idolatry (Ezekiel 20:18).

The ideal? Parents who love God. Look for it in your own parents, and strive to *be* the kind of parents who make home a school for heaven.

---

* Leah Flynn, "Nuclear Family a Thing of the Past, New Research Shows," *Stuff*, August 29, 2016, https://www.stuff.co.nz/national/83658409/nuclear-family-a-thing-of-the-past-new-research-shows.

The Author of Life

"You shall not murder."

—Exodus 20:13

A study of the Ten Commandments is a study of the character of God. Each commandment, while prohibiting aberrant behavior among human beings, is also, in its negative, a statement about what God is like. When God forbids murder, He is asking us to value life as He does.

Back in the 1950s, Stanley Miller conducted a famous experiment in which he created a chemical soup meant to resemble the primordial conditions of the very ancient earth. He placed the soup in a closed system and exposed it to an electrical charge, which was meant to replicate the lightning that may have been present at the time. When he was finished, he checked his concoction for signs of life, hoping to explain how life could have emerged from nonliving components. He found a handful of amino acids, which are an important part of any biological organism, but they are not life.

Throughout recorded history, we have been curious enough to try and understand the nature of the world around us. Our curiosity has served us well: breakthroughs in chemistry and physics have made basic survival much more likely. But ultimately, our biggest enemy, death, has continued to defeat us. We have failed to grasp the essential nature of life.

We instinctively recognize life when we see it, understanding, for example, that flowers and squirrels are living things, but marbles and pebbles are not. We know life when we see it, but we struggle to understand what it is or where it comes from. We can see how the human body works when it is alive, but we are powerless to reactivate it once it is dead and past the point of resuscitation.

We can build many things, but we find ourselves powerless to create life. That is the province of God alone. Life exists only because God exists. Peter explains that Jesus is "the Author of life" (Acts 3:15, ESV), and Paul explains that Christ is not just the origin of life but the reason it continues: "And He is before all things, and in Him all things consist" (Colossians 1:17).

God's ownership of life is good news: He prizes your life highly and chooses day by day to sustain it. He considers you as His own and forbids everyone else to take what belongs to Him.

Our Light Regard for Life

"The God of Abraham, Isaac, and Jacob, the God of our fathers, glorified His Servant Jesus, whom you delivered up and denied in the presence of Pilate, when he was determined to let Him go. But you denied the Holy One and the Just, and asked for a murderer to be granted to you, and killed the Prince of life, whom God raised from the dead, of which we are witnesses."
—Acts 3:13–15

God's right to be worshiped is derived from the fact that He is the Creator. "You are worthy, O Lord, to receive glory and honor and power," the twenty-four elders declare, "for You created all things, and by Your will they exist and were created" (Revelation 4:11).

Our present light regard for life offers startling evidence of just how far the human race has strayed from the Creator God. We even entertain ourselves with death; each successive generation working harder to make death scenes more realistic. Long ago we passed the moral boundaries we set for ourselves in the film industry's Hays Code, which stipulated that murder must not be glorified or presented in a way that promotes graphic violence.

Perhaps the most striking exhibit of the depravity of sin went on display nearly two thousand years ago, when, as Peter points out, we demanded the release of a known killer, suggesting that his sins were trifling—and then calling for the death of our own Creator. If we could see the Cross from the point of view of the angels, we would understand why Calvary became the last straw, the point where the devil was finally and forever cast out (Revelation 12:10, 11). It was at the cross that Satan's rebellion and the utter depravity of sin were on full display; the place where God's own creatures channeled Satan's hatred against the Author of life and called for His crucifixion. At the cross, Jesus "endured such hostility from sinners against Himself" (Hebrews 12:3).

To break any of God's commandments is to sin, but perhaps it is here, on the issue of murder, where we can see the hideous nature of sin most clearly. This is the place where sinners most completely assault God's creation by destroying that which was made in His image.

And it is here, at the cross, where we can see the incredible generosity of God's love at its most brilliant. Not only did He raise His Son from the dead, but He offers to do the same for us: to reverse, completely, the wages of sin and one day raise us to new life in Jesus.

"And this is eternal life, that they may know You, the only true God, and Jesus Christ whom You have sent" (John 17:3).

No Back Door

"You shall not commit adultery."

—Exodus 20:14

Marriage seems to have fallen out of fashion. According to the US Census Bureau, the number of couples who chose to live together instead of get married increased more than tenfold between 1960 and 2000.[*] Cohabiting has become so popular that 43 percent of people in their twenties believe that employers should offer the same benefits to live-in partners that they offer to married couples.[†]

It raises an interesting question: Why should an employer be asked to invest in a relationship the couple themselves will not commit to? It has become popular to ask society to believe that living together is equivalent to marriage, but the numbers do not lie. Marriage and cohabiting are not equivalent at all. The odds that a marriage will break up in the first five years is about one in five, or 20 percent. The odds that a common-law couple will break up in the same period? Nearly one in two, or 49 percent. Roughly one-third of marriages end within ten years; the number jumps to 62 percent for those who choose to cohabit.

The biblical pattern for marriage is lifetime commitment. Given the way that Paul compares a marriage to the relationship between Christ and the church, Christians understand that the love expressed in a marriage is analogous to the love of God for His people (Ephesians 5:31, 32). God did not merely express feelings of fondness for His people; He entered into a covenant with them, which is an arrangement that does not merely last for life but for eternity.

Perhaps the reason marriage is designed to last for life is that it will take at least that much time to even begin learning to love another person the way that God loves us. When we treat cohabiting as equivalent to marriage, we are only cheating ourselves; the love of God is committed to the point of sacrificing one's own life for the sake of another. It is utterly impossible to reap the benefits of marriage when outside of marriage. A fling, even a long-term one, is not the way God loves. There is no back door, no escape hatch, as far as God is concerned.

Outside of marriage, we have failed to seize an incredible opportunity to learn the heart and mind of God.

---

[*] "Unmarried-Couple Households, by Presence of Children: 1960 to Present," United States Census Bureau, last updated November 2011, Excel spreadsheet, https://www.census.gov/population/socdemo/hh-fam/uc1.xls.

[†] "Statistics," Unmarried Equality, accessed March 15, 2018, http://www.unmarried.org/statistics/.

For the Passersby

For we are members of His body, of His flesh and of His bones. "For this reason a man shall leave his father and mother and be joined to his wife, and the two shall become one flesh." This is a great mystery, but I speak concerning Christ and the church.
—Ephesians 5:30–32

The place God chose as a home for the descendants of Abraham cannot possibly be an accident. Canaan was the crossroads of the ancient world; anybody traveling between Africa, Europe, and Asia would likely pass through the region and have the opportunity to see the temple and its services. The children of Israel were a gift to the whole world, a "light to the Gentiles" (Isaiah 49:6). Passersby would have the opportunity to witness the drama of salvation in the rich symbolism of the sanctuary and ask questions, the most important, of course, being: What does the lamb represent?

The temple has now been missing from our planet since Titus sacked the city of Jerusalem in A.D. 70; the focus of the believer's attention has shifted to the heavenly sanctuary where Jesus, our High Priest, is now carrying on the reality of the ministry that was foreshadowed in the temple.

Today, passersby still have opportunities to witness God's love for sinners on display in a very tangible place: our marriages. Paul points out that the love between a husband and a wife is a powerful reflection of the covenant relationship that exists between Christ and His church. Throughout Scripture, God's people are described in marital terms as the bride of Christ.

Not only do we reap incredible benefits from learning the heart of God within the sacred confines of marriage, but the world also has an opportunity to see the love of God on display in our homes. It is a real, nonsentimental love that negotiates the challenges of life on principle rather than feeling. It empties self for the good of another, to the point of sacrificing one's own life if need be. It stands through the inclement weather of hard times and basks in the gentle glow of happier days. It is a love that forgives, encourages, and commits.

It is a love, frankly, that is hard to find in our present world, so God has placed you as a light on a hill to offer your fellow human beings hope that such a thing truly exists. As we learn something of God's heart in the school of our marriages, we also whisper hope into the hearts of the broken: "Yes, I have loved you with an everlasting love" (Jeremiah 31:3).

Where the Thief
Learns His Art

"You shall not steal."

—Exodus 20:15

To steal is to take what does not belong to you. It is to follow in the footsteps of the original thief who wished to take what belonged exclusively to the Creator: the praise and worship of His creation. This thief may have failed in seizing the throne in heaven, but since his fall from grace and expulsion from heaven, Lucifer has been stealing what belongs to God. So blinded is he by his own sense of self-importance—the impulse that drives every thief—that he even attempted to wring worship away from God's own Son.

Having already seized the planet through the art of deception, he offered to sell back stolen property in exchange for the adoration that belongs to God alone. He was offering to remedy the original theft with an even greater one: "All these things I will give You if You will fall down and worship me" (Matthew 4:9).

Jesus, of course, rebuked the devil and refused to bow, but Satan has not given up. Before the end, when Jesus reclaims what rightfully belongs to Him, the dragon stages his last great attempt to usurp God's throne. With his usual tools of deception—spirits of demons performing signs (Revelation 16:14) and fire from heaven (Revelation 13:13)—and coercion (verses 15–17), he seizes what belongs to God alone. This is where the human thief learns his art: from the one who invented thievery in the first place. Not only is taking what does not belong to you a violation of your fellow human being, but it is also to use your life to display the character of fallen angels rather than the character of God. Theft is not only to take what possessions that do not belong to you, it is also permitting rebellious angels to take *you*. It is to willingly make yourself an accomplice in the theft of your own person: a human being originally created in the image of God for the purpose of displaying His glory. To follow in Lucifer's footsteps is to sell what does not belong to you and rob the world of the opportunity to see God in your life.

To be honest, on the other hand, is to show the world what God is really like.

To Fail to Love

*"The thief does not come except to steal, and to kill, and to destroy. I have come
that they may have life, and that they may have it more abundantly."*
—John 10:10

I walked up to the back door of my little house and immediately sensed that something was wrong. A split second later I realized what it was: the little window in the door was missing. When I opened the door, I found the window in a thousand pieces, all over the kitchen floor. I had been robbed! I made my way through the house cautiously; the perpetrators were long gone. A few of my meager possessions were missing.

A loss of possessions is not the worst part of getting robbed, because mere things can be replaced. The worst part of thievery is the statement it makes about the value of the victim. To steal is to devalue the life of another.

Consider the possessions that people accumulate as a sort of congealed form of life: we voluntarily give up significant portions of our lives in exchange for the things we use to provide a living for ourselves. When we buy a bed to sleep in, it is not merely an item; it is what we received in exchange for a week's work or more. It is what we traded our time and labor for, the congealment of our past.

When people steal items, they are not merely taking physical objects; they are also stealing time and labor, forcing someone to work involuntarily for their benefit. Theft is a form of slavery—and slavery, of course, is a form of theft. Thieves not only take your things; they assault the value of your person, diminishing your life. The arch thief, Jesus points out, also kills and destroys. Theft is contrary to the character of God, who refuses to use coercion and allows people free will, even if they abuse it. To steal is to value self above others, which is the antithesis of how God's kingdom operates.

But what of modern-day Robin Hoods, stealing from the rich and using the wealth to help the poor? It is still theft. How someone uses their possessions is not our judgment call to make; in God's order, on this side of the judgment, everyone is free to live for or against God. God expects that we will show the same respect to people that He shows.

To steal, in other words, is to fail to love.

Protect Thy Neighbor

"You shall not bear false witness against your neighbor."
—Exodus 20:16

If there is one commandment pushed to the front of popular culture during an election cycle, it is God's prohibition on tarnishing someone's reputation. Every day we are subjected to deliberately crafted half-truths and misrepresentations about candidates, and typically, before the election is finished, we find ourselves disgusted by it. If we are honest, however, we would have to admit that we are also guilty: all of us have mishandled people's reputations or delighted in repeating stories that cast people in poor light.

It is not a trifling matter. The one thing everybody owns, regardless of material wealth, is his or her reputation. Your reputation survives your possessions, continuing even after financial ruin. Reputation even survives death, becoming the one thing you truly leave behind when you die. Your possessions will quickly be distributed to others, but your good name will always belong to you.

Even the poorest among us can be wealthy when it comes to the matter of character. When we deface that character by creating—or repeating—falsehoods, we are taking away their most valuable possession. In that regard, the commandment against bearing false witness is related to the commandment against theft. It is also related to the commandment against murder because to defame other people is to chip away at their quality of life, diminishing the joy they find during their brief time on this planet.

I remember sitting with an elderly man who had been the victim of the rumor mill, accused of something he certainly had not done. The tears rolled down his cheeks as he described the pain of having his reputation, so carefully guarded his whole life, ruined in a matter of days. "It's like cutting open a pillow in the wind," he said. "Even when the person who did this admits he lied, you can never get all the feathers back."

When you consider the example of Christ, diminishing the worth of another becomes a no-go for the Christian: He considered Himself of no reputation so that He could, in spite of our sinful past, one day consider us to be kings and priests in His kingdom. Our role on this side of glory is to consider others as better than ourselves and protect our neighbors the way God has protected us (Philippians 2:3–7).

Guard Your Neighbor's Light

Look also at ships: although they are so large and are driven by fierce winds, they are turned by a very small rudder wherever the pilot desires. Even so the tongue is a little member and boasts great things. See how great a forest a little fire kindles! And the tongue is a fire, a world of iniquity. The tongue is so set among our members that it defiles the whole body, and sets on fire the course of nature; and it is set on fire by hell.
—James 3:4–6

When God forgives our sins, the Bible assures us that He casts them into the deepest part of the sea (Micah 7:19). He writes His own character, as described in His law, in our hearts, assuring us, "Their sins and lawless deeds I will remember no more" (Hebrews 10:16, 17). Then, amazingly, He sets us out for the world to examine, as lights on a hill, so that other people will see His character revealed in us: "Let your light so shine before men, that they may see your good works and glorify your Father in heaven" (Matthew 5:16).

It is really an astonishing display of God's love. Even though we struggle to trust Him, He still trusts us with His own reputation—a risk, it is safe to say, that few of us would take with people who had betrayed *us* in the past.

When it comes to our own ability to forgive, we are not in God's league at all. We may verbally assure someone we have forgiven them, but we find it hard to forget what they did. In fact, we find ourselves prone to repeat it.

Now consider what spreading stories about other people does to their experience with God. They, too, have the promise that their sins have been cast into the depths of the sea. They, too, have been asked by God to be reflections of His character. But when we repeat stories—even if we believe them to be true—we are compromising their ability to both enjoy their forgiveness and then live God's plan for them. Try as they might to share the love of God and show the world what He is truly like, the stories we spread prevent those who know these people from seeing the light God intends for them to see. Some will be blinded by our rehearsal of other people's faults or by the stories we concocted based on incomplete information. Not only will we have ruined others' reputations, but we also will have ruined their ability to be lights in the world.

It may seem like a little thing to us, but as James reminds us, it does not take much to fan the flames of the devil's work in this world.

Quietness of Heart

*"You shall not covet your neighbor's house; you shall not covet your neighbor's wife,
nor his male servant, nor his female servant, nor his ox, nor his donkey,
nor anything that is your neighbor's."*

—Exodus 20:17

It is easily one of the first negative traits we discover in our children: a self-centered desire that says *I want!* It is some of the clearest evidence we have that people are born with sinful natures, hardwired with a selfish orientation. If not kept in check, it is what leads to almost every other sin: we usually steal, kill, and commit adultery, after all, in order to obtain what we do not have.

It is such a serious problem that God has made it clear that the covetous cannot inherit the kingdom of God (Ephesians 5:5). Why? It is because God is love, and the citizens of the kingdom of heaven are hardwired like Him, with a priority placed on others. It was covetousness that created problems for Lucifer when he decided that he would like to have something that did not belong to him: the throne of God. He was removed for his transgression because it put the peace and happiness of God's entire kingdom at risk. We will scarcely be allowed in if we are intent on following in his footsteps.

When you covet, you assume that you are better than others, more worthy of the possessions they happen to have than they are. In telling yourself, "I deserve to have that!" you are implying that another person does not deserve it. It minimizes the worth of another human being, and it is also an assault on the character of God Himself: you are suggesting that God is somehow unjust and that He has not dealt rightly with you.

The problem with covetousness is that it becomes a bottomless pit because of the obsession with self. You might appropriate more material goods to yourself, but you will not have fed your appetite for self-gratification. The sinful heart is such a massive pit that you will never fill it. The book of Job reminds us that the person driven by greed "knows no quietness in his heart" (Job 20:20).

God spares us the never-ending agony of self-gratification, trying to scratch an itch that can never be relieved by our own efforts. By clearly identifying greed and removing it from the table, He frees us up to practice having the mind of Christ, who esteemed us more highly than He prized Himself.

The Art of Contentment

Not that I speak in regard to need, for I have learned in whatever state I am,
to be content: I know how to be abased, and I know how to abound. Everywhere
and in all things I have learned both to be full and to be hungry, both to abound
and to suffer need. I can do all things through Christ who strengthens me.
—Philippians 4:11–13

Think back a few years, and ask yourself a question: Are you happier today than you were back then? Of course, unless you faced something particularly traumatic in the past, the passage of time has a way of casting a bit of a glow around yesteryear, sometimes making it easier to remember good times than bad. But think back to when you were starting out or had very little. Were you less happy then than you are now?

When Jean and I were first married, we set up house with very little. We had secondhand couches from her parents and a kitchen table that was on loan from a friend. The only new thing we owned was the mattress on our bed. We had very little income, which meant that we could not afford to do some of the things we do today. There was no money for entertainment of any kind, and we could only afford the most basic of groceries.

But were we any less happy? Hardly. I look back on those years as some of the happiest of my life. We owned practically nothing, but we were happy.

Why is it so hard for people to learn that *things* do not bring happiness? True, poverty does not bring much joy, either, but the accumulation of things is hardly a recipe for joy. "Take heed and beware of covetousness," Jesus warned us, trying to spare us a lifetime of misery, "for one's life does not consist in the abundance of the things he possesses" (Luke 12:15).

The Greeks told the story of Sisyphus, a self-aggrandizing man who was punished with an impossible feat: rolling a massive boulder up a hill, only to have it roll back down on him. He would have to repeat the same thing every day for all of eternity. While not a biblical story, it is a fair description of the futility of coveting things: You will be trapped in a cycle of dissatisfaction and misery for the rest of your life. You will waste your years on things that do not matter; things that will not follow you into eternity.

Learn the art of contentment, as Paul did, and you will suddenly find yourself free to actually enjoy the life that God has granted you.

There Are No Others

And God spoke all these words, saying: "I am the LORD your God, who brought you out of the land of Egypt, out of the house of bondage. You shall have no other gods before Me."
—Exodus 20:1–3

One of the key things that set Abraham apart from his neighbors was his belief that there is but one God. To be sure, there were other monotheists in existence, like the enigmatic priest Melchizedek whose meeting with Abraham is recorded in Genesis 14: both of them worshiped "El Elyon," the Most High God.

But most of the ancient Chaldeans, whom Abraham came from, and the Canaanites, whom Abraham landed among, were polytheistic. They assigned various divinities to the natural phenomena that governed their lives: a god of the sun, the moon, rain, harvest, and so on. As God established His covenant with Abraham's descendants, reminding them of their liberation from Egypt, the first commandment must have struck a powerful note. Today, we live in a world where three of the world's most prominent religions are all monotheistic, professing to worship the God of Abraham. The first commandment does not seem novel or out of place.

But back then, as the Israelites made their way out of a land dominated by scores of Egyptian gods, the first commandment would have been notable. They were reminded that Abraham's God is not only above all other gods; He is, in reality, the only God there is, because only the Creator can be truly worshiped.

Today, the reminder is not quite as striking, as billions of us having been raised with a monotheistic tradition. But the number of competing gods has not diminished; if anything, the world offers more substitutes for a relationship with the Creator than ever before. Never in human history has there been a generation so distracted or so seduced by wrong priorities. Many of us now claim to worship nothing, yet somehow we are blind to the way that we worship ourselves; our egos elevating ourselves above the place that God should hold in our lives.

To violate this commandment is to miss the joy that knowing God brings and to never find the purpose for which you were created. A sense of meaning is one of the greatest needs that human beings have, and before God invites us to examine the rest of His moral law, He starts at the very beginning—helping us to discover who we are and where we belong.

To pursue other gods is to waste your life running after nothing, for in reality, there are no others.

Now, Before the Crisis

So they worshiped the dragon who gave authority to the beast; and they worshiped the beast,
saying, "Who is like the beast? Who is able to make war with him?"
—Revelation 13:4

The Bible offers clear evidence that someone is attempting to divert the worship that rightfully belongs to God away from the Creator to himself. The prophet Isaiah identifies him as Lucifer, the one who said, "I will be like the Most High" (Isaiah 14:14). When his rebellion in the courts of heaven failed, he was cast out and turned his attention toward those made in the image of God: the human race. He began by encouraging our first parents to doubt God's word, telling them they would not die if they should eat from the tree.

"For God knows that in the day you eat of it your eyes will be opened," he lied, "and you will be like God, knowing good and evil" (Genesis 3:5). The best way to achieve his dreams, the devil believed, was to lead us to covet God's throne as well.

The rest of the Bible provides the long, painful narrative of people who decided to assume God's throne for themselves, even for just a moment. Adam and Eve were perfectly happy in their original state but decided to second-guess God and plunged us all into thousands of years of slavery to fallen angels. Abraham and Sarah struggled to understand how a geriatric couple could have a child, so they decided to contribute to God's promise by taking charge. Sarah suggested that Abraham should have a baby with her servant. They may have only assumed God's place for a moment, but it led to untold heartache for centuries.

As sinners, we all tend to want to be in control and to impatiently take over where we feel that God may not have come through as expected. It is easy to point a finger to a nefarious character, such as the beast of Revelation 13, as a monster who demands worship, but we should probably ask ourselves why he is able to convince *us* to worship him. Is it because he offers the path of self-sufficiency? The path that appeals to our desire for control? Will he offer the world a solution that looks as if it can fix its worst problems without God's intervention?

The time to trust that God actually belongs on His throne is now, before a crisis convinces us to do otherwise.

The Shortcut of Idolatry

*"You shall not make for yourself a carved image—any likeness of anything
that is in heaven above, or that is in the earth beneath, or that is in the water
under the earth; you shall not bow down to them nor serve them."*
—Exodus 20:4, 5

One of the last things you would expect somebody to complain about is salvation, but that is exactly what the children of Israel did. Having been freed from Egyptian slavery and having just enjoyed a decisive victory over King Arad, the descendants of Abraham discovered the path around Edom to be difficult. As we are all prone to do when the going is tough, they began to complain: life in Egypt had been better than navigating demanding territory.

It was at that moment that God revealed that He had been protecting them. It was a land of dangerous serpents (Deuteronomy 8:15), and to this point, the Israelites had not had to deal with them. As they complained of God's plan to bring them home, His protection was lifted. The remedy? To restore the practice of trust in God and look toward the bronze serpent on the pole by faith.

It was, of course, a type of the faith we need to place in the saving work of Christ on the cross. Like Israel, we are on our way to the heavenly Promised Land, and most of us will find that the path of Christ is not an easy one. It involves self-denial, trials, and frequently, opposition. To complain about the Christian life is to wonder if going back to the world is not a better alternative.

The end of the story is shocking to the modern reader: God ordered the serpent on the pole destroyed, because the Israelites had, once again, quit placing faith in God's covenant and had begun to worship the image itself (2 Kings 18:4). There are many layers to the story; enough to keep a Bible student busy for many hours. But perhaps the most uncomfortable aspect is the fact that an object meant to foreshadow the Cross became a graven image: a carved representation was used as an object of worship.

A longing for ease can give way to idolatry, for idolatry is a shortcut—a religion devoted to a god you construct yourself and a religion designed to avoid the challenges of relating to Someone real. It would do us well to examine our faith in light of the Word so that we are certain we have not created easier paths for ourselves that do not actually lead home.

Written in Wet Cement

"For I, the LORD your God, am a jealous God, visiting the iniquity of the fathers
upon the children to the third and fourth generations of those who hate Me,
but showing mercy to thousands, to those who love Me and keep My commandments."
—Exodus 20:5, 6

It is popular to speak of DNA as a hardwired code; something permanently engraved at the core of who we are, compelling us to live helplessly by that code. We look for genetic causes for nearly every behavior, and such markers are often found. The conclusion that many people come to? We have little choice in what we do; it is written in our genes.

Recent studies have revealed, however, that our genetic code is not as entrenched as we previously thought. As Nessa Carey points out in *Natural History*, DNA is less like a mold than it is a script.★ Two directors can take the same movie script and create movies with entirely different feels and outcomes.

An extreme famine hit the Netherlands during the winter of 1944–1945, thanks to a harsh winter and the blockades put in place by the Germans. The situation became so desperate that people resorted to eating tulip bulbs. Pregnant mothers who were starved in the last few months of pregnancy gave birth, predictably, to small babies. The surprise came when those children grew up: they were never able to catch up and tended not to become obese later in life. The famine had caused a genetic change in the babies that carried on throughout their lives.

In other words, various genes can actually be turned off and on, if the need arises. Our genetic identity is not carved in stone; it is written in wet cement.

But it is still there. Many have noticed how the second commandment mentions the sins of parents being handed down through a number of generations. We are only starting to realize just how correct this is: The lives we live and the choices we make can actually have a *genetic* impact on our children. It can predispose them to certain behaviors.

If we create a religion to suit ourselves, our children can feel powerfully compelled toward the same error themselves. That is bad news. The good news? We are not forever condemned by our predispositions; they are not permanently engraved in stone. Only God's law, reflecting His character, is completely immovable. Our genes may be powerful, impossible to overcome on our own. But the original Creator of that code is far more powerful, never leaving us forever condemned by someone else's choices.

★ Nessa Carey, "Beyond DNA: Epigenetics," *Natural History*, http://www.naturalhistorymag.com/features/142195/beyond-dna-epigenetics.

Called by His Name

"You shall not take the name of the LORD your God in vain,
for the LORD will not hold him guiltless who takes His name in vain."
—Exodus 20:7

As a boy, I believed the third commandment was a prohibition against cussing, and I must admit that my youthful understanding had a dampening effect on my choice of playground epithets. But this commandment is about more than careless language. God's people do not merely *declare* His name with their voices; they actually *take* it. They *wear* it. As the Babylonian captivity was drawing to a close, Daniel prayed for Israel and Jerusalem: "Do not delay for Your own sake, my God, for Your city and Your people are called by Your name" (Daniel 9:19).

The city of Jerusalem, of course, was sacked by Nebuchadnezzar seven decades earlier because the people of God were no longer a light to the Gentiles—a living display of God's character. The abominations of their kings had led to the desolation of the temple.* The temple had become pointless because God's people were now wearing His name in vain, and their actions giving lie to the reason their nation existed. The name of God was embedded in the name of the people: *Israel*, "he who prevailed with God." Now, tragically, the world had prevailed with them.

It is easy to point an accusing finger at people who lived so long ago because the passage of centuries makes them seem distant, and we tell ourselves they were quite unlike us. But the Bible tells a different story. The book of Revelation predicts that New Testament woman will also descend into spiritual adultery.

Ever since first-century believers in Antioch began to wear the label "Christian" (Acts 11:26), we, too, have been a people called by His name. We, too, have been tasked with revealing the Creator to the world, calling people to "worship Him who made heaven and earth" (Revelation 14:7). To take the name of Jesus is to *be* like Jesus. "For we are God's fellow workers," Paul reminds us, "you are God's field, you are God's building" (1 Corinthians 3:9). "Do you not know that you are the temple of God and that the Spirit of God dwells in you?" (verse 16).

The temple in Jerusalem is gone, left desolate forever. But you—the temple where God desires to reveal His perfect name to the world? Still standing. Whether it stands in vain is up to you.

---

* See, for example, 2 Chronicles 33:2; 34:33; 36:8, 14.

He Wears Your Name

"Then you shall take two onyx stones and engrave on them the names of the sons of Israel: six of their names on one stone and six names on the other stone, in order of their birth. With the work of an engraver in stone, like the engravings of a signet, you shall engrave the two stones with the names of the sons of Israel. You shall set them in settings of gold. And you shall put the two stones on the shoulders of the ephod as memorial stones for the sons of Israel. So Aaron shall bear their names before the LORD on his two shoulders as a memorial."
—Exodus 28:9–12

Consider the immense privilege of bearing God's name. Has there ever been a people so unworthy as the fallen human race to call themselves by God's name? Our very being has been so warped by sin that we cannot help but distort the character of God in our daily activities. To think that someone would examine us in order to see God is beyond humbling.

Now consider the fact that the high priest wore the names of the twelve tribes on the stones of his breastplate, carrying them into the very presence of God. The high priest, of course, is a type of Jesus, which suggests that not only did God place His name on the children of Abraham, but Christ also has placed our names on Himself. The Son of God is also the Son of man. Not only was Adam a son of God (Luke 3:38), but Jesus Himself became a Son of Adam.

The covenant that God has made with the human race can be summarized in one powerful statement: "You shall be My people, and I will be your God" (Jeremiah 30:22). We, the undeserving, have been given the privilege of bearing God's name, having it written on our foreheads (Revelation 14:1). And Jesus, the deserving One, has humbled Himself beyond comprehension and taken our names, our very nature on Himself forever.

The point is reemphasized in the vision of the New Jerusalem. The names of the twelve tribes are posted above the twelve gates. The names of the apostles form the foundation. "And I heard a loud voice from heaven saying, 'Behold, the tabernacle of God is with men, and He will dwell with them, and they shall be His people. God Himself will be with them and be their God' " (Revelation 21:3).

What astonishing love! What kind of God is this, who agrees to wear *my* name in spite of who I am and where I have been, somehow unashamed to call me "brother" (see Hebrews 2:11)? If Christ wears *our* names without shame, the ones who once sought His life, how much more reason to wear His name with joy. "Therefore whoever confesses Me before men," Jesus taught us, "him I will also confess before My Father who is in heaven" (Matthew 10:32).

JUNE 29

Life's Pause Button

"Remember the Sabbath day, to keep it holy. Six days you shall labor and do all your work,
but the seventh day is the Sabbath of the LORD your God. In it you shall do no work: you,
nor your son, nor your daughter, nor your male servant, nor your female servant, nor your cattle,
nor your stranger who is within your gates. For in six days the LORD made the heavens
and the earth, the sea, and all that is in them, and rested the seventh day.
Therefore the LORD blessed the Sabbath day and hallowed it."
—Exodus 20:8–11

At the apex of the first table, the commandments that show us how to relate to God, stands the Sabbath. It sits at the very heart of the moral law, both a poignant conclusion to the first table and a powerful segue into the second. It reminds us that before we can learn to properly relate to our fellow human beings, we must first learn to relate to the God who made us all.

The Ten Commandments open with a reminder that to use our inborn desires for communion and worship by pursuing other gods is to waste them, for there are no other gods. "I am the LORD," the Creator reminds us, "and there is no other" (Isaiah 45:5). Then the second commandment reminds us that we are made in *His* image, not the other way around. We are not free to re-create God according to our own preferences, declaring Him to be what He is not, and reducing Him to less than He is. The third commandment invites us to consider what it means to bear God's name, to use our lives to reflect His perfect character to the world.

Then, once we have learned from the first three, God pushes the pause button on the world and invites us into His presence so that we have the time and space we need to truly understand who He is. He not only instructs us on the proper way to relate to Him, but He also carves out the time we need to both study and learn it. "Come and rest in My presence," He is telling us, "and consider what it means to be created and to have a loving Creator, what it means to be human and yet made in the image of God."

Therefore, we finish each week in God's presence, taking our trials and the lessons of life directly into His throne room. He gives us the space we need to consider who He is and who we ought to be, and He heals our hearts. Then, when the sun sinks below the horizon on Saturday night, we are prepared to reenter the world and engage with the rest of humanity because we understand a little more of what it actually means to be human and keep the last six commandments.

Learning to Rest

"Come to Me, all you who labor and are heavy laden, and I will give you rest.
Take My yoke upon you and learn from Me, for I am gentle and lowly in heart,
and you will find rest for your souls. For My yoke is easy and My burden is light."
—Matthew 11:28–30

In recent years, our nest has become progressively emptier, and I find myself wondering how the time slipped by so quickly. One moment your children are infants, completely dependent on you for every need, and the next they are claiming their lives as their own. It has given me much time to reflect on the role God assigned to me as a father, lending me His children for a brief period and asking me to raise them the way He might.

Occasionally, as I think back over the years, my heart suddenly runs cold as I remember times when I clearly failed to be everything a father should be. I wince, painfully, as I recall those moments when I was conquered by impatience or surrendered to an easier path. I flinch as I see some of my own traits passed on to my children. I recoil in horror at the thought that I should ever have to examine my record as a father in the presence of the Father Himself.

The other day, as I was walking through the neighborhood, allowing feelings of regret to overwhelm me, a voice suddenly whispered to my heart, *"Don't you think I know who you are? Do you really believe I thought you would be the world's first perfect father? Why can't you just rest in Me?"*

In this world, when our sinful condition suddenly presents itself, it is easy to give way to despondent feelings. We quickly cave under the heavy weight of hopelessness. The enemy of souls is always ready to remind us that we are not worthy, and as we listen to his accusations, our hearts become restless.

What incredible love that God has set aside dedicated time as a regular reminder that we do not have to despair because He knows who we are, and while we were yet sinners, He died for us (Romans 5:8). We will not finally enter the kingdom of God because we were good enough, but because Christ is good enough (Isaiah 28:20). Take the time each week to see who Jesus is, to see His immense love for you and His dedication to bringing you home, and you will finally learn to rest, even on this side of glory.

July

I look forward to the soon coming of Jesus and the blessed hope when "this mortal shall put on immortality." As I prepare to meet the Lord, I will witness to His loving salvation, and by life and word help others to be ready for His glorious appearing.

Not a Moment Too Late

*But when the fullness of the time had come, God sent forth His Son,
born of a woman, born under the law, to redeem those who were under the law,
that we might receive the adoption as sons.*
—Galatians 4:4, 5

When you study the prophetic passages of the Old Testament, it becomes obvious that the timing of Jesus' birth was no accident. Not only was the first advent of Christ timed to correspond to the 490-year probationary period of Daniel 9, but it was also carefully choreographed to dovetail with the political and spiritual environment of the planet. "Providence had directed the movements of nations, and the tide of human impulse and influence, until the world was ripe for the coming of the Deliverer,"★ Ellen White reminds us.

The world had become well connected by Roman roads and the Greek language. A large number of the Israelites were living in remote nations but would come to Jerusalem for the feasts. Faith in pagan religions was waning. Everything was perfect for Jesus to come.

Can there be any doubt that the same is true of the Second Coming? You and I do not have precise time-setting prophecies, such as the seventy-week prophecy which pinpointed the moment of Jesus' public ministry, but we have enough evidence, based on the same prophecy, to suggest that we are getting very close. The rise and fall of kingdoms in the visions of Daniel did not culminate with Christ's first advent but His second. The spiritual decline of the planet is falling into line with Paul's predictions in his letter to Timothy, when he warned us that "in the last days perilous times will come" (2 Timothy 3:1).

If there was ample evidence that the moment of Christ's first arrival was approaching, there is *more* prophetic evidence pointing us to the nearness of His second. We do not know the day or the hour, but we do know when it is close. No matter what happens in the world around us, whether war, disaster, or catastrophe, we can know that nothing about our situation escapes God's notice. When Jesus *does* come, it will be at the "fullness of the time," at precisely the right moment—not a moment too soon and not a moment too late.

Our role is to live by faith and keep about the work *until* that moment arrives—trusting that no matter what happens, when Jesus does finally light up the eastern sky, God chose the moment, and there could not possibly be a better one.

★ Ellen G. White, *The Desire of Ages* (Mountain View, CA: Pacific Press®, 1898), 32.

The Margin for Doubt

After that He was seen by over five hundred brethren at once,
of whom the greater part remain to the present, but some have fallen asleep.
—1 Corinthians 15:6

When Jesus rose from the dead, a *lot* of people saw Him. It was not just a handful of disciples, who could be accused of fabricating a story to save face in the wake of Christ's death. In addition to the twelve disciples, Paul informs us that another five *hundred* people saw Him. This was not like a modern Elvis sighting, where the random person claims to have seen the aging pop star shopping at Walmart or having lunch in a diner. There was widespread confirmation of Jesus' resurrection.

You will notice, however, that Jesus did not present Himself to the whole world when He came back from the dead. He specifically told the high priest that He would not see him again until the Second Coming, and that was for a specific reason: the high priest would receive visual confirmation that he had just condemned God's Son (Matthew 26:64). But not all who saw the risen Jesus were believers; the repeated mention of the crowds who followed Jesus would suggest that there were many believers who did not get a chance to see Him.

They would have to take the words of the witnesses on faith, just like we do. We have ample evidence in the Bible to suggest that Jesus is the promised Messiah: the prophecies, the intricate details of each story, and the undesigned scriptural coincidences in which various Bible writers unwittingly confirm each others' accounts. But we have not actually *seen* Him with our eyes. "Now faith is the substance of things hoped for," the author of Hebrews famously points out, "the evidence of things not seen" (Hebrews 11:1). Modern Christians examine the scriptural evidence, listen to the voice of Christ through the Spirit, and choose to accept His claims by faith, sight unseen. There is always a margin for doubt and the freedom to decide otherwise.

For now, we will have to content ourselves with the witness of those who saw Him and the reassuring presence of the Spirit in our midst. But *our* moment is also coming when the rest of us will join the five hundred and see the risen Jesus for ourselves—when He comes back in glory, and "every eye will see Him" (Revelation 1:7).

At that point, all margins for doubt will have disappeared forever.

Afraid of a Lamb

Then the sky receded as a scroll when it is rolled up, and every mountain
and island was moved out of its place. And the kings of the earth, the great men,
the rich men, the commanders, the mighty men, every slave and every free man,
hid themselves in the caves and in the rocks of the mountains, and said to the mountains
and rocks, "Fall on us and hide us from the face of Him who sits on the throne and from the
wrath of the Lamb! For the great day of His wrath has come, and who is able to stand?"
—Revelation 6:14–17

The closing scenes of the sixth chapter of Revelation are some of the most tragic recorded in Scripture because they exhibit human stubbornness and willful blindness at their worst. As the unprepared seek to hide themselves from the presence of Jesus, there are a number of things we should notice.

First, Jesus is presented as the Lamb. The language is not an accident. At the end, as history winds up, the last remaining rebels are being confronted with what Christ has done to secure their salvation. They are not lost because of ignorance; they are lost because they rejected the offer of salvation. God pulled out all the stops. He did everything imaginable to bring them into His kingdom, not even sparing the life of His own Son. You will notice that when they see Jesus coming in glory, they *know who He is.* The cry going up from the world is not, "What is going on?" No, they know Him well enough to refer to Him as the Lamb of God, and they seem aware that He would come. They have simply been caught off guard by how quickly the day came.

It reminds us that when the history of our rebellious planet closes, those who are lost will be so because they chose to be, and with a broken heart, God lets them have what they chose.

Second, we see the madness of sin on full display. You might expect people to be afraid of the Lion of the tribe of Judah, but who is afraid of a *lamb?* When is the last time you saw someone cower in the corner or seek safety because there was a lamb in the yard? It is absurd; you might just as well be terrified of puppies. It highlights how absurd it is to be lost when God has done so much to win us back. These people have ultimately chosen not to trust God, even in the face of abundant evidence that God is trustworthy—and so even the magnificent, loving character of Christ is lost on them.

This awful scene is a powerful reminder that it is pointless to be lost because, at the end, there is no reason not to be safe with the God who loved you enough to lay down His life for you.

Better Than Easy

But I do not want you to be ignorant, brethren, concerning those who have fallen asleep,
lest you sorrow as others who have no hope. For if we believe that Jesus died and rose again,
even so God will bring with Him those who sleep in Jesus.
—1 Thessalonians 4:13, 14

If you listen to the lineup of TV preachers who fill the airwaves each weekend, you will hear a lot of what some people call the "prosperity gospel." Follow Jesus, we are told, and life will become a lot easier; you can expect health, wealth, and a relatively trouble-free existence. It is a message that sells and brings in millions of dollars for those who preach it. There is just one really big problem with it: most of the believers profiled in the New Testament, the ones who *wrote* the Bible, did not have trouble-free existences.

What we have been offered in Jesus is not an easy life; even a cursory glance through the life of Jesus Himself should make that clear. Rather, what we have been offered is *hope*. As members of the first-century Thessalonian church began to die, their friends naturally began to mourn each painful loss. A modern Christian might be tempted to tell the Thessalonians not to shed tears at a funeral (I have heard it many times), but Paul says no such thing. He does not tell them not to sorrow but not to "sorrow as others who have no hope."

The Christian, for the time being, still lives in this world. We experience pain, suffering, and loss, just like every other human being. The rain, Jesus reminds us, falls on the just and the unjust alike (Matthew 5:45). If anything, believers sometimes have a *greater* burden to bear because we are reaping the natural consequences of living in a sinful world, and we also often have to shoulder the disdain heaped on us by those who do not care for our beliefs.

So yes, we sorrow. We live full, authentic human lives. We feel pain, as Jesus did. We know loneliness and rejection, as He did. We are often misunderstood, as Jesus was. We suffer, as Jesus suffered. But the quality of our sorrow is not like everybody else's because we know that Jesus has conquered our greatest enemy. The grave will come for each of us, but it will not hold us because it could not hold our Savior, and we know that Jesus will come again to bring suffering to a permanent end.

We have been given something far more valuable than an easy life.

God's Idea of *Soon*

He who testifies to these things says,
"Surely I am coming quickly." Amen.
Even so, come, Lord Jesus!

—Revelation 22:20

It can be frustrating for mere mortals to read the promise of a *soon* coming. For most of us, Jesus cannot come back quickly enough. We need Him to be here in time to bring our suffering to an end. We want Him to come back before we have to deal with life's ultimate reality: the grave. As John hears, "I am coming quickly," he gets excited: "Even so, come, Lord Jesus!"

It has become evident, however, after two thousand years, that my idea of "soon" and God's idea of "soon" are two different things. We are a microwave generation that wants our meals prepared in less than five minutes and instantaneous responses to our text messages. "Soon" means *right now*.

But in the grand scheme of eternity, millions of years from now, the duration of the great controversy will seem like a mere blip in the long history of God's universe—a significant blip, a game changer of a blip, to be sure, but a chronological blip nonetheless. From God's perspective, the controversy will have been wrapped up *very* quickly. It was allowed to exist as long as it took to demonstrate Lucifer's true nature and confirm the painful results of detaching ourselves from God. It will be long enough to ensure that no individual is missing from the kingdom unnecessarily. It will also be short enough to prove God's mercy.

It can be hard to understand Jesus' return as "soon" when you are trapped inside a short life span and living with pain. Our ability to see clearly has been compromised by the results of sin. Speaking of Christ's first coming, Ellen White once wrote, "But like the stars in the vast circuit of their appointed path, God's purposes know no haste and no delay."★

In other words, when Jesus returns, it will be the *perfect* moment to do so. One day sooner would be too soon, and one day later would be too late. Our role is to live by faith, trusting that if we saw the world from God's perspective, we would hold out a little longer too. At the same time, let our hearts swell with hope as it becomes more and more obvious that the day is just about here. We wait, our hearts alive with hope: "Even so, come, Lord Jesus!"

★ Ellen G. White, *The Desire of Ages* (Mountain View, CA: Pacific Press®, 1898), 32.

"Thy Kingdom Come"

Now Enoch, the seventh from Adam, prophesied about these men also, saying, "Behold, the Lord comes with ten thousands of His saints, to execute judgment on all, to convict all who are ungodly among them of all their ungodly deeds which they have committed in an ungodly way, and of all the harsh things which ungodly sinners have spoken against Him."
—Jude 14, 15

The book of Enoch was the work of several different writers and was in relatively wide circulation during the century before Christ's birth. Although a handful of early church fathers believed there was a divine quality to the book, primarily because Jude chose to refer to it, the Christian church has never considered the book to be Scripture.

We can safely assume, however, that the passage from the book of Enoch that Jude quoted under inspiration is accurate. It highlights an important point for modern Christians to understand: even though the influence of dispensationalists has made the Second Coming seem like an event that belongs exclusively to a final generation of believers, it is not. The complete restoration of all things is a hope that has inspired God's people from the very beginning. While it is true that Old Testament believers were looking forward to the first coming of the Messiah, they were ultimately anticipating God's kingdom.

It explains why there was confusion about Christ's first coming. By the first century, it was widely anticipated that when the Messiah came, He would overthrow human kingdoms and claim the throne of David as His own. The fact that the Romans, Daniel's fourth kingdom, already ruled over God's people made it easy to believe, and the popularity of the book of Enoch in the century leading up to Christ speaks to the growing sense of anticipation.

It is exciting that God the Son walked among us in human form, and the astonishing gift of the Cross is, of course, indispensable to God's plan to save sinners. But the ultimate hope of God's people throughout the long centuries of our rebellion has been the coming of Christ in glory, the end of our disastrous attempts to rule ourselves, and the permanent restoration of the kingdom we rejected in Eden. It is the tie that binds all believers of all ages together.

And soon enough, when Jesus returns with ten thousand of His saints, we will finally meet the believers who passed forward their hope to our generation and together enjoy God's presence, where we can share our stories of God's love and mercy forever. And what better time to start practicing those stories than now, as we pass *our* hope forward to those around us?

The Humble Kingdom

"When the Son of Man comes in His glory, and all the holy angels with Him,
then He will sit on the throne of His glory."
—Matthew 25:31

Alexander the Great's legendary exploits earned him a place in both the world's history books and—even before he was born—in Daniel's prophecy. Alexander fancied himself to be a continuation of the ancient age of heroes, even keeping a copy of Homer's *Iliad* by his bed as he slept. He believed he was the reincarnation of Achilles, the great hero of the Trojan War, even traveling to Troy to make a sacrifice to Athena, lay a wreath at Achilles's grave, and pick up some ancient Trojan armor for good luck.

Historians suspect that Alexander's breathtaking expansion across the ancient world was more a matter of adventure than conquest, and once he managed to defeat the Persians, he claimed for himself the lofty role of a Persian king. The Persians practiced *proskynesis*, which meant that subjects had to treat the king as a god, referring to him as "King of kings" and bowing and scraping in his presence. In a wildly unpopular move, Alexander asked for this same treatment from his men.

In time, he came to consider himself to be the son of "Zeus Ammon," a kind of hybrid supreme god styled after the Greek god Zeus and the Egyptian god Ammon (Amun), which meant that Alexander now went by two titles that Christians reserve for Christ: King of kings, and Son of God.

It ended badly for Alexander: By the time his exhausted men reached India, they pushed back against Alexander's delusions of grandeur and insisted on returning home. As they traveled back, the great conqueror became increasingly unhinged, behaving erratically and displaying signs of paranoia. When they reached Babylon, he intended to move south and conquer Arabia, but his lifestyle finally caught up with him. Weakened by injuries, an insatiable appetite for liquor, and possibly malaria, he died at thirty-three years of age.

So it goes with the empires of men, which stand in stark contrast to the kingdom of God. Christ, who truly is King of kings and the Son of God, did not exalt Himself but took the path of humility, and His kingdom will ultimately replace Alexander's—and every other kingdom mentioned by Daniel. The ambitions of men always fizzle out and end in disgrace, but the humility of Christ ends with a kingdom that will last forever.

The Fear of Death

Inasmuch then as the children have partaken of flesh and blood, He Himself likewise shared in the same, that through death He might destroy him who had the power of death, that is, the devil, and release those who through fear of death were all their lifetime subject to bondage.
—Hebrews 2:14, 15

It was only two decades ago when I used to carry a pocket-sized annual calendar in order to keep track of my appointments. Sometime around the turn of the millennium, that gave way to a Palm Pilot, followed by a cell phone, and finally a smart phone that syncs with my laptop—all within the space of a few short years. The art of time management seems to change as quickly as technology does, but one thing does not change: the need to budget carefully what little time we have.

At some point, we all realize that our time on earth is exceptionally short. When you are young, it seems as if life will be long enough to accommodate all of your dreams. Sometime after you pass the statistical halfway point, you begin to realize that there *is not* enough time to do everything you would like to accomplish; you will have to prioritize.

If you stop to think about it, it is amazing how many of our life decisions are driven by the fact that we are going to die. We make a point of spending time with people that matter to us because we know that none of us lasts forever. We arrange for our sunset years in advance, knowing that we will have specific needs as our bodies begin to deteriorate. We carefully plan how our worldly goods will be distributed after we die. We buy various types of insurance because we *know* that the grave will eventually claim us, either quickly or slowly.

Now imagine an existence that is *not* motivated by death. You do not have to budget your time because if you do not finish something today, you can always come back to it in a year—or a thousand years. There is never a need to plan for the worst because the worst will never come: God has removed painful realities such as pain, suffering, and death.

Through Jesus, we have not just been delivered from death but from "fear of death." We can live entirely different lives because we know that we have not even *begun* to live. We may have to endure a few short years on a fallen planet, but the real clock—the eternal one—starts ticking the moment Jesus comes back to claim us.

"When I Drink It New"

And as they were eating, Jesus took bread, blessed and broke it, and gave it to the disciples and said, "Take, eat; this is My body." Then He took the cup, and gave thanks, and gave it to them, saying, "Drink from it, all of you. For this is My blood of the new covenant, which is shed for many for the remission of sins. But I say to you, I will not drink of this fruit of the vine from now on until that day when I drink it new with you in My Father's kingdom."
—Matthew 26:26–29

As a child, I always found the Communion service at my parents' church a rather solemn affair, almost funereal. As the emblems were distributed, a holy hush would fall over the congregation, making even the occasional suppressed cough seem insolent. The somber atmosphere made perfect sense to me. We were, after all, commemorating the most horrific act in human history: the hateful death of God's Son. As an adult, I continue to appreciate the quiet solemnity of the moment, taking the time to cherish the high cost of my salvation and the profound depths of God's love for mere sinners.

Solemn? Yes. But as an adult, I also cannot help but notice that to Jesus' way of thinking, the Communion service is not just a memorial. It has been instituted as a forward-looking moment of hope that regularly reminds us of God's magnanimous intent: the broken body and shed blood of Christ mean that we will one day be made completely whole again.

"This will be the last time we eat together like this," Jesus told His disciples, "until we are safely in the kingdom." "For as often as you eat this bread and drink this cup," Paul later wrote, "you proclaim the Lord's death till He comes" (1 Corinthians 11:26).

At the age of six, I underwent a very painful surgical procedure on my feet. I still bear considerable scars, and when I see them, I can still feel the postoperative pain. But they also remind me of something very important: Because of that painful moment, today I can walk. No, I can *run*.

So it is with the Communion service. It points us back to our world's worst moment when the awful truth of sin was on full display and our human shame was at its deepest. A quiet moment contemplating the shame of the cross can be overwhelming, and to that extent, the Communion service is indeed exceptionally somber. Sinners *must* be still in the presence of divine love.

But the Cross was not the end of Jesus' plan for us; He intends to come for us and forever enjoy *our* presence. We eat the bread and drink the cup solemnly; but at that same moment, our hearts begin to sing because we know that Jesus *will* come again.

Better Than Correction

For our citizenship is in heaven, from which we also eagerly wait for the Savior, the Lord Jesus Christ, who will transform our lowly body that it may be conformed to His glorious body, according to the working by which He is able even to subdue all things to Himself.
—Philippians 3:20, 21

A few years ago the American Society of Plastic Surgeons revealed that nearly sixteen million Americans spent 13.3 billion dollars on plastic surgery in 2015. These were not procedures to deal with burns, injuries, or genuine deformities: they were *beauty* procedures.★ Add to this the fact that consumers spend in the neighborhood of forty billion dollars a year on cosmetics, and someone might start to get the idea that Americans are obsessed with physical appearance. (And before we begin clucking our tongues about hedonistic Americans, we should probably understand that similar numbers are emerging all over the Western world.)

We are a society obsessed with appearance. We *tell* ourselves that a beautiful character is more important than one's physical allure, but the world we have built makes liars of us. Our TV screens idolize the young and the beautiful. Consumer products, from clothing and cars to detergents and diapers, are sold to us by improbable models whose images have been manufactured by the wizards of Photoshop.

Nor are we the first generation to do this. The ancient Greeks may not have had digital technology, but their art also promoted what was believed to be the ideal human form—a form that is clearly human and beautiful but did not resemble most real people.

It is almost as if we suspect that something is amiss with the human race. And as we begin to age and the imperfect bodies we were born with become even *more* imperfect, our suspicion grows into fear, particularly as we see the black finish line of life drawing closer: our imperfect lives end with death and decay.

And so we slap on more makeup, trying to pretend that it is not going to happen, much the same way that we try to make believe that sin does not hurt. But the solution is not found in covering up; the solution is found in the blood that covers. God has told us all along that we are no longer *truly* human, at least not in the sense of how we were originally created. "But I have a solution," our heavenly Father reminds us, "and My Son has already paid for it. Stick with Me, follow My Son, and soon I will transform your lowly body so that it will be like His glorious body."

It is better than correction; it is restoration.

★ *2015 Plastic Surgery Statistics*, American Society of Plastic Surgeons, https://www.plasticsurgery.org/documents/News/Statistics/2015/plastic-surgery-statistics-full-report-2015.pdf.

God's Greatest Reward

For what is our hope, our joy, or crown of rejoicing? Is it not even you in the presence of our Lord Jesus Christ at His coming? For you are our glory and joy.
—1 Thessalonians 2:19, 20

People often speak of golden streets and mansions when they describe the rewards of heaven, and rightly so. The language of the New Testament mentions such things in its description of our future reward. But, as with the things that matter most here on this earth, it is not *things* that make life pleasant, it is people. That thought can create a moment of panic in introverts (of which I am one), because relationships in this world can be fraught with complication.

An old preacher friend of mine used to say, "To dwell above with saints we love, oh that will be glory. To live below with saints we know, well, that's another story." It is an amusing ditty because we all know difficult people; and it is likely that we *are* the difficult people in someone else's life. Try as we might to get along, there are always going to be individuals in any given group who rub each other's fur the wrong way. Even the apostles Paul and Barnabas felt the need to part company after a sharp disagreement (Acts 15:39).

But we should not fail to notice Paul's insistence that his greatest reward in the world to come will be the Thessalonian believers who met Jesus through his ministry. Daniel also emphasizes the same point when he writes, "Those who are wise shall shine like the brightness of the firmament, and those who turn many to righteousness like the stars forever and ever" (Daniel 12:3).

The book of Revelation points out that Jesus plans to share His reward—His throne—with us. "To him who overcomes I will grant to sit with Me on My throne," He promised John (Revelation 3:21). Contrary to earthly kings, however, it would seem that Christ's throne is not considered a reward because of the power it represents, but (at least in part) because of the people He was able to redeem. Jesus was willing to go to Calvary "for the joy that was set before Him" (Hebrews 12:2).

Right now, we are still oriented toward self, which makes living together interesting and, more than occasionally, challenging. But when we finally all stand on Mount Zion with the Lamb, with the Father's name (or character) engraved in our hearts, we will understand why *people* are God's greatest reward.

The Rest of the Harvest

*But each one in his own order: Christ the first fruits, afterward those who are Christ's
at His coming. Then comes the end, when He delivers the kingdom to God the Father,
when He puts an end to all rule and all authority and power.*
—1 Corinthians 15:23, 24

I once saw an online discussion of the following question: Can someone who
does not believe in the literal resurrection of Jesus still be considered a Christian. Of course, in the Wild West of online debate, every conceivable opinion made
it to the table, and those of a more liberal bent insisted that one does not need to
believe in the miraculous parts of Christ's ministry to consider oneself Christian. To
admire His teachings is enough, they insist.

In one sense, they are right. We would not call a church-goer who reads the
teachings of Jesus a "Buddhist," after all; the only appropriate category to place them
in is "Christian." Likewise, a religious cult built around an understanding of Jesus,
even if it is wildly heretical, would still be "Christian" in the loosest sense of the
word.

But would denying the bodily resurrection be the faith that Christ intended His
followers to have? Not according to the New Testament. In his magnificent letter to
the Corinthian church, Paul insists that "if Christ is not risen, then our preaching is
empty and your faith is also empty" (1 Corinthians 15:14). Our future hope lies in
the fact that Jesus has already physically come back from the dead; a sinless human
Being who has taken our sins upon Himself and then conquered death, our greatest
enemy. The resurrection of Christ is not merely an interesting historical occurrence;
it is God's down payment on our future.

At the Feast of Firstfruits, the priest would take a sheaf of grain from the earliest
part of the harvest and "wave the sheaf before the LORD" (Leviticus 23:11). It was
simultaneously an act of gratitude for God's provision and an act of faith that the
rest of the harvest would soon follow. The resurrection of Christ, Paul tells us, is the
true wave-sheaf offering. Because Christ has risen from the dead as one of us—as a
human being—we can have confidence that the rest of the harvest will follow: we,
too, will one day rise from the dead.

The Resurrection is not merely a historical fact; it is the very cornerstone of
our hope. As we look back to the Cross, we know that we have something to look
forward to because Christ is not our past but our future.

Your Most Extravagant Gift

For I am already being poured out as a drink offering, and the time of my departure is at hand. I have fought the good fight, I have finished the race, I have kept the faith. Finally, there is laid up for me the crown of righteousness, which the Lord, the righteous Judge, will give to me on that Day, and not to me only but also to all who have loved His appearing.
—2 Timothy 4:6–8

B ack in 2016, Ezekiel Elliott, a rookie running back for the Dallas Cowboys, bought his parents a new house. He explained to reporters that his parents had sacrificed over the years to help propel him to success, and he wanted to give them something in return. When I read the story, I quietly whispered to myself, as I am sure thousands of people did, "Wouldn't it be nice to be able to give a gift like *that*? A whole house!"

Then I read Paul's letter to Timothy, and I realized that I am capable of far greater extravagance. My bank account is modest, and my resources are few; but I have at my disposal the greatest gift a person can give: my whole *life*. Houses can be rebuilt. Money can be replaced. But you only get one lifetime, and once it has been spent, it is gone forever. It is easily the most extravagant gift you can give. "Greater love has no one than this," Jesus told us, "than to lay down one's life for his friends" (John 15:13).

And to whom would I dare give such an extravagant gift? There is only one logical choice: to the One who sacrificed so profoundly for my future because even my life cannot approach what He has done for me. To give up your one and only life for Christ is not an attempt to pay for salvation, for it cannot be purchased by your efforts. It is a gift of love, a reckless, lavish expression of gratitude.

You do not have to throw yourself on a grenade or take a bullet in order to lay down your life for someone else; you can give your life away consciously, moment by moment, allowing yourself to be poured out completely for the sake of the gospel. You have full permission to stop worrying about tomorrow, wasting your time trying to satisfy the impossibly deep demands of self. Between now and the moment when Jesus returns, you can afford to be breathtakingly extravagant with your life, for you have eternity at your disposal. Give away every last second. Offer everyone a mansion in your Father's house. "For whoever desires to save his life will lose it, but whoever loses his life for My sake will save it" (Luke 9:24).

Our Incorruptible Inheritance

Blessed be the God and Father of our Lord Jesus Christ, who according to His abundant mercy has begotten us again to a living hope through the resurrection of Jesus Christ from the dead, to an inheritance incorruptible and undefiled and that does not fade away, reserved in heaven for you, who are kept by the power of God through faith for salvation ready to be revealed in the last time.
—1 Peter 1:3–5

There is a thrill that comes with buying something new. When I was a teenager, boom boxes, or "ghetto blasters" as we called them back then, were all the rage. At first, they only included radios and cassette tape players, but when CD players were suddenly available as part of the package, I was determined to have one. I began to sock away every cent I could lay my hands on for many months. I knew it was going to be a while before I could manage to purchase my prize, because (as some of you will remember) the first CD players were prohibitively expensive.

At long last, the anticipated day finally arrived. I proudly walked into a shop and presented a stack of carefully counted bills to the cashier, who in turn produced a large white box containing the very latest in portable sound technology. I had enough left over to buy a single CD, which cost in excess of thirty dollars at the time. Less than an hour later, I had the ghetto blaster out of the box in my room, and I became one of the first kids in town to listen to a compact disc.

I will not deny that it was an exhilarating experience. But a few months later, as with most purchases we make, the CD player began to seem ordinary. I enjoyed it, but it was no longer thrilling. After a couple of years, one of the mounts for the detachable speakers broke off, and it became nonportable. A few moves ago I found the remains of that once-loved ghetto blaster in a box, and when it failed to operate, I finally threw it out.

And so it goes with almost every experience. The pleasure associated with the things we reward ourselves with in this life passes quickly, and we find ourselves pining for something new so that we can recapture the thrill we felt last time. New clothes become threadbare, cars morph into derelict jalopies, and houses begin demanding costly repairs.

It will not always be so. While this world continues to deteriorate apart from God, Jesus has laid aside an incorruptible inheritance for us: an eternity in the presence of an eternal, incorruptible God whose deepest thrill comes from giving us rewards we cannot earn and do not deserve.

What God Has Not Revealed

But concerning the times and the seasons, brethren, you have no need that I should write to you.
For you yourselves know perfectly that the day of the Lord so comes as a thief in the night.
—1 Thessalonians 5:1, 2

Well, of *course*, we can't know the day or hour, Pastor! But Jesus never said we couldn't know the *year* He would return!" Phil studied me carefully to see if I was buying his argument. I was not. He glanced back down at the hastily scribbled diagram he had created on a scrap of paper to convince me that the time of Christ's return could be calculated from a string of "evidence" he had found in Scripture.

"Listen," I said. "I'm just as excited as you are about the fact that Jesus is returning soon. I'd love to mark it on my calendar too—but God hasn't given us any more than *soon*, and I'm sure He has a good reason for that. If people knew *exactly* when Jesus was coming, they'd probably put important decisions off to the last moment. The important thing is not knowing *when* Jesus is coming, but knowing the One who is coming, and meaningful relationships just can't be hastily assembled in the last few minutes."

The New Testament teaches that Jesus comes as a thief in the night; not because He sneaks into the world, but His arrival comes as a surprise. "But know this," Jesus explained to His disciples, "that if the master of the house had known what hour the thief would come, he would have watched and not allowed his house to be broken into. Therefore you also be ready, for the Son of Man is coming at an hour you do not expect" (Luke 12:39, 40).

When the disciples asked Jesus when to expect the establishment of His kingdom, He told them that the exact timing is not our business. "It is not for you to know times or seasons which the Father has put in His own authority," He said. "But you shall receive power when the Holy Spirit has come upon you; and you shall be witnesses to Me in Jerusalem, and in all Judea and Samaria, and to the end of the earth" (Acts 1:7, 8).

In other words, we have not been tasked with deciding when Jesus returns; we have been tasked with carrying the gospel to the world as we wait. There is easily enough work to do so that we do not have time to worry about specifics God has not revealed.

Pale Blue Dot

But I saw no temple in it, for the Lord God Almighty and the Lamb are its temple.
The city had no need of the sun or of the moon to shine in it, for the glory of God
illuminated it. The Lamb is its light. And the nations of those who are saved shall walk
in its light, and the kings of the earth bring their glory and honor into it.
—Revelation 21:22–24

On February 14, 1990, after almost twenty-three years in space, the *Voyager 1* space probe had completed its mission and was about to leave our solar system. At the request of Carl Sagan, NASA had the probe's camera look back at earth one last time and snap a picture from 3.7 billion miles (6 billion kilometers) away. In the photograph, known as *Pale Blue Dot*, the earth appears as a tiny mote of bright blue dust caught in a band of sunlight, less than a single pixel in size. It is a sobering image, demonstrating just how insignificant our world seems next to the immense expanse of the universe.

Carl Sagan, who was not a believer, famously presented the photo to an audience at Cornell University and said, "The Earth is a very small stage in a vast cosmic arena. . . . Our posturings, our imagined self-importance, the delusion that we have some privileged position in the Universe, are challenged by this point of pale light."★

In the view of modern atheists, the human race is an accident, the result of physical and chemical reactions in the universe. Nobody planned for us to be here. When existence on earth becomes hard and the trials of life begin to weigh us down, there is no point crying out to the heavens as the psalmist often did, because there is nobody listening. We are alone, we are remote, and we are insignificant.

But the Bible presents a different view. Not only are we *not* alone, but we also are the focus of God's universe. Jesus is not only coming to take us to be with Him in His Father's house (John 14:3), but He is also planning to move His center of operations to this world after a millennium of living and reigning with Him in heaven. We are the fallen planet, the least deserving place in all of God's creation, and yet He has chosen to display the magnificence of His loving character most fully by becoming one of us and eventually making this planet His personal home.

Pale blue dot? To a camera made by human beings, yes. But to God the Son? Absolutely not—it is a place that has utterly enraptured the heart of the One who made all the rest of the universe.

★ Quoted in Carl Sagan, *Pale Blue Dot: A Vision of the Human Future in Space* (New York: Ballantine Books, 1997), 6, 7.

As He Really Is

Now after six days Jesus took Peter, James, and John his brother,
led them up on a high mountain by themselves; and He was transfigured before them.
His face shone like the sun, and His clothes became as white as the light.
And behold, Moses and Elijah appeared to them, talking with Him.
—Matthew 17:1–3

Jesus makes a cryptic statement in the sixteenth chapter of Matthew, which has baffled countless readers of the modern era. "Assuredly, I say to you," Jesus told His disciples, "there are some standing here who shall not taste death till they see the Son of Man coming in His kingdom" (Matthew 16:28). How could this be true? The disciples have been dead for nearly two millennia, and Jesus has still not come.

The problem disappears when you remember that chapter and verse divisions were not added to the biblical text until the late Middle Ages. The close of chapter 16, in other words, is an artificial distinction, and the reader was meant to continue reading into the next chapter, where the story is completed. At the Transfiguration on the mount, some of the disciples did indeed catch a glimpse of Christ's return: Peter, James, and John saw Jesus transfigured into His glorious appearance, accompanied by a resurrected believer (Moses) and a translated believer (Elijah).

It was the second time that a Voice from heaven claimed Jesus as God's Son. "This is My beloved Son, in whom I am well pleased. Hear Him!" (Matthew 17:5). The incarnate Jesus was so ordinary, so much like us that it must have been easy to forget that He was the One who created us in the first place. Jesus' opponents certainly did not appreciate His uniqueness by looking at His physical appearance. But when divinity flashed through Jesus' humanity, it was as if the lights had suddenly been turned on, and the fallen state of our world became all too obvious. God's presence promptly made us aware of how decrepit the fallen race had become. Jesus' appearance was so intense that the disciples were paralyzed by fear, and Jesus had to reassure them: "Arise, and do not be afraid" (verse 7).

The moment will soon be here when the world will see the Son of God as He really is. There will be two reactions: some will cry for the rocks to fall on them; others will celebrate the fact that Jesus has finally come. Our task is to reveal Jesus to the world so that when He finally breaks through the eastern sky, it will be a moment marked with recognition and joy and not by fear.

Of Lollipops and the Inevitable

"If a man dies, shall he live again? All the days of my hard service I will wait, till my change comes. You shall call, and I will answer You; You shall desire the work of Your hands."
—Job 14:14, 15

It was a cool summer morning, and I was walking along a sidewalk in Ventura, California, when I suddenly spotted a half-melted lollipop on the sidewalk. I stopped to examine it, wondering why it was only half melted. *Perhaps,* I thought, *it was dropped in the afternoon when the sun was hot, and before it could finish melting into the hot concrete, the sun set, the air cooled, and the process stopped.*

I looked up at the hills; the sun was rising quickly in the east, and it would not be long before the sidewalk was hot again, and the destruction of the lollipop would be completed. It occurred to me that I was a lot like that piece of candy. As middle age approached, my body began to melt, as the first indications of mortality took hold of me. My eyesight began to fail, and my body began to hurt in new places. I found myself tiring more easily, and at one point, I struggled against a mysterious illness that threatened to take me out.

And then the deterioration of my body was suddenly arrested, and everything seemed to level out. I grew used to the new normal, the half-melted state of my body, and life continues happily. But I am painfully aware of the fact that before long, the sun will rise again, old age will seize me, and the painful process will be completed.

I will *not* be the only human being to escape the ultimate reality of death.

But that is where a discarded piece of confectionery and I part company. The lollipop will simply melt and disappear. The ants will consume what is left, and it will be forgotten because it is unimportant. You and I, on the other hand, are *not* unimportant: the Creator, as Job points out, *desires* us. He cannot bear the thought that we will be lost to the ravages of death forever.

So we wait. First, we wait for death to catch up to us, but with confidence, because we know that after death we will wait a short while until God Himself calls us back because He cannot bear the thought of an eternity where we are missing. And in that place, the Light, God Himself, becomes a source of eternal life.

Left Behind

"For behold, the day is coming, burning like an oven, and all the proud,
yes, all who do wickedly will be stubble. And the day which is coming
shall burn them up," says the LORD of hosts, "That will leave them neither root nor branch.
But to you who fear My name the Sun of Righteousness shall arise
with healing in His wings; and you shall go out and grow fat like stall-fed calves."
—Malachi 4:1, 2

In the 1990s, a new wave of secret rapture books—the Left Behind series—became an overnight sensation, selling millions of copies. It was the latest iteration of a theory born in the mid-nineteenth century, an explanation of the Second Coming that would have been utterly foreign to the Christians who lived during the eighteen hundred years that preceded its birth. The title *Left Behind* comes from the theory's assertion that Jesus will come secretly for the church, mysteriously evacuating them from the planet before a final seven-year tribulation. Those who are not taken to heaven with Jesus are "left behind" to brave the horrors of the antichrist, during which time they will have one final opportunity to repent.

The theory is a late interloper into Christian thought, completely unsupported by the authors of the Bible, who would likely be astonished that we managed to wrangle such nonsense from their writings. But that is not to say there is not a legitimate "left behind" story in the Bible; there is one that I am quite looking forward to.

Malachi indicates that those who enter the kingdom will encounter a Savior who has "healing in His wings," and they will "grow fat like stall-fed calves." It is the language of a new beginning. We enter the kingdom with new potential—the ability to grow up like newborn calves. That means that upon rising from the dead, there will be something left behind in the grave: the infirmity laid on the human race by our rebellion. As you turn through the pages of Genesis, the effects of sin on humanity become painfully obvious: Life spans become shorter and shorter. Disease takes hold of a race whose attachment to the Source of life has been severely compromised. Our minds have been warped by selfishness and sin, and our ability to learn and grow dramatically undermined.

Just as Jesus left His burial clothes behind in the tomb, you and I will be leaving the horrible consequences of sin behind. Our impairment will become a thing of the past; we will be free to sit in the school of Christ, learning from the infinite mind of God for all eternity. This life will be left behind, and we will finally be truly human, in the way God intended us to be.

The Giant Leap

I know a man in Christ who fourteen years ago—whether in the body I do not know,
or whether out of the body I do not know, God knows—such a one was caught up
to the third heaven. And I know such a man—whether in the body or out of the body
I do not know, God knows—how he was caught up into Paradise
and heard inexpressible words, which it is not lawful for a man to utter.
—2 Corinthians 12:2–4

It was on this date in 1969 that human beings first set foot on the moon. In the now-famous words of Neil Armstrong, it was "one small step for man, one giant leap for mankind."* We had just set foot on another astronomical body, having broken the bonds that hold us to this planet. In the minds of many, we had just liberated ourselves from Earth, having taken the first tottering steps toward our cosmic destiny.

But when the euphoria of local space travel dissipated, we quietly recognized that going any real distance in space is nearly impossible. To cross the distance to the next star system would require many generations, and any population living aboard a spacecraft for that long would be subject to the brutal ravages of cosmic radiation and the other negative effects of living in space. The unlikelihood of long-range space travel has forced us to dream of wormholes, which are described as folds in the space-time continuum that provide much-needed shortcuts across the universe.

A human expedition to another star system, in other words, is simply not likely to happen—at least not if you do not know the One who hung the stars in space. Somehow, angels manage to cross huge swaths of space in mere minutes. If you read the prayer of Daniel 9 aloud, which states that Gabriel started toward Daniel at the beginning of the prayer and appears by the end, you will discover that he made the trip in minutes. The scope of the universe is not beyond the One who made it in the first place.

Paul was privileged to make an early visit to heaven. He speaks in the third person to avoid bragging, but at some point, he was able to see Paradise. The experience was so real that he could not be sure whether he had traveled there in person or had seen it in vision. But one way or the other, God reached across the cosmos and brought him there.

I will admit that I have always been a little jealous of Neil Armstrong. But wherever Paradise is, we know that Jesus is presently there, preparing a place for us. When He comes, we will all finally be free of this world, and we will witness things that Armstrong could scarcely imagine.

---

* In reality, Armstrong said, "That's one small step for *a* man," but the word *a* was lost in transmission.

Worth the Wait

Therefore be patient, brethren, until the coming of the Lord. See how the farmer waits
for the precious fruit of the earth, waiting patiently for it until it receives the early and latter rain.
You also be patient. Establish your hearts, for the coming of the Lord is at hand.
—James 5:7, 8

I am, by nature, a very impatient man. If my flight is at noon, I am at the airport by nine o'clock, pacing the floor, waiting for the gate agent to open the door and let me board. If I am driving somewhere, I rarely, if ever, take breaks along the way, preferring to push through to my destination as quickly as possible. I show up for meetings an hour early.

So you can imagine how I feel about the Second Coming. I know it is real, and I know it will happen soon, so I want it to happen *now*. I have had quite enough of life on a fallen planet, and I have studied the promises of Scripture thoroughly enough to know that I am ready to move on. And in that respect, all Christians are by nature impatient: we all yearn for the moment when we see Jesus face-to-face, and we are reunited with Him forever. It cannot come quickly enough.

But James, while recognizing that the return of Christ is "at hand," suggests that we will need to cultivate patience—the kind of patience a farmer exercises when waiting for his crops. The sanctuary services prophesied the entire plan of salvation over the course of the agricultural year: beginning with the spring festivals and the early rain and ending with the fall festivals. There is intentionality in God's plan to save us. The ministry of Christ begins with the Incarnation, the sacrifice at the cross, the Resurrection, and the birth of the church. Then the long summer passes, after which we experience the final warnings, the judgment, and the moment when Jesus will "tabernacle" with us forever. God is working out a plan that covers every conceivable eventuality.

Be patient, James says. The Second Coming is soon, and it will be well worth the wait.

Staring Into Heaven

And while they looked steadfastly toward heaven as He went up, behold,
two men stood by them in white apparel, who also said, "Men of Galilee,
why do you stand gazing up into heaven? This same Jesus, who was taken up from you
into heaven, will so come in like manner as you saw Him go into heaven."
—Acts 1:10, 11

Making prophecy charts is fun. The thrill of tracing Daniel's startling predictions over many centuries is hard to describe; it was this exercise that finally made a believer of me. The statue of Nebuchadnezzar's dream, the animals rising up from the sea in Daniel 7, the stunning time prophecies of Daniel 8 and 9—they are some of the most compelling written material ever authored, clear evidence that the mind of God drove the composition of the Bible.

The material is *so* compelling, in fact, that I can find it hard to drag myself away from my study to do the actual work Jesus gave us to do. While we are never to neglect the prayerful study of God's Word, our primary task is not to figure out every intricate detail of prophecy but to carry the gospel to a dying world.

As Jesus disappeared into the clouds, out of sight, the disciples naturally lingered on the mountaintop, trying to catch one last glimpse of the One whose life and ministry had changed them so radically. You and I would have done the same thing; even though Jesus had just promised to return, the thought of losing Him, even for the short term, would have been overwhelming.

Angels suddenly appeared to the disciples. Perhaps they had been among those who first appeared to the shepherds when Jesus was born, exuberantly announcing His entrance into our world. Now, at the close of Christ's earthly ministry, angels once again announced the next phase of salvation history: the church was to start its work right away. "Why are you standing here, staring up into heaven?" they asked. "He told you He'd come back, so it's time to head back down the mountain into a world that's waiting to hear from you."

By all means, never let a day pass by where you do not fill your heart with the hope of Christ's return. But as you wait, do not spend every last minute staring into heaven, wondering *when*. There is more than enough work to do, and precious few moments to do it. The task is all consuming enough to make the time fly quickly, and the voice of Jesus Himself will let you know when it is time to stop and look back up to the clouds.

When Will I Use This?

*Whatever your hand finds to do, do it with your might; for there is no work
or device or knowledge or wisdom in the grave where you are going.*
—Ecclesiastes 9:10

The saying "I know one thing: that I know nothing" has been apocryphally attributed to the Greek philosopher Socrates, even though Socrates himself wrote nothing, and Plato's account of Socrates does not include this statement. People use the statement to emphasize the idea that the more we learn, the more obvious it becomes how little we actually know. Confucius is remembered to have said something similar: "To know what you know and what you do not know, that is true knowledge."

I have often pondered the human thirst for knowledge, marveling that many of us spend our lives cramming our heads full of knowledge that will do us no good once we have died. I find myself drawn irresistibly to books; there are never fewer than ten or fifteen piled up on my night table, with Post-it notes protruding from the edges of pages I find meaningful. The more I read, the more my thirst for knowledge deepens. The pile of books in my basement, already thousands of titles deep, is doomed to swell by thousands more before the clock runs out on my life.

Have you ever found yourself wondering what the point of continual learning might be? It makes sense for a young person to learn; he or she will acquire knowledge that will serve throughout the short decades of life still ahead. But what good is there in picking up another book, learning something new, when you are past the age of eighty? When will you ever use it?

The author of Ecclesiastes expends considerable effort bemoaning the pointlessness of life. Everything you do, achieve, or learn will be washed away by the tides of time. A few generations from now everything you managed to accomplish with your life will be long forgotten or will have become meaningless to the few people who might remember your name.

So what is the point? The author gives the answer, "He has put eternity in their hearts" (Ecclesiastes 3:11). The grave might be the end for this life, but the character we develop now will prove to be a springboard for the eternal existence Jesus will grant us when He comes to rouse us from our sleep and start us on a life that will prove to be far more real than this one.

The Power of His Voice

"Do not marvel at this; for the hour is coming in which all who are in the graves will hear
His voice and come forth—those who have done good, to the resurrection of life,
and those who have done evil, to the resurrection of condemnation."
—John 5:28, 29

While the minds of modern human beings struggle to understand how our universe burst into existence—how something came from nothing—the book of Genesis knows no such struggle. To our forefathers, the secret of our existence is simple: "By the word of the LORD the heavens were made, and all the host of them by the breath of His mouth" (Psalm 33:6). God spoke, and the universe came into being.

It is that same Voice that eventually brings us back from the icy silence of death. Without exception, every human being who has ever lived will one day hear the voice of Christ beckoning them back to life. The power that called our world into existence and first breathed into our nostrils the breath of life is the same power that will reanimate our bodies for the grand climax of history.

During this life, not everyone will respond to the final call to "worship Him who made heaven and earth, the sea and springs of water" (Revelation 14:7). Not everyone will acknowledge Jesus as Lord. But we will all respond to His voice; some to the resurrection of life, and others to the resurrection of condemnation. We will all know, beyond any shadow of doubt, who the Creator is as He wakes each of us from our mortal slumber. Even those whose minds have rejected His lordship cannot help but have the very cells of their bodies respond to the prompting of the God who made them. At that moment, His power and His claim on us will be abundantly obvious to all. Every knee will bow, and every tongue will confess that Jesus Christ is Lord.

But not every person will be destined for the kingdom because while the very elements know the voice of their Maker, these people's hearts have rejected Him. Some will be raised in the "resurrection of condemnation." They have no future with a God they will not love, and rather than go on living a torturous existence apart from Him, God eventually removes them from creation altogether after the final judgment.

The task that lies ahead of us is of utmost importance: displaying the character of God so convincingly that our world begins to respond to the creative power in His voice even now, before the final call.

Willing to Lose Eternity

For I could wish that I myself were accursed from Christ for my brethren,
my countrymen according to the flesh.

—Romans 9:3

The early Celtic church—the one that existed before the Synod of Whitby in A.D. 664—was distinct from the organized church centered in Rome. It grew up in isolation, with passionate missionaries as its founders and hand-illuminated copies of Scripture as its founding document. As author Derek Wilson points out in his biography of Charlemagne, "Celtic Christianity was itself an indigenous expression of the 'faith once given' and not a carbon copy of the church life of Rome."★

One of the key differences between this remote church, which evangelized Europe from outside the boundaries of the empire, was its organizational structure. When the western Roman Empire collapsed, the church, which had been given privileged status after Constantine, began to fill the governmental void left behind as what was left of the Roman Empire progressively withdrew to Constantinople in the east. Clergy began to take over control of *dioceses*, which were managerial units of the empire; to this day, the more traditional Christian churches continue to divide their territories into these Roman units of power.

The Celts, on the other hand, seemed unconcerned with establishing power bases, choosing instead to establish humble monasteries across the continent. Instead of bishops, they had abbots, the heads of monastic settlements. Rather than establish large cathedrals and diocesan centers, they built modest stone huts where monks concerned themselves with copying manuscripts and teaching.

Their work was marked by willing deprivation and selfless sacrifice. Their passion was not organization; it was people. They were less concerned with worldly achievements than with heralding the kingdom of Christ. The European map is dotted with their settlements to this day, from the British Isles clear down to the Italian peninsula. As a result, they managed to preserve biblical Christianity through a period of time when the organized church of Europe began to compromise. To a large extent, we have ancient Celtic Christians to thank for the faith we now enjoy.

The spirit of selfless evangelism marks true biblical Christianity. Paul considered his own salvation less important than the salvation of his fellow countrymen and was willing to lose eternity if someone else could find it. And that, of course, is the spirit of Christ, who was willing to humble Himself if it meant that you could find a place in His kingdom.

★ Derek Wilson, *Charlemagne* (New York: Vintage Books, 2005), 18.

JULY 26

Not for One Moment

Also she had a great and high wall with twelve gates, and twelve angels at the gates,
and names written on them, which are the names of the twelve tribes of the children of Israel:
three gates on the east, three gates on the north, three gates on the south,
and three gates on the west. Now the wall of the city had twelve foundations,
and on them were the names of the twelve apostles of the Lamb.
—Revelation 21:12–14

It is to our detriment that modern Christianity has de-emphasized the Old Testament, treating it as something transitory, with little to offer the more enlightened believer who has access to the New Testament. To the contrary, it is nearly impossible to understand the New Testament without the Old, and one of the most fascinating fields of study is to be found in the rites and rituals of the Old Testament sanctuary service.

Almost every detail reveals something important about Christ, including the layout of the camp itself. According to the second chapter of Numbers, when the children of Israel pitched camp en route to Canaan, they followed a very precise order. The tabernacle was erected in the middle of the camp, with the Levites in a tight circle around it. Then the remaining tribes pitched camp outside of that circle, with three tribes at each of the four points of the compass. The Shekinah glory—the presence of Christ Himself—would descend into the tabernacle and take up residence in the Most Holy Place.

It was as close an approach to the presence of God as human beings could have on this side of eternity and was a visible reminder that God's ultimate purpose was to bring them fully back into His presence, one day reopening the way to the tree of life.

As John is shown the New Jerusalem, he sees the fulfillment of God's promise. There are twelve gates to the city, each of which is labeled with the name of one of the twelve tribes. Similarly, the foundations are named for the apostles. The gates are not sealed but are open, and like the Most Holy Place, the city itself is fashioned in the shape of a cube. God's people, at long last, have been brought back into close communion with their Creator.

It provides a breathtaking picture. God did not abandon us to our doom when we chose to rebel against Him but chose, instead, to keep us as close as possible until the controversy between Christ and Satan had come to a close, and He could throw open the gates and bring us home. Not for one moment have God's people been left to their own defenses, and the moment is soon coming when no defenses will be needed at all.

No Cold Interests

"Men, why are you doing these things? We also are men with the same nature as you,
and preach to you that you should turn from these useless things to the living God,
who made the heaven, the earth, the sea, and all things that are in them,
who in bygone generations allowed all nations to walk in their own ways.
Nevertheless He did not leave Himself without witness, in that He did good,
gave us rain from heaven and fruitful seasons, filling our hearts with food and gladness."
—Acts 14:15–17

As far as evangelistic projects go, Paul and Barnabas's mission to the city of Lystra looked like an unmitigated disaster—at least by modern standards. A lame man was miraculously healed, and the citizens of the city took it as a sign that the pagan gods had suddenly appeared in their midst. They hastily prepared to worship Paul and Barnabas.

Paul, however, recognized what was happening. The people of Lystra were so hungry for truth that they jumped at the first thing that looked right to them. Their response was wildly inappropriate, but their motive appeared to be right. Pay careful attention to Paul's response, because it holds valuable keys for sharing our faith today. First of all, Paul preached a message similar to the first angel's message: worship Him "who made the heaven, the earth, the sea, and all things that are in them." Second, he framed his presentation in the context of the great controversy: "who in bygone generations allowed all nations to walk in their own ways." Finally, he pointed to what is perhaps the most important evangelistic principle: God "did not leave Himself without witness."

Turn through the pages of the book of Acts, and you will find something that comes as a surprise to many modern Christians: There are no cold interests. Every time the disciples baptized someone, it was someone already responding to the Holy Spirit. On the Day of Pentecost, Peter baptized "devout men." Saul had an encounter with Jesus before Ananias was sent in to work with him. Cornelius, the first Gentile convert, is described as "a just man, one who fears God."

We do not *convert* people; that is beyond our capacity. Rather, we *appeal* to those God is already converting. Perhaps the best skill you can cultivate when it comes to sharing your faith is to *listen*—to determine where God has already been at work with someone. Long before you make contact with someone who is interested in Jesus, God has already been there, stirring the heart. You are the last piece of the puzzle, the one God uses to appeal to people to act on the conviction that God has already created.

Lord, open our eyes so that we can learn to see the people around us who are already waking up.

#Forgiven

"For I know that my Redeemer lives, and He shall stand at last on the earth;
and after my skin is destroyed, this I know, that in my flesh I shall see God, whom I shall see
for myself, and my eyes shall behold, and not another. How my heart yearns within me!"
—Job 19:25–27

Justine Sacco, once the head of global communications for a successful digital media company, made an incredibly thoughtless mistake. As she waited for her plane at London's Heathrow airport, she tweeted an ill-conceived and tasteless joke to her 170 Twitter followers. It was an AIDS joke apparently meant to mock racism, but it came off as racist to the many people who saw it. She slept on the long flight to South Africa, blissfully unaware of what was taking place online.

When she landed, she turned on her phone and received a text from a friend. "I'm so sorry to see what's happening," it read. It was more than a little baffling. But in the next few minutes, she discovered that she had become the number one trending hashtag on Twitter: #hasjustinelandedyet. Her tweet had gone viral; millions of people around the world had been waiting for her flight to land, so they could revel in the public shaming she was about to receive. Someone snapped her picture in the airport and posted it online to let the world know their victim had arrived.

Was her tweet tasteless? Absolutely. Did she deserve the online pile on she received, which included violent language and death threats? No. She ended up losing her job, was unemployed for a year, and had to resort to online reputation managers to try and recoup what was left of her life.

Her experience says a lot about human nature. We are often dark, heartless, and unforgiving, willing to destroy a stranger with the click of a mouse. We love to punish people we do not even know from afar, protected by the anonymity that the internet offers us.

Justine's story points us forward to another day. All of us struggle through one short lifetime, accumulating many mistakes along the way. Our life record is besotted by sin, and at the end of it all, we sleep. But when we wake up, Someone is waiting for us—Someone who knows full well what we did. But because He loves us, He already bore all of our shame for us. And while we slept, He prepared a brand-new life where we get to leave every mistake behind forever and hold our heads high at His expense.

Oh, how my heart yearns within me.

"Eye Has Not Seen"

But as it is written: "Eye has not seen, nor ear heard, nor have entered into the heart of man the things which God has prepared for those who love Him."
—1 Corinthians 2:9

I do not know whether there is anything more tragic than an unfinished life. Every day millions of people slip into silence, their lives unfinished. Some had always meant to write a book; their thoughts, some of which were important, have now vanished and are permanently unavailable. Some had great symphonies etched in their hearts that never made it to paper, let alone an orchestra pit. There were those who might have been surgeons, philosophers, teachers, engineers; but because life is too short to engage more than one discipline well (except for those rare exceptions), we will never know what they might have accomplished.

Some people I have encountered, who have had a premature brush with death, have reported how it was not the possibility of dying that frightened them; it was the idea that they had been cheated of time. There were things they had always meant to do: children to raise, people to talk to, sights to see, and things to achieve. They were surprised by the clock, not expecting that they would run out of time as quickly as they did, and they experienced painful regret at the thought of a mostly unfinished to-do list.

The Christian has the gift of knowing that what this world has to offer will pale in comparison with what is in store. No symphony written on this side could ever compare to what might be possible in the earth made new. No book written could ever affect an audience like one written across the vast reaches of eternity, with the very presence of Christ available for inspiration. No project undertaken could ever mean as much as one that is finally free from the taint of sin.

We do not have to face the grave believing that much has been lost; at our next conscious moment, we will realize just how much there is to gain. "Eye has not seen, nor ear heard," Paul wrote, "nor have entered into the heart of man the things which God has prepared for those who love Him." Perhaps some of your dreams have been planted in your heart not for this life, where they would be tepid, but for the life to come, where they will shine. The philosopher once wrote, after all, that God has already "put eternity in [our] hearts" (Ecclesiastes 3:11).

"Behold, This Is Our God"

And it will be said in that day: "Behold, this is our God; we have waited for Him, and He will save us. This is the LORD; we have waited for Him; we will be glad and rejoice in His salvation."

—Isaiah 25:9

One of the deepest longings of the human heart is the desire to understand who we truly are. When we are children, the answer comes easily; we are the child of So-and-So, and we are five years old. Our place in the universe is obvious. As we grow a little older, we choose a career path, and we define ourselves by how we spend our days: *I am a dentist. I am a carpenter. I am a PhD student.*

But eventually the moment comes when the easy answers start to disappear, and we become less certain of who we are and where we belong. We find that the things we do and the people we know do not easily define who *we* are. We begin to ache for something deeper, more meaningful, and we miss the easy certainty we enjoyed when we were younger.

Millions can identify with the existential angst expressed by the bleak twentieth-century Marxist philosopher Jean-Paul Sartre (whose philosophy I quote by way of illustration, not endorsement): "I want to leave, go to some place where I will be really in my own niche, where I will fit in.... But my place is nowhere; I am unwanted."★

Your own struggle might not be as discouraging as his, but chances are you have at least occasionally felt what he described. *Who am I?* may just be the most frequently, albeit silently, asked question. Sure, we understand some of our roles: we are parents, employees, bosses, siblings, and/or friends. But beyond that, we struggle to understand the core essence of who we really *are*, longing to know exactly why we have been placed in this world. We do not just want to know our function; we want to know our place.

But all such questions will vanish in a heartbeat when the Son of man finally breaks through the eastern sky, "in the glory of His Father with His angels" (Matthew 16:27). Those whose hearts have become entwined with His over the course of a lifetime will look up and instinctively recognize Him. The deepest hungers of our hearts will suddenly be satisfied as we see our Creator's face, and at that very moment, we will know exactly who we are and precisely where we belong.

Behold, this is our God.

★ Jean-Paul Sartre, *Nausea*, trans. Lloyd Alexander (New York: New Directions, 2007), 122.

The Way Heaven Sees

Say to those who are fearful-hearted, "Be strong, do not fear! Behold, your God will come
with vengeance, with the recompense of God; He will come and save you."
Then the eyes of the blind shall be opened, and the ears of the deaf shall be unstopped.
—Isaiah 35:4, 5

Beethoven is rumored to have said, "Beethoven can write music, thank God, but he can do nothing else on earth." Music was his passion and his reason for living. If he really spoke these words, it only serves to underscore the magnitude of his personal tragedy: he eventually lost the ability to hear the very music he composed. There are a number of theories about *why* he lost his hearing: some blame disease, others blame the severe beatings his father used to give him as a boy, and still others suspect lead poisoning because the substance was discovered in a lock of his hair.

Whatever caused it, it is doubtless one of the most heart-wrenching stories from the nineteenth century: arguably the greatest composer who ever lived became deaf. It is a thought that has often plagued me because it seems so unjust.

At least, the great composer was able to hear music in the earlier stages of his career and knew what it *should* sound like. There are those among us who have suffered worse: They see our lips moving, they notice us responding to music, and they see our heads tilt back in silent laughter. Because they were born deaf, they have no idea what it sounds like. The same holds true for those born blind: we can try to describe the colors of a sunset to them all we want, but they have no point of reference and cannot imagine what we have been privileged to see.

God's promise is that the suffering comes to a permanent end when Jesus returns. He promises that "every eye" will see Jesus return (Revelation 1:7), and "the eyes of the blind shall be opened, and the ears of the deaf shall be unstopped." Imagine this: the very first thing some people will hear is the voice of Jesus, and the first thing they will ever see is His face.

As for the rest of us, who now "see in a mirror, dimly" (1 Corinthians 13:12), I suspect we will also be surprised at how much better we see and hear once this world of sin recedes into the distant past. We might just find that we were also virtually blind and deaf when we begin to see the world the way heaven does.

August

I accept the biblical teaching of spiritual gifts and believe that the gift of prophecy is one of the identifying marks of the remnant church.

In the Hands of God

Can the Ethiopian change his skin or the leopard its spots?
Then may you also do good who are accustomed to do evil.
—Jeremiah 13:23

At the dawn of the twentieth century, the Western world was brimming with hope. The nations of Europe had enjoyed a long period of peace, free from the kind of warfare that had marked their earlier history. Significant advances had been made in scientific knowledge and the mechanization of industry, and the ranks of the middle class began to swell. Politicians became fond of making optimistic speeches about the utopia that lay ahead in the twentieth century; it was widely anticipated that many of the ills that plagued the human race would disappear.

They could not have been more wrong. The twentieth century proved to be one of the bloodiest in human history, with more than two hundred million meeting their demise through warfare. The mechanization of industry made us far more efficient at killing, and scientific thinking took a twisted turn as we applied the dark science of eugenics to people groups deemed undesirable or problematic. We may have produced inexpensive consumer goods on a mass scale, but we also opened death camps to systematically slaughter millions. Atomic energy was used to kill before it was used to power our homes.

The human heart, left to its own devices, can be a frightening thing. Sin, it turns out, is not merely a dirt smudge on our souls but a baked-in problem that we cannot eliminate. We may have been created in the image of God originally, but apart from a relationship with the Creator, the creative gifts and ingenuity we have been blessed with invariably turn toward selfishness and evil. We are as helpless to change our sinful ways as we are to change the color of our skin.

In the hands of God, however, the human heart becomes a wondrous thing. It begins to shed its dark cloak of selfishness and turn outward again, focusing on the welfare of others. Our abilities are transformed into spiritual gifts, which are used to display the selfless, loving character of God in such a way that people are irresistibly drawn toward Him. We provide rather than horde and heal rather than kill. Instead of preaching futile optimism in human progress, the godly practice of spiritual gifts gives the world genuine hope in a kingdom that will sweep away the vain utopian efforts of human kings and empires.

AUGUST 2

The Image of God

So God created man in His own image;
in the image of God He created him; male and female He created them.
—Genesis 1:27

In stark opposition to the meaningless origins of the human race posited by modern disciples of Darwin, we find God's assertion that we were made in His image. While there is a definite demarcation between human beings and God, and God is quite distinct from His creation, His fingerprints can be found on each of us. Our ability to be creative, for example, displays the creative nature of the One who made us, and our capacity to love stems from our genesis at the hands of the One whose very existence defines love.

Our ability to reflect the nature and character of God has been sharply compromised by our fall into sin. With a sinful nature, we prefer to love self instead of others. We invent and create to our own glory, rather than the glory of our heavenly Father.

But in the practice of spiritual gifts, we have been given a unique opportunity; we can once again use our God-given abilities to glorify the Creator. Consider the days of Creation. On the first day, God brought light into existence by simply uttering the words, "Let there be light" (Genesis 1:3). You and I do not have power over the elements, for we are mere creatures, yet we have been privileged to practice a similar creativity. "You are the light of the world," Jesus explained to His disciples (Matthew 5:14). By using spiritual gifts such as teaching, preaching, and godly living, we have been given the chance to shed light in a world that has been horrifically darkened by sin.

During the Creation week, God separated the dry land from the water and covered the earth with vegetation and endless varieties of animal life, creating the perfect habitat for our first parents; so perfect, in fact, that it was paradise. Among the spiritual gifts mentioned in the New Testament, we find exhortation, generosity, and mercy (Romans 12:8), gifts that are focused on the well-being of others. We will never have the ability to speak an actual garden into existence, but we have been given the ability to create a sanctuary for others as we wait for Jesus to return.

Spiritual gifts, in other words, are an act of re-creation, where the image of God once again begins to shine through us.

As He Wills

But one and the same Spirit works all these things,
distributing to each one individually as He wills.
—1 Corinthians 12:11

One of the greatest modern misunderstandings of spiritual gifts is handily refuted by a single passage from Paul's letters. Many years ago, before I became a full-fledged Christian believer, I was invited to a church service by a friend. It was quite unconventional and unlike anything I had seen growing up in a Dutch Calvinist congregation. Instead of an actual church building, the group had rented a commercial storefront, which has become more commonplace today but was rare at the time. During the service—perhaps the word *program* would be more accurate—nobody opened a Bible, and there was no expository preaching of its contents.

Instead, a man stood at the front and explained how a very special spiritual gift was available to everyone in the audience if they only learned how to exercise it. To receive the gift, he explained, all you had to do was "clear your mind" and "just let it happen." Alarm bells immediately sounded in my head: I might not have been a practicing Christian at the time, but I knew better than to clear my mind and mindlessly accept the influence of anything.

The special gift, it turns out, was uncontrollable laughter that incapacitated those who came under its influence. All around me people started dropping to the floor, convulsing with wild giggle fits. It was more than a little disconcerting, to say the least. As with "speaking in tongues," the charismatic fad of the earlier twentieth century, the manifestation of "holy laughter" was offered as indisputable proof of having been "baptized in the Spirit."

Never mind that you will find no such "gift" manifesting itself in the New Testament church; the entire premise is wrong. The Bible does not describe a single spiritual gift that all must have as proof of the Spirit's presence, and it certainly does not teach that we can decide which gifts we receive from God. The Holy Spirit decides which of the spiritual gifts He wants each of us to have, "distributing to each one individually as He wills."

If you think about it, it is the best arrangement. God knows you better than you know yourself and will never make a mistake in how He decides you can best play a powerful role in revealing His character to the world.

Called to Be You

*There are diversities of gifts, but the same Spirit. There are differences of ministries, but the same
Lord. And there are diversities of activities, but it is the same God who works all in all.*
—1 Corinthians 12:4–6

There has been a disturbing trend in recent years to silence dissent on university campuses. Students demand "safe spaces" where they can be sheltered from or recuperate after being "triggered" by ideas that run contrary to their preferred way of thinking. Sometimes, the hostility toward dissent even spills over into physical violence and riots. It is eerily reminiscent of the world George Orwell anticipated in his novel *1984*, in which the government even regulates and rewrites language to maintain conformity of thought.

It is a disturbing trend because coerced conformity of thought is a signature characteristic of authoritarian regimes; in order to maintain their grip on power, totalitarians have generally disallowed differences of opinion. Christians should be especially alert to such trends as the world careens toward the moment when all the world marvels and follows the beast (see Revelation 13:3).

There is another place where Christians should be vigilant against group-think. We often tend to see certain personality traits as universally desirable, and we judge the quality of others' spirituality by whether or not they seem to have certain gifts and abilities. The ideal Christian man or woman is easy to imagine. Heavily influenced by the growing preference for extroversion that emerged in the West at the beginning of the twentieth century, we often expect our fellow believers to follow in the footsteps of Dale Carnegie. We believe a good Christian should be a gifted leader and a skilled prayer warrior; he or she must be comfortable striking up conversations with strangers, be willing to open his or her home for Bible study, must be good with children, must be willing to transparently share a personal testimony at the drop of a hat, and so on.

It is not the picture of the church presented in the Bible, however. Far from presenting uniformity of thought and action as the ideal for the church, Scripture underlines how, while we all worship one God and are influenced by one Spirit, we still retain our individuality. God does not expect us to mimic famous Christians when we use our gifts. He does not call us into His work because we are *like* everybody else; He uses us in the work because we are *not* like everybody else. You are called by God, in other words, to be *you*.

All Gates Open

*Also she had a great and high wall with twelve gates, and twelve angels at the gates,
and names written on them, which are the names of the twelve tribes of the children of Israel:
three gates on the east, three gates on the north, three gates on the south,
and three gates on the west. Now the wall of the city had twelve foundations,
and on them were the names of the twelve apostles of the Lamb.*
—Revelation 21:12–14

The Holy City—the place where God will dwell with His people forever—
has the names of the twelve tribes of Israel on its twelve gates. It doubtless
hearkens back to the arrangement found in the camp of Israel, where three tribes
were positioned on each side of the tabernacle, and the dimensions of the city likely
reflect the dimensions of the Most Holy Place, which was equal in height, breadth,
and depth.

The twelve tribes and the twelve apostles had similar commissions. The twelve
tribes were to serve as a light to the Gentiles, inviting them into a relationship with
God (Isaiah 49:6). The apostles were commissioned to go and make disciples of all
nations (Matthew 28:19). The names inscribed on the city—on the foundations and
on the gates to the city—are the names of those who live with God forever but are
also the names of those who were tasked with the work of evangelism.

Each of the tribes of Israel was known for distinctive characteristics. When they
pitched camp, they each flew their own standards (Numbers 2:2), and they were all
described as having unique characteristics by Jacob (Genesis 49). You are not expected to be exactly like everyone else in your service to God; you are unique while,
at the same time, part of the one city of God. What matters is that you become a
gate to the city, using your gifts to invite the world into a saving relationship with
Christ. You have not been asked to surrender your identity to become a carbon
copy of someone else, because God intends to use you to serve as an access point to
the kingdom for someone else. To be sure, Christ is the only way back to the Father,
but God uses many different people as an introduction point to Jesus.

When a church relies solely on the pastor or an evangelist for outreach, it is
missing the mark. Any given individual only appeals to a certain number of people,
and when evangelistic effort relies on one or two people, you have dramatically
narrowed the number of available gates. Open all of the gates, however, and use
everyone's gifts, and you will watch far more people move through them into a
saving relationship with Jesus.

AUGUST 6

It Takes a Chorus

For as we have many members in one body, but all the members do not have the same function,
so we, being many, are one body in Christ, and individually members of one another.
—Romans 12:4, 5

Beethoven's Ninth Symphony, from which we derive our hymn "Ode to Joy," is certainly one of the most recognizable compositions in history, and there are many who consider it to be among the finest works of all time. Few people fail to be stirred when they sit through a live performance; it speaks profoundly to the human heart. Even though many of the listeners might not possess a musical education and thus the grammar of the art form, we still all instinctively understand the language of music.

But imagine a solo performance of the symphony. The "Ode to Joy" movement cannot be performed with a single voice. A soloist might be able to produce a recognizable melody, alerting you to the fact that the tune was born of Beethoven's mind. But the recital will feel thin and incomplete, and the true mind of the composer will not be revealed the way he intended. There will be something of Beethoven there, but it will not truly be Beethoven.

Now consider spiritual gifts. Paul compares our gifts to body parts, emphasizing that together, we make up a single body—that of Christ. It has become popular to believe that Christians can dispense with organized religion and perform the works of the kingdom on their own. But God did not bless any single individual with all of the gifts of the Spirit, intending instead that we use them in concert with others.

To be sure, a single individual acting alone can still produce something that reveals a glimpse of Jesus, but it will be thin and incomplete, like a soloist attempting a choral symphony alone. A single voice will not truly reveal Christ in all His fullness, and the intended audience—the nations, kindreds, tongues, and peoples of this world—will be deprived of the majestic work that God designed for them to hear.

Not even God, you will notice, is a solo act. The Bible reveals the one true God as Three Persons who act in perfect concert with each Other, each assuming different roles in the performance of God's will. Can we expect any less of God's people? As we use our gifts in harmony with others, an unmistakable image begins to emerge, a picture of Christ so rich that it instinctively stirs the hearts of all who witness it.

In Need of Others

"How you are fallen from heaven, O Lucifer, son of the morning! How you are cut down to the ground, you who weakened the nations! For you have said in your heart: 'I will ascend into heaven, I will exalt my throne above the stars of God; I will also sit on the mount of the congregation on the farthest sides of the north.' "
—Isaiah 14:12, 13

One of the finest gifts a Christian can possess is the gift of discernment. It is a gift that gives you the ability to detect theological falsehood at a glance and enables you to diagnose trouble before it starts. There is another form of discernment that is also incredibly useful: the ability to know when someone else is more suited to a particular task than you are.

The Bible reveals that while Lucifer held one of the highest stations in heaven—he was a covering cherub, positioned immediately next to the throne of God—he became dissatisfied with his post. Instead of being grateful and content with his position as a highly exalted creature, he became jealous of the fact that he was not a member of the Godhead. He chose to stop believing that God was better suited to the throne than he was.

We can find something of Lucifer in our own jealousies. Instead of recognizing and rejoicing when someone has been discovered to be uniquely gifted for a role in the body of Christ, we can often feel dissatisfied with our own unique roles and covet what others have. The ugliness of pride will often surface around nominating committee time when we sometimes see people clambering for what are perceived to be the more noble posts in the church.

Even a brief look at the business world shows us what is wrong with that. The world's most successful chief executive officers are not usually successful because they possess every ability needed to run an effective company; they are potent administrators because they know how to surround themselves with people who are capable of doing what they cannot do half as well.

The exercise of spiritual gifts is an act of faith. Rather than grow envious of others, we must learn to believe that the gifts we have been given are crucial to the work of the church.

"And the eye cannot say to the hand, 'I have no need of you,' " Paul reminds us, "nor again the head to the feet, 'I have no need of you.' No, much rather, those members of the body which seem to be weaker are necessary" (1 Corinthians 12:21, 22).

Not only do you need the church, but the church needs you.

You Already Have It

Then Moses answered and said, "But suppose they will not believe me or listen to my voice;
suppose they say, 'The LORD has not appeared to you.'"
So the LORD said to him,
"What is that in your hand?"
He said, "A rod."

—Exodus 4:1, 2

Perhaps it has something to do with the way the church has become consumer oriented in much of the Western world—a situation that encourages laypeople to play spectator and watch the "professional" ministers do the work of the church. As a result, many church members feel inadequate to do the work of evangelism. They are not naturally comfortable with public speaking, they lack seminary degrees, and more than occasionally, they feel as if they do not know enough to share Christ with someone else.

In the world of spiritual gifts, however, God does not give us everything we need up front, making us comfortable before we get started. If you were perfectly comfortable and confident all the time, you might be tempted to think that your giftedness is what wins people to Christ. One of the hallmarks of successful soul winners is the fact that nearly all of them recognize that, left to their own devices, none of them have what it takes to bring someone to Christ. Instead, they acknowledge that what they witnessed in the miracle of conversion was completely out of their hands.

Do not wait until you feel gifted to get started. Evangelism, after all, is the school of faith. God gives us the impossible task of sharing Christ with a world where hearts are turned against Him. When you see someone accept Jesus under those circumstances, you become keenly aware that it is a genuine miracle—and your faith grows. You come to accept that God is in charge, and He really *will* keep His promises.

Believe that God has called you, exactly as you are, because He sees potential in the gifts you already have, even though you might not have used or cultivated them yet.

Moses felt so utterly inadequate to the task of approaching Pharaoh that he tried to escape going, and in response, God pointed to the humble rod in his hand: "What is that in your hand?" He asked. No onlooker would believe for a moment that a simple shepherd's staff would be all Moses would need to take on the king of Egypt. But in the hands of God, what you already have, the gifts you have already been blessed with, are all you need to get started and begin witnessing genuine miracles.

Your "Now" Place

"For the kingdom of heaven is like a man traveling to a far country, who called his own servants and delivered his goods to them. And to one he gave five talents, to another two, and to another one, to each according to his own ability; and immediately he went on a journey."
—Matthew 25:14, 15

As Jesus was preparing to leave for heaven, He left us an incredible and well-loved promise: "I go to prepare a place for you" (John 14:2). In a world where human existence has been stripped of meaning by those who insist that life is the product of chance, the followers of Christ can know with certainty that they mean something to God, and they have a place in His kingdom.

According to Jesus' parables, you do not have to wait for the Second Coming to claim a definite place in God's kingdom. In the parable of the talents, you will notice that Jesus—the Man traveling to a far country—gave talents to His servants. The word for "servant" is a little stronger in the original Greek; it is *doulos*, which is a "bondservant" or a slave. Those who have accepted the gift of salvation have been purchased at a very high price (1 Corinthians 6:20; 1 Peter 1:18, 19) and willingly become God's property.

Each of Christ's servants are entrusted with His goods, which He expects us to use in the work of growing His kingdom. Some are trusted with more gifts than others, but there is not a single follower of Jesus who lacks the gifts necessary to do something meaningful with their lives in Christ's service. In other words, you *already* have a meaningful place in the kingdom. Jesus is preparing an eternal place for you, but He has also positioned you in a place *now*.

What could be more significant than to be entrusted with that which belongs to the Creator? "Not more surely is the place prepared for us in the heavenly mansions than is the special place designated on earth where we are to work for God," Ellen White pointed out.★

People in this world attach meaning to the high stations they reach in human corporations or governments, but no position of worldly importance can rival the privilege of taking your place in the army of God and using the specific gifts that the Almighty has chosen especially for you. In this world, people promote their status by adding title and letters to their names; you have been given the unbelievable opportunity of having Jesus write the Father's name on your forehead (Revelation 14:1).

★ Ellen G. White, *Christ's Object Lessons* (Battle Creek, MI: Review and Herald®, 1900), 327.

Use It, Or Lose It

" 'For to everyone who has, more will be given, and he will have abundance;
but from him who does not have, even what he has will be taken away.' "
—Matthew 25:29

A very long time ago I was something of a musician. In fact, I studied music formally for many years and used to spend upwards of three hours a day practicing. There was a time when my fingers moved naturally over the instrument, effortlessly producing music. But alas, that was many years ago; and thanks to a dramatic change in life plans and an incredibly busy schedule, I have not practiced in more than three decades.

On the very rare occasions when I sit down at the same instrument and attempt to play, it does not respond to my touch like it used to. The music does not come naturally, and I often lament the fact that it sounds like I am wearing mittens when I play. I have lost the gift I once had through lack of use.

So it is with the talents that Christ has given you; if you do not exercise them, they do not grow, and they will eventually disappear. "A man who would refuse to exercise his limbs would soon lose all power to use them," Ellen White reminds us. "Thus the Christian who will not exercise his God-given powers not only fails to grow up into Christ, but he loses the strength that he already had."★

The first few faltering steps in Christ's service can be intimidating; nobody who understands the magnitude of the work feels adequate to the task. But in exercising the gifts that God has already given you, your faith begins to grow, and you learn to trust that He will use the abilities He has given you to work great things in His cause. The more you use your gifts, the more confident you become, not in yourself, but in God's graciousness.

The parable of the talents underlines that it is not only to your benefit to exercise your gifts; God *expects* it. It is one of the first acts of faith you will perform as a new believer, and according to the parable, it is yours until the moment Jesus returns, as long as you continue using it to God's glory.

If you could do *anything* to God's glory, anything at all, what would it be? And what exactly is keeping you from doing it *now*?

★ Ellen G. White, *Steps to Christ* (New York: Fleming H. Revell, 1892), 91, 92.

Preferring Others

Be kindly affectionate to one another with brotherly love,
in honor giving preference to one another.
—Romans 12:10

As we prepare ourselves during our younger years to navigate life, we tend to hone the skills we will need to compete in the marketplace. When we apply for a job, we present ourselves as being a better option than someone else; our résumé listing the characteristics we possess that distinguish us from the competition. When we run a company, we make sure the buying public understands that we are better than other options.

There is nothing wrong with this. If you are going about the business of making a living, it is wise to be competitive. A problem emerges, however, when we import the same kind of corporate thinking into the church, which is all too common.

To be sure, we want to be competitive in the larger marketplace of ideas. We *want* people to understand why our message is unique, and we have been charged with the task of calling people out of Babylon—helping people to understand the key differences between the remnant message and other voices in the religious marketplace.

That is not the problem. The problem emerges when we use our God-given talents to compete with each other *inside* the church. We are often not content to merely sing to God's glory, for example; we crave the kind of affirmation that lets us know that people thought we were *better* than most. We are not happy to quietly shoulder the responsibility of leadership; we secretly want to know that we were the very best option the church had. And worst of all, we sometimes harbor the green monster of envy when someone else shines—and we think *we* would have done a better job.

Spiritual gifts are not to be used in competition with each other. They are to be used the same way the Members of the Godhead operate: in loving, selfless concert with each Other. Paul's advice flies in the face of our fallen natures. It rubs our sinful fur the wrong way: do not just make room for others, give *preference* to them.

Not only is the work of the church an opportunity to learn faith, but also humility—and in that regard, we will likely find that the church was a rich opportunity to practice for heaven.

The Testimony of Jesus

And I fell at his feet to worship him. But he said to me, "See that you do not do that!
I am your fellow servant, and of your brethren who have the testimony of Jesus.
Worship God! For the testimony of Jesus is the spirit of prophecy."
—Revelation 19:10

There are a couple of important things we can learn from John's interaction with the angel in Revelation 19. First of all, pay attention to the angel's humility: he is utterly horrified at John's act of obeisance, insisting that he is no worthier of worship than is John himself. Angels of God, in spite of their lofty status (we were, after all, created "lower than the angels" [Psalm 8:5]), are still our fellow servants.

Second, the angel offers us a clear definition of what the "testimony of Jesus" represents in Bible prophecy—the spirit of prophecy. Some modern translations, however, have muddied the angel's meaning, suggesting that he is merely saying that the gist of all prophecy is to reveal Jesus. While that is certainly true, this passage is also clearly speaking of the prophetic gift.

Further on in Revelation, John makes the same mistake and again bows down to the angel. The angel replies with *nearly* identical words but makes an important change. Instead of saying he is "of your brethren who have the testimony of Jesus," he now says, "Of your brethren the *prophets*" (Revelation 22:9; emphasis added). What can we conclude from this? It is the *prophets* who have the "spirit of prophecy"!

The identification of "the testimony of Christ" as the prophetic gift is further demonstrated by Paul's opening words to the Corinthian church, where he thanks God that "the testimony of Christ was confirmed in you, so that you come short in no *gift*" (1 Corinthians 1:6, 7; emphasis added). At the opening of the book of Revelation, John describes what he is about to write as a prophetic message from God, and he refers to bearing witness "to the testimony of Jesus Christ" (Revelation 1:2).

That the prophetic gift should be found among God's last-day people, in other words, should not come as a surprise to careful students of Scripture. (It is, after all, listed in each major biblical list of spiritual gifts: Romans 12; 1 Corinthians 12; and Ephesians 4.) That it has happened in our midst is another clear indication of how close we are to the finish line of history.

Not Just a Show

"However, when He, the Spirit of truth, has come, He will guide you into all truth; for He will not speak on His own authority, but whatever He hears He will speak; and He will tell you things to come. He will glorify Me, for He will take of what is Mine and declare it to you."
—John 16:13, 14

One sure sign that something has gone wrong with a church's spiritual gifts is when they appear to be used for self-gratification or entertainment purposes. Years ago I attended a workshop (the topic had nothing to do with spiritual gifts) where a speaker started talking about how the Holy Spirit had "blessed their church": "The Spirit just fell upon us, and it was like electricity running through our bodies. He took over the room and people just bathed in His presence for hours and hours." He went on to describe some other-worldly manifestations, such as becoming paralyzed, speaking in a mysterious language, and uncontrollable emotional outbursts.

There is nothing wrong with enjoying God's presence; in fact, who *does not* enjoy those moments when God feels especially close? Personally, I have been moved to tears of joy on a number of occasions simply because God's presence was almost palpable. But we should never forget that the gifts of the Spirit are given for a specific purpose: to glorify Christ. They are for the work of evangelism; they are special abilities granted to the church to make outreach more effective.

When the gifts turn inward, there is a problem. When they become primarily about experiencing emotion, they have missed the mark. Remember that the reason the tongues of fire fell on the heads of the disciples on the Day of Pentecost was because there were people present "from every nation under heaven" (Acts 2:5). The event lead into a public sermon by Peter, who urged the crowd to believe in Jesus: "Therefore let all the house of Israel know assuredly that God has made this Jesus, whom you crucified, both Lord and Christ" (verse 36). And then the story closed with baptisms—thousands of them.

As you read the book of Acts, it becomes evident that God performs the miraculous for the purpose of revealing Himself to those who are still on the edge of the kingdom, waiting to come in. Miracles serve as invitations, as do the gifts of the Spirit. As with the character of God, they are outwardly focused, designed to glorify Jesus and win hearts to the Way, the Truth, and the Life. Anything else is likely just a show and not a gift of the Spirit at all.

Almost Home

Surely the Lord GOD does nothing, unless He reveals His secret to His servants the prophets.
—Amos 3:7

God is heavily invested in you. You are not a cosmic accident or an after-thought. You are not merely something that God *must* deal with in order to get what He wants; you are somebody that God *wants* to save.

He is not like the whimsical gods of pagan mythology who use human beings for sport or allow human beings to suffer the brutal consequences as they amuse themselves with cosmic games. We do not have to live anxiously, wondering when the next random event might wipe us out, because God has already seen the end from the beginning, and He promises it will work out well.

We do not head into the future blindly because what is important to know has already been revealed. The rise and fall of worldly powers, the trends we now see taking place in the world of politics and religion, the destabilization of the natural world—enough of it has been revealed in advance to help us understand that none of it is catching God by surprise, and thus none of it should ultimately worry us.

Years ago I lived in a place where winter could last eight months of the year, and occasionally, when I was driving home at night, whiteout conditions on the highway were so bad that you could not find the edge of the road. I would drive slowly, highly alert, with white knuckles. Mile after agonizing mile passed, leaving me no certainty as to my progress. And then I would suddenly see it: the red light on a radio tower off to my right. I knew that within minutes, I would see the glow of my town on the horizon, and shortly after that, I would be home.

Jesus may now physically reside in the presence of His Father, but He has never left us. Through the gift of the Spirit, He continues to be Immanuel: God with us. He has lived here among us and knows firsthand what it means to exist in a broken world. Every so often, He pulls back the curtains of the universe and allows us to see the glow on the horizon. He gives someone the gift of prophecy and whispers in his or her ear, for all of us, "Hang in there, you're almost home."

Our Safe Place

"If there arises among you a prophet or a dreamer of dreams, and he gives you a sign or a wonder, and the sign or the wonder comes to pass, of which he spoke to you, saying, 'Let us go after other gods'—which you have not known—'and let us serve them,' you shall not listen to the words of that prophet or that dreamer of dreams, for the LORD your God is testing you to know whether you love the LORD your God with all your heart and with all your soul."
—Deuteronomy 13:1–3

Unfortunately, we human beings are easily impressed. Years ago a friend tried to encourage me to attend religious meetings where they were performing "signs and wonders."

"You *have* to check this out," he insisted.

His excitement was unstoppable. I had already heard of the meetings and knew for certain that what was being preached was resoundingly unbiblical. I pointed out the concerns I had, and my friend quickly brushed them aside. "This *has* to be from God!" he insisted. "The other night someone I didn't even know slipped me a note, telling me that God had given him a message specifically for me. When I opened the note, it not only had my name on it, but it also gave intimate details about my life that nobody could possibly know. How do you explain that?"

"Easy," I said, pointing him to Deuteronomy 13. "Do you think that only God sees what happens in your private life? Or is it possible that fallen angels also might be keeping an eye on you?"

The miraculous is not proof of God's involvement, particularly in the last days. We must never forget that in the final moments before Christ returns, it is the first and second beasts who perform the miraculous, even bringing fire down from heaven (Revelation 13). It is "spirits of demons, performing signs, which go out to the kings of the earth and of the whole world" (Revelation 16:14).

When people claim to have the prophetic gift, even if what they predict *does* happen, we must always remember that predictive ability is not the only test we need to apply. If their messages run contrary to Scripture, they have not been gifted by the Holy Spirit because the Spirit simply will not contradict what He inspired the authors of the Bible to write. If their "ministry" has the effect of leading people away from the truth rather than into it, then we can be certain that we must have nothing to do with them.

My friend had been dazzled by something that appeared to be a supernatural message. Perhaps it was, but from the wrong side of the great controversy. It only serves to remind us that *Scripture* is the supreme authority for our faith, the only safe place to stand as the end of the world bursts upon us.

Nine Percent

"When a prophet speaks in the name of the LORD, if the thing does not happen
or come to pass, that is the thing which the LORD has not spoken;
the prophet has spoken it presumptuously; you shall not be afraid of him."
—Deuteronomy 18:22

Nostradamus, the sixteenth-century seer from France, may be the best-recognized name in the world of prognostication in our own century. Forced to quit school in Avignon during an outbreak of the plague, he took it upon himself to research natural medicine and eventually became an occult practitioner, which led to his fame as a so-called prophet.

His prophecies are written as four-line poems, known as *quatrains*. Most of them are vague enough that you could apply them to any number of historical incidents, and his devotees are adept at doing just that—with five hundred years of history to search through to find some kind of fulfillment. To be sure, there are a number of forecasts he made that are spookily similar to real people and events, such as his much-touted prediction of someone named "Hister" who would be a "child of Germany" and would start a war in western Europe.

It is undeniably close.

But close is not good enough to qualify as a prophet of God. Of the 449 major prophecies laid out by Nostradamus, 18 have been proven to be absolutely wrong. Of course, 18 mistakes only means a 4 percent error rate, which is admittedly impressive until you factor in all of the predictions that simply do not match any known historical event; there are 390 of those. Suddenly, Nostradamus's supposedly brilliant accuracy rate drops to a measly 9 percent, which utterly disqualifies him as a prophet of God.

If it "does not happen or come to pass," God reminds us, "that is the thing which the Lord has not spoken." The gift of prophecy has been given to God's church for a number of reasons; one of those reasons is to demonstrate that "there is a God in heaven" (Daniel 2:28)—a God who can declare the end from the beginning (see Isaiah 46:10). It is meant to inspire confidence that the future of humanity is in reliable hands and that we can trust God's promises.

That is why the test requires getting it right 100 percent of the time: because an all-knowing God does not get it wrong. You would not trust a surgeon with a 9 percent accuracy rating; neither should you trust your eternal future to someone who is wrong more than nine times out of ten.

Test the Spirits

"As for the prophet who prophesies of peace, when the word of the prophet comes to pass, the prophet will be known as one whom the LORD has truly sent."
—Jeremiah 28:9

Some years ago a young man at a convention stopped me in the exhibit hall and excitedly said, "You must be *so* thrilled to be a part of the visions!" I found myself mystified by his comment because I had no idea what he was talking about. My bewilderment continued until I received a letter from a lady who asked me an unusual question: Had I received any dreams or visions from God about a man who claimed to have the prophetic gift?

I had not. It turns out that the individual in question had claimed to receive a direct message from Jesus that He would connect the fledgling prophet with me. "Is there someone I can be connected with so that these messages can go out faster?" he asked Jesus in the purported vision. That is when my name came up; I would be the one to help launch his prophetic ministry around the world.

The lady who wrote me the letter had been experiencing a growing suspicion that perhaps the fledgling prophet's claims were fraudulent, so she decided to put them to the test. To this day—well over a decade later—I have received no such communication from the Lord. It has become obvious that I was not an instrument to hasten the spread of his messages.

The "prophet" in question was subsequently discovered to be an utter fraud. He had lied about the supposed miracle story he posited as evidence that God had called him, and he was discovered to have been impersonating the supposed witnesses to his "gift" online.

Jesus warned us clearly that in the last days "many false prophets will rise up and deceive many" (Matthew 24:11). We are to carefully "test the spirits, whether they are of God; because many false prophets have gone out into the world" (1 John 4:1). When someone claims to have a message from God, and that message is proven to be utterly false, we can know with confidence that God has not spoken to that person, because God simply does not get things wrong. While we must be careful not to "despise prophecies" (1 Thessalonians 5:20), we must be slow to accept seemingly miraculous manifestations, always painstakingly testing them, and be careful to never, ever cede our spiritual lives to a mere human being.

To Know a Phony

Then He said, "Hear now My words: If there is a prophet among you, I, the LORD, make Myself known to him in a vision; I speak to him in a dream."
—Numbers 12:6

Back in my college days, I used to repair carpets, which brought me into thousands of peoples' homes. Sometimes, I met people who seemed to be lifted right out of an episode of the *Twilight Zone*. One lady who had damaged the carpet in her rental apartment watched as I attempted to remove a rather nasty stain.

"God speaks to me through peoples' auras," she suddenly said, "and I can see yours."

She proceeded to tell me all about my life, based on a supposed haze of color around my body. Her description of my life was fascinating—in that she got nearly every detail utterly wrong. There was no gift and no message from God.

In spite of the fact that many modern psychics believe they have been gifted by God (some even declaring that their tarot cards and séances are God's way of revealing secrets), the Bible is clear about how God chooses to speak to someone who has the genuine gift: He uses dreams and visions. The stories in the book of Daniel illustrate this powerfully.

If you think about it, it makes perfect sense: a dream or vision eliminates the possibility of tampering because it is a closed-circuit form of communication. When Solomon dedicated the original temple, he pointed out that only God "know[s] the hearts of all the sons of men" (1 Kings 8:39). The forces of darkness do not have direct access to the human heart and cannot interfere with a direct communication from the Holy Spirit to the mind. Any other so-called prophetic tool, from crystal balls to séance tables, becomes immediately suspect: outside forces can influence what happens.

That does not automatically mean that all dreams are of God, however. Over the course of a lifetime, sinful human beings willingly absorb information that can radically distort perception and compromise spiritual discernment. Additionally, sometimes dreams are just dreams: the process by which the human brain moves short-term memories into long-term storage. So even when a dream or vision is emotional, powerful, and inexplicable, we still must carefully compare it to the Word of God, which is the final arbiter of all truth.

To know the Bible, to spend time communicating with God in prayer, is to know a phony when you meet one.

God's Keen Interest

The LORD has purposed to destroy the wall of the daughter of Zion. He has stretched out a line; He has not withdrawn His hand from destroying; therefore He has caused the rampart and wall to lament; they languished together. Her gates have sunk into the ground; He has destroyed and broken her bars. Her king and her princes are among the nations; the Law is no more, and her prophets find no vision from the LORD.
—Lamentations 2:8, 9

The book of Lamentations provides a postmortem of a disobedient nation. When Jeremiah was warning God's people that certain destruction was on its way, his detractors pointed to the temple as evidence that nothing could possibly happen. "Do not trust in these lying words," Jeremiah reminded them, " 'The temple of the LORD, the temple of the LORD, the temple of the LORD are these' " (Jeremiah 7:4).

The trappings of religion mean little when they are not symbolic representations of a genuine saving relationship with God. This is a point that God makes abundantly clear: "Will you steal, murder, commit adultery, swear falsely, burn incense to Baal, and walk after other gods whom you do not know, and then come and stand before Me in this house which is called by My name. . . ?" (verses 9, 10).

When the people's hearts turned away from God, there was no need for the temple, and so God permitted Nebuchadnezzar to seize the temple vessels and take them—along with the people—to the land of Babylon. In effect, they were being returned to their ancestral home, to Chaldea, the land Abraham had left. And in the wake of their captivity, the prophetic gift in their midst suffered: "her prophets find no vision from the LORD." (To be sure, there were still prophetic voices after the Exile, such as Daniel and Ezekiel—canonical prophets whose writings were included in Scripture. But the day-to-day prophetic gift ceased to function.)

Alignment with God's will and the gift of prophecy are also connected for God's last-day people: They "keep the commandments of God and have the testimony of Jesus Christ" (Revelation 12:17). They are a people "who follow the Lamb wherever He goes" (Revelation 14:4). They are keenly interested in God, and they discover that God is also keenly interested in *them*: He provides continual guidance, helping them on their path to the kingdom because they cherish His counsel.

The gift of prophecy points us to a God of love; a God who will not force people into His kingdom against their will. He wants to pour all of heaven's resources into us when it becomes evident that we would like to stand on Mount Zion with the Lamb of God and one day worship the King in heaven's temple itself.

Jonah and the Remnant

But Jonah arose to flee to Tarshish from the presence of the LORD. He went down to Joppa,
and found a ship going to Tarshish; so he paid the fare, and went down into it,
to go with them to Tarshish from the presence of the LORD.

—Jonah 1:3

Jonah was likely wise enough to know there is no place on earth to truly escape God's notice. So why does the Bible say he was fleeing the "presence of the LORD"? Diligent Bible students have noticed something they refer to as the *rule of first mention*: the first time the Bible introduces a concept, it helps establish an understanding for how that concept is used throughout the rest of Scripture.

The first time someone leaves the "presence of the LORD" is when Cain's departed from Eden, when he "went out from the presence of the LORD and dwelt in the land of Nod" (Genesis 4:16). Again, Cain could not possibly find a location where God no longer saw him, but when you consider what God had established at the gates of Eden, the verse suddenly makes a great deal of sense.

There was an early model of the sanctuary at Eden. Hugh Martin, the nineteenth-century Scottish commentator, makes an important point about Jonah: "To be banished from the holy place, or from the holy territory, is equivalent to, is described as, being banished from the presence of the Lord. It was in this sense, accordingly, that Jonah sough to flee from the presence of the Lord. Especially if there be any truth in a tradition that the Jews believed the spirit of prophecy to be confined to the sacred territory, we see the reason why, . . . he should desire to escape from the land of Israel."[*] You will notice that when Jonah repents, he mentions returning to the temple twice (chapter 2).

The gift of prophecy and evangelistic mission are intimately linked with the temple because the temple is where God's presence is housed. In these last days, the prophetic gift is intricately linked to the heavenly sanctuary, where our High Priest works on our behalf. You may have noticed that of all the remnant church's doctrines, the ones that seem to come under fire the most often are the unique ones: the heavenly sanctuary and the spirit of prophecy. Could it be that the book of Jonah has a veiled prophecy—a warning for the remnant church?

May we never be like Jonah, trying to flee the presence of the Lord. That presence is the key to finishing the work.

---

[*] Hugh Martin, *Jonah* (London: Billings and Sons, 1870), 38.

No Place for Schadenfreude

"Say to them: 'As I live,' says the Lord GOD, 'I have no pleasure in the death of the wicked, but that the wicked turn from his way and live. Turn, turn from your evil ways! For why should you die, O house of Israel?' "
—Ezekiel 33:11

Schadenfreude is a German word that means "harm joy." It has been imported into the English language to describe a feeling of pleasure people get from witnessing the downfall of others. Lord Byron coined another phrase to describe the same phenomenon: the *Roman holiday*, which describes the pleasure of a crowd that has the day off to watch a Roman gladiator die in an arena.

It is a sentiment that does not belong in the kingdom of God. Far too often we find among God's people those who exult when wicked people reap the consequences of their poor choices. God, on the other hand, warns His people in tears: "I have no pleasure in the death of the wicked." Isaiah describes God's punishment of the wicked as "His unusual act" (Isaiah 28:21), because it hurts the heart of a loving God to see His rebellious children finally lost and to have to put them out of their misery.

One of the hallmarks of the genuine gift of prophecy is a heart for people—a heart that breaks when God's children reap the consequences of sin. There is a stunning example of this in the ministry of Ellen White, who had repeatedly warned that American cities were on the verge of judgment. Two days before the great San Francisco earthquake of 1906, she received a vision: "During a vision of the night, I stood on an eminence, from which I could see houses shaken like a reed in the wind. Buildings, great and small, were falling to the ground. Pleasure resorts, theaters, hotels, and the homes of the wealthy were shaken and shattered. Many lives were blotted out of existence, and the air was filled with the shrieks of the injured and the terrified."★

After the devastating quake in April 1906, there was no "I told you so" speech from Ellen White. There was no exulting, no gloating, and no finger-pointing. Instead, she had a driver take her through the smoldering ruins so that she could see them for herself, and those who were with her recorded that she wept. The genuine gift of prophecy, inspired by the Spirit, will showcase the heart of God. All spiritual gifts, for that matter, should do the same.

There is no place for *schadenfreude* in the church of the Living God.

★ Ellen G. White, *Testimonies for the Church* (Nampa, ID: Pacific Press®, 2002), 9:92.

Until It's Over

And so we have the prophetic word confirmed, which you do well to heed as a light that shines in a dark place, until the day dawns and the morning star rises in your hearts.
—2 Peter 1:19

It makes abundant sense that the gift of prophecy would be in operation during the last days of this earth's present history. Throughout the plan of salvation, God has made sure that human beings knew when tectonic changes were about to take place, in keeping with His promise that He would do nothing without revealing His secret to the prophets (see Amos 3:7).

The first prophecy recorded in the Bible was tendered the moment our first parents were escorted from the Garden. The Seed of the woman, God told us, would come to bruise the head of the serpent (Genesis 3:15). Prior to rebooting human history with a catastrophic deluge, God sent Noah to warn the world. (Some scholars have even found "when he dies, it will come" in the meaning of Methuselah's name, suggesting that people knew *before* Noah that something was coming.) Jeremiah warned his people that Nebuchadnezzar's advance from the north was not to be taken lightly. Daniel gave us enough information to know, with astonishing accuracy, when the Messiah would begin His public ministry.

At every phase of the great drama, God has made sure that His people knew that something big was coming. The final generation, we are told, will face cataclysmic changes unrivaled since the beginning of the story. Daniel forecasted a final "time of trouble, such as never was since there was a nation, even to that time" (Daniel 12:1). When the record shows that God has never left His people without prophetic guidance, what are the chances the final generation will be left in the dark without a word from the Lord?

The first coming of Christ was thoroughly anticipated by the Old Testament prophets, and there were those who were not authors of Scripture, such as Simeon, who nonetheless received a prophetic message from God regarding Jesus' birth. To discover that God's last-day people "have the testimony of Jesus" should surprise no one who is familiar with God's interaction with us. In fact, Joel made it abundantly clear that we should *expect* it (Joel 2:28).

"Here," God is in effect saying, "it's going to get stormy out just before you come home, so let Me hold your hand until it's over."

When Prophecy Ends

Love never fails. But whether there are prophecies,
they will fail; whether there are tongues,
they will cease; whether there is knowledge, it will vanish away.
For we know in part and we prophesy in part.
But when that which is perfect has come,
then that which is in part will be done away.
—1 Corinthians 13:8–10

The gift of prophecy is a bit of a double-edged sword. The fact that it exists is evidence of God's desire to keep us safely on the path to the kingdom. Its presence among God's people can be a reassuring reminder that they are moving in the right direction. The Holy Spirit, after all, was given to the church as a "guarantee" of things to come: "Now He who has prepared us for this very thing is God," Paul writes, "who also has given us the Spirit as a guarantee" (2 Corinthians 5:5). The word he uses for "guarantee" is *arrabon*, which means "down payment."

The spiritual gifts, then, are a deposit God gives us against the future. They represent God's presence among His people here in this world before we go to reside in *His* presence forever.

So what is the other edge of the sword? Had we not sinned, the gift of prophecy would not have been necessary. We had direct, face-to-face communication with God in Eden, but our sinful rebellion drove a wedge between us and made such direct interaction impossible. In place of personal visits, God sent messages through the prophets, and some of them had their words recorded in Scripture for all generations. Then God appeared in our midst as a human being. We could not enter behind the veil into the Most Holy Place, so the Son of God stepped out onto our side of the veil as one of us, making the glory of the second temple greater than the first. "They shall come to the Desire of All Nations," Haggai prophesied. "The glory of this latter temple shall be greater than the former" (Haggai 2:7, 9).

The good news is that the prophetic gift will not be necessary forever. "Whether there are prophecies, they will fail," Paul points out. "But when that which is perfect has come, then that which is in part will be done away." The sharp rift between sinful humans and the Almighty God will be healed forever when "the tabernacle of God is with men, and He will dwell with them, and they shall be His people. God Himself will be with them and be their God" (Revelation 21:3).

I am deeply grateful for the gift of prophecy, but come quickly, Lord Jesus!

Reluctant

O LORD, You induced me, and I was persuaded; You are stronger than I,
and have prevailed. I am in derision daily; everyone mocks me. For when I spoke,
I cried out; I shouted, "Violence and plunder!" Because the word of the LORD
was made to me a reproach and a derision daily. Then I said, "I will not make mention of Him,
nor speak anymore in His name." But His word was in my heart like a burning fire
shut up in my bones; I was weary of holding it back, and I could not.
—Jeremiah 20:7–9

I have met a number of people over the years who craved the prophetic gift or sometimes even claimed to have it, wearing it as a badge of their prestige in the church. They enjoy the status they assume such a calling would bring. A quick glance at the careers of genuine prophets, however, reveals that few have actually wanted the job.

Jeremiah began his prophetic career by protesting that he was too young for such a calling. "Behold," he replied to God's calling, "I cannot speak, for I am a youth" (Jeremiah 1:6). God's answer, however, exposed that the real issue was not youth or inexperience, it was fear. "Do not be afraid of their faces," He told Jeremiah, "for I am with you to deliver you" (verse 8). Moses was similarly horrified by his call to the prophetic ministry, arguing at length that he was not suited for the post, and finally suggesting, "O my Lord, please send by the hand of whomever else You may send" (Exodus 4:13). Jonah's reluctance—and unfortunate disobedience—is one of the best-known stories of the Bible.

Ellen White's ministry was marked by the humility and reluctance you would expect to find when the gift is genuine. She did not seek the title of prophet: "To claim to be a prophetess is something that I have never done," she stated.★ She found the call to share what she was shown in vision overwhelming: "I prayed earnestly for several days, and far into the night, that this burden might be removed from me and laid upon someone more capable of bearing it."†

Throughout history, those who were called to the prophetic ministry knew what it would mean: it is not a place of prestige but a call to humility and often humiliation. Those who seek the office likely do not understand what it entails, or their hubris makes them unfit for it. There is no place for pride in the gift of prophecy. After all, when Lucifer's sense of worth was exaggerated by arrogant pride, he was removed from his post as a cherub and escorted from the property.

Genuine spiritual gifts are treated with reverence and a deep sense of unworthiness by those who understand what they are and why they have been given.

★ Ellen G. White, *Selected Messages*, bk. 1 (Hagerstown, MD: Review and Herald®, 2007), 34.
† Ellen G. White, *Testimonies for the Church* (Nampa, ID: Pacific Press®, 2002), 1:62.

People of the Book

To the law and to the testimony! If they do not speak according to this word,
it is because there is no light in them.

—Isaiah 8:20

For those who grew up outside of the church, discovering Ellen White's prophetic gift is thrilling, to say the least. The sheer volume of material she produced is astonishing: she wrote more than fifty *thousand* pages. The content is nothing short of astonishing, and it is easy, once it dawns on you that she really *did* hear from God, to get swept up in her writings to the extent that you begin to neglect reading the Bible itself. It is, after all, a much easier task to read Ellen White's comments than to spend careful hours digging for gems of truth in Scripture.

But to major in Ellen White and minor in the Bible is to make a grave mistake. The prophetic gift never supersedes what God has revealed through the biblical prophets; in fact, the Bible is crystal clear that the prophetic gift must be tested by Scripture, and never the other way around.

Ellen White herself was straightforward on this. She never expected her writings to become a substitute—or even an equivalent—to the Bible. "In our time there is a wide departure from their [the Scriptures'] doctrines and precepts, and there is need of a return to the great Protestant principle—the Bible, and the Bible only, as the rule of faith and duty."★ "God's Word is the unerring standard," she wrote in 1890. "The Testimonies are not to take the place of the Word. . . . Let all prove their positions from the Scriptures and substantiate every point they claim as truth from the revealed Word of God."†

Then, quoting today's passage from Isaiah in the introduction to *The Great Controversy*, she wrote, "The Spirit was not given—nor can it ever be bestowed—to supersede the Bible; for the Scriptures explicitly state that the word of God is the standard by which all teaching and experience must be tested. Says the apostle John, 'Believe not every spirit, but try the spirits, whether they are of God.' "‡

Do you reach for Ellen White more than you reach for your Bible? By all means, cherish Mrs. White's counsels. Read them often; it would be foolish not to take advantage of them. But at the same time, remember that God's people, ultimately, are a people of the Book.

★ Ellen G. White, *The Great Controversy* (Nampa, ID: Pacific Press®, 2002), 204.

† Ellen G. White to Brother and Sister Garmire, Petoskey, MI, August 12, 1890, Letter 12, 1890, in Ellen G. White Writings Website, https://m.egwwritings.org/en/book/5994.2000001#1.

‡ White, *The Great Controversy*, vii.

"By Their Fruits"

"Beware of false prophets, who come to you in sheep's clothing, but inwardly they are ravenous wolves. You will know them by their fruits. Do men gather grapes from thornbushes or figs from thistles? Even so, every good tree bears good fruit, but a bad tree bears bad fruit. A good tree cannot bear bad fruit, nor can a bad tree bear good fruit. Every tree that does not bear good fruit is cut down and thrown into the fire. Therefore by their fruits you will know them."
—Matthew 7:15–20

A part from Christ, nobody is perfect, not even those with the prophetic gift. Even a casual scan of the Bible will reveal that some of the top names in the history of faith have had some less-than-perfect moments. John the Baptist, named as the greatest of prophets by Jesus (Luke 7:28), struggled with doubt because Jesus had not released him from prison—he had doubt about his own prophetic message! Peter, who authored two books of the Bible and led so many to Christ at Pentecost, had to be chastised by Paul about duplicitous behavior—he would only eat with Gentiles if none of his Jewish friends were around (Galatians 2:11, 12).

No, prophets are not perfect, so to test the prophetic gift by examining every last jot and tittle of people's lives and dismissing them because of the occasional fault would be a mistake. (Of course, if the mistake happens to be the fact that they invented their gift in the first place and were lying about their "prophetic visions," that is another story.) But if they make the same kinds of minor mistakes that most Christians make, that would not rule them out.

What matters is the general tenor of a prophet's life. What, if anything, is the outcome of the prophet's ministry? Jesus made it clear that one way to determine the validity of the prophetic gift is the fruit a prophet bears. A good tree, He points out, does not bear bad fruit.

So what kind of woman was Ellen White? Those who knew her repeat the same description: She was gentle and Christlike. She was never embroiled in scandals or immorality that sadly destroys so many preachers today. Even one of her most determined critics conceded this point when, at her funeral, he broke down. After walking past the casket once, he went back to his seat but could not stay put. He went back a second time, heartbroken. Those present tell us he "put his hand on the edge of the coffin and looked down into that sleeping face. With tears rolling down his cheeks, he said: 'There is a noble Christian woman gone.' "★

Spiritual gifts were given to the church by Christ (Ephesians 4:8). It only makes sense that those who possess the genuine article would be Christlike.

★ W. A. Spicer, "The Spirit of Prophecy in the Advent Movement—No. 2," *Advent Review and Sabbath Herald*, January 13, 1938, 10.

Visionary Checkpoints

But he, being full of the Holy Spirit, gazed into heaven and saw the glory of God,
and Jesus standing at the right hand of God, and said, "Look! I see the heavens opened
and the Son of Man standing at the right hand of God!"
—Acts 7:55, 56

The seventy-week prophecy of Daniel 9 has such sweeping ramifications that it holds a place of special significance among prophetic passages. It is, for starters, such a clear endorsement of Jesus as the Messiah that the reading of the passage has been forbidden in some circles where people are afraid it will lead to faith in Christ.

In addition to that, it lays out a clear prophetic time line for the probation of God's covenant people. They had transgressed God's Sabbath-year requirements for 490 years;* they would be given another 490-year probationary period. At the end of that time, the responsibility for promulgating the gospel was given to the Gentile nations.†

What is fascinating is how God not only launched the 490-year probationary period through the prophetic gift, He also marked significant milestones the same way. Take, for example, the first segment of the prophecy (the seven weeks or forty-nine years) that marked the reconstruction of Jerusalem. During that time, God's people were encouraged by prophetic lights such as Ezra and Nehemiah. When it finally came time for the Messiah to appear, the Spirit whispered to prophets such as Simeon and Anna. When the Messiah appeared at His baptism in A.D. 27, at the conclusion of the sixty-nine weeks, it was John the Baptist, the greatest prophet in history, who introduced the Messiah to the world.

Then, at the close of the seventy weeks, in A.D. 34, Stephen is given a prophetic message just prior to martyrdom. After reviewing God's faithfulness to Israel, he is given a vision of Jesus standing in heaven's sanctuary.

Each checkpoint along the way was marked by God's reassurance through the prophetic gift. Seventh-day Adventists have long recognized that the twenty-three hundred–day prophecy of Daniel 8 is intimately linked with the prophecy of Daniel 9. Should we expect God to confirm its completion through the prophetic gift? Consider this: the day after the Great Disappointment in 1844, the Spirit revealed the truth about the heavenly sanctuary to Hiram Edson, and in December of that same year, Ellen White experienced her first vision.

It would have been surprising to *not* hear from God at the close of history's longest time prophecy, and the fact that He *did* speak is yet more evidence that we have not followed "cunningly devised fables" (2 Peter 1:16).

---

* See 2 Chronicles 36:20, 21. The Captivity lasted seventy years in order to make up for all the broken Sabbaths. Given that Sabbaths represent one-seventh of time, this would represent a period of transgression that lasted 490 years.
 † See, for example, Matthew 22:1–10; Acts 13:46.

But Have Not Love

Though I speak with the tongues of men and of angels, but have not love, I have become sounding brass or a clanging cymbal. And though I have the gift of prophecy, and understand all mysteries and all knowledge, and though I have all faith, so that I could remove mountains, but have not love, I am nothing. And though I bestow all my goods to feed the poor, and though I give my body to be burned, but have not love, it profits me nothing.
—1 Corinthians 13:1–3

Perhaps you have met them online—the argumentative ones. The ones who compose every other word of their angry posts with the Caps Lock key engaged so that you understand just how right they are and how wrong you are. The ones who cannot let a matter drop, and when you choose to disengage their irritated rhetoric for the sake of peace, they will triumphantly crow that they have been vindicated. The ones who resort to name-calling in order to silence someone who might disagree.

Sadly, some (or maybe even *many*) of them profess to be Christians, but you would be hard-pressed to find the Spirit of Christ emanating from their keyboards. Perhaps they are kinder in person, and they merely struggle to express themselves appropriately in an environment where the cues and context of personal contact are missing. Perhaps. Or, as is often the case, they find the relative anonymity of the internet liberating, allowing them to utter things they would never dare say in person.

Rarely, if ever, do they actually fulfill the gospel commission and sacrifice their pride for the sake of introducing a sinner to Christ. They spend more time trying to reconcile people to their point of view than they do fulfilling the true "ministry of reconciliation" given to the church (2 Corinthians 5:18). They seem more engaged in bringing people to *their* feet than to the foot of the cross.

At the heart of Paul's discussion of spiritual gifts lies an important key to fulfilling the gospel commission. You can be the most talented member of the church, he insists, and still miss the mark if your ministry is not permeated with love. In the work that Jesus assigned to the church, it is more important to display the love of Christ than it is to be skilled, brilliant, accomplished, or right. (Of course, being *wrong* is not helpful either. It *is* important to understand Scripture, rightly divide the word of truth, if you are going to share it with someone else.)

As you head out into the world to fulfill the commission Christ gave the church, ask yourself this question: When have I ever seen an online argument end with someone utterly capitulating and saying, "I guess you're right. I'm ready to join your church now"?

It just does not happen.

The Unity of the Spirit

I, therefore, the prisoner of the Lord, beseech you to walk worthy of the calling with which you were called, with all lowliness and gentleness, with longsuffering, bearing with one another in love, endeavoring to keep the unity of the Spirit in the bond of peace.
—Ephesians 4:1–3

In each of Paul's three major comments on spiritual gifts—Romans 12; 1 Corinthians 12; and Ephesians 4—he makes an effort to underline an important point: if you are using spiritual gifts correctly, they trend toward unity in the congregation rather than division. Before mentioning the fact that Jesus left gifts for the church when He returned to heaven, Paul asks the congregation in Ephesus to "endeavor" to keep unity.

Unity, in other words, does not happen passively among sinful human beings. We do not naturally suppress our personal wants and wishes in order to acknowledge others, nor do we submit easily to the wisdom or ability of others. In his address to the church in Rome, after Paul counsels the church members to push the envelope in the exercise of their God-given gifts, he quickly follows up by saying, "Be kindly affectionate to one another with brotherly love, in honor giving preference to one another" (Romans 12:10). "Do not set your mind on high things," he continues, "but associate with the humble. Do not be wise in your own opinion" (verse 16).

The exercise of spiritual gifts is an opportunity to understand, to a limited extent, how the Godhead works together. Father, Son, and Holy Spirit live and work together in selfless harmony. Each of us has been granted spiritual gifts that we have been told to use in harmony with others. There is a reason none of us has been given all of the gifts; to exercise them properly, we must learn to use them in concert with the gifts God has given to those around us. It creates a situation where we must learn to discern when it is appropriate to lead and when it is more appropriate to follow. We must also learn to see the bigger picture, asking God to reveal the work of the church to us as *He* sees it so that we can understand where God intends for us to fit in.

The exercise of spiritual gifts, then, becomes a training ground for heaven, where self-exaltation and pride will have been set aside. When we insist on working alone, we never see how the larger body of Christ more faithfully represents who He is to the world than one person ever could.

For the Work of Ministry

And He Himself gave some to be apostles, some prophets, some evangelists, and some pastors and teachers, for the equipping of the saints for the work of ministry, for the edifying of the body of Christ, till we all come to the unity of the faith and of the knowledge of the Son of God, to a perfect man, to the measure of the stature of the fullness of Christ.
—Ephesians 4:11–13

The twenty-first century world has, particularly in the West, come to think of church in terms of a consumer product. We advertise our events, like any other event that comes to town. We keep track of growth metrics, such as attendance, baptisms, and tithe. And we far too often tap into the West's obsession with personality-driven ministry. Our pastors become celebrities, and we rely on personal attributes, such as charisma, eloquence, and talent, to drive the growth of the church. The members of the congregation become spectators and fans, sitting in the stands while our favorite team scores all the goals.

The New Testament model of ministry, however, is radically different. The gift of pastoring, you will notice, is more like the role of a coach than a star team member. Apostles, prophets, evangelists, pastors, and teachers exist in the body of Christ "for the equipping of the saints for the work of ministry." If the saints are watching the aforementioned do the work of ministry as paid professionals, something is wrong.

Pay close attention to the ministry of Ellen White in the role of prophet, for example. The bulk of her writings are directed to the members of the church, encouraging them to be faithful in carrying out the gospel commission. The pastor falls under the same category, according to Paul. In time, as the church becomes healthier and the members become the agents of ministry, the pastor should be able to move on to establish other congregations because the present church no longer needs as much oversight.

If you have been waiting for your pastor to turn the church around singlehandedly, you have missed the point of spiritual gifts. The actual work of ministry is not the pastor's job, it is yours! God expects all hands on deck. "It is a fatal mistake to suppose that the work of saving souls depends alone on the ordained minister," Ellen White explains. "All to whom the heavenly inspiration has come are put in trust with the gospel. All who receive the life of Christ are ordained to work for the salvation of their fellow men."★

Read the list of spiritual gifts carefully: they are the attributes of an entire body of believers, equipped to light the world with the glory of Christ.

★ Ellen G. White, *The Desire of Ages* (Mountain View, CA: Pacific Press®, 1898), 822.

The Gift of the Magi

When they saw the star, they rejoiced with exceedingly great joy.
And when they had come into the house, they saw the young Child with Mary
His mother, and fell down and worshiped Him. And when they had opened their treasures,
they presented gifts to Him: gold, frankincense, and myrrh.
—Matthew 2:10, 11

It should be carefully noted that it was outsiders who seemed most excited by the birth of Christ. Humble shepherds received the first announcement ahead of the dignitaries in Jerusalem, and wise men from the East—foreigners—seemed more attuned to the nuances of Bible prophecy than those to whom the prophecies had been given. How did the wise men come to discover the Messianic prophecies? We can only guess, but there is at least an even chance that the influence of Daniel may have had something to do with it.

The scene that unfolds in Herod's palace when the wise men arrive is tragic. Outsiders discovered that those who had been given the gift of God's covenant were not only ignorant of the prophecies they had found so thrilling but felt personally threatened by the arrival of the long-awaited King of heaven. Before the story is over, God has to warn them in a dream not to return to the palace.

It is a lesson for the church. So many eye the outside world with suspicion while squandering the gifts they have been given. We use our spiritual gifts to entertain and enrich ourselves, and sometimes, we find newcomers—who are usually enthusiastic about their newfound faith—a threat to the status quo. Occasionally, you will hear someone wistfully hope that the new people will eventually "settle down" and get used to life in the church.

Over the years, however, I have noticed that the most vibrant churches are the ones that go out of their way to seek God's children and welcome them home. They have become keenly aware of the fact that God has many children who are still not home, many of whom are already more faithful believers than we are.

When those people arrive in our midst, they provide us with a powerful reminder that spiritual gifts are not ours to keep but a God-given opportunity to give something back to Jesus. Like the wise men of old, they enthusiastically embrace the mission of the church, throw themselves into the work, and give their very best in service to the Lord who gave so much for them. May we follow such wise men to the manger and remind ourselves why God has placed us in the church.

September

I believe in church organization. It is my purpose to support the church by my tithes and offerings and by my personal effort and influence.

Spiritual Hermits

And the LORD God said, "It is not good that man should be alone;
I will make him a helper comparable to him."
—Genesis 2:18

From the very beginning, even before sin, God determined that it was not good for human beings to be alone. When Adam stood in Paradise alone, God considered that he was incomplete, in need of appropriate companionship. Man, in other words, was created as a social being, which remains true to this day. When we come across someone who completely withdraws from the rest of human society and cuts off all contact, we refer to that person as a "recluse" or a "hermit" because we instinctively recognize that it is not the normal order of things. After a while, many hermits begin to exhibit odd behaviors because their choice of lifestyle eventually leads to psychological changes.

It is not the normal order of things in the exercise of the Christian faith either. Prior to His ascension, Christ did not establish a loose collection of individuals who were to serve Him independently of each other; He established a church. The blessings of Pentecost did not fall on hundreds of independent individuals who were scattered throughout the land; they fell on the church. The thousands Peter baptized that day were not merely marked as Christians and released into the wild, they were "added to the church" (Acts 2:47).

Healthy Christianity is lived in the body of Christ, the church, where a believer can use his or her gifts in harmony with the gifts of other members. In contact with other believers, we can constantly check our thinking against others, making sure that we have not, in isolation, followed a theological rabbit trail to the point of distorting the gospel. The testimonies of others can bolster our faith when we happen to be passing through a dark moment ourselves.

Alone, we are limited in exhibiting the character of Christ, for we are only able to express His love from our own perspective. But when in contact with others, we begin to see facets of God's character that we would have never experienced or understood on our own, because we have been exposed to the greater mosaic of the body, where the Spirit reveals Christ more fully.

It is still not good to be alone; the spiritual hermit simply cannot achieve what God intended to accomplish on the earth as we wait for Christ to return.

Living in the Fire

And let us consider one another in order to stir up love and good works,
not forsaking the assembling of ourselves together, as is the manner of some,
but exhorting one another, and so much the more as you see the Day approaching.
—Hebrews 10:24, 25

There is an old story about the great revivalist Dwight L. Moody: he went to visit two members of his church who had not attended for a while. Their absence had been keenly felt by the church because they had been especially active before they quit coming. They informed Moody that attending church was not important because you can worship God anywhere, including in the privacy of your home.

Moody said nothing. Instead, he leaned forward, grabbed the tongs from the fireplace, pulled two coals out of the fire, and placed them on the hearth, where they continued to burn brightly. After a few moments, however, the red glare of heat dissipated, and the coals became black. They got the point: it is hard to maintain your fervor while separated from the fire.

The tongues of fire that fell on Pentecost were the launching point of Christ's New Testament church. "You are going to go from Jerusalem to Judea, from Judea to Samaria, and from Samaria to the uttermost parts of the earth," Jesus had explained to His disciples days earlier. "But I want you to wait here in Jerusalem until you receive the Promise of the Father" (see Acts 1:4–8). They were not to begin their work until the Holy Spirit had fallen on them.

God placed the fire of His presence in the church, and when we choose to separate ourselves from the body of believers, we will find it difficult to keep our own light burning. Over the years, I have met many people who insisted, for one reason or another, that they could go it alone and almost invariably I later find out that they have left the Christian faith altogether. And if they have not left the faith, their passion for the work Christ gave us has certainly cooled off.

It is not always easy to coexist with the saints. While human interaction and living in a community comes with challenges, these challenges are worth it because living *in* the fire is one of the key ways God intends to keep the fire of your faith burning.

Level Ground

*Then I saw a strong angel proclaiming with a loud voice, "Who is worthy
to open the scroll and to loose its seals?" And no one in heaven or on the earth
or under the earth was able to open the scroll, or to look at it. So I wept much,
because no one was found worthy to open and read the scroll, or to look at it.
But one of the elders said to me, "Do not weep. Behold, the Lion of the tribe of Judah,
the Root of David, has prevailed to open the scroll and to loose its seven seals."*
—Revelation 5:2–5

L et me tell you about one of the first impressions I had when I first visited
this church," Karen told me. I braced myself; most of the time when people
had a burden to share their first impressions, it was not good. Perhaps she had been
offended by someone. Maybe someone had refused to make room in a pew for her.
Worse yet, maybe church members had gathered in their characteristic huddles, and
she had been ignored. It was bound to be *something*; after all, the way some people
talk about churches hardly anything ever goes right.

I was pleasantly surprised. "You see that man over there?" Karen asked, gesturing
across the sanctuary to a man in his early sixties. "He's a well-known doctor in the
community. Everybody knows him, and he's really well off." She looked back at me.
"When I first came to this church, I noticed that everybody kneels for prayer, and
I was sitting next to him. In this community, I'm truly a nobody, but we both knelt
together. In front of God, we were exactly the same."

She was right. The communion of saints is the great leveler of humanity. Perhaps
you have seen those motivational posters that show someone standing jubilantly on
a mountain peak, having accomplished his or her goals. The implication, of course,
is that before you accomplish your goals you exist at a lower level than you do
afterward. It may be true for the business world and even in the arena of self-
improvement; but in the kingdom of God, the ground is level.

Picture a person on a valley floor, another one halfway up a mountain, and another at the mountain's top. From our worldly perspective, the difference is considerable. But then zoom out to heaven's perspective, and you will notice something
interesting: there is absolutely no discernible difference. In the church, we are all
reminded where we stand next to the Son of God. We are a community of broken
sinners—all with the same problem and the same Solution.

Living out your Christianity in a church community is an important reminder
that in front of the cross there are no exceptional people, just an exceptional Savior.
In all this universe, there is only One who is ultimately worthy, and it is not any of
us.

The Greatest Among Us

Then He came to Capernaum. And when He was in the house He asked them, "What was it you disputed among yourselves on the road?" But they kept silent, for on the road they had disputed among themselves who would be the greatest. And He sat down, called the twelve, and said to them, "If anyone desires to be first, he shall be last of all and servant of all."
—Mark 9:33–35

The kingdom of God turns worldly values completely upside-down. In the corporate world, the early bird gets the worm. The trophy goes to the fast, the strong, and the one who outwits everybody else. At the Olympics, there are three boxes, of differing heights, for the gold, the silver, and the bronze medal recipients. When you beat out everybody else here on planet Earth, you get a higher place: more prestige, more money, and/or more power.

But the kingdom of God takes what we hold dearest and turns it on its head. As the disciples were traveling with Jesus, they were understandably excited by the prospect of the coming kingdom. As with most of us, they began to wonder how the highest and best positions might be doled out. Who would hold the highest places of honor? Surely, they would be at the top of the heap, because after all, they had been hand-picked by the Messiah Himself. But who, among the Twelve, would hold the greatest place after Jesus claimed His throne?

"What were you talking about back there?" Jesus asked them. Ouch. They instinctively understood—as do most of us—that what they had been discussing was out of sync with the character of Jesus, who gave up the glories of heaven and condescended to become one of us. They were silent, and nobody dared to utter a word. It was just too embarrassing.

"Let Me explain how this works," Jesus told them. "If anyone desires to be first, he shall be last of all and servant of all." The kingdom of Christ does not honor self-achievement. It does not place a blue ribbon or a gold medal on the one who distinguishes himself or herself as better than the rest. It is a place where self is set aside and people live for the sake of others' joy. It is a place where God lives for our good and we live for His glory.

To be sure, there are rewards to be given when Jesus returns, but they will not be assigned based on personal net worth or how often one has appeared on the covers of magazines. Rewards are given to those who emptied themselves of self and gave up their lives to become vehicles through which Christ could show His love to the world.

The God Who Serves

Then He came to Simon Peter. And Peter said to Him, "Lord, are You washing my feet?"
Jesus answered and said to him, "What I am doing
you do not understand now, but you will know after this."
Peter said to Him, "You shall never wash my feet!"
Jesus answered him, "If I do not wash you, you have no part with Me."
—John 13:6–8

Peter is the disciple who probably gets the most negative press after Judas. He is headstrong, impulsive, and always shooting from the hip. It was Peter who pulled out his sword and slashed off the ear of the high priest's servant. That is not what a pragmatist does; the office of the high priest could make a lot of trouble for people like Peter. Peter is the one who bragged that, while the other disciples would likely lose their courage, he would *never* forsake Jesus—and then proved to be the one who denied knowing Jesus at all. Peter was the one who clucked his tongue when the rich young ruler walked away, proud that *he* had been able to give up *his* livelihood for the sake of the gospel.

So when we see Peter refusing Jesus' attempt to wash his feet, it is easy to be critical; it is just another example of Peter acting before he thinks. But read the story carefully. How comfortable would *you* be if Jesus knelt to wash your feet? Every biblical prophet who was escorted into the throne room of heaven was suddenly painfully aware of his sinful deficiencies and felt utterly unworthy. Be honest: Would *you* not squirm if the King of heaven insisted on acting as your servant? What have you done to deserve service from Him? Nothing. And that is the point.

It is hard to maintain our pride-driven disposition when the One who formed us in the first place kneels in front of us to wash the dirt from our feet. It becomes even harder when He further submits Himself to the Roman whip, allows us to drive nails through His feet and hands, and sinks into the dark abyss where He can no longer feel the presence of His Father—all because He prefers our salvation to His own well-being.

There is no room for pride in the Christian church and no places of honor except for Jesus. As Jesus rose from the floor, He told us to never forget what we had seen and to follow in His footsteps. "For I have given you an example," Jesus said, "that you should do as I have done to you. . . . If you know these things, blessed are you if you do them" (John 13:15, 17).

SEPTEMBER 6

Heaven's Chisel

*Coming to Him as to a living stone, rejected indeed by men, but chosen by God
and precious, you also, as living stones, are being built up a spiritual house,
a holy priesthood, to offer up spiritual sacrifices acceptable to God through Jesus Christ.*
—1 Peter 2:4, 5

One of the most vivid descriptions of the church found in the Bible is Peter's temple-building analogy: Jesus is the Cornerstone; the rest of us are "living stones" being added to the structure. It brings to mind the patient work of stone-masons, who endlessly sort through piles of stones, looking for exactly the right piece to fit into a gap in a wall. They pick up each stone, turn it this way and that, holding it in the gap to determine if it is the best fit for the position, and then finally cement it in place. By the time the temple has been completed, all of the stones have been used.

Not all of the stones, however, are a perfect fit. In addition to a trowel, the stone mason also has chisels in order to chip away superfluous edges that stand in the way of a perfect fit. As we are right now, we are not fit for the kingdom of heaven. As Christ forgives us and finds our place in the church, He begins the process of chipping away the rough edges that have no place in the kingdom to come.

Perhaps some of the most talented stone workers in the world were the Incas, who built breathtaking palaces in the sky. Of special note are the ruins of Sacsay-huaman, where some six thousand cubic meters of stone, of various sizes and shapes, have been pieced together into stunning walls that are more than three meters tall. No two stones are alike. Some are small and (almost) manageable; the largest of them weigh as much as two hundred tons. In spite of the huge variety and formidable sizes of the stones, modern engineers marvel at how well they fit together. In many places, the seams between the stones are so tight that it is impossible to slip a sheet of paper in between.

In order to live in a community, we will invariably be placed next to other "lively stones," and the Master patiently works on our characters until we fit so well in the body of Christ that, without sacrificing individuality, it is nearly impossible to tell where one stone ends and the next one begins. Sinners do not naturally exist in harmony, but with heaven's chisel, God is shaping our characters until we do.

When Bad Things Happen

And when they had preached the gospel to that city and made many disciples, they returned to
Lystra, Iconium, and Antioch, strengthening the souls of the disciples, exhorting them to continue
in the faith, and saying, "We must through many tribulations enter the kingdom of God."
—Acts 14:21, 22

The life of the apostle Paul was many things, but it certainly was not boring. When he preached the gospel in the city of Lystra, a man who had been crippled from birth was miraculously healed, and the citizens of the city reacted so enthusiastically that it created a serious problem. Convinced that they had just come in contact with the gods, the people tried to worship Paul and Barnabas as Hermes (Mercury) and Zeus (Jupiter). After Paul managed to diffuse that situation, Jews from Antioch and Iconium pulled into town and managed to persuade the crowds in the opposite direction, which resulted in the stoning of Paul.

Paul left the city to preach elsewhere, which is perfectly understandable. What is harder to understand is the fact that after Paul had established a congregation in the nearby city of Derbe, he returned to Lystra. Why? He wanted to encourage the church. Although they had witnessed a genuine miracle in the healing of the lame man, they had also witnessed the fickle nature of crowds and had seen the attempt to kill Paul.

Even after God has intervened in our lives miraculously, the trials and obstacles we face can quickly eclipse the happy moments and make living the Christian life seem, at times, overwhelmingly difficult. In the twenty-first century, we are no less easily dissuaded from the joy of faith by the trials we face than were the ancient Lystrians.

Occasionally, something will happen to us at church that makes us hesitant to return. But notice Paul's Christlike attitude: He was more worried about the courage of the Lystrian Christians than he was about his own safety. He knew that his stoning would serve to discourage many of the new believers, who would have to continue living out their faith in the same city where the great apostle had nearly been murdered. So in spite of any personal misgivings he might have, he returned.

When bad things happen—and in a world engulfed in spiritual warfare, they are bound to—we should consider the possibility that fallen angels are attempting to remove us from a place where we are needed. There are others in the congregation who could use encouragement, and your continued presence in the church can become a ministry of healing for others.

SEPTEMBER 8

The Heart of the Camp

My God, My God, why have You forsaken Me? Why are You so far from helping Me,
and from the words of My groaning? O My God, I cry in the daytime, but You do not hear;
and in the night season, and am not silent. But You are holy, enthroned in the praises of Israel.
—Psalm 22:1–3

The heart cry of the psalmist has become one of the best-known passages in the Bible because it foreshadowed Jesus' darkest moment as He hung on a cross, unable to detect His Father's presence. It was an agony that none of us will truly understand because we have never been as intimately connected with the Father as has the Son. But that does not mean that we do not feel the words of David keenly because every Christian eventually passes through the "valley of the shadow of death" (Psalm 23:4). Every Christian passes through moments when the voice and presence of God appear to be absent.

It is then that we should pay careful attention to the words that follow: "But You are holy, enthroned in the praises of Israel." There are a few things we can learn from this statement. First, when the moment seems dark, we can immediately draw closer to God by praising Him in spite of our circumstances. It is amazing what a song or prayer of gratitude can do to quickly dispel the dark clouds of discouragement. To sing a hymn of praise, like Paul and Silas did at midnight in the Philippian prison (Acts 16:25), can suddenly break open the prison of doubt and discouragement. It is to echo the determination of Daniel's three friends, who told the Babylonian king that they would continue to worship God alone, even if it meant they would face the fiery furnace, and then they found the presence of Jesus in the flames. We are never closer to God than when we worship Him.

There is a second principle that should not escape our notice. The psalmist does not say that God is enthroned in *my* praises; he says that God is enthroned in the praises of *Israel*. It is a corporate statement. In the wilderness experience, the She-kinah glory did not take up residence in Aaron's or Moses' tent; He placed Himself in the heart of the camp, with the twelve tribes encircling His presence.

Something special happens when God's people gather for the act of worship. Every believer ought to spend time with God alone, engaged in daily worship of heaven's King. But the experience is incomplete unless we combine it with corporate worship, where God's people find hope together.

266

A Group Assignment

Therefore, when Paul and Barnabas had no small dissension and dispute with them,
they determined that Paul and Barnabas and certain others of them
should go up to Jerusalem, to the apostles and elders, about this question.
—Acts 15:2

I don't need to join a church," Simon told me. "I'll be God's 'secret agent,' and I'll effect change from the outside." He had been resisting the idea of becoming part of the church for weeks, and now he had decided that he would go it alone, effecting change in the world by himself.

Unfortunately, Simon's thinking about church is not all that uncommon. Millions of people describe themselves as spiritual but have no formal religious affiliation, and even when presented with the gospel of Christ, they still see no need to become part of a church. Chalk it up to cynicism born of centuries of church-state abuse or perhaps to a generation that finds long-term commitments risky. Many of those same millions, after all, are also hesitant about the marriage covenant.

So can Christians go it alone? Some have had to because they happen to be the only believers in the vicinity. But given a choice, the New Testament is clear: Christians were not meant to exist in isolation. When Jesus told His disciples that they were to go and make disciples of all nations, He told them as a group. Then He told them to wait in Jerusalem for the outpouring of the Spirit as a group. After Pentecost, many of them set out for the mission field, but when disputes arose—such as what to do with Gentiles who wanted to come into the church—the church reconvened, again as a group.

In the landscape of the New Testament, Paul looms large and is perhaps the most influential of the apostles. He certainly wrote the largest portion of the New Testament. But even the great apostle, commissioned by Christ Himself, submitted himself to the judgment of the church community. When questions were raised about his evangelistic methods among the Gentiles, he made the trip to Jerusalem, where the larger group could consider the matter.

Solitary Christians run the risk of heading down theological rabbit trails or making decisions that may not be wise. And solitary Christians, none of whom possess all of the gifts of the Spirit, also have no hope of carrying the everlasting gospel to every nation, kindred, tongue, and people. That is the job Jesus gave to the whole group to carry out together.

Organized Religion

And they continued steadfastly in the apostles' doctrine and fellowship,
in the breaking of bread, and in prayers.

—Acts 2:42

One of the more damaging aspects of the marriage of church and state that took place during the Dark Ages is the degree of mistrust that continues to exist when it comes to organized religion. Many people who do not wish to be formally affiliated with an organization continue to describe themselves as "spiritual." They do not object to the idea of God. They may not even question the accuracy of Scripture. They simply do not wish to belong to organized religion.

The alternative, of course, is *disorganized* religion. Over the years, I have had many people come to large evangelistic meetings and enthusiastically tell me that they enjoy coming to the meetings more than they like "organized religion." They are almost always caught by surprise when I point out that a meeting with thousands in attendance is most certainly organized, and it requires hundreds of volunteers working in concert with each other. There are ushers, greeters, registration volunteers, stage managers, prayer coordinators, and many more people involved.

Any honest reading of the Bible quickly reveals that the work of propagating the gospel has always been organized, because that is the way Jesus intended it. Right from the start, in the wake of the Pentecost miracle, the new believers continued to meet with the apostles. They studied together, they prayed together, and they shared meals with each other. They did not disperse and go back to their individual lives. It was not a loose collection of believers that was born on the Day of Pentecost; it was a *community* of believers.

Of course, in a world ruled by the Romans, who, by the latter half of the first century, would come to view the Christians as a threat to the stability of their empire, the community would prove to be all important. When society begins to ostracize you, it is helpful to have a large support network in place. That community is no less important today than it was two thousand years ago, and as final events continue to fall into place, the global network of believers will become even more vital.

To practice biblical Christianity is to practice it in a community. Instead of bemoaning the supposed evils of organized religion, we ought to be asking ourselves how *we* might be able to help organize it even better.

Hardened

*Beware, brethren, lest there be in any of you an evil heart of unbelief in departing
from the living God; but exhort one another daily, while it is called "Today,"
lest any of you be hardened through the deceitfulness of sin.*
—Hebrews 3:12, 13

When I typed today's date at the top of the page, I paused. A mere two decades ago the date had no special significance. It was just another day of the year, bound to pass without much notice. But since 2001, the numbers 9/11 have become iconic; it was the day that terrorists took thousands of lives as they flew airplanes into the Twin Towers, the Pentagon, and a field in Pennsylvania. While there have been many horrific acts of mass murder throughout history, what happened on 9/11 was relatively new to the Western world. Because it was an open attack on the home soil of the most powerful nation on earth, it was an absolute game changer: the world would never again be the same.

Since that time, we have conditioned ourselves to live with mass surveillance, intrusive pat-downs at the airport, and many other things Westerners would have found unacceptable before 2001. It also changed patterns of church attendance: Immediately following the attacks, church pews suddenly swelled with numbers that had not been seen in years. Interest in Bible prophecy spiked dramatically, and evangelistic halls were full of people seeking answers because many sensed there was likely something more behind the attacks than a simple act of war.

It was, in many ways, a turning point. Prior to 9/11, it was hard for people to imagine how many of the scenarios laid out in the book of Revelation could happen anytime soon. After the collapse of the towers, however, there was a renewed awareness that some of the biggest changes to world circumstances can happen overnight.

In a matter of weeks, however, most of the new faces in the church started to disappear. As life returned to the "new normal" and people became engrossed in their routines, fear-based interest in the church waned.

It is too bad those people did not stay. One of the key functions of the church is to make sure we never accept the pain of this sinful world as normal. The author of Hebrews instructs us to "exhort one another daily" so that our hearts do not become hardened. This happens in a Bible-based church community, where the gospel remains as vivid and powerful in quiet times as it does in times of global distress.

SEPTEMBER 12

Of Servitude and Tithing

Honor the LORD with your possessions, and with the firstfruits of all your increase;
so your barns will be filled with plenty, and your vats will overflow with new wine.
—Proverbs 3:9, 10

Money, it is said, is congealed life. We accept it in exchange for the precious hours of our lives that we give away for the sake of someone else's goals. It is what we receive for giving up a significant fraction of the only lifetime we have been given; across the average working career, about one hundred thousand hours are yielded in exchange for cash.

Society then takes a percentage of those hours in the form of taxes, applying them to what someone else determines is the "common good." In other words, you are *again* asked to work for someone else's benefit; this time with even less control and possibly no benefit to yourself.

From a Christian perspective, however, it is not just *you* that loses something when such a huge portion of your life is yielded to other people. We believe that because God is the Source and Sustainer of life and because He paid such an exorbitant price for our redemption, our lives ultimately belong to Him. Paul asks, "Do you not know that your body is the temple of the Holy Spirit who is in you, whom you have from God, and you are not your own? For you were bought at a price; therefore glorify God in your body and in your spirit, which are God's" (1 Corinthians 6:19, 20).

To live in a sinful world is to live, to some extent, a life of servitude. We will always be working for someone else. But when we give the firstfruits of our increase back to God, we are turning our servitude on its head. The hours we exchange for money suddenly become a way to work for God even when we are technically on the clock for someone else.

In the very beginning, before sin, our first parents were free to spend their days carrying out tasks that showcased the majesty of God. They did not report to another human being but directly to the Creator, and they could use their talents for His glory all day long. In giving our tithes to God, the first 10 percent of each day becomes a protest against the fallen state of the world and a daily reminder that one day soon we will once again be able to give God the *whole* day.

Pierced With Sorrow

For the love of money is a root of all kinds of evil, for which some have strayed
from the faith in their greediness, and pierced themselves through with many sorrows.
—1 Timothy 6:10

Born in Russia in 1905, Alisa Rosenbaum was an especially bright child. By the age of ten, she had already begun writing novels, and by the time she was sixteen, she was a history major at Petrograd State University. In 1917, she witnessed the Bolshevik Revolution and when her father's pharmacy was confiscated by the Communists, she became vehemently opposed to the dehumanizing ideology of Communism, a system that was willing to sacrifice human dignity—and even humans—for the "good of the people."

In 1926, she obtained permission to visit the United States, and she never returned. She changed her name to Ayn Rand, and she founded a distinctly anti-Communist school of philosophy known as Objectivism, in which the pursuit of an individual's self-interest is considered the highest good. In common with the Communists, however, she rejected the idea of God.

She wrote a number of powerful books, such as *The Fountainhead* and *Atlas Shrugged*, which continue to influence millions of policy makers to this day because they emphasize individual rights over coercion and collectivism. For many years, Ayn Rand enjoyed a degree of popularity. When she died, a six-foot-tall floral wreath shaped into a dollar sign was placed next to her casket: the ultimate symbol, she believed, of self-interest.

For Ayn Rand, Paul's words to Timothy were prophetic. She rejected the worship of the state embraced by the Communists and replaced it with the worship of self—and ended up piercing herself "through with many sorrows." She died penniless and even began to embrace some of the behaviors she had opposed her entire life, even attempting to control what her followers were permitted to read.

We all worship something, and while the freedom enjoyed in the West has obviously produced the highest standard of living enjoyed by any generation to live on planet Earth, the worship of *things* will always lead to heartbreak. We may not be tempted to bow before carved idols, but the temptation to bow before the dollar is powerful. To be sure, God does not object to money, or even wealth—some of His most notable followers, such as Abraham and Job, have been very well off. But if the pursuit of gain replaces the pursuit of God, then many sorrows are sure to follow.

Foolproof Investment

Come now, you rich, weep and howl for your miseries that are coming upon you!
Your riches are corrupted, and your garments are moth-eaten. Your gold and silver are corroded,
and their corrosion will be a witness against you and will eat your flesh like fire.
You have heaped up treasure in the last days.

—James 5:1–3

Money: in theory, it is only a medium of exchange. Long ago someone figured out that it was much more convenient to trade things such as eggs for cash than to swap them for firewood. What if the woodcutter did not want or need your eggs? Then what? Do you first barter the eggs for something he *does* want? Money could be taken anywhere and exchanged for anything.

Today, what we call "money" is only a promissory note, theoretically backed by something of actual value. At one time, it was backed by physical gold, but now money is no longer backed by much of anything, which is why its value constantly fluctuates. And now promissory notes are beginning to disappear: in some countries, paper currency is being phased out, and when this happens, what we call "money" will be little more than ones and zeros in the internet's cloud.

In America, a dollar in the year 2000 was worth only about one-twentieth of what a dollar was worth in 1900. (It took more than twenty dollars to buy what a single dollar would have purchased in 1900.) Money, in other words, has been losing its value steadily for more than one hundred years. When it was no longer backed by gold, its value became less certain.

The value of the things we work for is subject to all sorts of forces that are beyond our control: inflation, natural disasters, war, artificial market bubbles, and countless other potentially devastating factors. Our worldly goods and our bank accounts can suddenly be devalued, robbing us of a lifetime of saving.

It is, of course, wise to save and prepare for the future, but at the same time, we should be aware that there is nothing certain about money—with one exception. When we take the resources that God has put at our disposal and invest them in the work of evangelism, the dividends suddenly become immeasurable and are absolutely guaranteed. A human being saved for the kingdom will never depreciate. In fact, as the ceaseless ages of eternity unfold in the presence of Christ, I suspect that the people you had the privilege of introducing to Jesus will seem more and more valuable with each passing year. It is the one investment that is guaranteed to appreciate in value forever.

Giving Quietly

*"Take heed that you do not do your charitable deeds before men, to be seen by them.
Otherwise you have no reward from your Father in heaven. Therefore, when you do a charitable
deed, do not sound a trumpet before you as the hypocrites do in the synagogues
and in the streets, that they may have glory from men. Assuredly, I say to you,
they have their reward. But when you do a charitable deed, do not let your left hand
know what your right hand is doing, that your charitable deed may be in secret;
and your Father who sees in secret will Himself reward you openly."*
—Matthew 6:1–4

In the kingdom of heaven, the reason you give is as important as the gift itself. It is one thing to give to God, Jesus points out, and quite another to give for the sake of public acknowledgment. If your primary objective is to have people notice your generosity, then the applause you receive, the structure named in your honor, the plaque on the wall—these things will become your reward in full. You were, after all, giving for the sake of yourself, and with public recognition, you have achieved your goal.

A gift for the sake of love, however, is something altogether different. Consider the case of a man who buys his friend a gift, only because he knows that he needs to move in a month and his friend owns a truck. Once his friend discovers that he had ulterior motives, the gift suddenly becomes meaningless, and the loan of the truck becomes only the repayment of a favor. Help on moving day is all the reward the man will reap; he has done nothing to deepen their friendship. (In fact, he probably created resentment when his friend felt manipulated.)

It is pointless to try and curry favor with God by giving Him things. To begin with, He already owns everything. Second, you already have God's favor through the gift of the Cross. The purpose of giving to God is not to try and buy God's love but to express love for *Him*. If there is an ulterior motive, it is not a gift at all.

Nor is it an act of love if the point of giving is to gain the applause of your fellow church members. When your ambition is to seek prestige in the congregation through public acts of largesse, God may well allow you to have public recognition out of pity because it might just be all the reward you will ever have. After all, pride, the original problem that led to sin, is still an issue. But to give to God quietly is something God always notices because He knows there was only one reason to do it: you love Him, and you long to see His kingdom.

When you give, Jesus says, do not let your left hand know what your right hand is doing.

The Size of the Heart

So He said, "Truly I say to you that this poor widow has put in more than all;
for all these out of their abundance have put in offerings for God,
but she out of her poverty put in all the livelihood that she had."

—Luke 21:3, 4

If human beings have always been wired the same—and I suspect they have been—the gifts of the wealthy at the temple must have turned a lot of heads. "Wow! Did you see how much that guy put into the offering this week? I only wish *I* could give that much!"

People have often been impressed with the charitable deeds of the wealthy. Buildings are dedicated to wealthy families, plaques are placed on walls, and foundations are named for people who have the means to contribute substantial gifts. While the rest of the crowd may have been impressed with the gifts of the affluent, their faces lighting up with wonder, Jesus remained unimpressed. Then came a poor widow who threw in a couple of pennies, and *Jesus* lit up. "Wow! Did you see *that*?"

See what? A poor person tossing a few cents into the plate? So what? How much good could that paltry sum possibly do? You are not going to build a hospital with that money or even start a soup kitchen. It is negligible. What is so impressive about *two cents*?

It was the fact that the poor widow gave it *all*. The wealthy were accustomed to putting large sums in the offering, but they had not given *everything*. The act of complete self-denial warms the heart of God because it means that His own character is being reflected in the heart of a human being. Jesus Himself, after all, gave everything. He gave up the glories of heaven for a life in a world wracked with pain and suffering. He stepped away from the adoration of angels to be mocked and rejected by people whose lives depended on His creative power. He even gave up His own life—absolutely everything He had—to save sinners.

"Let this mind be in you which was also in Christ Jesus," Paul reminds us, "who, being in the form of God, did not consider it robbery to be equal with God, but made Himself of no reputation, taking the form of a bondservant, and coming in the likeness of men" (Philippians 2:5–7).

It is not the number of digits on the check that puts a smile on the face of God; it is the size of the heart that gives it.

God Is a Giver

"Give, and it will be given to you: good measure, pressed down,
shaken together, and running over will be put into your bosom.
For with the same measure that you use, it will be measured back to you."
—Luke 6:38

The billboard was in an unusual place: on a seldom-used road through an industrial park in Washington State. *Who's going to see that here?* I wondered to myself, forgetting the fact that *I* had just seen it. The message? "Become the rich eccentric relative you wish you had!"

It was part of an ad campaign to encourage people to start saving, or to "feed the pig," as the advertisers put it—a reference to putting money in your piggy bank in order to save for old age. Saving money, of course, is sound advice, as a debt-ridden generation will tragically discover as they reach their golden years with nothing in the bank.

Saving money is one of the reliable keys to financial security, but the Bible offers another important key that does not make much sense to most people: *give.* "If you want to be perfect," Jesus told the rich young ruler, "go, sell what you have and give to the poor, and you will have treasure in heaven; and come, follow Me" (Matthew 19:21).

It might not lead to fabulous wealth, but it does lead to security. "For the eyes of the LORD run to and fro throughout the whole earth," we are reminded in 2 Chronicles 16:9, "to show Himself strong on behalf of those whose heart is loyal to Him."

When we adopt a lifestyle of giving, rather than taking, God smiles because it closely aligns with who He is. God is a giver. He gave us this world at Creation as a splendid home for the human race. He gave His life to secure our salvation. And in spite of the pain and suffering we have caused by our rebellion, He intends to restore us to Paradise and give us everything we tossed aside to pursue fallen angels. His "generous Spirit" offers us salvation and sustains us (Psalm 51:12).

So by all means, put something away for your golden years; it is sound advice. But at the same time, discover the joy of spending this one life you have on behalf of others to whom the offer of salvation has also been made. Give for the sake of others, and you will discover that God knows how to keep you in business.

Generosity and Forgiveness

*"But that servant went out and found one of his fellow servants
who owed him a hundred denarii; and he laid hands on him
and took him by the throat, saying, 'Pay me what you owe!' "*
—Matthew 18:28

L ife in the body of Christ could be considered a training ground for heaven. We are, after all, planning to spend eternity with the people who occupy the same pew in church. If we can learn to coexist in this life, when circumstances are less than ideal, it will likely bode well for us in Paradise.

One of the key lessons the schoolroom of the local congregation can offer us is in the art of generosity, which is something that extends well beyond the financial contributions we place in the offering plate. Once we have learned to be generous with our means, we can move on to learn how to be generous with people.

To be generous with your time means placing yourself at someone else's disposal, which, given human nature, will likely require the cultivation of patience. To be generous with your gifts and talents will likely mean learning to give your best even when someone else is calling the shots and you would likely do things differently if you were in charge. To be generous with opportunity means giving someone who might not do things perfectly the chance to participate and grow, even when there are others who would be more experienced and thus more efficient.

To put it another way, participating in the life of the church means learning to live as a family with people who are not related to you by any blood other than the blood of Christ. And in that regard, perhaps the greatest lesson life in the church has to offer is the chance to be generous with *forgiveness.*

As a minister, I have noticed that the number one reason people seem to give for quitting church is the treatment they received from other church members. A church-board decision did not go their way. Someone said something cutting and cruel, and it got back to them. They were not invited to hold a particular office in the church they felt suited—and perhaps called—to.

It happens to all of us; rather than resign from church life, we can take advantage of a unique opportunity to respond to other people with the same generous selflessness that God has extended to us. It is an opportunity to become distinctly more like Christ and perhaps begin to understand the depth of His love. We should do unto others as we would have them do unto us (see Luke 6:31; Matthew 7:12).

To Be Like Tabitha

*Then Peter arose and went with them. When he had come, they brought him
to the upper room. And all the widows stood by him weeping, showing the tunics
and garments which Dorcas had made while she was with them.*
—Acts 9:39

Tabitha, also known as Dorcas, was one of those church members that pastors love to have around. Her contributions to the congregation and the larger community were such that her death was practically considered a showstopper. It was enough of an emergency that messengers were sent to Peter to beg him to come as quickly as possible (Acts 9:38). When the apostle arrived, the death chamber had become a showcase of her considerable talents and contributions.

Almost every congregation has one: that person who always says *yes*. If there is a work bee scheduled for early in the morning, he or she will arrive first and will likely be the person who organized it. The lawn is mowed; the sanctuary is cleaned during the week; and when nobody else will volunteer to lead a project, the local Tabitha will always step up to the plate.

It causes me to ask a question of myself: If I should die tomorrow, would my discontinued participation in God's church be noticed? Since coming to Christ, has my life really been about the kingdom of Christ, or has it more or less remained about me? Do I live for the advancement of the gospel or the advancement of my own ambitions? With Tabitha, there was little question that she lived for Jesus.

There is another question the story raises: Why does the burden of church work always seem to fall on one or two people, while the rest of us take their contributions for granted? How do we allow a handful of people to pick up so much responsibility that we are at a loss when they are no longer there? Should the life of the church depend so heavily on a few individuals that the congregation is never more than one or two funerals away from going out of business?

To be sure, we do not know that this was the case with the congregation at Joppa. It may just be the case that the whole church was very active, and Tabitha happened to be one of those extraordinarily gifted people. But imagine what might happen if we *all* resolved to be like Tabitha! It could just be that once again Christians would be known as the people who turn the world upside-down (Acts 17:6).

Giving Everything

But Jesus said, "Let the little children come to Me,
and do not forbid them; for of such is the kingdom of heaven."
—Matthew 19:14

On more than one occasion, Jesus indicated that of all the humans who live on planet Earth, little children most closely resemble citizens of the kingdom of heaven. And children have any number of traits that make them inherently more Christlike than your average adult: humility, trust, honesty, and gracious dispositions. Children, you may have noticed, also tend to be more generous than the rest of us.

When my daughter was eight years old, she walked into the room one morning counting her way through a stack of one-dollar bills. I was immediately suspicious that such a young child should have come into such a sizable windfall, and I asked her where she had found the money. She had *earned* it, I discovered, by offering her services to neighbors returning from the grocery store. "I help people carry their bags to the door, Daddy, and they usually give me a dollar!"

I could not help but feel a little swell of fatherly pride that she had thought of a way to supplement her allowance all on her own and that she had worked for her money. She had already accumulated twenty-two dollars. When I asked her what she planned to do with the money, she told me it was for buying toys.

"But you do remember that some of that goes to Jesus, right?"

"Yes, Daddy—I know. Ten percent." She asked how much that was, and I told her it was $2.20. "What's He going to do with the two dollars and twenty cents?" she asked.

"He's going to send ministers and missionaries out into the world to tell people how much He loves them," I explained.

"And will they give people Bibles too?" she asked, suddenly very interested. I assured her that it often happened that people received Bibles. "Well then," she said with a note of determination, her hand holding out the entire wad of bills, "take it *all.*"

I know that adults have things such as rent, bills, and mortgages to pay; but aside from your financial obligations to your family, ask yourself a question: When was the last time I gave it all? Children do not worry about where the next dollar is going to come from; they simply cannot see any reason not to give Jesus everything they have and everything they are.

Just One Master

"No one can serve two masters; for either he will hate the one and love the other, or else he will be loyal to the one and despise the other. You cannot serve God and mammon."
—Matthew 6:24

Christianity and money have always seemed to have a bit of an uneasy relationship. From the fund-raising schemes of the sixteenth century that helped to trigger the Protestant Reformation to the religious hucksters of our own century, who see media ministry as a formidable opportunity to sell false hope, the world has had countless opportunities to see the truth of Jesus' statement firsthand: if you serve money, you are not serving God.

The prominent scandals of the last twenty centuries have made it awkward for churches and Christian organizations to raise the money they need to operate; the modern public is immediately suspicious about anybody who asks for funds—and obviously with good reason. The matter of finance (especially when coupled with sexual scandal) is one area where the devil has been remarkably successful in bringing the cause of Christ into disrepute.

It means that above all people, sincere Christians must be exceptionally careful to avoid any hint of impropriety in financial matters. We must remember that while our personal conduct may be above board, in the public's eye, we are all wearing the treachery of the past. Once you identify yourself as a Christian, you are no longer operating on a level playing field; you will be held to a higher standard. Ask yourself how many times you have heard an angry person sputter the words, "And he claims to be a Christian!" You will suddenly realize that the world looks at us differently. Everyone else is out to make a dollar, too, but your motives will be scrutinized by a different standard and on a different level.

Is that fair? Probably not. But then again, the world has never dealt with Christians fairly, and the higher level of scrutiny does provide us with an opportunity to remind ourselves that we have not been placed in this world to accumulate possessions. None of them will survive the Second Coming. Not only should the way we handle money be circumspect enough to avoid the appearance of impropriety, but it should also make it obvious to the world that our priorities are radically different from everyone else. It should be clear to anyone looking in from the outside that our real treasure has nothing to do with things and everything to do with the Pearl of great price.

Indispensable

But now indeed there are many members, yet one body. And the eye cannot say to the hand,
"I have no need of you"; nor again the head to the feet, "I have no need of you."
No, much rather, those members of the body which seem to be weaker are necessary.
—1 Corinthians 12:20–22

When you first become a part of Christ's church, it can be a little over-whelming to consider that you have just taken your place alongside some pretty big names. You are no less a part of the church than were the original twelve disciples or the great luminaries that lived between the first century and now. You are no less valuable to Jesus than the men and women whose names grace the pages of historical books or the martyrs who gave their lives for the sake of the gospel. You are as much a part of fulfilling the gospel commission as any of them.

It is natural to ask the question: But what have *I* got to offer? Next to the seem-ingly great feats of famous believers, our potential for contribution can seem minus-cule in comparison. We feel like the toddler who is given an "important job" to do alongside his mother in the kitchen so that he can feel as if he is a valuable part of the team, but in reality, he has been given an insignificant task to perform to keep him from getting underfoot.

Paul explains that in the work of the church there are no people who are merely "Mommy's special helper." Nobody occupies a station in the work of the church such that he or she can disregard the contributions of others as unimportant. We have not been sent into the world as a loose collection of individuals but as the body of Christ. On an individual basis, no one's efforts amount to much, but when as-sembled together, we become the presence of Jesus to the world—a complete body.

In reality, the contribution *any* human being can make is minuscule in com-parison to the service of angels, whose abilities exceed our own considerably. But the way Scripture reads, it is hard to come to the conclusion that angels find our participation in the great controversy meaningless.

The key thing to remember when you engage in God's work is that He did not call you to be someone else; He called you because of who *you* are. Your place in the family of Christ is unique and can only be filled by you because God considers you as indispensable as any other part of His church.

What You Stand to Give

By covetousness they will exploit you with deceptive words;
for a long time their judgment has not been idle, and their destruction does not slumber.
—2 Peter 2:3

Any time I am tempted to think that the church of the twenty-first century has more problems than previous generations, a bit of time spent reading the New Testament makes me realize that there is nothing new under the sun. Much of the material found in the New Testament letters was originally composed to address issues within the church, including the words from Peter's second letter that we are studying today.

Peter warned his audience that false teachers and prophets were just as likely in the New Testament era as they were in the Old, and he identifies "covetousness" as their motivating factor. They are preying on the church, in other words, for the sake of personal gain. Perhaps that perceived gain included things such as power and position; but in our day and age, it almost certainly includes money.

Peter's warning should make us think twice any time we catch ourselves viewing the local congregation as a source of income. While there is certainly nothing wrong with doing business with a fellow church member, if we start to view the church directory as a list of sales leads, something might be amiss. We do not have to be teaching false doctrine or seeking a position in the church to cross the line into being motivated by covetousness.

Years ago I knew a man who became involved in a multilevel marketing scheme, and his "upline" representative encouraged him to recruit the members of his church, so he dutifully called every name in the church directory. It utterly ruined his relationship with everyone because few people trusted his motives after that. Every time he made contact, people mentally questioned whether he was thinking about the work of the church or whether he was just generating sales leads. His motives for church membership had been compromised, and he managed to generate more distrust and ill will than anything else. His actions had effectively isolated him from fully participating in the life of the church—to the point where church members wondered if he was really sharing the gospel or merely trying to make more contacts.

Perhaps the test of our motivations is as simple as asking ourselves if our actions within the church are more about what we stand to gain or what we stand to give.

Your Profound Ability

Then Moses said to the LORD, "O my Lord, I am not eloquent,
neither before nor since You have spoken to Your servant;
but I am slow of speech and slow of tongue."
So the LORD said to him, "Who has made man's mouth?
Or who makes the mute, the deaf, the seeing, or the blind? Have not I, the LORD?
Now therefore, go, and I will be with your mouth and teach you what you shall say."
—Exodus 4:10–12

Most of us can completely identify with Moses' hesitation to serve as God's spokesperson in Pharaoh's court. In fact, we might even be suspicious of someone who believed himself to be completely qualified for the job: "What took You so long, God? I'm the *perfect* man for the job!" It is the kind of pride that disqualifies a person for spiritual leadership.

The story of Moses, however, is good medicine for those who feel incompetent to serve in God's kingdom. Walking close to Christ can make you keenly aware of your shortcomings, like bright lights have a way of making flaws more obvious. But the story of Moses demonstrates that serving in God's church is one of the ways that He grows our faith.

When Moses realized that he was being asked to speak and that he was being asked to do it in very prominent circles, he recoiled in horror. "Have You *heard* me, Lord? I'm about the worst choice available for this assignment!"

Pay careful attention to God's reply because it proves important to your own calling. "Didn't I make you in the first place?" He asks. God is well aware of our shortcomings, and He reminds us of an important fact: He is the Creator. Our personal shortcomings are the result of the human race's willful separation from God; but when we choose—by faith—to place ourselves back under His care and control, He can make new and wonderful creations of us.

The Bible promises that we can become "a new creation" in Christ (2 Corinthians 5:17). He can restore to us the qualities that sin corrupted and bring us back to His original design. In God's hands, you are capable of more than without Him. But in order to see what God is planning to do through you, you must begin serving by faith. Your new capacity for service will not manifest itself privately at home; it grows through use.

Many people feel that they are not able to do great things in God's kingdom, and so they never try. Forgetting that their Master is the Creator, they simply assume that they cannot contribute. Never say *no* until you have tried; you might be amazed at what God is waiting to do through you.

Everything

Then Melchizedek king of Salem brought out bread and wine;
he was the priest of God Most High. And he blessed him and said:
"Blessed be Abram of God Most High, possessor of heaven and earth;
and blessed be God Most High, who has delivered your enemies into your hand."
And he gave him a tithe of all.

—Genesis 14:18–20

The exchange between Abraham and Melchizedek is one of the briefest and yet most fascinating encounters in the Bible. While we believe Melchizedek to be a human being and not a Christophany (a preincarnate appearance of Jesus), it seems fairly evident that he is a *type* or symbol of Christ. One of the strongest indications that he is meant to foreshadow Jesus is found in the gifts he presents to Abraham: bread and wine.

Those two gifts just happen to be the elements of the Communion service, representing the body and the blood of Christ. The fact that a priest and representative of the Most High God presents these elements to the friend of God is not likely a coincidence. Abraham's entire journey to the Land of Promise, as well as that of his descendants who later escaped Egypt, points forward to the eventual exodus of God's people from spiritual Babylon and Egypt to the heavenly Canaan and the New Jerusalem. Christ's all-important contribution to our salvation is His very life at Calvary.

In that context, Abraham's tithe makes a powerful statement. It demonstrates what true gratitude looks like. The bread and the wine point us to what God is willing to invest in our salvation, which is absolutely *everything*. And in return, when we tithe our income, we are not suggesting that we can earn our salvation. (You will notice the act of tithing came after Melchizedek freely gave Abraham the emblems.) It is rather an act of gratitude; one that says, "All that I am and all that I have belong to You."

It shows us that our relationship to God is not merely a legal transaction; it is a profound relationship in which both God and man are completely sold out to each other—much the way (as Paul points out in Ephesians 5) that husband and wife are so completely sold out to each other that they essentially become one person. Jesus so completely identifies with us that He has assumed human identity forever and plans to live among us eternally in the earth made new. We so completely identify with Jesus that we are counted as Abraham's seed (Galatians 3:29), take on the name "Christian," and reckon that everything we own in this life belongs to Him.

What God Really Wants

But a certain man named Ananias, with Sapphira his wife, sold a possession. And he kept back part of the proceeds, his wife also being aware of it, and brought a certain part and laid it at the apostles' feet. But Peter said, "Ananias, why has Satan filled your heart to lie to the Holy Spirit and keep back part of the price of the land for yourself? While it remained, was it not your own? And after it was sold, was it not in your own control? Why have you conceived this thing in your heart? You have not lied to men but to God."
—Acts 5:1–4

The story of Ananias and Sapphira may be one of the most troubling episodes in the book of Acts. The penalty for publicly misrepresenting their charitable contribution was immediate death. Over the years, I have heard some people suggest that the couples' crime was holding back part of the proceeds of the sale, as if it is a serious crime against God not to give everything you own to the church.

The context, however, suggests otherwise. "After it was sold," Peter asked, "was it not in your own control?" In other words, they were not *required* to give any of the funds to the church. The money was theirs to do with as they saw fit.

It tells us something of the nature of giving in the church. There are religious groups who assess church members either by a percentage of their income or by a percentage of the church budget in order to finance their work, which makes giving more a matter of membership dues than freewill giving. Peter's response to the dishonest couple makes it clear that God considers giving voluntary. While Malachi indicates that withholding tithe is a form of robbery (Malachi 3:8), it is still up to the individual whether to give or not. God does not coerce; the gift given freely is worth far more than the one given grudgingly.

"So let each one give as he purposes in his heart," Paul reminds us, "not grudgingly or of necessity; for God loves a cheerful giver" (2 Corinthians 9:7).

So with Ananias and Sapphira, what was the crime? They were giving for the sake of personal recognition, even lying in an attempt to elevate the esteem in which the congregation held them. Their gift had nothing to do with gratitude to God or the furtherance of the work; they were quietly attempting to make a profit. Not a financial profit, perhaps, but it was still a personal gain nonetheless. They were also planning to steal from the others. The funds collected were combined to support all the believers, and if they were believed to have yielded everything, they were entitled to live from the common pool while secretly keeping a significant portion for themselves.

The story underlines an important fact: God does not need our finances; rather, He wants our hearts.

Better Together

"I pray for them. I do not pray for the world but for those whom You have given Me, for they are Yours. And all Mine are Yours, and Yours are Mine, and I am glorified in them. Now I am no longer in the world, but these are in the world, and I come to You. Holy Father, keep through Your name those whom You have given Me, that they may be one as We are."
—John 17:9–11

It can be a remarkably difficult thing to submit to the decisions and will of the church. Most of us, after all, tend to trust our own perceptions and judgments more than those of other people. For the independent minded, it often seems best to strike out on our own and do the work of the gospel in a way that seems right to us.

Years ago I participated in a group exercise, even though I am not naturally wired to enjoy such things. In a thought experiment, each individual was told that he or she would have to survive in the middle of the Sonoran Desert for a number of weeks and was asked to choose a handful of items they deemed helpful from a long list. After each person's list was complete, the room was divided into small groups, each of which was asked to compile a second list of items through the process of negotiating around the table. When both lists were complete, a survival expert assessed each list and determined that the majority of people in the room would perish quickly with their individual lists, but most people would probably survive if they used the lists compiled by the groups.

The intended lesson was simple: few people are as resourceful alone as they are in groups. A variety of perspectives, thought processes, and talents made more solutions available to every individual. The same can be said of the church: individuals who attempt to fulfill the gospel commission on their own might meet with some success; but when the body of Christ works together and all of the gifts of the Spirit are assembled in one place, suddenly, far more is possible.

You will notice that as Jesus prayed for the church, one of His key concerns was that we remain united—as closely bonded to each other and to Christ as Jesus is with His Father. Working together can prove challenging at times, and apart from outright apostasy, it will sometimes mean that for the sake of keeping the body united we have to acquiesce to a decision we do not personally feel is best. Over time, we will notice that the gifts the Spirit has chosen for us will become far more effective when synchronized with gifts He has chosen for others.

Enabled

Then Moses said to the LORD, "O my Lord, I am not eloquent, neither before
nor since You have spoken to Your servant; but I am slow of speech and slow of tongue."
So the LORD said to him, "Who has made man's mouth? Or who makes the mute,
the deaf, the seeing, or the blind? Have not I, the LORD? Now therefore, go,
and I will be with your mouth and teach you what you shall say."
But he said, "O my Lord, please send by the hand of whomever else You may send."
—Exodus 4:10–13

I have often supposed that the word *reluctant* would be a good way to describe my life in public ministry. People often assume when you frequently stand at the front that you are comfortable there. I am anything but. In fact, I am a lifelong, off-the-charts introvert; a man who continues to live in sheer terror of public speaking.

When I am asked to do something in the public eye, my first instinct is to think of someone else who could do it better. In that regard, I can sympathize with Moses as he wrestles with the commission to go and speak with Pharaoh. "Please, send someone else," he argues. "I am not eloquent, and I *know* I'm going to do a horrible job of this."

Chances are that you can relate. Studies reveal that roughly one-third of us are introverts: people who crave more time alone, not more time in front of the masses. Introverts prefer books and essays, not speeches and presentations.

The difficult part of the story is God's reaction to Moses. "Didn't I make your mouth?" He asks. "Don't you believe that I can enable you once you're standing in front of the king of Egypt?" With the benefit of hindsight, you and I can observe what Moses is struggling to see: he has just spent forty years in the wilderness, being meticulously trained by God for this moment.

You will find the same thing, if you will only exercise your faith. Your commission is much like the one Moses received: you have been asked to share the gospel, the message of freedom, with the world around you. One day, in the courts of glory, you will be able to look back, the way we can look back at Moses' story, and see that God has used all of the circumstances of your life to prepare you for this moment. It is time to step out in faith and believe that God made you. He knows what He is doing. Your gifts were given to you—and not someone else—specifically. You are called. As the old saying goes, "God's calling is God's enabling."

It is not just a saying; it is a promise: "He who calls you is faithful, who also will do it" (1 Thessalonians 5:24).

Reveal the Conductor

Now, therefore, you are no longer strangers and foreigners, but fellow citizens with the saints and members of the household of God, having been built on the foundation of the apostles and prophets, Jesus Christ Himself being the chief cornerstone, in whom the whole building, being fitted together, grows into a holy temple in the Lord, in whom you also are being built together for a dwelling place of God in the Spirit.
—Ephesians 2:19–22

It should be carefully noted that when Jesus left for heaven, He did not leave behind a single individual who had been divinely nominated to be His representative on earth. Instead, He left behind twelve disciples (Judas having been replaced) who would form the earliest nucleus of the Christian church—the entity through which Jesus would continue to be present on earth. Led by the Spirit and made up of diverse individuals, the combined presence of Christians on earth would make Jesus visible to the world.

No one person alone can truly represent Jesus to the world because none of us possesses every one of His attributes. But as Paul points out, the church becomes the dwelling place of God when we work in harmony with each other. Millions of believers serving together can better represent the infinite character of God than any one individual can.

When we choose to work alone, it is far too easy for our efforts to take on the flavor of our own personality. With just one person, the "church" (if one person can be called a church) is created in one's own image more than that of Jesus. It more easily reveals self to the world than it does the majestic person of Christ. That is not to say that there are no Christlike individuals in the world; I have met many who reflect the character of Jesus beautifully. But the efforts of a single individual will never be as broad a portrayal of Jesus as the labors of many people combining their God-given gifts and influence.

It is not unlike the difference between a soloist and a full orchestra. A soloist can produce astonishingly beautiful music, and fans will quickly learn to identify his or her unique sound. The music has been flavored by the soloist's personality. But a full orchestra is different. When many instruments combine their sounds together, the result is much larger and fuller; it reveals the character of the conductor rather than any one player or singer.

Our task is to reveal the Conductor to the world, and that becomes much easier when we follow His prompting and combine our efforts in order to light up the planet with God's glory in the last moments before Jesus returns.

Every Bit of You

*And when Simon saw that through the laying on of the apostles' hands the
Holy Spirit was given, he offered them money, saying, "Give me this power also,
that anyone on whom I lay hands may receive the Holy Spirit."
But Peter said to him, "Your money perish with you, because
you thought that the gift of God could be purchased with money!"*
—Acts 8:18–20

We find it easy to be hard on Simon, the former sorcerer. "Imagine that!" we tell ourselves. "He thought he could buy the gift of the Holy Spirit!" It seems so obvious to us that what Simon was doing was wrong. But before we contentedly contrast ourselves with him, assuring ourselves that we belong in a different—and more enlightened—category of believer, perhaps we should take stock of our own belief systems.

Simon's reaction to the gift of the Spirit was the product of the world he had just left, where nothing came for free, and everything and everybody could be bought. It was not unlike the world we live in, where money talks, and it is assumed that every person has his or her price. If someone resists our request in the twenty-first century, we sweeten the deal, knowing that eventually most people's resistance will wear thin.

We take our experiences from that world into the church, just like Simon did. We may not offer cash for the gifts of the Spirit (because we would not be sure where to offer it at any rate), and we may not bribe the nominating committee with legal tender, but we still bring a negotiation mind-set to Christianity.

Most of us do it quietly, bargaining directly with God. "Lord," we pray, "if only You'd do *this* for me, then I'd do *that*. Get me through this event, or help me accomplish that task, and I'll help more at church or give more in the offering." From heaven's perspective, such bargaining must seem ridiculous. What can a mere mortal offer God that He does not already have?

The act of tithing can be a rich corrective to such thinking. It reminds us that everything we have is already a gift from God, and He asks us to contribute a mere fraction as a reminder that we are in a lopsided partnership with the Creator: He provides absolutely everything. We did not purchase or earn our salvation; He did. We do not secure the blessing of heaven by balancing the scales of giving. God blesses *us* because He loves us.

It is not our *things* that God seeks; it is our heart. Ultimately, He does not want some of your possessions—He wants every bit of you.

October

I believe that my body is the temple of the Holy Spirit, and will honor God by caring for it, avoiding the use of that which is harmful; abstaining from all unclean foods; from the use, manufacture, or sale of alcoholic beverages; the use, manufacture, or sale of tobacco in any of its forms for human consumption; and from the misuse of or trafficking in narcotics or other drugs.

Healing in His Wings

And Jesus went about all Galilee, teaching in their synagogues, preaching the gospel of the kingdom, and healing all kinds of sickness and all kinds of disease among the people.
—Matthew 4:23

It is hard to imagine the kind of heartbreak that our broken world must have presented to Jesus when He walked among us. The Creator Himself was in our midst, with a front-row seat to human suffering. Eyes that had been created to enjoy the spectacular beauty of creation were darkened. Ears that were made to hear the music of the universe and the approach of God in the cool of the evening were oblivious. Legs that were made to carry a person over the next hillside to witness another breathtaking horizon were limp and useless. Instead of joy, peace, and contentment, the human race was afflicted with sorrow, pain, and anxiety.

The Bible record indicates that Jesus was engaged in two key activities during His time on earth: teaching and healing. Some Bible students have estimated that Jesus may have spent more time healing than teaching, and if their estimates are correct, it speaks volumes about the character of Christ and His intentions toward us. When Jesus came to town, the tide of suffering was suddenly pushed back. Cases that had baffled the physicians were miraculously resolved. Families who were preparing to say goodbye to a loved one with a terminal illness had their fortunes suddenly reversed.

Even the dead came back to life, but not every person was healed and not every death reversed. What Jesus accomplished during His short tenure on earth can be considered a down payment on what He will do for all of us once the judgment has come to a close and He lays claim to His prize. When He returns then, His feet will finally touch the planet (Zechariah 14:4), which is the sign that He has been awarded permanent ownership of the planet:★ "and the LORD shall be King over all the earth" (verse 9). Any claim that the devil has made on the planet or on the human race will have been utterly refuted, and the healing work of God will be complete. With Lucifer eliminated, the human race will once again be free to live as God originally intended.

"But to you who fear My name the Sun of Righteousness shall arise with healing in His wings; and you shall go out and grow fat like stall-fed calves" (Malachi 4:2).

★ The foot is often used as a symbol of ownership in the Bible. Cf. Genesis 13:17.

The Synergy of Healing

"Is this not the fast that I have chosen: to loose the bonds of wickedness, to undo the heavy burdens, to let the oppressed go free, and that you break every yoke? Is it not to share your bread with the hungry, and that you bring to your house the poor who are cast out; when you see the naked, that you cover him, and not hide yourself from your own flesh?"
—Isaiah 58:6, 7

Isaiah addressed the words in today's Bible verse to people who were very religious and were careful to offer sacrifices and observe rituals, yet God found their fasting vacuous. "You participate in religious rituals," He told them, "and yet you do nothing to assist with the suffering of your fellow man."

I must confess that when I read these words, I have to plead guilty. It is so much easier, so much more convenient, to pretend that we do not see the suffering of people around us because to acknowledge it—and do something about it—often means compromising our own comfort and security. Not long ago, while I was traveling in rural Italy, a young man approached me as I walked out of the grocery store and asked me for a bottle of water. I had just purchased the water because I was going to spend the day working in the mountains and would not have access to water for about fourteen hours. To yield the bottle would mean going back into the store and waiting in line to buy another one, so my first instinct was to refuse him.

But as he walked away, a little voice whispered the words from Isaiah 58 into my heart. *"It would have been so easy to be the presence of Jesus for that young man,"* the voice reminded me. I repented and handed him the water, understanding that any inconvenience I might experience paled in comparison to life on the street.

Many of us ask God to heal us of various afflictions, and rightly so. We have been invited to boldly enter His throne room and present our requests (Hebrews 4:16). But we should never forget that while we are proficient at asking, we have also been asked to be someone else's answer to prayer.

It appears to be a synergistic relationship; our willingness to be agents of healing for others brings healing to our own lives. God uses our participation in ministry to bring about change in our lives because when our focus is directed outward, toward others, we truly get out of the way so that He can work on us. "Then your light shall break forth like the morning," Isaiah 58:8 continues, "your healing shall spring forth speedily."

You Were Heard

Now a certain woman had a flow of blood for twelve years, and had suffered many things from many physicians. She had spent all that she had and was no better, but rather grew worse. When she heard about Jesus, she came behind Him in the crowd and touched His garment.
—Mark 5:25–27

There were a lot of people crowding around Jesus when a suffering woman desperately wanted to make contact. I have seen something similar to this many times during an evangelistic series: At the close of a meeting, there are scores of people who want to tell me something. Most of them want to share a story that seems similar to one I just told, a clever interpretation of a Bible passage, or even a dream they once had. As they talk to me, I will often see a shy person in the background, a guest, who clearly has an issue that needs addressing but is far too timid to interrupt.

The suffering woman of Jesus' day faced a similar problem: she desperately wanted to interact with Him, but the crowds made access seem impossible. *Maybe if I could just touch His garment,* she thought to herself, *that would be good enough.* So she pushed her way through the crowd just to the point where she could reach through the moving people and quickly touch Him.

Perhaps the most exciting part of the story is the fact that Jesus noticed. "Who touched My clothes?" He asked (see Mark 5:30). He had been bumped and jostled hundreds of times by curious onlookers; but when a humble woman made a quiet request by faith, Jesus recognized it as different. She was not merely curious; she *needed* Him.

The story gives incredible hope to the suffering. There are more than seven billion people on this planet; yet when you bring your deepest need to Christ, He hears your voice among all those countless millions. He instantly recognizes the plea of faith and the desperate cry for wholeness. Suffering does not escape His notice, and neither does faith.

While not everyone is granted instantaneous healing, it is guaranteed at some point. God has seen what this broken world has done to you, and He instantly recognizes your plea for healing. It does not escape His notice. Jesus suddenly stopped the crowd, and I suspect He still stops everything for a moment when the plea of faith reaches Him. And one day, in the earth made new, you will know for sure that your cry did not go unheard, because your faith, like that woman's, will have made you whole.

Read the Manual

"If you diligently heed the voice of the LORD your God and do what is right in His sight, give ear to His commandments and keep all His statutes, I will put none of the diseases on you which I have brought on the Egyptians. For I am the LORD who heals you."
—Exodus 15:26

I once had a good friend who told me he had found an amazing deal on collapsible lawn chairs. "They were only ten dollars each!" he boasted. When I saw them, I understood *why* they were so inexpensive: they were designed for little children. Somehow, he had failed to notice. Later that week, as we set our chairs around the campfire, he sat in his bargain, and over the course of the next ten minutes, the legs of the chair slowly bent underneath his weight until the chair collapsed to half its previous height.

My friend was not amused. "What a piece of junk!" he indignantly exclaimed, disgusted with what he believed to be shoddy workmanship. (Even if the chair *had* been designed for adults, he probably should have asked himself why it was so inexpensive.) "I'm going to demand a refund!" There was, of course, no refund due, because he had been using the chair improperly; it had never been designed to hold his weight.

The same holds true for the human body. Day in and day out, we punish the human machine, using our bodies in ways that God never intended when He designed them. We skate by on barely enough sleep. We fuel our bodies with processed junk foods. We ingest substances that create short-term feelings of euphoria but take a toll on the system that far outweighs any perceived benefit. And then, when it all breaks down, we shake our fists at heaven and blame the Creator for allowing us to get sick.

You will notice, however, God's prescription for living a fuller, healthier life. As Israel was departing Egypt, God told them how to avoid the diseases that were prevalent among the Egyptians: live in harmony with the Creator. "If you do what is right in My sight," God explained, "I will put none of the diseases on you."

The counsel is simple: Pay attention to the Manufacturer's instructions. Start using the marvelous biological machine God has given you in the way He intended, and you will find that it does not collapse under a weight that it was never designed to hold. It simply cannot be a coincidence that those who follow the Bible's advice are world-renowned for living up to ten healthier years than everyone else.★

★ Dan Buettner, "The Secrets of Long Life," *National Geographic*, November 2005.

Borrowed

Or do you not know that your body is the temple of the Holy Spirit who is in you,
whom you have from God, and you are not your own?
—1 Corinthians 6:19

When I first asked my wife out, I was a poor college student who did not own a car. Desperate to make a good impression, I approached a good friend who owned a nice sports car and half-heartedly asked whether I could borrow it, knowing that the chances he would place it in my care were slim to none. To my surprise, he consented.

As you can imagine, I was *very* careful with his car. Not only did I drive cautiously, but I also took it to be detailed when the date was over so that I could return it in better condition than I had received it. When you do not own something, there is added incentive to take care of it.

The Bible teaches that the Christian does not own his or her body. As Paul encourages the Corinthian believers to avoid sexual immorality, he explains that our bodies are the temple of the Holy Spirit and we have surrendered any claim to ownership when we joined the Christian church. "You are not your own," he states.

When we come to Christ, we place ourselves at heaven's disposal, joining the army of angels who delight to do God's bidding. We use the days we have in this world to bring honor to His name, to display His character to the world, and to invite people to become part of Christ's family. And because we do not own our bodies, we have a responsibility to keep them in top running order so that our efforts in God's service will be more effective and last longer.

But it is not simply a matter of being used by God. God also knows that by living in harmony with Him, we will enjoy far more abundant lives. There are many diseases in our day and age that are brought on by lifestyle, and they rob their victims of many years of joy, forcing them instead to wait out their days through disabling pain.

The owner of the car smiled when I returned his car in pristine order, happy to have loaned it to me. We ought to make it our goal to return these bodies of ours to Jesus the same way—as pristine as possible—having used them in ways that make Him smile.

Your Price Tag

For you were bought at a price; therefore glorify God in your body
and in your spirit, which are God's.
—1 Corinthians 6:20

People tend to have a skewed understanding of what their possessions are actually worth. Over the years, individuals have made very generous donations to some of the ministries I have been a part of, including things such as homes and cars. Often, however, they have been disappointed when the item sells for less than they believed it to be worth.

Such was the case with a vehicle that a lady donated. Its expected value kept dropping as potential buyer after potential buyer discovered things that needed to be repaired. At one point, we realized that it would never pass an emissions test, and the only way we were going to be able to sell it was to drive it to a jurisdiction that did not require the test. By the time we finally sold it, we realized only about a third of the price she had expected.

She was visibly disappointed when I told her. "But it's worth much more!" she protested.

Unfortunately, no matter how attached we might be to a particular item, it is never worth more than what people are willing to pay for it. I can insist that my humble, aging hatchback is worth twenty thousand dollars, but if nobody will pay more than fifteen hundred dollars for it, that is all it is worth.

Now ask yourself what price God was willing to pay to secure your salvation, and it will give you some idea of the estimate God has placed on you. Paul reminds us that we have been "bought at a price," and that price was Calvary. You have been deemed so valuable to the kingdom that God did not spare His only begotten Son in order to save you.

Many people have such a low estimate of their own value that they cause themselves harm as a result. They abuse the one and only body they have been gifted, never realizing what they are truly worth. "God has paid an infinite price for you," Paul reminds us, "therefore glorify God in your body and in your spirit."

As it turns out, you are not an old, rusty hatchback sitting neglected in an abandoned garage. You are more like a performance vehicle, so valuable to God that He gave everything He had to obtain you. That ought to change how you handle yourself.

Abundant Life

*"The thief does not come except to steal, and to kill, and to destroy. I have come
that they may have life, and that they may have it more abundantly."*
—John 10:10

In one short sentence, Jesus rips the veil off the great controversy and shows us
exactly who is doing what on planet Earth. While much of the human race
continues to blame God for the death and destruction we are faced with every day,
it is actually "the thief"—Satan—who is the instigator of human suffering. And it is
not as if he is causing suffering incidentally, as he engages in other tasks. Jesus points
out that it is Satan's objective: he has come to steal, kill, and destroy.

Jesus, on the other hand, came into the world to reveal the true nature of God.
"He who has seen Me," He explained to Philip, "has seen the Father" (John 14:9).
And what are God's intentions toward us? "That they may have life, and that they
may have it more abundantly."

A clear line of demarcation is drawn between the destroyer and the Creator.
When we suffer, it is not because disease and suffering were part of God's plan. It is
because an enemy has tampered with creation in an effort to cast God in a bad light.
If we blame God for our misfortune, we will continue to question His character, as
we did when Satan first suggested to Eve that God had not been forthright about
the tree in the Garden.

The sad result, of course, is that when we hold God responsible for the suffering
that we brought on ourselves by accepting the lies of the destroyer, we damage our
chances at a more abundant life even further. Not only is our connection to the
Source of life compromised, but we also deliberately resist Him and push away the
only solution available.

There is a promise in the words of Jesus. He has not only come to secure our
salvation but to give us better, fuller lives, even as we wait for His return and our
complete restoration in the earth made new. We can begin living now as if we are
already in the kingdom, laying claim to some of the benefits that will be ours eternally when we live in the immediate presence of Christ. And our ultimate reward
is not only to live eternally but with Jesus Himself, which will make life richer and
more abundant.

Our Collective Problem

Now as Jesus passed by, He saw a man who was blind from birth.
And His disciples asked Him, saying, "Rabbi, who sinned,
this man or his parents, that he was born blind?"
Jesus answered, "Neither this man nor his parents sinned,
but that the works of God should be revealed in him."

—John 9:1–3

Very little about human nature has changed since the day Jesus had to explain to His disciples that a man's blindness was not the result of personal sin. Even today, people seem to have a habit of trying to assign blame when something goes wrong.

Years ago a good friend of mine was diagnosed with a very aggressive cancer that first caused an amputation and later cost him his life. Shortly after he received his diagnosis, a meddlesome church member decided that he knew why my friend was suffering and dropped by the house to question him: "You ate cheese, didn't you?"

It was an absurd suggestion. Every day millions upon millions of people eat cheese without contracting a lethal disease. The visitor, like the disciples, had assumed that illness must somehow be the fault of the sufferer, and since my friend's life was exemplary, he narrowed down his options to the occasional consumption of cheese. Needless to say, my friend's wife was suddenly possessed of a strong desire to physically remove the meddler from the house.

One of the worst things you can do when someone is suffering is to suggest that it must be self-inflicted. It is a useless discussion because most sufferers have already considered that possibility as they pass through the stages of grief and explore the "why" of personal suffering. About all you can accomplish by suggesting fault— usually from a position of ignorance—is to make their suffering worse.

"Rabbi, who sinned, that this man should be born blind?" the disciples asked. "Was it him or his parents?" To be sure, all suffering is the result of human sin, but that is true in the collective sense: Our well-being as a race has been compromised through sin and rebellion. Our systemic disconnect from the Creator has resulted in brokenness. In that sense, we are as much at fault for someone's suffering as the sufferer. This is *our* problem, not any single individual's, and even the best among us eventually succumb to disease.

It would be so much more constructive to take the approach of Jesus and look at someone's suffering as an opportunity to demonstrate God's intention to restore wholeness and to do what you can to share the burden and alleviate the suffering.

"Not Now"

Concerning this thing I pleaded with the Lord three times that it might depart from me.
And He said to me, "My grace is sufficient for you, for My strength
is made perfect in weakness." Therefore most gladly I will rather boast in my infirmities,
that the power of Christ may rest upon me.
—2 Corinthians 12:8, 9

Nothing seems quite as unjust as death. Theoretically, Christians understand that it *is* just: Death is the result of sin. We deserve it. But to witness it or to experience it, that is the moment when it seems patently unfair. You spend your life accomplishing things, improving your skill set, building your knowledge, and then it all disappears into the grave.

It can be especially difficult if you have prayed for healing and the result is still death. Over the course of more than two decades, I have seen some spectacular answers to prayer—a tumor disappears, a deformity is corrected, and a man wakes up unexpectedly from a coma. But I have also seen some prayers appear to go unanswered. The first person for whom I performed an anointing service was also the first funeral I conducted; we did not seem to get the answer we were looking for.

When you pray for healing and it does not happen when you would like, it is tempting to think that perhaps something is wrong with your prayer life or perhaps there is even something wrong with *you*. When I have prayed for someone's healing and it did not happen, I have often asked God if perhaps there was something in *my* life that stood in the way of an answer.

It is important to understand that sometimes God says, "Not now." The promise of healing is guaranteed—all believers receive complete restoration at the resurrection—but the timing is not. We are not entirely certain what Paul's affliction was (some have speculated that it was his eyesight), but we do know that after praying for deliverance three times, he did not receive the answer he wanted.

If a great hero of faith like Paul did not get the answer he wanted, we should be slow to assign blame when our prayers do not yield the result we hoped for. Rather than worry that something is wrong with our faith, we should continue trusting as Paul did, understanding that in the grander scheme of the great controversy, there is a good reason that God has not given us what we want when we want it. If we are not healed in this lifetime, remember that God is strong enough to carry us to the finish line, where we *will* be made whole.

The Misery Industry

Wine is a mocker, strong drink is a brawler, and whoever is led astray by it is not wise.
—Proverbs 20:1

Few things have left as much death and destruction in their wake as alcohol. In the United States alone, apart from maternity and intensive care patients, up to 40 percent of hospital beds are used to treat people suffering from alcohol-related maladies. Something like 2.5 million years of potential human life are lost annually because of alcohol.★ Ask police officers how many of the calls they receive on a Saturday night involve alcohol consumption, and you might get a good idea of why the author of Proverbs levels such a straight warning at his audience.

Few of us live lives that have not been impacted by the negative consequences of the liquor trade, ranging from ruined homes to the death of loved ones. For me, perhaps the most impactful moment was the day I received news that a good friend, an only child, had been killed in a car accident. I went to visit his parents. After a few awkward exchanges in the house, my friend's father walked with me to the street in front of the house. I knew he wanted to discuss something, and I was right: he was hoping I would act as a pallbearer.

It was the moment I decided that alcohol simply cannot be part of any Christian's life. He struggled to find the words, barely able to mouth them in a hoarse whisper. His entire world had collapsed in a heartbeat. Their marriage fell apart shortly after the devastating loss, and the last I heard, he had turned to the bottle himself to drown out his sorrow.

I have heard Christians defend the use of alcohol, suggesting that a few drinks in moderation are harmless. And for some people, one or two drinks are as far as it ever goes. But in light of the fact that we serve a loving God—a Healer by nature—what place does alcohol have in our lives? How can Christians possibly support the misery industry?

Jesus came to give us more abundant lives, but short of a few moments of reckless euphoria (followed by a hangover and often regret for those acts committed while under the influence), what abundant life is to be found in drinking? How do the dollars spent on liquor bring restoration to our broken world?

★ "Facts About Alcohol," National Council on Alcoholism and Drug Dependence, https://www.ncadd.org /about-addiction/alcohol/facts-about-alcohol.

The Serpent's Bite

At the last it bites like a serpent, and stings like a viper.
Your eyes will see strange things, and your heart will utter perverse things.
—Proverbs 23:32, 33

Those who flirt with alcohol consumption should probably ask themselves why many casinos offer free drinks to their clients. In addition to the well-known physical risks of alcohol are the facts that alcohol lowers inhibitions and circumvents the processes in the brain that normally inform people that they are about to engage in risky behaviors. Add a few drinks to a night of gambling, and people are willing to make wagers that would seem a little too precarious to sober minds.

The same holds true for other risky behaviors. While a sober person might recognize the perils of a one-night stand, someone fueled by alcohol is far more likely to indulge, which is why predatory men typically like to buy women a few drinks in the hopes that their targets will be more willing to compromise their morals.

There are many arguments in favor of abstaining from alcohol, but perhaps one of the most persuasive is the fact that drinking—even in moderation—makes it easier to sin. We live in a world that seems to be more saturated with temptation than ever, to the point where even the most mundane objects are sold using sex appeal. It is hard enough to keep your mind on godly things when you are sober, let alone when you have chemically compromised your ability to think clearly.

"Be careful," the wise man advised us many centuries ago. "If you follow this path, you will not escape injury. Those seemingly harmless drinks are eventually going to bite like a venomous serpent, and your heart will be corrupted to the point where it utters perverse things."

Thousands of years of tragic human history have proven the book of Proverbs right. How many unwanted pregnancies and sexually transmitted diseases have come on the heels of a night of compromised reason? How many needless injuries have people sustained because they were not thinking clearly when they climbed behind the wheel of a car? How many marriages have been painfully scarred because of careless words that would not have been uttered had fallen angels not been given amplified access to the mind?

Clear thinking—the voice of the Spirit to the heart—is a gift far too valuable to be sold for a mere beverage.

Treasure Good Things

"A good man out of the good treasure of his heart brings forth good things,
and an evil man out of the evil treasure brings forth evil things."
—Matthew 12:35

When it comes to the personal computer, I must admit that I was a reluctant adopter. Quite content with the typewriter that had helped me through college, I did not see the need for a computer. But my wife convinced me that it would likely alleviate much of the frustration I felt when I came to the end of a page, only to make a mistake, as I would then have to rip the paper out of the machine and start all over.

She was right (of course!): The first computer we purchased was a godsend. Not only did it cut my preparation time in half, but it also meant that we could keep detailed records of nearly every ministry activity we had been involved in. Eventually, I noticed a problem: the more I used the computer, the slower it ran. Over time, it began to develop operational problems that would occasionally result in the "blue screen of death"—a crashed system.

Why? In part, it was because I had a bad habit of recklessly installing all kinds of software on it; some of which conflicted with the computer's operating system. Over time, the machine's ability to function became sufficiently compromised and caused serious problems.

Many people are conscientious about the kinds of foods they put in their bodies, hoping to enjoy better health and forestall the inevitable. But fewer people are conscientious about taking care of the human brain, which is easily the most important organ we possess. All day long we carelessly feed them all kinds of conflicting information and then marvel when our brains return confused or even dark thoughts. We bemoan the tempting thoughts that plague us, wondering where such horrible ideas come from. But the fact is that our astonishingly efficient brains retain every bit of data they receive through our senses. Wicked thoughts do not simply materialize in our minds; we willingly absorb the ideas from which they are composed.

Jesus points out a profoundly simple principle: You get from your heart—your mind—what you feed it. Feed it immoral content, and that is what it will produce. Make a point of treasuring good things, of feeding your mind quality information, and you will find that the world's greatest computer will serve you well, long past the day the laptop on your desk outlives its usefulness.

Lest They Forget

It is not for kings, O Lemuel, it is not for kings to drink wine, nor for princes intoxicating drink;
lest they drink and forget the law, and pervert the justice of all the afflicted.
—Proverbs 31:4, 5

Many years ago I received a parking ticket I believed I would be able to challenge successfully in court. My wife had gone into labor while I was out of town, but fortunately, my mother was in the house at that time and drove her to the hospital. Once the patient had been dropped off, she parked the car on a side street—right under a No Parking sign. The sign was partly obscured by tree branches.

As I waited my turn in court, I heard a teacher admit guilt but plead for mercy over his own ticket; he had been waiting for students to come back from the library when his meter expired. The judge dismissed his case. *Oh good!* I thought. *He's a merciful and understanding man. If he let this man go, he's bound to show mercy for a wife in labor!*

When my turn came to appear before the judge, I took the same approach as the teacher before me. "I know the car was parked illegally," I explained, "but my wife was in labor, and I was out of town. My mother took her to the hospital and, in her haste, made a mistake." The judge looked at me for a minute and then declared me *guilty.* I could hardly believe it: surely *my* case was more pressing, yet I was stuck paying the full fine!

In fairness, the car was parked illegally, but I cannot help but question the judge's perception of the day. Was he thinking clearly?

Christians above all people should strive to be fair and equitable in their dealings with others. The author of Proverbs warns Lemuel to abstain from alcohol because he dare not compromise his judgment or his mercy for the afflicted. As kings and priests who will reign with Christ, we owe it to ourselves—and our fellow human beings—to keep our thinking as sharp as possible, especially in a world that is described as being drunk on the wine of Babylon. It is just one more good reason to shun anything that compromises our capacity for justice and mercy and our capacity to display the character of God to the world. The ideal? When people deal with us, they should leave knowing that God is everything He has ever claimed to be.

The Cutting Edge

And God said, "See, I have given you every herb that yields seed which is on the face of all the earth, and every tree whose fruit yields seed; to you it shall be for food."
—Genesis 1:29

A noticeable portion of the academic community, ranging from philosophers to scientists, seems prone to dismissing the claims of the Bible as antiquated mythology. "It is the natural tendency of the ignorant to believe what is not true," the famous American scholar and satirist H. L. Mencken once said of religion. "To admit that the false has any standing in court, that it ought to be handled gently because millions of morons cherish it and thousands of quacks make their livings propagating it . . . is to abandon a just cause to its enemies, cravenly and without excuse."★

It is a sentiment that is all too common in our own generation. Spend a few moments reading the comment threads below any news story that involves religious belief, and you will find thousands, with their fangs bared, ready to pounce on even the briefest mention of faith. The Bible is ridiculed as mythology about "an imaginary friend in the sky," while human reason, echoing the cries of the French Revolution, is exalted to almost godlike status.

You will notice that much of the derision, however, does not stem from the text of the Bible itself. Few of the critics have actually *read* the text, at least not in its entirety. Rather, most of the criticism seems to stem from the words and deeds of professed believers—some of which does invite ridicule.

But the Bible itself has stood the test of time. Take, for example, the medical community's insistence in our own time that a plant-based diet would help to ameliorate many of the lifestyle diseases that have become common in the West. "If you're eating mostly or only fruits, vegetables, nuts, beans, whole grains, and meat substitutes like soy, you may cut your odds of getting heart disease, high cholesterol, high blood pressure, and type 2 diabetes, compared to a diet that includes a lot more meat," the popular WebMD site states when discussing the benefits of a plant-based diet.†

It seems like cutting-edge advice to much of our generation because we know it comes from the world of white coats and test tubes. Science has proven it, so we find it novel. But it is something careful students of the Bible have known for a very, very long time.

★ H. L. Mencken, "Counter-Offensive," review of *Is It God's Word?*, by Joseph Wheless, *American Mercury*, May 1926, 124, http://www.unz.com/print/AmMercury-1926may-00123/.

† "Plant-Based Diet for Heart Health," WebMD, last updated July 21, 2016, http://www.webmd.com/heart-disease/guide/plant-based-diet-for-heart-health.

OCTOBER 15

The Pain of Editing

For You formed my inward parts; You covered me in my mother's womb.
I will praise You, for I am fearfully and wonderfully made;
marvelous are Your works, and that my soul knows very well.
—Psalm 139:13, 14

Perhaps one of the most frustrating experiences a writer can have is what happens to his or her work in the hands of an ambitious editor. A good editor is an essential step in the publishing process because even the best writer makes a lot of mistakes. What is clear to the author is not always clear to the reader, and the right editor can bring clarity to the work that would not exist without him or her.

But an ambitious editor—one who feels the need to add his or her own perspective or content to the work or eliminates portions that might be key to the topic but do not seem that way to the editor—can be a frustrating experience. In the hands of the wrong person, what comes off the press may be only a dim shadow of the author's original intent.

Imagine the frustration God must feel when He sees the way His creation has been edited by sin and rebellion. What was once a perfect expression of His will has become a mere shadow of what used to be. We can still find clear evidence of the Master Designer's plan in our world, but it has obviously been degraded. Human beings created in the image of God are now plagued by deterioration and disease, and to make matters worse, Satan, the fallen "editor" who has laid claim to this world, has convinced us to blame God for our suffering.

What kind of God gives children cancer? is a common sentiment found in online discussions. Skeptics will raise this question in an attempt to discredit the Christian faith. It springs from a tragic lack of understanding and from the belief that the broken world we live in today is the way it has always been.

But in spite of our broken state, the human body is still a marvel. Doctors will tell you that they do not actually heal anyone; they merely create conditions that are conducive to the body's natural ability to heal itself. And in a relationship with Christ, it is possible, even on this side of Christ's return, to recapture some of the Author's original intent. Despite the flaws we imposed through sin, we can still see that we are, indeed, fearfully and wonderfully made.

Sitting: The New Smoking

Then the LORD God took the man and put him in the garden of Eden to tend and keep it.
—Genesis 2:15

The Western world is notoriously sedentary. According to the Centers for Disease Control and Prevention, only about one in five adults engages in the recommended amount of physical activity each day—in spite of the fact that it is well known that physical activity can mitigate a host of diseases, such as heart disease, stroke, type 2 diabetes, and even depression.*

While sedentary occupations have given us relief from the rigors (and dangers) of a purely physical existence, they are most certainly taking a toll on us. Members of the medical community constantly remind us to get up and move. We even sell digital devices, worn like watches, that buzz and vibrate periodically throughout the day to encourage us to get up from our desks.

You will notice that when God first created the human race, He gave them physical work to do. Undoubtedly, Adam and Eve were also created with the capacity for intellectual achievement, but God did not set them in a classroom or office at the launch of human history. He placed them in a garden and gave them the responsibility to keep it and tend it. They were not to be idle but active, which is a great indication that God designed our bodies to move.

A 2012 Harvard study revealed that a sedentary lifestyle, or "sitting disease" as some people call it, leads directly to some five million deaths per year worldwide. Inactivity is so harmful to the human body that it is now considered as dangerous as smoking!† It also rates with high blood pressure, obesity, and high blood glucose as a health hazard.

As it turns out, staying physically active is not only good for your body, it is also good for your mind. In a study done at the University of British Columbia, researchers discovered that regular aerobic exercise enlarges the portion of your brain responsible for language and learning.‡ Given that the mind is where God communicates with us, this provides even more incentive to stay active. The physically active person thinks more clearly; and in a world where fallen angels are working overtime, a clear mind can prove invaluable.

Perhaps it is time to hide the TV remote and disconnect from the internet for an hour each day and get outside and meet with God.

---

* "Facts About Physical Activity," Centers for Disease Control and Prevention, https://www.cdc.gov/physicalactivity/data/facts.htm.

† Cory Quirino, "The Risks of Sedentary Living," Inquirer.net, March 14, 2017, http://lifestyle.inquirer.net/257213/risks-sedentary-living/.

‡ Heidi Godman, "Regular Exercise Changes the Brain to Improve Memory, Thinking Skills," *Harvard Health Blog*, Harvard Health, updated March 14, 2018, https://www.health.harvard.edu/blog/regular-exercise-changes-brain-improve-memory-thinking-skills-201404097110.

The Gift From the Well

"Behold, God is my salvation, I will trust and not be afraid; 'For YAH, the LORD,
is my strength and song; He also has become my salvation.' "
Therefore with joy you will draw water from the wells of salvation.
—Isaiah 12:2, 3

Depending on its size and physical condition, the human body can survive for several weeks without food, but it can only survive for a matter of days without water. So essential is water to human survival that God chooses it to demonstrate how vital it is to have a living connection with Him. Just as your body cannot survive without access to water, your heart ultimately cannot survive without access to God.

You will find water at the very beginning of the Bible, in the Creation story, where "the Spirit of God was hovering over the face of the waters" (Genesis 1:2). It is also found at the very end of the Bible, where God invites "him who thirsts" to "take the water of life freely" (Revelation 22:17). Through the pages of Scripture, water is used as a symbol for life again and again: from the showers of blessing mentioned in Ezekiel 34:26 to the invitation Jesus gave to the Samaritan woman to drink water that would prevent her from thirsting ever again (John 4:13). God's chosen people were to be placed among the nations "like dew from the LORD, like showers on the grass," sharing the life-giving news of salvation with their neighbors (Micah 5:7).

The Bible uses water as a symbol of life hundreds of times because it makes it easy for us to understand how essential God is to our spiritual well-being. When it comes to health, then, we should be able to reason backward to the fact that water itself is essential to good physical health. Your body is mostly water, and when it is not replenished adequately, your body begins to malfunction. Water is critical to brain function, metabolism, maintaining a healthy weight, muscle function, waste elimination, skin tone—just about everything your body does.

In fact, water is so critical to good brain function that studies have demonstrated that dehydrated drivers make twice as many mistakes as those who drink enough water, which is similar to intoxicated driving.* It may just be that drinking enough water is as important to health as avoiding alcohol and other toxic substances!

A key part to living the abundant life that God intended is to fill our bodies with the one beverage found in the rivers of Eden.

---

* "Studies on Hydration Suggest Dehydrated Drivers May Pose Hazard on the Road, and Majority of Children Don't Drink Enough Water," Mercola, June 29, 2015, http://articles.mercola.com/sites/articles/archive/2015/06/29/kids-not-drinking-enough-water.aspx.

Solar Life Support

So He brought me into the inner court of the LORD's house; and there,
at the door of the temple of the LORD, between the porch and the altar,
were about twenty-five men with their backs toward the temple of the LORD
and their faces toward the east, and they were worshiping the sun toward the east.
—Ezekiel 8:16

Sun worship is a nearly universal feature of pagan religions, from the ancient Sumerians in Mesopotamia to the Incas, Aztecs, and Mayans in the Americas. Most of the adoration for the star at the center of our solar system stems from the understanding that it supports life on earth, which led many cultures to consider it the life-giver. Without the sun, crops would not grow, and life could not exist on earth.

This belief was so prevalent that when Israel failed to clear the Promised Land of false religion, they were easily enticed into worshiping the sun along with their Canaanite neighbors. The tragic story recorded in Ezekiel reveals that solar worship was one of the main reasons that led to the Babylonian captivity: God's own people were worshiping the sun as it rose in the east.

As Christians, we reject the notion that the sun is the originator of life, even though we live in a world where we are told that each of us is made of ancient star dust—a by-product of the big bang. Instead, we worship the One who made the sun and set it in the sky as a way to mark signs and seasons (Genesis 1:14).

While we do not worship the sun, we still understand that sunshine is a key part of maintaining life. While it did not give birth to us, the sun was provided by God as a way to promote and sustain life. "Pure air, sunlight, abstemiousness, rest, exercise, proper diet, the use of water, trust in divine power," Ellen White reminds us, "these are the true remedies."[*] When we are physically sick or mentally depressed, sunlight is a natural aid to recovery: "By such employment and the free use of air and sunlight, many an emaciated invalid might recover health and strength."[†]

False religion has simply failed to look past the star itself to find the true Source of life and healing, the "Sun of Righteousness" who arises "with healing in His wings" (Malachi 4:2). While rejecting pagan idolatry, we can still deeply appreciate the life that God supports by means of daily exposure to the sun's rays, and we can thank Him for the gift of life He has granted us.

---

[*] Ellen G. White, *The Ministry of Healing* (Nampa, ID: Pacific Press®, 2003), 127.
[†] White, *The Ministry of Healing*, 246.

Self-Control

But the fruit of the Spirit is love, joy, peace, longsuffering, kindness,
goodness, faithfulness, gentleness, self-control. Against such there is no law.
—Galatians 5:22, 23

What comes to mind when you think of someone who has great self-control? Life of the party? Fun to be around? Probably not. When most of us think of someone who practices the biblical quality of temperance, most of us think of subdued, uninteresting people. Recent studies, however, paint a completely different picture: people with great self-control tend to be *happier* and enjoy life more than the rest of us.

Why? Psychologist Jeremy Dean explains, "Instead of agonising over whether to indulge in fattening foods, extra-marital affairs or cheap reality TV, people with high self-control find it easier to make the right choice. This is part of the reason they are happier. That and the fact they got better grades at school, earn more money, have better physical and mental health and so on."*

In other words, the practice of temperance leads to delayed gratification. While most people are looking for a quick fix, their level of satisfaction is fleeting. The excitement of easy choices wears thin quickly, leaving a deep sense of dissatisfaction, and often creates a drive to ramp up thrill seeking to new levels. But those who consistently make wise choices that deny self in the short term have the satisfaction of reaping rewards that last a lifetime: better health, more meaningful accomplishments, and so on.

The Christian life itself is geared toward delayed gratification. The faith chapter in the book of Hebrews explains that God's people have always put self aside in favor of waiting for the kingdom of Christ. Moses, for example, cast aside a life of ease in Egypt to suffer with God's people in the wilderness, knowing that the ultimate reward would be much greater.

One of the fruit of the Spirit, Paul explains, is self-control. In this life, passing up short-term delights in favor of a longer, more vibrant life is one of the things that contributes to having the more abundant life that Jesus promises. While there is no harm in the occasional treat, favoring self-control means living longer and healthier in the long run; and as studies are now demonstrating, it not only means better health but also a much deeper level of life satisfaction.

---

* Jeremy Dean, "What Can Self-Control Do for You? 10 New Studies Provide Surprising Answers," *PsyBlog*, July 8, 2013, http://www.spring.org.uk/2013/07/what-can-self-control-do-for-you-10-new-studies-provide-surprising-answers.php.

The Breath of Life

"Who among all these does not know that the hand of the LORD has done this,
in whose hand is the life of every living thing, and the breath of all mankind?"
—Job 12:9, 10

The story of the human race begins with a gasp of air, when God "formed man of the dust of the ground, and breathed into his nostrils the breath of life" (Genesis 2:7). If you have dived too deep into some water and have suddenly become anxious to reach the surface, you know full well the body's overwhelming need for oxygen. As daylight becomes visible above you, a desperate fire rages in your chest and your legs kick frantically to speed your return to the air. Your survival instincts will compel you to do whatever it takes to breathe.

Less obvious is your body's cry for clean air. As you move about the compromised atmospheres of indoor spaces, your body does not tell you that you are drowning, but the effects of being denied good, clean air nonetheless take their toll on your well-being.

Day after day, year after year, more and more of us toil away daily under fluorescent office lighting, breathing air pumped through heating or cooling systems. After work, we climb into our cars and drive back to air-conditioned houses where we continue to breathe indoor air all night long. The countless chemicals and plastic products that fill our homes even further diminish the quality of the air we breathe.

We used to be concerned about outdoor air pollution, but now, in many places, our indoor work and living environments are sometimes more polluted than the air outside. Pesticides, fire retardants, and mold and mildew (just to name a few) have become common in our living spaces. While we are not entirely certain why, it is interesting to note that asthma appears to be on the rise in many parts of the globe.

We may not be literally drowning, but we *do* appear to be compromising our access to clean air. "Impure air does not afford the necessary supply of oxygen," Ellen White points out, "and the blood passes to the brain and other organs without being vitalized. . . . To live in close, ill-ventilated rooms, where the air is dead and vitiated, weakens the entire system."★

For many people, it might just be the case that a more abundant, healthier life can be had simply by opening the windows or heading outdoors more often.

★ Ellen G. White, *The Ministry of Healing* (Nampa, ID: Pacific Press®, 2003), 274.

A Little Shut-Eye

It is vain for you to rise up early, to sit up late,
to eat the bread of sorrows; for so He gives His beloved sleep.
—Psalm 127:2

From about the age of eight onward, I cannot remember having slept through the entire night uninterrupted. It has always taken me upwards of two to three hours to fall asleep, and very rarely do I sleep until an alarm clock rings. Perhaps it started with my poor sleep habits as a child: I lived in a northern town where there was light throughout most of the night during the summer, and I was able to read for hours on end when I should have been sleeping.

Life on the road has taken its toll on my ability to get adequate sleep as well. Airline schedules rarely accommodate temperate living, and shifting between time zones is lethal to good sleep habits. But I cannot blame everything on hard work and travel. I must also admit that I am a chronic worrier, with a mind that will not shut down until I have solved all of the day's problems.

That, the Bible assures me, is "vain" behavior. Sitting up late to "eat the bread of sorrows" is not the way God intends for us to live. The human body needs far more sleep than most of us are getting. According to one study, as many as one-third of us are not logging enough hours in bed.[*] If it is not anxiety keeping us awake, it is the blue light emitting from the countless electronic devices that tell our brains it is still daytime when we should have been asleep long ago.

Harvard University reports that sleep deprivation is leading to disease as well as compromising our ability to exercise sound judgment.[†] Perhaps, instead of viewing sleep as something that robs us of productive time, it is time to reclaim it as the gift that God planned it to be. One day in seven, after all, is dedicated to rest, so we know that God intends downtime to be a much-needed blessing.

Perhaps if we ended the day earlier, became insistent on retiring at a regular time, viewed sleep as something desirable, and thanked God for the gift of rest, we would begin to see that sleep really *is* something that God gives His beloved.

Go ahead: turn everything off and turn in early tonight. You have God's blessing.

---

[*] Centers for Disease Control and Prevention, "1 in 3 Adults Don't Get Enough Sleep," press release, February 18, 2016, https://www.cdc.gov/media/releases/2016/p0215-enough-sleep.html.

[†] "Consequences of Insufficient Sleep," Harvard Medical School, http://healthysleep.med.harvard.edu/healthy/matters/consequences.

The Joy of Trust

Now may the God of hope fill you with all joy and peace in believing,
that you may abound in hope by the power of the Holy Spirit.
—Romans 15:13

The human race's original disease was breaking our trust with God. While pride is the underlying cause of all sin, the incident in Eden was fueled by a loss of trust in God's word. The serpent craftily encouraged Eve to doubt what God had said by asking one simple question: Did God really say that? From that moment forward, we have been listening to the devil's lies and struggling to regain trust in God.

That lack of faith led to our expulsion from the Garden and a deep divide between God and us. We have chosen the word of fallen angels over God, and we have opted to go our own path outside of God's will. Additionally, Satan has managed to convince most of us that God is the author of our misfortune and the source of suffering. We project the faults of others onto God, and to learn to trust God is a struggle for most.

I remember visiting with Ray, who had experienced a horrible childhood: his family members repeatedly lied to him, belittled him, and failed to keep their word. His introduction to the world was an environment of mistrust, and he found it incredibly difficult to believe that anybody—God included—could be trusted. His adult life was marked by constant anxiety, suspicion, and fear, and his stress levels eventually took a toll on him physically.

When he finally chose to believe God and constantly opted to believe God's promises, regardless of circumstances, there was a marked change. The stress levels dropped, and—as Paul promised—he found "joy and peace in believing." His outlook improved, and eventually, so did his health.

A key part of the Christian walk is to learn to trust again, even on the days when the evidence of your senses might suggest that God has forgotten His promises. We can willfully choose to believe, just as we willfully choose not to. And once you begin to comprehend that Someone really does have your life in His hands, you can relax and get about the business of *living* instead of worrying. In Christ, your future is so secure that you can afford to laugh off most of life's problems because you know they will mean nothing a million years from now.

The Restoration

"Repent therefore and be converted, that your sins may be blotted out, so that times of refreshing may come from the presence of the Lord, and that He may send Jesus Christ, who was preached to you before, whom heaven must receive until the times of restoration of all things, which God has spoken by the mouth of all His holy prophets since the world began."
—Acts 3:19–21

It generally does not take your average human being much time to discover that something is wrong in this world. If you were lucky enough to be born without any health challenges, the broken world you were born into will ultimately take its toll on you. Something will eventually give out.

It leaves you longing for something better. As the years take their toll on my own body, I find myself yearning for my younger days, when healing was faster and issues were fewer. But of course, what the human heart is longing for is not childhood, but the world we lost when we broke faith with God. Human beings are born with a memory of Eden; as the book of Ecclesiastes puts it, God "has put eternity in [our] hearts" (Ecclesiastes 3:11).

It is the reason we can recognize imperfection and brokenness when we see it. None of us were born into a perfect world, so we do not have a reliable reference point against which to check our imperfect existence. Sure, we remember when we had more energy and when things did not hurt as much. But the real reason we quietly protest even mild suffering is because we were born with enough memory of God's original plan that we know we do not have to accept the status quo as God's will. There *was* something better, and there *is* something better coming.

Peter, in his landmark sermon on the mission of Christ, makes it plain: When Jesus returns, it will be the "times of restoration of all things." Our rebellion will be at an end. Pain and suffering will be completely reversed, and we will once again step into Eden. In the meantime, those aches and pains—and even the more serious issues—can serve as daily reminders that something better is coming. Like the global turmoil predicted in Matthew 24, pain and illness can be understood as clear indications that our world is about to throw off its broken state and become new. The planet is experiencing things such as earthquakes, famine, and war—the pains of a failed system that is dying. Think of illness this way: your body is experiencing its own signs of the times. But the restoration of all things is almost here.

Modern Witchcraft

*Now the works of the flesh are evident, which are: adultery, fornication,
uncleanness, lewdness, idolatry, sorcery, hatred, contentions, jealousies,
outbursts of wrath, selfish ambitions, dissensions, heresies, envy, murders,
drunkenness, revelries, and the like; of which I tell you beforehand,
just as I also told you in time past, that those who practice such things
will not inherit the kingdom of God.*

—Galatians 5:19–21

The disconcerting thing about Paul's list of "the works of the flesh" is that all of us can find something on the list that applies to us personally. Perhaps you have not participated in such flagrant, public sins as fornication or adultery, but have you ever been involved in contentions? Outbursts of wrath? Dissensions? It would be the rare human being indeed who could claim a lifetime exemption from such things.

Any sin, frankly, bars you from inheriting the kingdom of God. Fortunately, there is a cure for the problem: there is nothing on the list that cannot be handled by Christ. You can find forgiveness for any issue on the list—or even all of them—if you repent and bring the problem to Jesus.

While we are unfortunately familiar with most of the things Paul lists, there is one item on the list that might seem curious to modern audiences: sorcery. Older translations have rendered the same word as "witchcraft." Modern sorcery or witchcraft, of course, is a completely non-Christian system of religious belief with deep roots in paganism. Few Christians, if any, could think of someone in their church circle who was practicing such things.

But before we dismiss it as irrelevant to our own lives, it might be useful to examine the word Paul used. The Greek is *pharmakeia*, which is where we get our modern word *pharmacy*. What Paul is describing is recreational drug use—and that *is* a problem in our twenty-first-century world. Mind-altering substances keep us from engaging in the real world, they compromise our ability to make sound moral judgments, they ruin family relationships, and they dramatically impair our ability to engage in a relationship with God. As with alcohol, sin begins to seem less sinful when using these substances. And of course, without a relationship with Christ, the kingdom of God becomes unobtainable.

That is the bad news. The good news is that recreational drug use is not the unpardonable sin. Those who struggle will find forgiveness, understanding, compassion—and the power to break free—at the cross of Christ. It is just one more chain the devil has wrapped around our lives that Jesus is eager to break so that we can step into the abundant life God would love for us to have.

Claiming Victory

But thanks be to God, who gives us the victory through our Lord Jesus Christ.
—1 Corinthians 15:57

The human brain rewards behaviors that cause you to feel good, no matter how fleeting that "feel good" sensation is. Certain things, including alcohol, drugs, and even sugar, are processed through the brain's reward circuitry, causing your system to dump abnormally massive amounts of dopamine, a feel-good chemical, into the regions of your brain responsible for emotions and motivation.

When the high wears off, your brain demands that you do it again. It also adjusts to the new levels of dopamine, which might be ten times the normal amount, and it convinces itself that what it just experienced is normal. Over time, if you continue to feed your body the dopamine-inducing chemicals, the brain reacts by reducing the number of dopamine receptors in your body and that means you will need more of the drug to produce the same high.

Addiction, in other words, can be tough to beat, because your body has become rewired to need the substance you have been abusing. Anyone who has tried to quit smoking can testify to the suffering that follows in the wake of denying your brain what it believes it needs.

Fortunately, the Bible offers something much more powerful than quitting. Quitting a bad habit relies on human will, which often flounders in the face of the brain's demands. Instead of asking you to quit, God offers you victory as a gift. Instead of telling you to struggle your way back to normal, fighting every inch of the way, God is willing to simply declare the whole matter finished. You are not a quitting smoker with God; you are a nonsmoker because He declares it so.

We are not asked to struggle for victory; we are asked to claim it and accept it as a gift. You can tell yourself that through Jesus, you are a nonsmoker, a nondrinker, or a nondrug user right now. Your role is to accept the gift by faith and to remind yourself continually that this gift is yours because God has promised it. You do not have to live "in recovery" for the rest of your life, telling yourself that you will never truly be free; you can claim to be free every minute of every day because there is no chemical on earth greater than God's miraculous healing power.

Dead Indeed

*Likewise you also, reckon yourselves to be dead indeed to sin, but alive to God in Christ Jesus
our Lord. Therefore do not let sin reign in your mortal body, that you should obey it in its lusts.*
—Romans 6:11, 12

Over the years, I have worked one-on-one with more than twelve hundred
people who wanted to give up their cigarette habits, and the vast majority,
once they understood that accepting victory as a gift from God is a much better path
than struggling to quit, have found lifelong freedom. It *is* as simple as understanding
that God can give you freedom as a gift. Your role is to choose to believe it, much
the way a five-year-old eagerly tears the paper from a birthday present. You do not
usually have to convince a child that a present belongs to him or her.

Our role in the process is to eagerly grab the gift. Pretend that you are that five-
year-old child, and rip the paper from the present. Thank God that He has made
you a nonsmoker, a nondrinker, or a non-whatever-your-bad-habit-is. Live every
minute as if you believe the promise.

It does not mean that fallen angels will not attempt to convince you otherwise.
Ever since Eden, they have been mastering the art of raising doubts about God's
word. Just as surely as Satan asked Eve, "Did God really say that?" he is going to do
the same to you: "You don't have victory. You're an addict! You have no choice in
the matter!"

That is the moment to practice what Paul describes. Because you choose to
believe that God's word is true, you can reckon yourself "to be dead indeed to sin."
Remind yourself, "I don't *have* to do that because God has given me victory over
it. In fact, I am dead to it." If it helps, imagine a dead person trying to practice your
former habit. A dead person cannot smoke, gorge on junk food, or drink a beer.
Through God's grace, you are just as dead to that habit as an actual dead person.

When temptation comes—and it probably will—your role is to say, "No, I'm dead
to that. Thanks be to God who gives me the victory!" You will be amazed at what
just a few days of gratefully accepting God's gift minute by minute, out loud if you
have to, will do to send you down the path to a brand-new life.

What You Don't Need

But put on the Lord Jesus Christ, and make no provision for the flesh, to fulfill its lusts.
—Romans 13:14

I'm just going to keep this one pack on top of the fridge to remind myself that I have victory over smoking!" Blake had told me that he wanted to claim victory over his smoking habit. He understood that claiming victory was different than quitting and that his job was to reckon himself "to be dead to sin" (Romans 6:11).

The choice, of course, was his to make. But by placing a pack of cigarettes on top of the fridge, he was already planning to fail. If you truly choose to believe that God, through His creative power, can declare you a nonsmoker, there is no need to keep anything associated with your previous bad habit. A nonsmoker does not *need* cigarettes. For that matter, a nondrinker does not need alcohol, and a nonwhatever does not need whatever used to hold him or her in bondage.

The practice of faith means that you choose to live as if God's promises are true, even on the days when you do not particularly *feel* it. If you choose to believe that God can remove your harmful habit from your life and give you complete and utter victory over it, faith says that it is time to remove all traces of that habit from your life. Paul explains that our role as believers is to "make no provision for the flesh, to fulfill its lusts."

I shared Paul's words with Blake and explained, "Blake, your job is to live as if you believe God's promises are true. A nonsmoker does not keep cigarettes in his house, and so they really have no place in your home." He quietly handed them over to me so that I could dispose of them, and he never smoked again.

Victory over harmful habits, whatever they are, really can be yours. But it is up to you to start living as if you believe God's promises are true. Perhaps there is something that has been bothering you for years. Today is the day to accept God's gift of victory, reckon yourself dead to it through God's creative power, and remove that harmful thing from your life.

The beautiful thing about a relationship with God is that, even before Christ returns, you can start living your life as if you are already living in the kingdom.

What Defiles a Man

So He said to them, "Are you thus without understanding also? Do you not perceive that whatever enters a man from outside cannot defile him, because it does not enter his heart but his stomach, and is eliminated, thus purifying all foods?"
—Mark 7:18, 19

Over the years, I have heard quite a number of people present today's Bible verse, which is a short statement from Jesus, as evidence that unclean meats are now permissible to eat. They point to the statement where Mark mentions "purifying all foods" as proof that God has changed His mind about eating pork and shellfish.

That understanding, however, runs into immediate trouble when read in the context of the whole Bible. Take, for example, Peter's vision of Acts 10, in which he sees a blanket being lowered from heaven with unclean animals on it. When told to eat them, he protests, "Not so, Lord! For I have never eaten anything common or unclean" (verse 14). If Jesus had already given blanket permission to eat bacon, why would Peter bother to protest?

In Mark's account, you will notice that flesh foods are never specifically mentioned because the subject is not meat. Earlier in the same account, the Pharisees had witnessed the disciples eating bread with unwashed hands (Mark 7:2, 5). "For the Pharisees and all the Jews do not eat unless they wash their hands in a special way," Mark explains (verse 3).

The issue was not pork chops; it was ceremonial washing. Nobody present that day would have considered pigs or shrimp to be food at all. Jesus is simply pointing out that human beings have a knack for taking simple things and piling so many man-made traditions on top of them that they become a burden.

We would do well to pay attention. While we might not engage in ritual washing before a potluck meal, we do tend to police what other people eat as a means of calling their spirituality into question. I have heard people openly question what someone else has on their plate, whether it be eating vegetables and fruit at the same time or eating a piece of cheese.

Often, the person raising such questions has a bigger spiritual issue than the victim. "What comes out of a man, that defiles a man," Jesus explains (verse 20).

May God grant us the gracious disposition of Christ and the good sense and courtesy to mind our own business.

Angry?

So the LORD said to Cain, "Why are you angry? And why has your countenance fallen? If you do well, will you not be accepted? And if you do not do well, sin lies at the door. And its desire is for you, but you should rule over it." Now Cain talked with Abel his brother; and it came to pass, when they were in the field, that Cain rose up against Abel his brother and killed him.
—Genesis 4:6–8

Pastor, did you see what those people brought for lunch?" Sarah was clearly upset as she cornered me near the kitchen in the church basement. "They brought fish!"

"Well, that was generous of them, don't you think?" I gently responded. The people in question were brand-new church members, and when they heard that potluck was vegetarian, they chose to bring fish because to some people's way of thinking, fish does not qualify as meat. Sarah was not having any of it. "We *have* to do something!" she insisted.

"No, we don't," I replied. "By all means, you don't have to eat it, but you *do* have to keep your mouth shut." She persisted, insisting that eating fish was a grievous sin, at which point I shared Luke's account where Jesus ate fish in His resurrected body (Luke 24:42, 43). She sputtered and fumed, then marched off to find a more sympathetic ear, likely writing me off as a hopeless compromiser.

I have often marveled at how some people allow the actions of others to anger *them*. I struggle to understand why the content of someone else's lunch would incite wrath. If you were being force-fed foods you did not want, I could understand why that would cause frustration; but what someone *else* does?

It does not make sense—unless, of course, you are struggling with issues of your own. When Cain's faithless offering was rejected by God, he grew angry. But you will notice he did not just grow angry with God; he took his wrath out on his brother. Abel was murdered, not because of what *he* had done, but because of the condition of Cain's heart.

Perhaps, when we find ourselves getting angry about the actions of others, even when those actions do not affect us personally, we should take a personal spiritual inventory. I have discovered that those who seem to be frequently angry with others are often dealing with personal spiritual problems, but they seem to be unconsciously blaming others for their own issues. Honestly, each of us has enough to deal with in our own lives that we do not have time to police each other. And of course, all that pent-up anger will be worse for your health than someone else's meal choices are.

Idolatry of the Stomach

For many walk, of whom I have told you often, and now tell you even weeping,
that they are the enemies of the cross of Christ: whose end is destruction, whose god
is their belly, and whose glory is in their shame—who set their mind on earthly things.
—Philippians 3:18, 19

When someone mentions false gods, most believers think back to the wooden and stone idols of yesteryear; pagan deities that served as substitutes for worshiping the Creator. In the modern context, we might think of money or material success as an idol—maybe even pop stars and cultural icons. But few people would consider the stomach to be an idol. And yet there it is, clearly identified by Paul as a false god.

In this passage from Philippians, Paul is lamenting people who have detached themselves from the will of God and have chosen the path to destruction. Their "glory is in their shame," he says, which is another way of saying that some people seem to relish a licentious life, viewing their rebellion against the Creator as a form of liberty. Their stomachs become gods when they practice gluttony and the wanton indulgence of appetite. These are people who live to satisfy their primal urges, paying no attention to consequences, always in search of the next adrenaline rush.

Those kinds of stomach worshipers are easy to identify. But there are others who worship the stomach in another way, making abstemiousness rather than indulgence an idol. It is one thing to learn the health message, put its principles into practice, and rejoice in God's care for your physical well-being, but it is another thing to become obsessive about diet to the point where the health message begins to look like the ticket to heaven.

I have met them: hollow-eyed, sallow-skinned devotees to self-denial who view *any* variance from strict dietary rules as a sin. If eggs are not the best dietary choice, then you must *never* eat them. If dessert is generally not a good idea, you must *never, ever* eat it—ever!

I know of one mother whose son wandered away from the church. Weeks before he announced his decision, she had seen him eat a candy bar. Not a *bag* of candy bars, mind you, but one. "That's why he's lost!" she lamented.

No, it is not. Health principles are a God-given guideline, but we must be careful not to make them a substitute for a saving relationship with Jesus. Anything becomes an idol if it offers you a substitute path to heaven apart from the saving blood of Christ.

God's Showcase

Sing to the LORD a new song, and His praise from the ends of the earth,
you who go down to the sea, and all that is in it, you coastlands and you inhabitants of them!
Let the wilderness and its cities lift up their voice, the villages that Kedar inhabits.
Let the inhabitants of Sela sing, let them shout from the top of the mountains.
Let them give glory to the LORD, and declare His praise in the coastlands.
—Isaiah 42:10–12

The last cry to our planet, the message of God's remnant people, is a plea to "fear God and give glory to Him" (Revelation 14:7). When God first created this world, everything was a clear expression of His glory, from the flora and the fauna to the human race itself. "In their original perfection," Ellen White reminds us, "all created things were an expression of the thought of God."★

Now that sin has gripped our race, the original beauty of creation has been compromised. The human race is no longer a perfect reflection of God's image. Instead of naturally expressing God's glory through our thoughts and actions, we have come to the point where we shake our fists at heaven and blame God for the ills that have befallen us. When we lose our health, we demand that God explain why He let it happen, instead of mourning the fact that our human rebellion against the Creator has led to our present situation.

When we come to Christ, however, our perspective changes. We recognize that we have a new opportunity to use our lives to bring glory to God. Our thoughts, our actions, and our deeds can all be vehicles through which we can place the goodness of God on display for others to discover. That includes our physical bodies, of course, which are God's purchased possessions, having been redeemed by the blood of Christ.

In this present life, we will still be subject to sickness, aging, and death, but by placing our broken bodies at God's disposal, allowing Him to use us however He wills, we can still become a showcase of His goodness. Following God's principles will always yield better results. We might not escape illness altogether, but we can improve our lot. Our health can improve, our outlook can become more positive, and our lives can be more abundant.

Let your whole life give glory to God and declare His praise. You can become a showcase of God's intention for the human race—an advertisement for the world that is coming. Living well is not only for our own benefit but also for the benefit of all those around us who need to notice that God is alive and well on planet Earth and that He wants the best for us.

★ Ellen G. White, *Christ's Object Lessons* (Battle Creek, MI: Review and Herald®, 1900), 18.

November

I know and understand the fundamental Bible principles as taught by the Seventh-day Adventist Church. I purpose, by the grace of God, to fulfill His will by ordering my life in harmony with these principles.

I accept the New Testament teaching of baptism by immersion and desire to be baptized as a public expression of faith in Christ and His forgiveness of my sins.

Which Jesus?

For if someone comes and proclaims another Jesus than the one we proclaimed,
or if you receive a different spirit from the one you received, or if you accept
a different gospel from the one you accepted, you put up with it readily enough.
—2 Corinthians 11:4, ESV

Doctrine stands in the way of people coming to Christ," the lecturer explained while gesturing toward a simple drawing on his chalkboard. The picture was a stick man on his knees, as if praying, and in front of him stood a large pile of bricks with the word *doctrine* written across them. On the far side of the brick pile stood the cross.

"You can teach all the doctrine you want," he concluded, "but what people need is Jesus."

Which Jesus? I quietly thought to myself. There is the Jesus of the New Age movement, who is little more than a cosmic master who came to show us how we, too, can become enlightened. There is the Jesus of Islam, who is a mere prophet and did not actually die on the cross. There is the historical, academic Jesus who is unquestionably a significant influence on world history but who has been greatly exaggerated by His followers. There is even the Jesus of the flying saucer movement, who descends from a race of super beings planted here by aliens from another world.

How do you distinguish the Jesus of the New Testament from *those* pictures of Christ? It is simple: by His teachings. In the twenty-first century, *doctrine* has become something of a dirty word, particularly among millennials, who (according to some studies) claim they want to see the church become more homelike and less school-like. Christians across the world speak of "doctrines that divide us."

Paul chided his congregation in Corinth, however, that they were not discerning enough. "If someone comes along and preaches a different Jesus," he tells them, "you just put up with it!" How can you tell the difference? By comparing their teachings with the doctrines of the Bible.

Doctrine simply means teaching. Truth be told, you cannot even preach the Cross without doctrine: it requires the doctrine of man, the doctrine of sin, the doctrine of salvation, and the list goes on.

As our world approaches the last gasp of history, Jesus warned that there will be many false prophets and false Christs (see Matthew 24:24). The only safe place to stand in the moments before Christ returns is on the Bible. Remember that Jesus said the Scriptures "are they which testify of Me" (John 5:39).

Amazed by Doctrine

And when the unclean spirit had convulsed him and cried out with a loud voice,
he came out of him. Then they were all amazed, so that they questioned among themselves,
saying, "What is this? What new doctrine is this? For with authority
He commands even the unclean spirits, and they obey Him."
—Mark 1:26, 27

If you are a frequent student of the Bible, it becomes difficult to maintain the modern myth that there is some sort of ideological chasm between the person of Jesus and the doctrines of the Bible. While much of modern Christianity is crying, "Less doctrine and more Jesus!" the Bible speaks of crowds marveling at the doctrines of Jesus.

Doctrine, of course, is simply a set of teachings, and there is little doubt that Jesus offered the world a divine curriculum. Of course, Jesus' critics also offered doctrine and plenty of it. In addition to the plain words of Scripture, they offered their audiences a lot of man-made traditions intended to place a sort of fence around the teachings of the Bible and keep people from even getting *close* to violating one of God's commandments. But their teachings were lackluster and powerless. Rather than creating passion for God, they served as a spiritual soporific, lulling the masses into a careless spiritual slumber.

So lifeless were their teachings that the demon-possessed were able to attend the synagogue and not be bothered by what they heard. But when the Son of God opened the Scriptures and taught, fallen angels cried out through the lips of their victims because they recognized that the truths Jesus taught would be their undoing. With a mere verbal rebuke, they were obliged to leave the room.

It left the audience astounded. "What new doctrine is this?" they asked. They knew the passages that Jesus preached but never before had they seen the power behind them. With Jesus, the teachings of the Bible were not mere theories but practical truths meant to be lived out in daily life. They were transforming truths, powerful enough to pierce through the drunken haze of sinful thought and enable us to see the world—and life—from God's perspective.

When people speak of doctrines that keep us from coming to Christ, they are likely referring to the lifeless theorizing of so-called religious experts who know much about the text of the Bible but little of the life-giving power of its Author. The problem is not doctrine; it is misplaced doctrine. Bible doctrine as Jesus teaches it? It will ruin the work of fallen angels, who need lies to keep you in the dark.

Parachute Christianity

For the time will come when they will not endure sound doctrine, but according to their own desires, because they have itching ears, they will heap up for themselves teachers; and they will turn their ears away from the truth, and be turned aside to fables.
—2 Timothy 4:3, 4

Christianity is one of those things you can only truly understand by *doing* it. The Christian faith is not merely a matter of mentally assenting to a list of teachings; they mean little unless you apply them to your daily life.

It is not unlike skydiving. Anybody can do the math and conclude that a parachute will slow a descending mass enough to prevent catastrophe on the ground. It is simply a matter of measuring drag, mass, and other factors. But to say that you truly believe a parachute will stop you from becoming a splatter mark on the ground seems less than convincing. What would convince everyone that you believe it? Jumping from a plane with a parachute.

It is one thing to say you believe that it is a historical fact that Jesus rose from the dead. But it is a hollow claim unless it changes the way you live. The fact that Jesus conquered death, coupled with the fact that He is God in human flesh, ought to have a profound impact on the way you execute your daily living. For the genuine believer, the teachings of Jesus will become all important. If you really believe, you will want to know everything Jesus has ever said, recommended, or commanded. You will be convinced that He knows what is best for you.

In the last days, Paul warns, there will be a lot of people who are willing to sign a document saying they believe in Christ. There will be people who assert that the Bible is the Word of God, perhaps even suggesting they believe that the Bible is the foundation of Western civilization and should be respected as such. But for all their insistence, they will not strap on the parachute and jump. They will not *live* the claims of the Bible.

Seventh-day Adventists have long asserted that the Christian faith is more than mental assent to a list of doctrines. "You believe that there is one God," James explains. "You do well. Even the demons believe—and tremble!" (James 2:19). To believe your faith is one thing. To choose to *live* your faith and allow the creative power of God to change you through and through? To believe God's Word and live it? That is the essential difference between demons and Christians.

The Plank in Your Eye

"And why do you look at the speck in your brother's eye, but do not consider the plank in your own eye? Or how can you say to your brother, 'Let me remove the speck from your eye'; and look, a plank is in your own eye? Hypocrite! First remove the plank from your own eye, and then you will see clearly to remove the speck from your brother's eye."
—Matthew 7:3–5

What do you think of someone who knits in church?" The woman eyed me, waiting for an answer. Unfortunately for her, I had learned long ago to be wary of "What do you think of . . ." questions because they are often asked in an attempt to entrap the pastor. She obviously disapproved of someone knitting in church and was hoping I would say something to fortify her position, thus dragging me into the matter. I did not wish to be quoted as being against a woman I had never met. For all I knew, the supposed violator of sanctuary sanctity had a nervous disposition or an anxiety disorder that was mitigated by the simple act of knitting.

"I would imagine I would be glad she was in church," I answered.

"I think it's *wrong*," said my disappointed questioner.

The curious thing about the question was the nature of the one asking it. People have often tried to drag pastors into their disputes, framing their questions in such ways as to make it "obvious" that the pastors should take their side. But I also knew that for all her concern about decorum, the woman asking the question had issues of her own. She was an avid coffee drinker, had been heard encouraging young church members that coffee drinking was harmless, was known to consistently knock Adventist beliefs, and had also been known to drink wine. In fact, based on what I knew, I would have been obliged to bar her from holding church office had she been *my* church member.

When Seventh-day Adventists pledge to live by the teachings of the Bible, some people seem to get the idea that they have been assigned to police the behavior of others, making sure that everybody *else* toes the line. In reality, each of us has far more than we can handle when it comes to monitoring ourselves. Given the plank in our own eye, it is surprising that we can detect the specks of dust on others, but somehow sin warps our perception such that our pride easily blinds us to our own faults. In light of Jesus' teaching on specks and planks, when it comes to living biblically, we ought to be as generous as possible with others and as fastidious as possible with ourselves.

Fire in Your Bones

Then I said, "I will not make mention of Him, nor speak anymore in His name."
But His word was in my heart like a burning fire shut up in my bones;
I was weary of holding it back, and I could not.
—Jeremiah 20:9

Living biblically can be remarkably challenging. Jeremiah had been commissioned by God to take a final warning to His rebellious people, and after spending a night in the stocks, he was tempted to give up his mission. Hardship, rejection, and mockery made his ministry seem like a failure.

That's it, he thought to himself. *I'm finished speaking. Why put myself through the trouble? These people aren't listening anyway!*

He found himself incapable of silence, however. "His word was in my heart like a burning fire shut up in my bones; I was weary of holding it back, and I could not." The prophet was so saturated with the Word of God that keeping silent became painful. It was harder, in fact, to keep quiet than it was to keep preaching.

So it is with living biblically. When the believer immerses himself or herself in the Word of God daily, living by the principles of Scripture becomes natural. Even though the world ridicules people who choose to live principled lives (and more so with each passing year), and it sometimes appears to be more convenient to compromise with the world, a heart saturated with the Bible will find it difficult to stop doing the right thing.

It is not unlike an exercise program. When you start working out, it seems easier to quit than to get up early, strap on your running shoes, and head out the door. But after about three weeks of consistently exercising, you begin to feel anxious if you *do not* do it because it has become a key part of who you are. Skip a day of exercise, and your body will notice it.

In the beginning, living by scriptural principle takes conscious effort. You will have to consider carefully each moral decision life throws at you, searching the Bible for godly wisdom. But in due time, as you immerse yourself in the atmosphere of heaven through daily contact with God, doing the right thing becomes such a vital part of who you are that choosing the right path happens almost automatically. Even on days when the right thing seems difficult or imposing, and your first reaction is to shirk from duty, the fire in your bones will irresistibly push you to keep walking the narrow path with Christ.

Inspiring Confidence

But we all, with unveiled face, beholding as in a mirror the glory of the Lord,
are being transformed into the same image from glory to glory, just as by the Spirit of the Lord.
—2 Corinthians 3:18

There is an old story of two travelers who found themselves stranded on a lonely road late at night. After walking some distance, they came upon a humble cabin and decided to ask if they could spend the night. To their delight, the old prospector who answered the door not only agreed to host them in a small guest room overnight, but he also gave them a hot meal and proved to be good company.

When it came time to retire for the night, however, the two men grew nervous because they were carrying a substantial sum of cash. They both agreed to sleep in shifts, taking turns guarding the money. The first man to stand watch noticed a light under the door in the middle of the night and decided to see what the old prospector was up to. He quietly tiptoed from his bed and cracked the door. When he peeked through the opening, he saw the old man at the kitchen table, reading a copy of the Bible.

He softly closed the door again and went to wake his travel companion. "I think we can both sleep soundly tonight," he said. "We're in no danger in this house."

What inspired such confidence? Would he have said the same thing if the prospector had been reading a copy of *Playboy* or Charles Darwin's *The Descent of Man*? Our modern world has unfortunately been conditioned, through constant mockery and horrific portrayals of the clergy, to distrust Bible-believing Christians. But it was not always so. There was a day in the not-so-distant past when most people still recognized the moral value of the Bible's teachings. They understood that people who studied Jesus intently started to reflect His character.

Perhaps the Christian community has earned some of the mistrust. During the latter part of the twentieth century, the world of religion was rocked by high-profile scandals carried out by members of the clergy. Trust was shattered, and it became easy to mock the Christian faith.

But imagine if more of us actually *lived* the Bible. Imagine if our faith guided our public conduct. Perhaps we could offer this world another opportunity to catch a glimpse of Jesus and inspire hope that with Bible-believing Christians around, things are going to be OK.

NOVEMBER 7

"Do You Hear Me?"

So then faith comes by hearing, and hearing by the word of God.
—Romans 10:17

I am not really a fan of audiobooks. As a bibliophile, I have tried to squeeze as many books as possible into my short lifetime, and I thought that perhaps listening to books would enable me to aggregate even more knowledge. But it did not work. As I listened, I would start to daydream, wandering down any number of tangential rabbit trails, only to realize twenty minutes later that the book was still playing, and I had missed much of it.

Good biblical preaching that drives me to a careful examination of the Bible, however, continues to arrest my attention. In explaining the urgency of evangelism, Paul underlines how critically important it is that Christians verbally share the gospel with others. "How shall they believe in Him of whom they have not heard? And how shall they hear without a preacher?" (Romans 10:14)

Then he points out that "faith comes by hearing, and hearing by the word of God." Some conclude, then, that all we need to do is to *listen* to the words of the Bible in order to grow. Listen to enough sermons, read enough Bible passages, and you will become more Christlike.

It is true that reading changes who you are. Studies have repeatedly demonstrated that reading rewires and grows important regions in the human brain and increases intelligence—and some parts of your brain even have a tough time distinguishing between a real experience and one that you imagined while reading a book. So *reading* your Bible is unquestionably valuable.

But the point of the Christian experience is not the mere accumulation of knowledge. God intends to grow our faith, and for that to happen, we must *live* the principles we discover in the Bible. When Paul says our faith comes by hearing, we should probably understand that the same way we understood it when our mothers or fathers used to correct us by saying, "Do you hear me?" They were asking if we were going to *apply* what we had heard.

The most effective way to understand the Bible is to read what it says and then test its principles in our daily life. Eventually, we begin to realize through experience that God's Word is infallible, and God becomes more real to us, and our faith in Him deepens.

"Can These Bones Live?"

Again He said to me, "Prophesy to these bones, and say to them, 'O dry bones, hear the word of the LORD! Thus says the Lord GOD to these bones: "Surely I will cause breath to enter into you, and you shall live. I will put sinews on you and bring flesh upon you, cover you with skin and put breath in you; and you shall live. Then you shall know that I am the LORD." ' "
—Ezekiel 37:4–6

In a vision, God took the prophet Ezekiel and set him down in a valley full of long-dead people. They had been dead so long that their bones were dried, bleached, and strewn about the valley floor. Ezekiel describes them as "very dry" (Ezekiel 37:2). "What do you think, Ezekiel?" God asks him. "Do you think these bones can live?"

Impossible. If someone has been clinically dead for a few minutes, you might stand a chance at resuscitating him or her. If the heart stopped beating seconds ago, you could apply a defibrillator's paddles and hope for the best. But after the body has decomposed and the bones are sun bleached? Impossible.

Unless, of course, the creative power of God is applied to them. Ezekiel is told to *preach* to the bones, to apply the "word of the LORD" to them. It was God's word that first gave birth to the universe, and it is the voice of the Word of God that will call the dead back to life at the Second Coming. Between those two events, the Word of God resuscitates sinners, bringing them back from spiritual death. No matter how long your spiritual decline has been in effect, no matter how deep your spiritual malaise, God's Word can breathe new life into you.

The same appears to be true for churches as a whole. During the early part of the twentieth century, there was a sharp decline in biblical preaching in mainline Protestant churches. The hope was that by watering down distinctive biblical doctrines, churches would seem more accommodating and arrest the decline. The opposite happened: churches in slow decline entered a death spiral.

But churches that faithfully preach the Word continue to grow in the face of mounting secularism. "If we are talking about which belief system is more likely to lead to numerical growth among Protestant churches," researcher David Millard Haskell explains about a study of Canadian churches, "the evidence suggests that conservative Protestant theology is the clear winner."★

Such churches, of course, are far more likely to be evangelistic, and they prove what Ezekiel knew long ago: living by the power of God's Word, which has always been invested with creative power, is the real secret to spiritual life and growth.

Oh, dry bones, hear the Word of the Lord!

★ Kate Shellnutt, "The Mainline's Saving Grace," *Christianity Today*, May 2017, 14.

NOVEMBER 9

A Cloud of Witnesses

*Therefore we also, since we are surrounded by so great a cloud of witnesses,
let us lay aside every weight, and the sin which so easily ensnares us, and let us run
with endurance the race that is set before us, looking unto Jesus, the author
and finisher of our faith, who for the joy that was set before Him endured the cross,
despising the shame, and has sat down at the right hand of the throne of God.*
—Hebrews 12:1, 2

Well before the American Revolution began, founding father John Adams sensed that something monumental to the history of the world was about to happen, and he asked his wife Abigail to start saving his correspondence. He kept all of his letters in a folio he purchased in June 1776, knowing that future generations would find them important.

So it was with most of the American founding fathers. They instinctively understood that their revolution would change the world. It would have huge ramifications for both future generations of Americans and the world at large. The American bid for independence was unique in the landscape of revolutionary movements; unlike the French Revolution, it did not turn violent against its own people shortly after the overthrow of the monarchy. The struggle to draft a Constitution and form a nation involved heated debate among various factions with diverse interests, yet it was marked by civil discourse rather than bloodshed.

As we study the Bible, we, too, will recognize that something monumental is about to happen. There are many good reasons to sculpt our characters by the biblical principle, not the least of which is the way that scriptural living draws us into closer contact with the Author of the Book. But it is also prudent to consider the cloud of witnesses, past and future, that will watch our moment on the stage of God's last-day remnant movement. At some point in the not-too-distant future, those who went before us will open the books of heaven and examine our conduct, as will the generations after us (should time last) who will pick up the work when we have finally laid it down.

Unfortunately, life in the church has always been marked by human disputes; that much is evident from the content of the New Testament letters. Much of what Paul wrote to first-century churches was in response to challenges. How we handle disputes in our own time—and how we choose to live—will speak volumes about how willing we were to allow the Spirit of God to steer us. For future generations who look back to this moment, our conduct will either challenge the notion that this is *God's* movement or underline it.

Worth the Risk

"Again, the kingdom of heaven is like a merchant seeking beautiful pearls, who,
when he had found one pearl of great price, went and sold all that he had and bought it."
—Matthew 13:45, 46

In the library at the Voice of Prophecy, there is a very special book—one of the most unique on the planet. It does not have a beautiful leather binding, the type is less than perfect, and the pages certainly are not archival quality, yet it might be more valuable than the beautiful editions of the Bible produced at Cambridge. Those beautiful Bibles, you see, were produced in perfect freedom on presses capable of high-speed reproduction.

This book was not. It is a copy of Arthur S. Maxwell's *Your Bible and You*, produced on a typewriter in Bulgaria during the reign of Soviet Communism. Faithful church members would load seven sheets of paper into the typewriter, with carbon paper in between each of them, and then under cover of night, in a carefully arranged room away from prying ears, painstakingly hammer one key at a time to be sure that it imprinted on all seven sheets.

The result is a document 531 pages long, representing countless hundreds (if not thousands of hours) at the typewriter. If they had been caught, it would have meant prison—or worse. But the flames of the gospel were so brilliant in their souls that no mere human threat could keep them from producing such works. And there were people willing to risk everything to obtain a copy.

It was not even a Bible; it was just a book *about* the Bible.

Most of us have multiple copies of the Bible in our homes. The shelves of almost any secondhand bookshop feature dozens, if not hundreds of copies; most of which have never been used. We have easy access to the Scriptures on our phones, tablets, and laptops—yet there may be no generation of Christians so negligent of the Bible as ours. We can read it in freedom, without fearing heavy fists knocking on our doors in the middle of the night, yet we do not.

Perhaps we should ask ourselves why our forefathers in the faith were willing to risk everything to land a copy of the Book we so carelessly set aside in favor of Netflix. Not only did they live by biblical principle, but they also found that experience so valuable they were willing to *stop* living, if need be, to keep that privilege alive for their children.

Recreated

Create in me a clean heart, O God, and renew a steadfast spirit within me.
—Psalm 51:10

Have you ever made a New Year's resolution that you actually kept? Most of us, when it comes to the substantive issues, usually find ourselves powerless to make any real changes. Habits established over decades of living can prove to be nigh on impossible to conquer. Emotional issues such as anger or anxiety continue to imprison us no matter how many self-help books we wade through.

Sometimes, infrequently, we succeed. We plan to exercise, and we do. We plan to lose weight, and it happens. But with the deeper issues, we still discover that our sinful hearts cannot be changed by mere willpower. David did the unthinkable: He committed adultery and then had the wronged husband put to death on the battlefield. He knew it was wrong, and after the prophet Nathan confronted him with what he had done, he felt great remorse. The fifty-first psalm was born of his deep regret.

There is a reason his plea with God sounds so desperate: he knew that without divine intervention, his heart would not change, and he would do the same thing again. His painful sentiments were echoed by Paul centuries later: "But I see another law in my members, warring against the law of my mind, and bringing me into captivity to the law of sin which is in my members. O wretched man that I am! Who will deliver me from this body of death?" (Romans 7:23, 24).

A theologian might refer to this as the doctrine of depravity: the fact that our human hearts are so stained by sin that we are powerless, like a leopard that wishes to change its spots (see Jeremiah 13:23).

There is great hope in David's plea, however. When he asks God to "create" a clean heart in him, he uses the Hebrew word *bara*, which is precisely the same word that is used to describe the creation of the world: In the beginning God "created" (*bara*) the heavens and the earth. And how did He accomplish that? By speaking them into existence.

God's Word has creative power: to live by it is to be daily changed, gradually re-created in the image of Christ. The psalmist declares, "Your word I have hidden in my heart, that I might not sin against You" (Psalm 119:11).

Big Tent Christianity

That we should no longer be children, tossed to and fro and carried about with every wind of doctrine, by the trickery of men, in the cunning craftiness of deceitful plotting.
—Ephesians 4:14

It is popular now to refer to "big tent" Christianity. The imagery hearkens back to the days of traveling revivalists who set up tents on the edge of town. The townspeople, regardless of their religious background, would converge on the tent each evening in search of a deeper experience. It is a generous image, and one that seeks to include a much broader base of people in the life of the church.

Likewise, some refer to "generous orthodoxy," which suggests that the bare essentials of Christianity remain nonnegotiable (such as the basic plan of salvation or the divinity of Christ), but the traditional bounds of doctrine that serve the church—sometimes appearing to be more like a fence—are moved further outward to include more points of view.

It is a pleasant thought and has something to it: Jesus was always generous when it came to the people He was willing to engage with and love. We could learn much when it comes to how broad we are willing to make our circle of personal associates. The doors of the church *should* be open, and people from every walk of life ought to feel welcome and comfortable with us. Every church service ought to be a "big tent" evangelistic outreach.

When it comes to minor issues, silence is often eloquence. Some hills really *are not* worth dying on, and there is plenty of room for personal discretion and understanding of Bible principle in God's remnant church.

But as the rest of the world jettisons biblical doctrine in favor of broader inclusivity, the last-day remnant church cannot afford to forget that we *do* have a distinctive message—the three angels' messages—which will always be nonnegotiable.

When Seventh-day Adventists pledge to order their lives in harmony with Bible principle, we are declaring common doctrinal ground on which we will not compromise. We understand that we have been given a unique role in this last generation: to hold out distinctive truth, to call God's people out of the errors of Babylon, and to exhibit a clearer, much more compelling picture of Jesus than can be found in the world of last-day religious compromise.

Yes, our tent must always be big, but not so doctrinally undefined that it is no longer a tent at all.

Of One Mind

"These are of one mind, and they will give their power and authority to the beast.
These will make war with the Lamb, and the Lamb will overcome them, for He is Lord of lords
and King of kings; and those who are with Him are called, chosen, and faithful."
—Revelation 17:13, 14

Many people see in the ominous prediction of the ten horns of Revelation 17 a last-day revival of the church-state marriage that grew out of the post-Constantinian city of Rome. But the crowns that were prominent on the horns in Revelation 13 appear to be missing in Revelation 17, suggesting that this revival takes place in a day and age when monarchies may have become somewhat irrelevant, and "kingly" political powers have taken their place.

Our present day, of course, answers neatly to the description. Since the early part of the twentieth century, particularly after the Great War, monarchs have largely become figureheads and the days of empire have retired to our history books. The modern nations of Europe seem to live in a constant state of turmoil, uncertain (at the time of this writing) regarding issues of migration and the challenges to the European Union itself. The ugly prospect of war continues to rear its head. It is not hard to comprehend a situation in which sovereign nations compromise and fall in line behind the one power that held them (somewhat) together in the medieval period—the papacy.

As Seventh-day Adventists, we should pay particular attention to the prediction that these nations will be "of one mind." Whatever their present differences, they will establish common ground and find unity under the beast power. Their belief systems will merge, and they will know what they believe in common.

Can the remnant movement be any less decisive about the clear doctrines of the Bible? There are only two movements in the end, and according to Revelation 14, God's last-day people will also be of one mind, standing on Mount Zion with the Father's name inscribed on their foreheads. They unite behind the Lamb who leads them and also behind a final message they are tasked with delivering to the world.

Our biblical beliefs are not incidental to our fellowship; they are the reason the fellowship exists. If it were not for the clear teachings of Christ as found in Scripture, there would be no Seventh-day Adventist Church. We do not always have to agree on every little point, but when it comes to Jesus and His teachings—and our commission—we must always be of one mind.

Once Delivered

Beloved, while I was very diligent to write to you concerning our common salvation,
I found it necessary to write to you exhorting you to contend earnestly
for the faith which was once for all delivered to the saints.

—Jude 3

There are at least two schools of thought when it comes to the nature of God's church in the twenty-first century. One school says that the teachings and scriptural understandings of the Christian church must be dynamic, always changing with the times. It views the life of the church through an evolutionary lens, suggesting that as history carries us to new frontiers, our understanding of the message of the Bible must adapt to suit. Tradition carries a lot of weight for Christians who subscribe to this view because tradition changes with the times, and the supposed wisdom of each generation is added to the canon as circumstances dictate.

The other school of thought says that the original faith that was handed down to us matters and is far more authoritative than any thoughts that might be added by later generations. This was the position held by Jude, who warned his audience of "certain men [who] have crept in unnoticed . . . ungodly men, who turn the grace of our God into lewdness and deny the only Lord God and our Lord Jesus Christ" (Jude 4). He identifies dark influences in our world that attempt to change the essential message of Christianity, stripping it of some of its most important elements. The world cannot share the gospel because it will distort the message; instead, we must "contend earnestly for the faith which was once for all delivered to the saints."

In other words, there are essential doctrines in Christianity that never change. They have been the same since the inception of the church and will remain the same forever. These are the teachings that unite us as believers, not just across our modern communities but across the centuries. Christians today essentially believe what Christians believed in the first century, when Jesus first sent His disciples into the world. While we have to learn to *apply* the message of the Bible to each cultural context we face across time, the *essence* of Christian doctrine remains the same in spite of the world around us.

The face of God's church simply cannot change because the face of Jesus does not change. And, as the author of Hebrews reminds us, "Jesus Christ is the same yesterday, today, and forever" (Hebrews 13:8).

The Prosperous Way

"This Book of the Law shall not depart from your mouth, but you shall meditate in it day and night, that you may observe to do according to all that is written in it. For then you will make your way prosperous, and then you will have good success. Have I not commanded you? Be strong and of good courage; do not be afraid, nor be dismayed, for the LORD your God is with you wherever you go."
—Joshua 1:8

There were a number of key political "footballs" on the field during the earliest years of the American republic, including a plan for the federal government to assume state debts and the location of the nascent nation's capital. While these might seem like small issues, at times the frenzied debate over them threatened to rend the new republic in two. Both problems were, of course, settled; but there was another issue, a far more important one, that remained embarrassingly unresolved: slavery.

There were plenty of voices petitioning Congress for abolition in 1790, including some Quaker delegations and the Pennsylvania Abolition Society, whose petition was signed by no less a luminary than Benjamin Franklin. A number of state constitutions also included a prohibition of slavery.

Tragically, the issue remained virtually untouched for another seven decades, until the Civil War forced it. Members of Congress knew that slavery was antithetical to the Declaration of Independence, which insisted that "all men are created equal" and have a right to liberty. But sufficient numbers of them knew that to tackle slavery in 1790 would be to risk the republic, as some states threatened to secede if it became an issue. In 1787, the Constitution itself prohibited stopping the slave trade for a period of twenty years, until 1808. They opted to be pragmatic, clinging to the 1787 provision.

Two parties emerged: those who pushed for abolition based on the Declaration of Independence, and those who procrastinated based on political concerns. "One's answer," author Joseph J. Ellis points out, "depended a great deal on which founding moment, 1776 or 1787, seemed most seminal."★ For the moment, political concerns won over principle. It is a blight that tarnishes the founding of the freest republic on earth and continues to plague it to this day.

As Christians, we can learn something from the slavery debate. From time to time, controversies break out in the church, as they have from the very beginning. The question is whether we will allow political concerns to drive the discussion or whether we will refer to the core principles as explained in our founding document, the Bible. Political concerns almost invariably lead to compromises that can take many years to straighten out; operating by God's Word, on the other hand, "will make your way prosperous."

★ Joseph J. Ellis, *Founding Brothers: The Revolutionary Generation* (New York: Vintage Books, 2003), 88.

The Way Back Home

Then Jesus came from Galilee to John at the Jordan to be baptized by him.
And John tried to prevent Him, saying, "I need to
be baptized by You, and are You coming to me?"
But Jesus answered and said to him, "Permit it to be so now, for thus
it is fitting for us to fulfill all righteousness." Then he allowed Him.
—Matthew 3:13–15

Try to imagine the gut-wrenching discomfort of being asked to baptize the One you know to be the Son of God. He is the "Lamb of God who takes away the sin of the world" (John 1:29), and you have been openly calling sinners to be baptized as a public symbol of repentance. What sense does it make to baptize the only One who has never sinned?

"When Jesus came to be baptized," Ellen White points out, "John recognized in Him a purity of character that he had never before perceived in any man. The very atmosphere of His presence was holy and awe-inspiring."★

"I can't do this!" John protests, insisting that it would be far more appropriate for Jesus to baptize *him*. Peter reacted much the same way when Jesus later tried to wash his feet: "You shall never wash my feet!" (John 13:8).

It makes perfect sense, humanly speaking. I cannot imagine that I would react any differently, knowing who I am and who Jesus is. He deserves eternity, and I deserve death. Instead, Jesus is put to death on a cruel instrument of torture, and I receive eternity because of His humiliation.

"John, I want you to do this," Jesus replies, "because it is fitting for us to fulfill all righteousness."

Jesus was baptized because it was the right thing for *us* to do, not because *He* needed it. He had appeared on earth as the "last Adam" (1 Corinthians 15:45), the new Head of the human race. Like a parent who personally demonstrates a new task for a young child, He knew that our minds were so clouded by sin that we would never understand the way back home without an example. We were utterly incapable of redeeming ourselves from the horrible situation we created through our rebellion, so He came to lead us back to the kingdom in person—much the way He had personally led the Israelites to the Land of Promise in a pillar of cloud.

As Jesus steps into the Jordan, He is not merely asking John to baptize Him, He is also asking you to follow Him. "I know you're lost," Jesus says, "so here: follow Me. This is the way back home."

★ Ellen G. White, *The Desire of Ages* (Mountain View, CA: Pacific Press®, 1898), 110.

Your First Day of Ministry

When all the people were baptized, it came to pass that Jesus also was baptized;
and while He prayed, the heaven was opened. And the Holy Spirit descended
in bodily form like a dove upon Him, and a voice came from heaven which said,
"You are My beloved Son; in You I am well pleased." Now Jesus Himself began
His ministry at about thirty years of age, being (as was supposed) the son of Joseph.
—Luke 3:21–23

Over the centuries, many Christians have wondered why Jesus seems to do so little before His baptism. Some have conjectured that He would not have been accepted as a teacher until He had reached the age of full adulthood; men under thirty were not considered ready for public life. There may be some truth to this assertion; Jesus would have been taken more seriously after thirty than before.

Others, unhappy that we have so few details from Jesus' earlier years, have tried to fill in the blanks, inventing childhood stories such as a Jesus raising the future thief on the cross from the dead or bringing a clay bird to life.

The Bible, however, provides a good reason that Jesus did not begin His ministry earlier: it was not time. Many centuries earlier Daniel had seen it in vision. "Know therefore and understand," Gabriel explains to him, "that from the going forth of the command to restore and build Jerusalem until Messiah the Prince, there shall be seven weeks and sixty-two weeks" (Daniel 9:25). The decree to rebuild the city came in 457 B.C., under the Persian king Artaxerxes. Sixty-nine weeks into the future, or 483 prophetic days, ended in A.D. 27—the very moment when Jesus was baptized.

It was supposed to be obvious to any student of Scripture when Messiah the Prince had arrived. There could be no mistaking who Jesus was; at His baptism, the Father publicly announced His Son, declaring that the moment had at long last arrived.

You will notice that Jesus began His public ministry with baptism. Now consider the fact that you have also been called into ministry. Every church member has been given a commission to carry the gospel to the ends of the earth. When you are baptized, you are not only publicly declaring that *your* moment has arrived—that you have chosen to step into the kingdom of God—you are also beginning *your* public ministry.

Know that when you came up out of the waters of baptism, the Father also smiled and said, "This is My beloved child, in whom I am well pleased." Your baptism was not the finish line but the start of something big. Get out there and share what you know: God intends for the world to see you.

Jesus Won

Then Jesus was led up by the Spirit into the wilderness to be tempted by the devil.
And when He had fasted forty days and forty nights, afterward He was hungry.
—Matthew 4:1, 2

Even though His baptism marked the launch of His public ministry, the first thing Jesus did after coming up out of the Jordan was to head to the wilderness for forty days. Before He began ministering to crowds, He took the time to "brace Himself for the bloodstained path He must travel."★ Satan seized upon His isolation and self-denial as an opportunity to derail His mission.

All told, it was an ordeal that lasted forty days—a period of time that should arrest the attention of good Bible students. In his first letter to the Corinthians, Paul compared Israel's safe passage through the Red Sea to baptism: "all our fathers were under the cloud, all passed through the sea, all were baptized into Moses in the cloud and in the sea" (1 Corinthians 10:1, 2). And of course, Paul also pointed out that the Rock, Jesus Himself, was with them through that experience.

Not only was Jesus present with Israel in the cloud, but the wilderness experience also foreshadowed His future ministry. After passing through the "baptism" of the Red Sea, the children of Abraham wandered in the wilderness for a period of forty years. The parallels are unmistakable: the entire nation of Israel was a type of Christ, who also left Egypt, was baptized in the Jordan, and entered the wilderness for forty days. "When Israel was a child," God explained to Hosea, "I loved him, and out of Egypt I called My son" (Hosea 11:1).

In addition to the clear parallel, however, there is also a striking contrast to consider. The Israelites' wandering was the result of having *failed* in the face of temptation. "They could not enter in because of unbelief," the Bible explains (Hebrews 3:19). Jesus, on the other hand, deflected the devil's lies by clinging to an "it is written."

The message is clear: Jesus, the Son of man, has utterly triumphed where we have utterly failed. He walked the same path we did but prevailed where we had surrendered. He lived our existence but without sin. Today, our own baptism stands as a public declaration, letting the world know that we believe Jesus has already won and the Promised Land can be ours, not because of our own accomplishment but because of His.

★ Ellen G. White, *The Desire of Ages* (Mountain View, CA: Pacific Press®, 1898), 114.

The Descender

"Are not the Abanah and the Pharpar, the rivers of Damascus,
better than all the waters of Israel? Could I not wash in them and be clean?"
So he turned and went away in a rage. And his servants came near and spoke to him,
and said, "My father, if the prophet had told you to do something great, would you not have
done it? How much more then, when he says to you, 'Wash, and be clean'?"
—2 Kings 5:12, 13

It was bad enough that the prophet failed to come to the door in person when Naaman the Syrian general called on him; the messenger he sent insisted that the cure for his leprosy was to bathe in the Jordan. His pride was wounded, and he became furious, insisting that his own homeland had far better rivers than the miserable little stream Elisha had suggested.

Naaman's story, of course, has been included in the Bible for our benefit. His leprosy illustrates our sin, for we have all been condemned to die an ignominious death as a result of the plague that fell on us when we broke our trust with God. Naaman's leprosy, however, is not the only thing we have in common with him; there is also a proud Syrian general in each of us who refuses to believe that the path to the kingdom is through self-denial. Sin has placed our ego on a pedestal, and it warps our perception to the point where we have come to believe that the cure for what ails us most is to feed our pride rather than squash it.

"That muddy, miserable stream. Never! Elisha should have come out, paid me respect, and just waved his hand over me!"

Fast-forward through the centuries to the General of heaven's army, who approaches that same muddy, miserable stream and, against the protests of John the Baptist, insists on humbling Himself in spite of the fact that He does not suffer from pride.

The very name of the river is profound: *Jordan* means "the descender," because it winds its way down through the land until it empties into the Dead Sea. The real Descender, however, was the One who stepped down from heaven's glory into our existence; a Creator who was not too proud to take our muddy problems on Himself. Before it was over, He would descend all the way to the grave.

What chance does our sinful pride have in the face of such selfless love? How can we cherish our egos and feed our pride when the sinless Son of God Himself was more willing than Naaman to step into the Jordan? It leaves us no further rationalization for sin: we have no choice but to step into the same muddy, miserable river ourselves.

The Starting Line

Peter said to Him, "You shall never wash my feet!"
Jesus answered him, "If I do not wash you, you have no part with Me."
Simon Peter said to Him, "Lord, not my feet only, but also my hands and my head!"
Jesus said to him, "He who is bathed needs only to wash his feet,
but is completely clean; and you are clean, but not all of you."
—John 13:8–10

I once knew a man who had attended church for more than twenty years, yet he had never joined the church through baptism. Anytime I hinted at the subject, no matter how subtly, he grew agitated and would invariably change the subject. I was tempted to think (and shame on me for thinking it) that perhaps he had some horrible, unconfessed sin in his life that kept him from making a full commitment to the cause of Christ. Cherished sin, after all, can prove a formidable barrier to repentance.

It turns out that was not the case at all. He did not *cherish* sin; he *resented* it because he understood the pain and suffering that our sins brought to Jesus. He feared he would profess repentance in baptism and then sin again afterward. He did not want to risk making a mockery of what was, to him, a sacred and profound rite.

It was the story of Peter that brought him relief. "Phil,"★ I said, "look at the story of Peter. When Jesus came to wash his feet, he was as horrified as John the Baptist had been when Jesus requested baptism. At first, he refused. When Jesus told him that he could have no part in the kingdom unless He washed him, the pendulum swung sharply in the other direction, and Peter wanted to be washed all over."

Phil blinked a couple of times and then looked up at me. "Here's what you need to see," I explained. "Peter had already been baptized and had begun his walk with Christ. But baptism isn't the finish line; it's just the beginning. Peter went on to make many mistakes afterward, not the least of which was denying Christ the night of His trial. So I can promise you: you *will* make mistakes after this, because on this side of glory, we all do. It's not what we want, but it's going to happen occasionally. As Jesus washes Peter's feet, He's reassuring a stubborn fisherman that He can handle our sins *after* baptism, just as well as He can handle them before. We don't have to start all over every single time we slip."

"And if anyone sins," John reminds us, "we have an Advocate with the Father, Jesus Christ the righteous" (1 John 2:1).

★ Not his real name.

A Promise Kept

*For as many of you as were baptized into Christ have put on Christ.
There is neither Jew nor Greek, there is neither slave nor free, there is neither male
nor female; for you are all one in Christ Jesus. And if you are Christ's,
then you are Abraham's seed, and heirs according to the promise.*
—Galatians 3:27–29

With nothing but God's promise to go on, Abraham uprooted his family and left the comforts of Chaldea for an uncertain existence in a strange land. "You are going to have so many descendants," God explained, "that they will be like the sand on the shore or the stars in the sky."

The author of Hebrews points out that Abraham, like other giants of faith, went to his death never having seen God's promise fulfilled (Hebrews 11:39, 40). When his wife died, he had to buy land to bury her because he had not come into possession of the Promised Land. When he died, he did have heirs, but they would have been easy to count.

Did God fail him? Not at all. Every one of God's promises is rock solid. You can take them to the bank. For many long centuries after Abraham's death, God continued to produce heirs, and He continues to add countless millions to the number even today.

The day you were baptized, God was making a promise to you: your sins have been forgiven, and when Jesus returns, He will be coming for you. But He was also *keeping* a promise to His good friend Abraham (see James 2:23). The day you were baptized, you see, you "put on Christ." And all those who have "put on Christ" become "Abraham's seed, and heirs according to the promise."

You are a promise kept. As Abraham was contemplating specks of sand by the water or distant points of light in the night sky, wondering who his future descendants might be, God was thinking of *you*. It may have seemed like only a few people sitting in the pews at church witnessed your baptism, but you can be sure that all of heaven witnessed it and that angels rejoiced because God's Word had proven faithful yet again.

"After these things I looked," said John, "and behold, a great multitude which no one could number" (Revelation 7:9). He looked forward through time in a vision and also saw God's promise come to pass—too many descendants to count. It makes me wonder, as John scanned that massive crowd, if he did not also happen to see your face.

Be sure to introduce yourself to Abraham in the kingdom. You are, after all, immediate family.

Added to the Church

Then those who gladly received his word were baptized;
and that day about three thousand souls were added to them.
—Acts 2:41

The record of the earliest church is clear: people who were baptized into Christ were also baptized into His church. It has become fashionable in recent years to suggest that we ought to simply baptize people "into Christ," without insisting on church membership, and leave them to find their own expression of faith. In an era where the label *nondenominational* has been displayed as a badge of honor, it seems appropriate to many to simply baptize new believers into an abstract, ill-defined larger "body of Christ."

It is a little like baptizing people into the internet's cloud, I suppose; they are just placed somewhere on the spiritual internet, without a specific home.

It was not the pattern of the first-century church, however. The three thousand baptized at Pentecost were "added to them," that is to the church. Individual Christians do not exist in a spiritual vacuum, independent of each other, but are expected to fulfill the gospel commission together, using their individual gifts in concert with other believers.

The instructions Jesus left His disciples make this clear. Baptism was not a rite of closure but an initiation into the life of the church. After baptism, the disciples were to teach people "to observe all things that I have commanded you" (Matthew 28:20). That would not be possible if we simply released people into the wild.

If someone told you that he or she had been "baptized" into any other religion, you would rightly assume that the person had subscribed to the beliefs of that religion. It is no different with Christianity. When we are baptized, we subscribe to the doctrines of Jesus, one of which is *belonging*. "As You sent Me into the world," Jesus prayed, "I also have sent them into the world" (John 17:18).

Our mission is to mirror Jesus, with a key difference. Jesus is unique, a perfect expression of God all by Himself. You and I are not, but together we make up Christ's presence in a fallen world.

"I do not pray for these alone, but also for those who will believe in Me through their word; that they all may be one, as You, Father, are in Me, and I in You; that they also may be one in Us, that the world may believe that You sent Me" (verses 20, 21).

A Public Matter

"Therefore whoever confesses Me before men,
him I will also confess before My Father who is in heaven."
—Matthew 10:32

Can't it just be you and me, in private?" Peter studied my face, hoping to detect signs of agreement.

I understood Peter's hesitancy immediately. "I can understand your desire for privacy, Peter, and we don't have to have a *lot* of people there. But there do need to be witnesses. Baptism is not a private ritual; it is also meant to be a witness to the world around you. You are telling the whole world that you believe Jesus died for your sins and that you also believe He rose from the dead and lives today. More than that, you are also telling the world that you believe that God has buried the old sinner and raised you to a new life in Christ."

For Peter, it was a matter of introversion. For others, however, the desire for a quiet baptism stems from a wish to keep their Christianity quiet. In countries where Christian profession can earn you a death sentence, it makes some sense to be discreet; but in the free West, it does not.

Many years ago I drove a young lady to a beautiful oceanside park, walked her to a small lake full of swans, and got down on one knee to ask her to marry me. She was, to my great relief, excited, even breaking into tears of joy. She could not wait to start planning and sending out invitations so that the world could share in our joy.

But let us suppose I stopped her enthusiasm. "I'm happy to get married," I state, "but I wouldn't want my friends thinking I'd gotten all weak kneed and sloppy for some girl. So let's just go to city hall and do this privately, and afterward, we'll keep it quiet."

What girl in her right mind would accept such a proposal? Christianity is not a private affair; by its very definition, the faith of Jesus is outward focused. Everything we do and say concentrates on saving a world lost in sin. Jesus came to "seek and to save that which was lost" (Luke 19:10), and as our desires merge with His, that becomes our mission as well.

We begin our life in Christ as active Christians, telling the world what He has done for us the very moment we come up out of the water.

Death, Burial, Resurrection

Or do you not know that as many of us as were baptized into Christ Jesus were baptized into His death? Therefore we were buried with Him through baptism into death, that just as Christ was raised from the dead by the glory of the Father, even so we also should walk in newness of life. For if we have been united together in the likeness of His death, certainly we also shall be in the likeness of His resurrection, knowing this, that our old man was crucified with Him, that the body of sin might be done away with, that we should no longer be slaves of sin.
—Romans 6:3–6

A young soldier was called away to war, and as time passed, he became worried that his girlfriend might lose interest during his absence and move on to some other suitor. When his discharge was imminent, he wrote her a letter. "I'll be coming home soon," he explained, "and the train will pass right by your yard. If you're still interested in me, tie a yellow ribbon around the old oak tree. Then I'll know that you still care, and I'll get off the train. If it's not there, I'll understand, and I'll just keep riding to the next town."

The story has become immortalized in a popular song. As the train passed by his girlfriend's house, he nervously looked out the window and discovered a tree *covered* with yellow ribbons.

But let us suppose the girlfriend read his letter and began to change the instructions. "It's wartime," she tells herself, "and yellow ribbon is *so* expensive. I'll just use some of this black material I have lying around. And it's *so* dangerous and inconvenient to climb a ladder into a tree, so I'll just tie it to the fence."

What would happen? The soldier would never get off the train.

God's symbols are important. They are meant to convey very specific messages, which is why He has been so particular about them over the centuries. Cain tampered with the symbolism of the sacrificial lamb and robbed the rite of the Christ-centered meaning God had assigned it. The tabernacle had to be built exactly the way God instructed Moses, without freedom of expression, because every little detail pointed forward to Jesus.

During recent centuries, we have managed to convince ourselves—even though we kept the symbol virtually intact for the first twelve hundred—that perhaps the symbolism of baptism is not all that important. We have created dozens of divergent expressions, from sprinkling to pouring, that do not convey what God originally intended: according to Paul, baptism is a death, a burial, and a resurrection.

Only immersion tells *that* story. God intends for the story of redemption to be told millions of times, as each new believer steps into the waters of baptism and shows the world what God has done. Each of us, in other words, is a yellow ribbon for the world to find on the tree of life.

"What Hinders Me?"

Now as they went down the road, they came to some water.
And the eunuch said, "See, here is water. What hinders me from being baptized?"
Then Philip said, "If you believe with all your heart, you may."
And he answered and said, "I believe that Jesus Christ is the Son of God."
—Acts 8:36, 37

Matthew, recently divorced, asked if he could be baptized on an evening when he had custody of his son. "I want him to see it," he explained.

When Matthew arrived with his five-year-old boy, the boy suddenly made a beeline for me. "You the preacher?" he asked with wonder. I nodded. "My daddy's getting baptized tonight!" he beamed. "And so am I!"

He was a little too young to fully understand what baptism entails, but I had learned that you never, ever say *no* to someone who wants to do the right thing. It is wise to always encourage people to keep moving in the right direction, so I opted to affirm him. "That's wonderful!" I gushed. "We're going to have to start Bible studies right away, like your daddy did so that you can get ready."

His face fell. "No, I want to do it *now*," he said. He had never studied the Bible and had no idea what it meant to follow Christ. To go ahead would not have been right; but obviously, I wanted to be careful not to discourage him.

"I'll tell you what," I said. "I'll bet you'd like to be in the water with your daddy when he does this." He nodded. "And I'll bet you'd like to wear a robe like his." He nodded again. "So tonight, you can come in the water to support your daddy, and when you get baptized, he can be in the water to support you."

He was thrilled; he had only been worried that he might not be included in the special evening. We only had an adult-sized robe, but he happily put it on and climbed into the pool with his father. As Matthew came up out of the water, the little boy beamed. And then, as everyone was getting ready to climb out, he suddenly stuck his little arm in the air and then baptized *himself*.

He would go on to be baptized in later years, but I know heaven smiled at his enthusiasm. Children, after all, remind Jesus of the citizens of heaven (Matthew 19:14). It hearkened back to an Ethiopian treasure two thousand years ago: "See, here is water. What hinders me from being baptized?"

We all ought to find Jesus that irresistible.

A Moment of Dark

*Then Saul arose from the ground, and when his eyes were opened he saw no one.
But they led him by the hand and brought him into Damascus.
And he was three days without sight, and neither ate nor drank.*
—Acts 9:8, 9

Y ou have to wonder what kinds of thoughts passed through Saul's mind as he sat in the dark for three days, fasting and waiting for God's next move. It can be a devastating experience to discover that you have been playing for the wrong side of the universe your entire life. Saul of Tarsus was a promising young man who knew exactly what he wanted out of life: he wanted to defend the faith of his fathers and put a stop to the burgeoning sect of Christ followers who promised to upset everything. He was so right about his convictions that he even had papers from the high priest confirming his right to round up the "radicals."

It all changed suddenly on the road to Damascus when the God he thought he was defending stopped him short and challenged his entire worldview. He was questioned by the very One who had spoken with Abraham and shown that he had been working *against* God, not for Him.

It happens to all of us: during the conversion process, the voice of the Spirit whispers to our hearts (or sometimes *shouts!*), showing us that our understanding of the world is radically skewed by sin. He shakes our self-confidence and reveals our radical blindness. In a heartbeat, or sometimes over the course of weeks, months, or years, He tears down the priority system of a fallen world and shows us who God really is—in contrast with who we are.

As we pass under the surface of the water into baptism, we enter a brief moment where the world falls quiet: our eyes are usually closed, and the sights and sounds of the world around us disappear. It is almost as if we have passed into darkness with Saul. I have seen some candidates ask the pastor to keep them submerged for a few moments, so they have time to contemplate everything that is passing away—everything they are forsaking for Christ. When they are ready, they signal the pastor that it is time to come back up.

Every believer has been arrested on the road to Damascus, figuratively, and the old self passes into a watery grave, left behind forever. Saul the persecutor became Paul the apostle; the same has now happened for you.

Gone for Good

Then Jesus said to His disciples, "If anyone desires to come after Me, let him deny himself, and take up his cross, and follow Me. For whoever desires to save his life will lose it, but whoever loses his life for My sake will find it."
—Matthew 16:24, 25

The field of quantum mechanics emphasizes how little we know about the universe. Early on in the twentieth century, physicists learned that the subatomic world runs on an entirely different set of physical laws than the larger world around it. The famous double-slit light experiment, for example, appears to demonstrate that particles can exist in more than one place at once. Even more curious is the fact that the mere act of observing the subatomic world can change outcomes: it is the act of *looking* at a particle that determines where it will be.

It has led some theoreticians to consider the prospect that there are countless parallel universes, where all possibilities exist simultaneously: a multiverse. Perhaps you turned down a job in Paris; the theory suggests there is a universe out there where you accepted that job.

The theory is debated fiercely among physicists and has given rise to countless science-fiction movies. The words of the Bible, however, assure us that it is not true. There are not multiple versions of yourself, living all of your possible choices simultaneously.

There is little question that there is much more to the universe than we presently understand, but the rite of baptism sheds light on what God's perspective on the multiverse might be. When you choose Christ and pass through the waters of baptism, the old you is dead and buried. It does not exist elsewhere, continuing to reject Christ and living in sin.

If all possibilities always coexist, the ability to choose means little. The Bible assures us that with God, the matter is closed, and your salvation is secure. Your decision to accept the gift of Christ has eternal weight: you have been adopted into the family of God and are destined for the kingdom. You have "lost" your old life and found a new one in Jesus.

You can bank on it.

Pay It Forward

Therefore, when the Lord knew that the Pharisees had heard that Jesus made and baptized more disciples than John (though Jesus Himself did not baptize, but His disciples). He left Judea and departed again to Galilee.

—John 4:1–3

It is a curious fact that Jesus never actually performed the rite of baptism Himself but left it to His disciples. John 3 makes it clear that Jesus was indeed baptizing people (verse 22), but it appears that people were responding to His invitation, while the disciples performed the actual ceremony.

The Bible never explains why, but given human nature, it is not hard to guess. Perhaps Jesus understood that if some Christians had been baptized by the Son of God Himself, it might create the impression of a hierarchy in the church: those who were baptized by Jesus, and those who were baptized by mere mortals. The last two thousand years of Christian history certainly demonstrate our tendency to do such things.

Perhaps if Jesus had performed the rite Himself, baptism would have seemed more sacramental than symbolic, with people assuming that the act of being immersed by God's Son was the method by which we are saved. Again, the last two millennia have shown us that this is possible; we have many cases in which people assumed the act of baptism itself saves us, rather than serving as an outward witness of an inward acceptance and change. Those who were later baptized by mere disciples after Jesus returned to heaven might not have felt their baptism was as valuable.

Whatever the reason, the fact that Jesus left the work of baptizing new believers to His disciples does underline something important: Baptism is a distinctly *human* ritual. It is performed by forgiven sinners *for* forgiven sinners. It is evangelistic in nature, involving the whole church. Choosing Christ is not merely a private matter, but something that happens in the context of a community. You are immersed in the water, and at that same moment, you become immersed in the life of the church.

Baptism is a pay-it-forward proposition. You have been forgiven, and you have now been charged with bringing others into the community of faith. Of course, it is always Jesus Himself who brings people to the foot of the cross, but you have been given the incredible privilege of inviting—and welcoming—other sinners into the family. Jesus has not just shared the joy of the kingdom with you but also the joy of growing it.

First Generation

*Jesus answered, "Most assuredly, I say to you, unless one is born of water
and the Spirit, he cannot enter the kingdom of God."*

—John 3:5

The Pharisees had a hard time with John the Baptist's preaching. Tax collectors and other societal pariahs had heard John preach and had repented of their sins, gladly stepping into the waters of baptism. "But the Pharisees and lawyers rejected the will of God for themselves," Luke explains, "not having been baptized by him" (Luke 7:30). To suggest that Pharisees were on the same level as mere tax collectors? Ridiculous!

Tax collectors worked for the occupying Roman government, which led most people to consider them as traitors who had betrayed the heritage of Abraham, Isaac, and Jacob. They had forsaken their national identity for the sake of money and were unworthy of the kingdom. The Pharisees, on the other hand, were the guardians of national greatness, ever vigilant to make sure that nobody ever crossed the lines of propriety, thereby compromising Israel's ability to one day throw off the Romans. The contrast between tax collectors and Pharisees could not be more obvious, especially to the Pharisees.

In the quiet hours of the night, however, Jesus pointed out to Nicodemus just how level the playing field truly is. Any perceived difference between human beings is insignificant in the eyes of heaven. Nobody, He explained, will arrive in God's kingdom simply because he or she is a genetic descendant of Abraham. To be admitted into God's family requires repentance and a change of heart.

I have met many Adventists over the years who seem to feel that their multigenerational heritage in the church affords them some special status. "I'm a fifth-generation Adventist!" they remind me with a note of pride. Truth be told, I often wish *I* was a fifth-generation Adventist because of the incredible treasures to be found in this movement.

But according to Jesus, there are only first-generation believers. The baptistry is a powerful reminder that we are all of the same stature in God's sight. We have all fallen short of the glory of God, and we must all pass through the same water, regardless of our lineage. The terms of admission are the same for all of us: we all need Jesus, who is the only One who knew Abraham in person, and has been there through every generation.

"Behold, He Is Praying"

So the Lord said to him, "Arise and go to the street called Straight, and inquire at the house of Judas for one called Saul of Tarsus, for behold, he is praying. And in a vision he has seen a man named Ananias coming in and putting his hand on him, so that he might receive his sight."
—Acts 9:11, 12

Saul of Tarsus had been a Pharisee prior to his conversion (Acts 26:5). The Pharisees were known for their proud and public prayers. "God, I thank You that I am not like other men," prayed the Pharisee of Jesus' famous parable, "extortioners, unjust, adulterers, or even as this tax collector. I fast twice a week; I give tithes of all that I possess" (Luke 18:11). It was the kind of prayer so tainted with pride that heaven finds it repugnant.

After Saul's encounter with Jesus on the road to Damascus, however, his prayers became so radically different that God made a point of mentioning them to Ananias. "I want you to go and visit Saul," He said, "because he's busy praying." The model Pharisee had suddenly learned to pray like the tax collector: humble, repentant, and in desperate need of a Savior.

I have visited many places where church members seem to feel that before someone can be baptized, they must attend church for months (sometimes years!) and prove their dedication to the church. While it is understandable that a congregation would not want to take baptism and church membership lightly, this attitude completely ignores that almost all of the baptisms in the New Testament happened quickly.

God did not prove Saul's readiness for inclusion in the church by pointing out his public deeds in behalf of the church. He did not say to Ananias, "Behold, he sings loudly, takes part on the platform, and serves as a greeter," even though taking part in the life of the church *is* important to our Christian experience. What made heaven sit up and take notice on this occasion was Saul's humble prayer. He was *repentant*.

It is true that baptism requires understanding the essential teachings of the church, and it is important that candidates understand what they are agreeing to in joining. That much is understood. But at the same time, we must be sure that we are not waiting for people to act like the Pharisee in Jesus' parable before we agree to welcome them into the family. What we are looking for are the tax collectors, the men and women who know they need Jesus and are clinging to Him desperately.

The road to Damascus teaches us that such things can happen rather quickly.

December

I accept and believe that the Seventh-day Adventist Church is the remnant church of Bible prophecy and that people of every nation, race, and language are invited and accepted into its fellowship. I desire to be a member of this local congregation of the world church.

Until We See Him

And the armies in heaven, clothed in fine linen, white and clean, followed Him
on white horses. Now out of His mouth goes a sharp sword, that with it
He should strike the nations. And He Himself will rule them with a rod of iron.
He Himself treads the winepress of the fierceness and wrath of Almighty God.
And He has on His robe and on His thigh a name written:
KING OF KINGS AND LORD OF LORDS.
—Revelation 19:14–16

In 1944, Lieutenant Hiroo Onada and a small group of soldiers were sent to seize control of a little island in the Philippines for the Japanese Imperial Army. When Lieutenant Onada arrived, he discovered the island had already been taken over by the Allies, and his mission was hopeless. Not one to shirk responsibility, however, he took his men into the jungle and conducted guerrilla raids on Allied installations, stealing supplies and damaging infrastructure under cover of night.

Then in 1945, his men suddenly discovered some pamphlets on the jungle floor, encouraging them to come out of hiding because the war had ended. "Sir," they urged their commanding officer, "it seems that we can go home now. It's over."

Onada, however, had pledged to never surrender unless *his* commanding officer told him to. "It's obviously a lie!" he insisted and pressed his men to continue fighting. He continued the struggle for nearly three decades. Then a college student camping on the island discovered him and went back to Japan to find his commander, who now worked in a bookshop: "You've still got a man fighting out there!"

Onada was one of the last men on earth to fight World War II, finally surrendering his sword in 1974. He had been wrong about the war ending, but he was absolutely right about one thing: you do not lay down arms until your Commander tells you to.

As the world heads for its final chapter, persuasive voices are urging us to give up the fight for truth. "That struggle ended long ago," they suggest, "and it's time for Christians to lay aside doctrine and compromise for the sake of unity." On the surface, this has great appeal: we are supposed to be united, after all.

But we are to be united in truth, not compromise. The pamphlets on the jungle floor *are* lying to us: the war has not ended. When Jesus returns, He comes with a sword—the Word of God—in His mouth. The need to stand against the tide of falsehood and hold out the truth to a dying world does not let up until the Commander of heaven's host returns. Until then, the world needs a people who will never quit until their Commanding Officer tells them it is over.

With the Lamb

Then I looked, and behold, a Lamb standing on Mount Zion, and with Him
one hundred and forty-four thousand, having His Father's name written on their foreheads.
—Revelation 14:1

The focus of God's people in the last days is Jesus. It is not the church that John first notices standing on Mount Zion; it is the Lamb of God. The others found on Zion are there because of Jesus; they are there *with* Him.

Because it is a revelation of Jesus, the Bible is a two-edged sword that pierces "even to the division of soul and spirit, and of joints and marrow, and is a discerner of the thoughts and intents of the heart" (Hebrews 4:12). It is a fire that burns away the sin in our hearts and a hammer that smashes our arrogance and confusion (Jeremiah 23:29). Read the Bible without seeking Jesus, however, and it becomes just another book, another work of ancient poetry, or another noble saga from another ancient culture.

Because the church is the bride of Christ, it "is the one object upon which God bestows in a special sense His supreme regard. It is the theater of His grace, in which He delights to reveal His power to transform hearts." Because she is married to Christ and reveals Christ to the world, "the church of God has been as a city set on a hill."★ Without Jesus, the church is just another social club—a charitable organization or society for like-minded individuals.

It was not losing Eden that hurt most when we fell into sin; it was losing our close communion with Christ. The point of the Garden was not its beauty or its bounty; it was the way it revealed the Creator and drew us closer to Him.

Many have worshiped institutions or have enshrined intellectual facts pulled from a mere scholastic approach to the Bible as the sum of their religious lives. Do not misunderstand: the church is essential, an indispensable movement launched by Christ Himself, and the Bible is the all-important Word of God that nourishes our souls. But leave out a personal relationship with the Creator God, and you have missed the point. You are trying to stand on the mountain alone; but the only path there is, is "the Lamb who is in the midst of the throne [and He] will shepherd them and lead them to living fountains of waters" (Revelation 7:17).

★ Ellen G. White, *The Acts of the Apostles* (Nampa, ID: Pacific Press®, 2002), 12.

To Stand on Zion

LORD, who may abide in Your tabernacle? Who may dwell in Your holy hill?
He who walks uprightly, and works righteousness, and speaks the truth in his heart.
—Psalm 15:1, 2

The book of Revelation portrays God's last-day remnant people standing on Mount Zion with Christ. They have a number of character traits that the Bible carefully enumerates before going on to the last-day message they deliver to the world: They have the Father's name (or character) written on their foreheads; they are redeemed from the earth (having accepted the gift of salvation); they follow Jesus wherever He goes; they are virgins (not having compromised with false spirituality); and there is no deceit found in their mouths (Revelation 14:1–5).

It bears a close resemblance to the character traits described in Psalm 15. The entire psalm is well worth contemplating; it shows us what God's people *should* look like in the last days. God's people are jealous of the well-being of others, just as God is, and their word is dependable because God's character is etched in their hearts: "He who does not backbite with his tongue, nor does evil to his neighbor, nor does he take up a reproach against his friend; . . . he who swears to his own hurt and does not change; he who does not put out his money at usury, nor does he take a bribe against the innocent" (verses 3, 5).

They are pure of heart, having come to the point where they hate sin and love right, seeking the company of others who love Christ: "In whose eyes a vile person is despised, but he honors those who fear the LORD" (verse 4).

The descriptions boil down to one thing: the Father's name on their foreheads. The character of God is so meaningful to these people that they have become *like* Him. It is not through their own grit-one's-teeth-and-do-better efforts that they become this way but through close contact with Jesus, who changes them into His likeness a little more each day.

"But we all, with unveiled face," Paul explains, "beholding as in a mirror the glory of the Lord, are being transformed into the same image from glory to glory, just as by the Spirit of the Lord" (2 Corinthians 3:18).

With Mount Zion as the finish line and the grace of Christ as your undefeatable strength, who *would not* want to enter this final race?

The Ancient Remnant

*Now Adam knew Eve his wife, and she conceived and bore Cain,
and said, "I have acquired a man from the LORD."*
—Genesis 4:1

The idea of a remnant church is as old as the story of salvation. Some people, reading the key remnant passages of Revelation, mistakenly assume that "the remnant" is a body of believers who appear in the last days of earth's history, but the first story that takes place after Adam and Eve's expulsion from the Garden suggests otherwise.

Our first parents were removed from the Garden to reap the consequences of their choice to rebel, but they were not escorted to the gates without hope. "The Seed of the woman will come," they were promised, "and He will bruise the head of the serpent" (see Genesis 3:15). The Savior would not be an outsider, but someone who came from the "woman"—from that segment of the human race that chose to cling to the promise that He would come.

The birth of Cain underscores how tenaciously Adam and Eve clung to that hope. "I have acquired a man from the LORD," Eve says, as if she is merely thankful for the birth of a child, but the full impact of her statement has been lost in translation. The original Hebrew reads, "I have gotten a man, the Lord."★ The promise of the coming Deliverer was fresh in their minds, and there was every reason to believe that their firstborn child might be the promised One. They were the world's first remnant church, even though they were the world's only people at the time: a people who not only lived in expectancy of the Messiah but whose every hope depended on it.

As it turns out, their firstborn child proved to be of the serpent's seed. He was the world's first murderer, exhibiting the very traits of the beast's followers described in Revelation 13: he practiced a man-made, self-serving religion and used coercion against God's faithful follower, Abel, to the point of death.

There have only been two sides to the human race: those who follow the Lamb wherever He goes (Revelation 14:4), and those who wonder after the beast (Revelation 13:3). When you and I take our place in God's remnant church, we join a group that has existed since the beginning—a *very* long line of believers who cling tenaciously to the hope that the Messiah will come soon.

★ Francis D. Nichol, ed., *The Seventh-day Adventist Bible Commentary* (Hagerstown, MD: Review and Herald®, 2001), 1:238.

Not So Fast!

*Now there was a day when the sons of God came to present themselves before the LORD,
and Satan also came among them. And the LORD said to Satan, "From where do you come?"
So Satan answered the LORD and said, "From going to and fro on the earth,
and from walking back and forth on it."*

—Job 1:6, 7

Perhaps it should not come as a surprise that Satan showed up in the heavenly council. In the Garden, the human race had surrendered their God-given dominion, and now the devil claimed this world as his own. He felt he was the duly appointed representative of this planet.

"Where have you been?" God asked.

"From walking back and forth on the earth," he replied. This was not simply a matter of saying he had been out for a stroll; in Bible times, the foot was a symbol of possession. He was stating, in front of the universe, that the earth now belonged to him. The people created in God's image had chosen his government over God's.

"Not so fast," God answered. "You don't own *everything*. Have you considered my servant Job? There is none like him on the earth, a blameless and upright man, one who fears God and shuns evil" (Job 1:8, paraphrased).

There were still people whose allegiance belonged to God. It might have been a small number—a remnant—but they were declaring with their lives that this planet, in spite of our sinful rebellion, was still our Father's world.

Although the precise time when the book of Job was written eludes us, it appears to date to the times of the patriarchs, and ancient tradition states that it was the first book of the Bible to have been written. It is the story of an early remnant—a man whose loyalty to God was firm, even in the face of the devil's determined attempts to turn him. It gives us a glimpse into at least one crucial role of God's remnant people: We give God the freedom to point to this world, in the face of the devil's continued insistence that it is his, and say, "No, this world still belongs to Me. These people are under the blood of My Son, who is now counted among their number as a human being, and these people, of their own free will, want Me to restore everything to the way it was before you destroyed it."

The devil may throw his worst at God's remnant people (Revelation 12:17), as he did with Job, but it will fail to unseat God's last-day witness on this planet. Jesus *will* come and take back what is rightfully His.

Noah's Results

On the very same day Noah and Noah's sons, Shem, Ham, and Japheth,
and Noah's wife and the three wives of his sons with them, entered the ark.
—Genesis 7:13

It is impossible to tell how many people might have been living on planet Earth the day the floodwaters came. Some Bible students have attempted to extrapolate from the data available in Genesis and have guessed that it might have been as many as a *billion* people.

How many responded to Noah's preaching? He publicly shared his final warning message for many years, and it mostly fell on deaf ears. The vast majority of the human race had passed the point of no return and rejected the final offer of mercy. After several decades, the only ones to enter the ark were the members of Noah's immediate family. Noah, in a manner of speaking, only managed to baptize his own children.

If he had been a modern-day evangelist, we might be tempted to pull him off the road for his lack of results: "Look at all that expense! We're just not getting any results! Time to pull the plug."

The story of Noah reminds us of something important: The designation "remnant" is not dependent on numbers. Small results do not negate the mission of the church; if nobody ever responded, we would still be responsible for proclaiming the three angels' messages. Fortunately, that is not the case; people are presently responding in record numbers. But if they were *not* responding, we would still be responsible for fulfilling our mandate of preaching.

Nowhere does the Bible ever suggest that our mission ceases to be important if our numbers are low: Noah would have been sinning had he stopped preaching God's message. We are not simply called to *do* something for God; we are called to *be* something: a voice in the last days that pleads with a lost race to come out of Babylon.

In the grand wrap-up of history, it will never be said that people did not have the opportunity to know better. It can never be claimed that someone did not have a chance; the door of mercy was held open as long as possible, as God is not willing that *any* should perish (see 2 Peter 3:9). When Jesus comes to claim that which rightfully belongs to Him, the judgment will record that there was never a time when there was not a voice crying in the wilderness, "Prepare the way of the LORD" (Matthew 3:3).

Wherever He Goes

These are the ones who were not defiled with women, for they are virgins.
These are the ones who follow the Lamb wherever He goes. These were redeemed
from among men, being firstfruits to God and to the Lamb.
—Revelation 14:4

Perhaps the chief characteristic of God's last-day remnant people is the fact that they "follow the Lamb wherever He goes." So closely are their hearts bound up with Christ that His will becomes their will. They have forsaken the human rebellion and have decided that "Thy will be done" is a much wiser course of action than "my will be done."

They walk in the footsteps of their father Abraham, who walked away from a life of ease and comfort, in one of the most opulent cities of the ancient world, to live the humble life of a nomad, preferring to head "for the city which has foundations, whose builder and maker is God" (Hebrews 11:10).

Abraham's hometown, Ur of the Chaldees, was the envy of the ancient Mesopotamian world. When Sir Leonard Woolley began his excavations of Ur in 1922, he was amazed by what he found: two-story homes with indoor bathrooms and elaborate water collection systems. The citizens of Ur were incredibly wealthy, thanks in large part to their easy access to the trade routes of the Persian Gulf. They wanted for nothing.

When Abram heard the call of God, however, he knew that nothing in Ur could compare with the riches that were to be found in Christ. If he were to stay, the influences of the city would dull his witness. He had to be separate—be called out. He became a "Hebrew," a name that signified someone who was called out from the other side of the river.

God wanted to establish him in the crossroads of the ancient world, in a place where the human race could see and hear the story of Christ in the rites and rituals of the temple, even before Jesus took on human form. The children of Abram were to be separate but not exclusive. The world was to be invited to join them in following the Lamb.

The same is true of the final generation of Abraham's descendants. We are in the world but not of it; "a peculiar people" (1 Peter 2:9, KJV) separate from the world but not elite or exclusive. Our role, like Abraham's, is to forsake the love of this world, follow the Lamb wherever He leads us, and hold open the door of invitation to every nation, kindred, tongue, and people.

Unlikely People

Nebuchadnezzar the king, to all peoples, nations, and languages that dwell in all the earth:
Peace be multiplied to you. I thought it good to declare the signs and wonders that the
Most High God has worked for me. How great are His signs, and how mighty His wonders!
His kingdom is an everlasting kingdom, and His dominion is from generation to generation.

—Daniel 4:1–3

The remnant church is made up of the most unlikely people. We would expect it to be a body of near-sinless saints, with sins so negligible that, *of course*, they belong in that group that God defines as His own. But a careful reading of the Bible suggests otherwise: the remnant of God is a body of forgiven sinners, "redeemed from among men" (Revelation 14:4).

Even the king of Babylon—the very city used by Inspiration to represent everything that stands contrary to the kingdom of Christ—was a convert. For many long years, God had labored with Israel to be a light to the Gentiles, to put the beautiful character of Christ on display. But as time went by, God's own people preferred the wine of Babylon, even coming to the point where they had begun to offer their own children to a fiery-hot idol named Molech (Jeremiah 32:35).

They did not want what God was offering them, so God sent them back home—in chains. It is no small coincidence that they were taken captive to Chaldea, the very place where Abraham had left in pursuit of Jesus. And while they were there, God showed them what had always been possible: the king of Babylon himself became a servant of the Most High God.

In fact, before the Bible finishes with his story, Nebuchadnezzar is found singing the song of Moses and the Lamb. "For His dominion is an everlasting dominion, and His kingdom is from generation to generation. . . . I, Nebuchadnezzar, praise and extol and honor the King of heaven, all of whose works are truth, and His ways justice" (Daniel 4:34, 37).

Compare that with Revelation 15: "Great and marvelous are Your works, Lord God Almighty! Just and true are Your ways, O King of the saints! Who shall not fear You, O Lord, and glorify Your name? For You alone are holy. For all nations shall come and worship before You, for Your judgments have been manifested" (verses 3, 4).

Imagine that: the king of Babylon among God's chosen people, making the same declaration as the angels in judgment (Daniel 7:14). Now imagine this: *you* among God's chosen people, singing the song of Moses and the Lamb.

Impossible? Not according to the king of Babylon.

Two Sets of Names

For I do not desire, brethren, that you should be ignorant of this mystery, lest you should be
wise in your own opinion, that blindness in part has happened to Israel until the fullness of the
Gentiles has come in. And so all Israel will be saved, as it is written: "The Deliverer will come
out of Zion, and He will turn away ungodliness from Jacob."
—Romans 11:25, 26

A careful reading of the Bible and the Spirit of Prophecy presents an intriguing possibility. God's last-day people are depicted as standing on Mount Zion, the place where the entire identity of God's people has long been focused. It was the place where Israel of old went to visit the temple, the holy hill of the Almighty.

The last-day remnant is a continuation of the woman presented in Revelation 12, who symbolizes God's people waiting for the Messiah to come. The church of the New Testament is a continuation of the church of the Old. We, the Gentiles, have been "grafted into" God's people, a wild olive tree that has been attached to the ancient root (Romans 11:24). We are now counted among the seed of Abraham because of our faith in Christ (Galatians 3:29).

But pay attention to Paul's argument in Romans 11: we have been grafted into Israel. Of course, it was always God's intention to bring all nations into His covenant family through Israel's witness (Isaiah 49:6; 60:3); but as Israel lost sight of its mission, and Daniel 9 finally came to pass in A.D. 34, God went directly to the Gentile nations with His New Testament church. It was a fulfillment of very old promises.

Paul suggests that Israel has been blinded until the "fullness of the Gentiles has come in." Ellen White, intriguingly, points to a final movement that will take place among the Jews before Christ returns. Many will join *us*: "There are among them many who will come to the light, and who will proclaim the immutability of the law of God with wonderful power." She writes, "These converts will aid in preparing the way of the Lord."★

There are many reasons to be faithful in keeping God's commandments, but among them is the possibility that we are to be a light to Israel the way Israel was supposed to be a light to us. We cannot be like other churches; we *must* be distinct enough that the genetic descendants of Abraham might recognize in us the fulfillment of God's promises to our mutual father.

There are two sets of names on the Holy City, after all: the twelve apostles, and the twelve sons of Israel.

★ Ellen G. White, *Evangelism* (Hagerstown, MD: Review and Herald®, 2003), 578.

DECEMBER 10

With Prophets of Old

Now it shall come to pass in the latter days that the mountain of the LORD's house shall be established on the top of the mountains, and shall be exalted above the hills; and all nations shall flow to it. Many people shall come and say, "Come, let us go up to the mountain of the LORD, to the house of the God of Jacob; He will teach us of His ways, and we shall walk in His paths." For out of Zion shall go forth the law, and the word of the LORD from Jerusalem.
—Isaiah 2:2, 3

Sometimes, because of our natural focus on last-day prophecies, it can be easy to lose sight of the fact that the divine plan revealed in Revelation is the culmination of many long centuries of effort. The last-day remnant does not stand alone, apart from history, but represents the closing chapter of a continuous work that has been in existence since the very first prophecy was given outside the gates of Eden.

The remnant church has a distinct message, which includes a call to "worship Him who made," and this message is put on full display for the world to observe by a people who "keep the commandments of God and the faith of Jesus" (Revelation 14:12). That message goes to "every nation, tribe, tongue, and people" (verse 6).

This is not an afterthought or a game plan that was devised because the developments of the Dark Ages and the medieval church caught God by surprise. The remnant church is not something that suddenly emerges out of necessity because the spiritual confusion of the last days demands it. The remnant church has always been there, taking various forms throughout the centuries, but it has always existed and has always had the same objective: to prepare the world for the inevitable moment when all "the kingdoms of this world have become the kingdoms of our Lord and of His Christ, and He shall reign forever and ever!" (Revelation 11:15).

Nearly twenty-eight hundred years before you were born, and more than eight hundred years before John was on Patmos, Isaiah described the work of the remnant church. "In the last days," he predicts, "there will be a call for all nations to come to the mountain of the Lord, and out of Zion will go forth the law." Compare it to the message of those who stand on Zion with Jesus in the last days, whose message goes with loud urgency to "every nation, tribe, tongue, and people."

There has always been a remnant church, and as you take your place among God's people in the last days, you are joining your voice to prophets of old, joining a loud chorus that has declared the righteous character of God's kingdom and Christ's right to reign since the very beginning of time.

"Of One Blood"

"And He has made from one blood every nation of men to dwell on all the face of the earth, and has determined their preappointed times and the boundaries of their dwellings, so that they should seek the Lord, in the hope that they might grope for Him and find Him, though He is not far from each one of us."
—Acts 17:26, 27

One of the marvels of the Seventh-day Adventist movement is its international, cross-cultural character. It not only preaches the key biblical message one would expect to find from a last-day remnant movement, but it also represents the response of "every nation, tribe, tongue, and people" to God's final call to this planet (Revelation 14:6). There is scarcely any place left on the planet where we cannot find Seventh-day Adventists faithfully carrying out the special commission God has laid on this movement.

Witness the quinquennial gathering known as the General Conference Session. I know that the issues discussed on the floor completely occupy the attention of many people, and some of them are important issues with important debates. But do not let the business of the church rob you of the prophetic spectacle that plays out at the session. It begins as people from every nation on the planet pour into the airport and continues as people from radically different backgrounds interact with each other, surmounting language and cultural barriers to find that they have in common a profound love for Christ and a desire to see Him return.

It is a humbling thing. It can be tempting to think of Jesus in terms of your own culture, allowing yourself to believe that He is part of your particular tribe. But Jesus is not Western or Eastern; He is not European, African, Asian, or American. He is the Son of man, the Head of the entire human race. He is not beholden to our cultural preferences; instead, He calls us to immerse ourselves in the culture of *His* kingdom, where we learn to see the world the way that He does.

Jesus once prayed that all of His disciples would be one (John 17:21). In searching for His last-day body of believers, one would expect to find a striking unity of purpose, passion, and love—all without sacrificing individuality. The members are from separate nations, with the freedom to be different, but made of one blood—together making up a much fuller picture of Jesus than any one group could muster alone.

The remnant church offers the world the most comprehensive picture of Jesus the planet has ever seen, right before He comes in person to reveal Himself completely.

Us and Them

And I heard another voice from heaven saying, "Come out of her,
my people, lest you share in her sins, and lest you receive of her plagues."
—Revelation 18:4

Human beings are very talented at dividing the world into "us" and "them." More than once in recent history, we have seen entire groups demonized to the point where they are no longer considered human. Before World War II, Nazi propaganda wormed its way into the textbooks of a nation, making Jews (and others) seem less than human; this made it plausible for average people to believe that something needed to be done about "those people." The same thing happened in Rwanda: before the slaughter of Tutsis began, the media depictions of tribe members made it easier for Hutus to demote them to subhuman status.

Of course, Seventh-day Adventists are not about to organize genocide campaigns, but there is something we can learn from these horrible episodes in history. It is easy for people to cloister in the safety of the church, never going out and interacting with—and befriending—people who do not share our faith perspective. We sometimes dehumanize them, speaking of them as if we are God's children and they are not.

We know what prophecy says about the final conflict on this planet, and we rightly recoil in horror when we see the monstrosity emerging from the coalition found in Revelation 13: Protestant America and the Church of Rome join forces to bring about the world's final great crisis, and it is awful. Our natural reaction? Stay behind the safety of church walls—keep your friends Adventist—and never venture out into foreign territory.

It is a mistake. Because we let go of our friendships with others, we stop seeing them as God's children and as human beings no more and no less sinful than ourselves, and we neglect the one task God gave His church: winning the world. We easily utter "amen" to a mission report delivered in church, but we forget that we have also *personally* pledged to invite people of every nation, race, and language into our fellowship.

To be the remnant church is to light the *world* with the final call, to invite God's people to come out. To be the remnant of prophecy is not to hide in our carefully crafted safe spaces, but to know and love others to the point where we "esteem others better" than ourselves and "look out . . . for the interests of others" (Philippians 2:3, 4).

When Nineveh Repents

Then word came to the king of Nineveh; and he arose from his throne
and laid aside his robe, covered himself with sackcloth and sat in ashes.
—Jonah 3:6

A reluctant prophet is an understandable phenomenon. The task assigned is insurmountably huge, and the audience is often unwilling to listen. Noah, for example, preached for years and had little to show for it in the way of conversions. Few of us relish the idea of preaching without tangible fruit for decades.

The remnant church is a prophetic movement with a distinctive assignment. We may not individually possess the prophetic gift, but we do have a prophetic role to fill as a collective body. The world must hear the three angels' messages and be given an opportunity to make things right with God. Many of us shrink from the magnitude of the task.

Jonah has a unique role among Old Testament prophets: he is the only one sent specifically outside of the nation to preach to a Gentile nation. The Ninevites, every Israelite knew, were vile. They were violent heathens who worshiped war and committed unspeakable atrocities on their captives. They were evil, that "great" and "wicked" city (see Jonah 1:2).

Jonah was much happier at home, like most of us. Over time, we all manage to build comfortable nests for ourselves, creating an environment in which we do not have to face our own tendencies toward evil or reckon with our shortcomings. It becomes easier and easier to convince ourselves that we are God's children and the "outsiders" are the real problem in this world.

So what does God do? He kicks us out of our nests and sends us out to meet every nation, kindred, tongue, and people. If we are faithful, we will make a remarkable discovery: many are desperate for a chance to come home and are more responsive to the Spirit than we have been.

The Ninevites repented dramatically. And then Jonah was forced to deal with the darkness in his own heart. He was the one who still needed to repent by the end of the story. It turns out that God's prophet needed more work than the king of Nineveh.

There is a reason God sends you into the world: it is to share the gospel. But it is also an opportunity, as you deal with the real world and your own emotions, to see yourself as you truly are; and it is an invaluable opportunity to allow God to draw you even closer.

While It Is Day

"Cry aloud, spare not; lift up your voice like a trumpet;
tell My people their transgression, and the house of Jacob their sins."
—Isaiah 58:1

The work of the remnant church is portrayed in the book of Revelation as a series of three angels who cry with a loud voice (Revelation 14:6, 9), much as prophets of old were asked to "cry aloud" when pointing out the errors of God's wayward people. The work is urgent: the final warning *must* be given to the planet before Jesus comes.

Fallen angels are none too happy to have their lies exposed before the world, so they work overtime to keep people wondering after the beast (see Revelation 13:3, KJV), too drunk on Babylonian wine to understand the dangerous trap of error that has been laid for them. If the truth gets out, their rebellion will be over.

The final battleground for our hearts and minds will clearly involve the issue of church and state: the beast's religious power is largely derived from its ability to bring the coercion of the state into play. Seventh-day Adventists should be watching the news from a different angle than the rest of the world, paying careful attention to developments that threaten to compromise our ability to be the loud voice that God intends. For God's people, the most important news coming out of governments has little to do with the popular issues of the day: we have been warned that the unhappy archenemy of Christ will do all in his power to silence our voices and arrest the spread of God's truth.

When we contemplate the legislation emerging from the halls of power, we must look past social and economic implications, no matter how seemingly important, and consider the matter of religious liberty. We must also have faith that God has people in unexpected places to keep our loud voices loud. "The enemy moves upon his servants to propose measures that would greatly impede the work of God," Ellen White explains, "but statesmen who fear the Lord are influenced by holy angels to oppose such propositions with unanswerable arguments. Thus a few men will hold in check a powerful current of evil. The opposition of the enemies of truth will be restrained that the third angel's message may do its work."★

May God grant us the spiritual eyesight to see the world's issues from heaven's perspective and the courage to work while it is still day.

★ Ellen G. White, *The Great Controversy* (Nampa, ID: Pacific Press®, 2002), 610.

Healthy Fear

The fear of the LORD is the beginning of wisdom;
a good understanding have all those who do His commandments.
His praise endures forever.

—Psalm 111:10

The opening line of the three angels' messages is a call for the world to "fear God and worship Him." It is not popular in the twenty-first century to suggest that human beings should "fear God." We are happy to ask people to *love* God, but *fear* Him? We are hesitant to suggest it.

Yet the Bible brings up the topic of fearing God repeatedly, and it holds it out as a good thing. To fear God is to find life: "The fear of the LORD is a fountain of life, to turn one away from the snares of death" (Proverbs 14:27). To *not* fear God is to find certain trouble: "God will hear, and afflict them . . . because they do not change, therefore they do not fear God" (Psalm 55:19).

Fearing God is a good thing. But does it mean we ought to be *afraid* of God? We have been quick to dismiss such notions in our generation. But Ellen White makes it clear that God *does* intend to get our attention from time to time with a little healthy fear: "A proper fear of God, in believing his threatenings, works the peaceable fruits of righteousness, by causing the trembling soul to flee to Jesus. Many ought to have this spirit to-day, and turn to the Lord with humble contrition, for the Lord has not given so many terrible threatenings, pronounced so severe judgments in his word, simply to have them recorded, but he means what he says."* Paul, likewise, speaks of "the terror of the Lord" (2 Corinthians 5:11).

Does God intend for us to live in abject terror? No, not after we come to Christ. "Perfect love casts out fear," John tells us (1 John 4:18).

Martin Luther once made a useful distinction between raw terror and the fear of the Lord. He spoke of *servile* fear, a prisoner awaiting torture and *filial* fear, a child's respect for his father. (*Filial* is from the Latin for sons and daughters.) It is not a fear of being destroyed, but a fear of not bringing honor to God's name, of having your life cast a shadow across His reputation.

To fear God is to return to your home as His child and defend His name with your life.

---

* Ellen G. White, "Danger in Rejecting Light," *Advent Review and Sabbath Herald*, October 21, 1890, 2 (642).

Self-Awarded Crowns

So on a set day Herod, arrayed in royal apparel, sat on his throne
and gave an oration to them. And the people kept shouting, "The voice of a god
and not of a man!" Then immediately an angel of the Lord struck him,
because he did not give glory to God. And he was eaten by worms and died.
—Acts 12:21–23

Read the story of Herod's demise carefully, and you will notice something interesting: his case resembles that of Lucifer, to the point where I wonder if Herod is not a type of the devil. Lucifer is destroyed from the inside out by fire (verse 18); Herod was destroyed from the inside out by worms. Both worms and fire are mentioned by Jesus as elements in the destruction of the wicked: "Their worm does not die, and the fire is not quenched" (Mark 9:44).

Perhaps Herod's crime gives us a useful way to think about Lucifer's rebellion. Herod was destroyed because "he did not give glory to God." The living creatures in heaven give glory to God by taking off their crowns, falling before the throne, and acknowledging God's right to rule the universe because He is the Creator.

Lucifer, on the other hand, manufactured his own crown and declared himself independent from God and of equal worth. To this day, he demands worship, and he is pushing the human race toward the grand climax found in Revelation 13, where the world will be coerced to bow before the beast. He will be destroyed for it.

The group of faithful believers who stand on Mount Zion with the Lamb, however, rush out to the world with an urgent call to "fear God and give glory to Him" (Revelation 14:7). It is a call to return to the throne of God and, with the living creatures, take off our self-awarded crowns and acknowledge that there is but one God. It is a call to reject man-made religion and circle around the only real throne in the universe.

To be part of God's remnant, however, is to understand that the real King is the One who never dressed Himself up but condescended to our level to win our love as a Lamb.

The Open Door

"And to the angel of the church in Philadelphia write, 'These things says He who is holy,
He who is true, "He who has the key of David, He who opens and no one shuts, and shuts and
no one opens": "I know your works. See, I have set before you an open door, and no one can
shut it; for you have a little strength, have kept My word, and have not denied My name." ' "
—Revelation 3:7, 8

After suffering the disappointment of 1844, the early Adventists continued to believe that Christ would return very soon. After Jesus had failed to return at the expected time, they became the recipients of ruthless ridicule, and some understood the mockery as evidence that the Spirit of God had been withdrawn from the earth and that the human race had reached the bottom rungs of depravity. The door of mercy in heaven, they reasoned, must have been closed "and that the work of Christ as man's intercessor before God had ceased."*

It was, in other words, too late for the unsaved to be made right with God. Probation had closed. When they comprehended, however, that the twenty-three hundred–day prophecy was pointing to something other than the Second Coming, it changed their understanding: Christ's ministry focus had shifted from the Holy Place to the Most Holy Place in heaven's sanctuary. The door of mercy was not closed, the judgment had begun, and the earth had moved into what Daniel calls "the time of the end" (Daniel 8:17).

It is easy to understand the tendency to write off those who mock our beliefs as hopelessly lost. But it is an attitude that throws the brakes on evangelistic work. Many of the early believers simply stopped preaching. Why continue to preach if the door has been closed?

Perhaps that is the reason that our assignment as the remnant church includes announcing when the judgment hour *begins* but not when it *ends*. It is not up to us to worry about when the door will shut; it will be abundantly obvious when the plagues hit. Our task is to be faithful until Jesus returns. "God has not revealed to us the time when this message will close, or when probation will have an end. . . . Let us not seek to know that which has been kept secret in the councils of the Almighty. It is our duty to watch and work and wait, to labor every moment for the souls of men that are ready to perish."†

It is over when the One who holds the key of David says it is over. May we ever be found at our post of duty, right up to that moment when Jesus says it is finished.

* Ellen G. White, *The Great Controversy* (Nampa, ID: Pacific Press®, 2002), 429.
† Ellen G. White, *Selected Messages*, bk. 1 (Hagerstown, MD: Review and Herald®, 2007), 191.

The Power of "We"

And I prayed to the LORD my God, and made confession, and said, "O Lord, great and awesome God, who keeps His covenant and mercy with those who love Him, and with those who keep His commandments, we have sinned and committed iniquity, we have done wickedly and rebelled, even by departing from Your precepts and Your judgments."
—Daniel 9:4, 5

Daniel's prayer has a surprise in it for careful readers: he includes himself among the sinners whose rebellion led to the sack of Jerusalem. Daniel was in his late teens when he was taken captive by Nebuchadnezzar, and the sterling character on display in the Bible makes it highly doubtful that he was an actual participant in the abominations that caused the desolation of the temple. It was not Daniel who broke the Sabbath or placed infants in the white-hot arms of Molech, yet he uses the word *we*.

It is a prayer of corporate responsibility and repentance, and it provides us with an important template for our task as the remnant church. Among the critical elements of the remnant's message, we find a duty to warn the world that "Babylon is fallen" (Revelation 14:8). God's people, of course, have been called *out* of Babylon (Revelation 18:4), so it is easy for us to fall into an "us and them" mentality: *we* are the chosen people of God, and *they* are Babylon. This can be a mistake in the public proclamation of our message. We are sent out to proclaim God's name (or character), not our own. The One to whom we direct all attention is the Lamb of God, not ourselves. If an audience senses that we believe ourselves to be superior, many will simply choose to write us off as yet another arrogant religious sect—a mistake we cannot afford to make.

Perhaps Daniel's example is a good way to broach the sins of Babylon with the public. Ultimately, we are all part of the problem: we have all sinned and come short of the glory of God. We may not have personally committed the sins of a fallen church, particularly the more gruesome ones that took place during the Dark Ages, but with Daniel, we should recognize that we are still part of the problem.

"This is our Christian history, and this is what *we* have done," we can tell people, "and now it's time for us to repent of it, ask God's forgiveness, and take our place in His efforts to save the world." There is no "us and them," just one sinner holding out a hand to others and showing them the way out.

"Everybody Worships"

"You alone are the LORD; You have made heaven, the heaven of heavens,
with all their host, the earth and everything on it, the seas and all that is in them,
and You preserve them all. The host of heaven worships You."
—Nehemiah 9:6

David Foster Wallace, the award-winning writer, once pointed out that everybody worships *something*. "There is actually no such thing as atheism," he declares in his essay *This Is Water*. "Everybody worships. The only choice we get is what to worship. And the compelling reason for maybe choosing some sort of god or spiritual-type thing to worship—be it JC or Allah, be it YHWH or the Wiccan Mother Goddess, or the Four Noble Truths, or some inviolable set of ethical principles—is that pretty much anything else you worship will eat you alive."*

He is, of course, utterly (and dangerously) wrong about just choosing any old religious figure to worship, but he is correct about our human compulsion to worship *something*. It is hardwired into us. We cannot help ourselves.

He is also *almost* correct when he states that most of the things people choose to worship will "eat you alive." The truth is, *everything* apart from God will eat you alive, including nearly his entire list of so-called appropriate choices. Idolatry is a lethal sin, riveting your focus on things that will ultimately destroy you if you worship them. If you worship wealth or material possessions, for example, you will fall into a cycle where you will never have enough, and your god will keep demanding more. Worship youth and beauty, as much of our world seems intent on doing, and the ravages of age will eventually make you realize that your god has callously tossed you aside.

The task of the remnant church is to call the world to worship the Creator, to remind the world that there is only *one* choice that makes sense: "Worship Him who made heaven and earth, the sea and springs of water" (Revelation 14:7). The remnant church holds out the Sabbath as important, not simply because it is a cosmic rule that must be followed, but because the world is worshiping all the wrong things, and people are destroying themselves because of it. The Sabbath is an opportunity to connect deeply with our Maker and to satisfy the longing in our souls that only God can fill. Our message is a compassionate declaration to the planet that the human race has been deceived into placing its affections in all the wrong places, and it is dying because of it.

---

* David Foster Wallace, *This Is Water: Some Thoughts, Delivered on a Significant Occasion, About Living a Compassionate Life* (New York: Little, Brown and Company, 2009), 100–102.

An Ancient Photograph

That was the true Light which gives light to every man coming into the world.
—John 1:9

On January 5, 1939, Amelia Earhart was officially pronounced dead. Her plane had gone missing over the Pacific Ocean in 1937, and both she and her navigator, Fred Noonan, were never heard from again. For nearly a century, what happened to her has remained a mystery.

In 2017, an old photo suddenly surfaced that appeared to show both Earhart and Noonan sitting on a dock, suggesting that they had survived the crash. The photograph seemed to confirm the testimony of locals who had been saying, for decades, that they saw the plane go down and also witnessed the two fliers being taken captive by the Japanese. However, this photo turned out to be another attempt to find Amelia that didn't pan out.

In a similar manner, throughout the twentieth century, there were many attempts to rediscover the "real Jesus." Many people have long had this sense that somehow, over the years, the original, authentic Jesus has been lost, buried under centuries of superstition and myth making. The sins of the official Christian church throughout the Dark Ages add weight to their misgivings; of course, as Seventh-day Adventists, we know that they are right: Christianity *did* go off the rails after the merger between the church and Constantine. Many false ideas were added to the body of Christian belief, which obscured the truth about who Jesus is.

But what if an old picture was to suddenly reemerge in these last days, an accurate picture of Jesus? What if, instead of digging relentlessly through the past in search of the "real Jesus," people could find Him living in their midst? What if there was a remnant body of people whose lives and teachings clung tenaciously to the original model set out in the New Testament? What if there were loud voices in this world, a church openly declaring that Babylon has fallen and calling the human race to come back and "worship Him who made heaven and earth, the sea and springs of water" (Revelation 14:7)?

Regardless of what actually happened to Amelia Earhart, one thing is certain: she *is* dead and gone. By contrast, however, the tomb of Jesus is empty, He is quite alive and eager for the world to know it, and He asks *us* to turn on the lights and reveal Him.

The End of War

And the dragon was enraged with the woman, and he went to make war with the rest of her offspring, who keep the commandments of God and have the testimony of Jesus Christ.
—Revelation 12:17

In the deeply disturbing phenomenon of war, we find nearly all of the ills that have befallen the human race wrapped up into one horrifying spectacle: murder, famine, pestilence, greed, raw hatred—you name it. It is one of the plainest exhibits of Satan's true character and his capacity for destruction. The book of Revelation discloses that all the woes in our universe began with the war he instigated in heaven, which is a war that he subsequently brought to this world.

After defrauding our first parents, he planted his flag on earth. To his deep chagrin, however, members of the deceived human race continued to pledge allegiance to their Creator, leaning on His promise that the Seed of the woman would come to crush the head of the serpent. Their hopes were realized when Christ was born as one of them, carried their sins to the cross, and rose victorious over death.

When Jesus returned to heaven, the Bible explains that the devil, blind with rage after losing the showdown with the Son of God, turned his wrath against us. He derailed the church by marrying it to the state throughout the Dark Ages, using it to twist the world's perception of God. Then he had God's faithful hunted like animals and put to death for "crimes" such as possessing a copy of the Scriptures.

Now, in the last days, God still has a people who "keep the commandments of God and have the testimony of Jesus," and the devil turns his wrath on them. Many people, raised in an environment where prosperity preachers promise the easy life after coming to Christ, are surprised to discover that life continues to be full of trials for those who are relentless in their pursuit of truth and their allegiance to Christ.

The war, they find, can be just as devastating as it was for our ancestors in the faith. Taking your place among God's remnant people will always mean that the devil hates you for exposing his lies, and he turns his wrath against you.

Do not let hard times get you down; the other thing that will always be the same is the devil's fate. He may have started the war, but Prince Immanuel will finish it because He finds war even more abhorrent than we do.

Flooding the Market

But the woman was given two wings of a great eagle, that she might fly
into the wilderness to her place, where she is nourished for a time and times
and half a time, from the presence of the serpent.

—Revelation 12:14

The amount of time God's people are forced into hiding is identical to the amount of time the beast power of Revelation 13 bears sway over the former western Roman Empire: 1,260 days, 42 months, or a "time, times and half a time." We recognize those years as the time span between A.D. 538 (when the authority promised to the bishop of Rome became a reality) and 1798 (when a Napoleonic general unseated the pope).

We should expect the woman to emerge from the wilderness after that time; and sure enough, early in the nineteenth century, William Miller began preaching the Second Coming, and the Adventist movement showed up shortly after that. It all fits too neatly to be a coincidence.

It is also probably not a coincidence that there was an explosion of "isms" in the nineteenth century. The forces of darkness were likely none too happy about the emergence of the last-day remnant movement, and there was a sudden flood of new religious ideas to accompany the birth of the Seventh-day Adventist Church.

When you study the content of these new religious ideas, an interesting pattern emerges. Darwinism offered people a theory that does not acknowledge the Creator. Mormonism offered a new understanding of the sanctuary with their temples and "prophet." Russellism (Jehovah's Witnesses) compromised the divinity of Christ. Spiritualism gave the world an alternative to the Bible's explanation of death. Marxism promised a man-made return to paradise. Christian Science offered a different health message.

The list of nineteenth-century "isms" is long, and when you compile a list of their major features, it begins to look a lot like the fundamental beliefs of the Seventh-day Adventist Church. Coincidence? Probably not. The Bible promised that God's remnant church would light up the world, "having great authority" (Revelation 18:1).

God intends for His final message to the world to be powerful. The remnant church has been granted "great authority." Satan certainly understands the incredible potential of this last-day movement and seems to have flooded the marketplace of ideas in a desperate attempt to silence its voice.

If only *we* comprehended how much potential God has invested in this final push—if the devil panics at the thought of what might happen—our courage should be unstoppable.

Cherish Your Liberty

But the earth helped the woman, and the earth opened its mouth
and swallowed up the flood which the dragon had spewed out of his mouth.
—Revelation 12:16

The Protestant Reformation sparked a wave of optimism across much of Europe. When Henry VIII broke away from Rome to establish the Church of England, many Bible-believing Christians hoped they would also find religious liberty. By the seventeenth century, however, it was obvious that the new church-state arrangement was nearly as bad as the previous one. People were technically free to *believe* what they wanted in seventeenth-century England; but when it came to religious practice, everyone was expected to conform to the Book of Common Prayer.

Some Dissenters, including the famous political philosopher John Locke, fled to the Netherlands in pursuit of religious liberty. Once there, they came in contact with Jewish scholars who had fled the Inquisition, and suddenly the Dissenters had access to some very old books—and learned to study in Hebrew. In the Old Testament, they discovered God's displeasure over Israel's demand for a king and recognized in God's warnings to Samuel that a king would seriously impede His people's freedom. *We've rid ourselves of the bishop of Rome,* they began to reason, *what if we also rid ourselves of human kings?*

The persecuted started to make their way to the Americas, in answer to the Bible's prediction that the earth would open up to help the woman. Once there, the writings of the Dissenters helped form the ideas found in the Declaration of Independence and, more important, the American Constitution, which rejects the idea of human monarchies and guarantees a number of crucial liberties—not the least of which is *religious* liberty.

In a very real sense, then, America *is* a Christian nation: its roots can be traced directly to the Protestant Reformation, which is why Ellen White refers to the American Constitution as a "Protestant" document.★ As a church, we should ever be vigilant to guard the liberties outlined by the American founders, regardless of the nation we call home, because liberty is the platform on which this movement was born. When the right to dissent, worship, and speak as we please eventually becomes compromised, we will have to do our work under much more trying circumstances.

Cherish your liberty, and resist the tide of evil that seeks to silence God's final call to the planet.

★ See Ellen G. White, *Testimonies for the Church* (Nampa, ID: Pacific Press®, 2002), 5:451.

A Voice in the Wilderness

The voice of one crying in the wilderness: "Prepare the way of the LORD;
make straight in the desert a highway for our God."
—Isaiah 40:3

Early Persian road builders used a fascinating technique to create straight roads. Two men would stand at a distance from each other and call to each other. A third man would find the middle point between them by listening to their voices, responding, and positioning himself accordingly. Then a fourth man would walk the line, listening to all three callers and marking trees that needed to be removed. By the time they were done cutting down the marked trees, they were left with an astonishingly straight line.

Some historians believe that perhaps Isaiah was referring to this ancient surveying technique when he illustrated the future work of John the Baptist: a voice crying and a straight road being prepared. His task was to announce to the world that the time for the Messiah's arrival had come. Jesus spoke of John as Elijah's return, which was an event predicted by Malachi: "If you are willing to receive it, he is Elijah who is to come" (Matthew 11:14).

In the Christmas season, people fondly remember John's work of preparing the way for Christ to arrive. His work was critical: the time for the Messiah had come, and God wanted the world to know it. In the Bible record, John's prophetic ministry essentially culminates when Jesus begins His ministry with a Voice from heaven announcing, "This is My beloved Son, in whom I am well pleased" (Matthew 3:17).

John's cry in the wilderness, however, was not the final or ultimate return of Elijah. It is no small coincidence that Elijah was forced into hiding from Jezebel for 1,260 days—the precise amount of time that a spiritual Jezebel forced the woman into the wilderness (Revelation 2:20). After the time had expired, Elijah reappeared and confronted falsehood on Mount Carmel. Elijah returned in John's ministry, but he also returns in ours.

"Elijah is coming first and will restore all things," Jesus explained, pointing forward to another fulfillment (Matthew 17:11). At the end of the Dark Ages, the woman suddenly emerged from the wilderness to prepare the way for Christ to come again. The task of the remnant is simple: walking in the footsteps of Elijah and John, our voices must help people to locate the straight path that leads directly into the kingdom of Christ.

In the Areopagus

Then Paul stood in the midst of the Areopagus and said, "Men of Athens, I perceive that in all things you are very religious; for as I was passing through and considering the objects of your worship, I even found an altar with this inscription:
TO THE UNKNOWN GOD.
Therefore, the One whom you worship without knowing, Him I proclaim to you:
God, who made the world and everything in it, since He is Lord of heaven and earth, does not dwell in temples made with hands."

—Acts 17:22–24

The story of Paul in Athens might seem like a strange choice for Christmas Day, but there is more of Christmas here than first meets the eye. Every year tensions emerge in Seventh-day Adventist churches around the world over the appropriateness of observing Christmas. The twenty-fifth of December, after all, is not the day that Christ was born, and most people recognize that the date was plucked from ancient pagan calendars when the Roman Empire was in the process of being Christianized.

The pagan roots of the day are enough to make some people dispense with Christmas altogether, and some become angry when others do not hold the same position. I have seen well-meaning Adventists berate their fellow church members and openly question their commitment to Christ because they acknowledged the day at all.

Should we discard Christmas because of its roots? That is a personal choice. There is no command to observe the birth of Christ in the Bible; neither is there a command forbidding it. If you choose to skip the celebration in order to honor the Lord, by all means do so. It is a perfectly biblical response. But it is also an entirely biblical response to do *something* with the day.

Pay attention to the fact that Paul was utterly comfortable appropriating a pagan altar in order to teach the crowds about the one true Creator God. He was also known to quote pagan poets to make a point. For one single day each year, the world around us is willing—no, feels an *obligation*—to talk about Jesus. Should the voice of the remnant be absent from that discussion?

Consider this: we have the prophetic word confirmed (2 Peter 1:19). There are scores of Old Testament prophecies pointing to the first advent of the Messiah, and we have a ready audience this time of year, willing to listen to those prophecies and be told that they were stunningly accurate. From this, there is a natural springboard to the second advent of Christ; we can show there are *more* prophecies to anticipate.

By all means, if you are uncomfortable, skip it. But be very slow this time of year to condemn those who are willing to stand in the Areopagus and point the world to Christ.

So Others May Live

For you know the grace of our Lord Jesus Christ, that though He was rich,
yet for your sakes He became poor, that you through His poverty might become rich.
—2 Corinthians 8:9

When my wife and I first moved to the United States, we were surprised that most of the American workforce returns to work on December 26. In our home country, Canada—a member of the British Commonwealth—the day after Christmas is Boxing Day, which is another holiday. As a child, however, I had no idea what Boxing Day was about; we were a family of Dutch immigrants. My father used to joke that it was the day when servant children were given the boxes from the rich children's Christmas gifts to play with.

In reality, the origin of Boxing Day has been largely forgotten. Most historians believe the holiday likely stems from the practice of British nobility giving their servants the day off, along with a box of gifts, to thank them for their year-long service and for having to work all day on Christmas entertaining the master's family and guests. Another tradition ties Boxing Day to the Feast of Saint Stephen, during which special offerings were taken for the poor.

In a few places, such as a military academy I recently stumbled across, the day is celebrated with role reversals: leadership trades places for the day with the people they lead. Servants become masters, and masters become servants.

In that sense, members of the remnant church celebrate a sort of Boxing Day every day of their lives. The book of Revelation portrays the last-day remnant church as "the ones who follow the Lamb wherever He goes" (Revelation 14:4), and that would include a willingness to give everything to ensure that sinners can inherit the kingdom of heaven. Jesus willingly became poor so that we can become rich, but this was no day-long exchange: His gift places us in heavenly places *forever.*

"Christ was treated as we deserve," Ellen White explains, "that we might be treated as He deserves. He was condemned for our sins, in which He had no share, that we might be justified by His righteousness, in which we had no share. He suffered the death which was ours, that we might receive the life which was His."★

You will know the remnant people of God when you find those who are willing to do the same—give selflessly so that others may live.

★ Ellen G. White, *The Desire of Ages* (Mountain View, CA: Pacific Press®, 1898), 25.

"Well Done"

Do you not know that those who run in a race all run, but one receives the prize? Run in such a way that you may obtain it. And everyone who competes for the prize is temperate in all things. Now they do it to obtain a perishable crown, but we for an imperishable crown.
—1 Corinthians 9:24, 25

A soldier who had been mortally wounded on the battlefield was barely clinging to life in a field hospital. The doctors knew he was not going to survive, and they marveled at his stubborn refusal to die. He was obviously holding out for something. When his commander arrived, they finally understood why he was still hanging on. Leaning over the cot, the senior officer gently asked, "How are you, Son?" knowing full well that the outlook was grim.

The young man looked up, and when he saw the face of his commander, his painful grimace vanished for a moment. "I'm going to be OK," came the weak reply, "but I need to know something. Is my commander pleased?"

"Yes. More than pleased. You've been an excellent soldier." A trace of a smile faintly passed across the soldier's lips for a moment; then he sighed deeply and let go of life.

When we become part of God's last-day movement, we are resigning from the world. Its values are no longer our values, and we no longer seek the applause of men. We willingly give up the all-too-human dream of seeing our name in lights or achieving what the world might consider success. The name of God is being written on our foreheads, and we willingly surrender the entire course of our lives to His cause.

As we navigate the challenges of life, there is but one form of applause we crave: we want to know that our Commander is pleased. We know that the world does not possess the eternal perspective or the right metrics with which to assess our characters. We do not care if we never make a splash on the evening news or have a star placed on Hollywood's Walk of Fame because we know that the applause of men is fleeting and meaningless. It is not a trophy, a plaque, or a recognition dinner that we desire; we wish to know that God is smiling as we pass to our rest. We want to hear the Spirit whisper, "Well done, good and faithful servant" (Matthew 25:21).

"A great name among men is as letters traced in sand," Ellen White reminds us, "but a spotless character will endure to all eternity."★

★ Ellen G. White, *Testimonies for the Church* (Nampa, ID: Pacific Press®, 2002), 5:578.

Just as We Are One

"I do not pray for these alone, but also for those who will believe in Me through their word;
that they all may be one, as You, Father, are in Me, and I in You; that they also may be one in
Us, that the world may believe that You sent Me. And the glory which You gave Me
I have given them, that they may be one just as We are one."
—John 17:20–22

Most Christians instinctively understand that God intends unity for His church, and we know that God expects us to get along. "By this all will know that you are My disciples," Jesus taught His followers, "if you have love for one another" (John 13:35).

When you consider Christian unity in light of Jesus' prayer, however, it becomes obvious that what God intends is much more than merely getting along. His purpose is far higher than a church that does not fight. He intends to have a church in which the close relationship between God the Father and God the Son is reproduced, to the point where the will of church members has been so completely intertwined with the will of God that the world will see a people who are "one in Us" and come to believe in Christ.

The doctrine of a triune God suddenly becomes much more than a theological mind-bender best left to seminary classrooms, when it has a practical application in the life of the church. The Bible reveals but one God ("Hear, O Israel: The LORD our God, the LORD is one!" [Deuteronomy 6:4]), but that single Godhead is comprised of Three distinct Persons. Those Three Persons work in such close harmony, however, that Their purposes are one. They are of one mind. They labored together with one purpose to bring the world into existence, to devise the plan of salvation, and to bring history to its rightful close, when the everlasting kingdom of Christ shall be established.

God intends for His people to be of that same mind and to be so closely connected to Him that we share His purposes on earth. It does not mean that we lose our individual identities, any more than the Members of the Godhead are individual Persons. The family of God is not a mindless, faceless collective; no, God has always treated individuals as unique and important. The church, rather, is a purposeful, voluntary blending of hearts that values every individual for who they are.

Perhaps that is part of what it means to have the Father's name inscribed on our foreheads. Our church will be what the Creator intended when together we impulsively share His purpose for this world—the salvation of sinners and the inauguration of the kingdom of Christ.

The Whole Thing

*Let us hear the conclusion of the whole matter: Fear God
and keep His commandments, for this is man's all.*
—Ecclesiastes 12:13

It is easy for Seventh-day Adventists to read the description of God's last-day people—"keep the commandments of God and the faith of Jesus" (Revelation 14:12)—and unconsciously substitute the words "keep the Sabbath" for "keep the commandments." It is understandable, I suppose, given the emphasis we must place on the Sabbath in a world where most Christians value the other nine commandments but treat the fourth as if it were a legalistic burden. It is one of the things that distinguishes our movement from much of the rest of Christendom, and so it naturally stays at the front of our awareness.

At the same time, we cannot afford to forget that the *whole* moral law of God is a snapshot of His character, and as such, the remnant church prizes it all. We might refuse to go to work on the seventh day of the week, but do we prize honesty the same way God does? Do we jealously guard our neighbor's reputation, the way God has guarded ours (in spite of what we have done)? Do we find ourselves asking if we *truly* value human life the way our Creator does, searching for better ways to show the world the inestimable worth of a man, a woman, or a child? Do we shrink from dishonesty so that the world can see that our word is our bond because our Father's Word is always truth? We might not rob banks or convenience stores or embezzle money from work, but do we value intangible things like intellectual property?

The list goes on; it goes on with ten major bullet points, to be exact. At the heart of the commandments is God's requirement to observe the Sabbath and worship Him as Creator, but among God's remnant people, we should find a hunger for the *whole* character of God. It is not merely "the Sabbath" that is written on our foreheads but the very name of God Himself.

Jesus told Philip, "He who has seen Me has seen the Father" (John 14:9) and then He prayed that the world would see Him in us (John 17:21). Our job is not only to present doctrinal truth but to allow the world to catch a glimpse of their Creator and learn to love Him.

Maybe Now Is Better

Then last of all He was seen by me also, as by one born out of due time. For I am the least of the apostles, who am not worthy to be called an apostle, because I persecuted the church of God.
—1 Corinthians 15:8, 9

When Paul identifies himself as the author of the letter to the Galatians, he spends a brief moment defending his position as an apostle: "Paul, an apostle (not from men nor through man, but through Jesus Christ and God the Father who raised Him from the dead)" (Galatians 1:1). His defensive posture is easy to understand: he was not like the other apostles in that he had not spent time with Jesus during His earthly ministry. His commission came later, on the road to Damascus.

When I first arrived at the doorstep of the Seventh-day Adventist Church, I marveled at the rich history behind the movement. As I pored through the stories of early Adventist pioneers, I marveled at the hardships they endured, the privations they suffered, and the sheer magnitude of their faith. I felt the occasional twinge of envy when I saw the answers to prayer they received and noted that they actually witnessed the prophetic gift in their midst.

I was a latecomer, an outsider who showed up after the heavy lifting had been done. I could not claim four or five generations in the church as many of my new friends could. Yet I could not help but notice that my arrival in the church was a fulfillment of prophecy: "Every nation, tribe, tongue, and people" were to be called to God's remnant church (Revelation 14:6). I was among *those* people.

My story may never be found in Adventist history textbooks, but it *was* told in the Bible: I am part of the great response John witnessed in vision. I am also far from alone. In the very near future, if it has not happened already, more than 80 percent of church members will have been born *outside* of the church.

The story of Paul reminds us that being late to the movement does not mean we have missed an opportunity. Paul went on to break open the Gentile world. You and I are now living in the moment our forefathers in the church *wished* they could have seen: the world lighting up with the glory of Christ as another mighty angel descends from heaven to propel this movement to its grand climax.

It would have been great to be there in the beginning; but come to think of it, this moment might even be better.

Welcome Home

Therefore remember that you, once Gentiles in the flesh—who are called Uncircumcision by what is called the Circumcision made in the flesh by hands—that at that time you were without Christ, being aliens from the commonwealth of Israel and strangers from the covenants of promise, having no hope and without God in the world. But now in Christ Jesus you who once were far off have been brought near by the blood of Christ.
—Ephesians 2:11–13

I will always remember the first time I walked through the doors of the Seventh-day Adventist Church. I had never attended a service, nor had I ever been inside the building, yet somehow, the whole place felt familiar. I was *home*—the home I had always known was out there somewhere.

My wife, Jean, and I had just finished taking part in a series of evangelistic meetings and were utterly stunned by the beauty and cohesiveness of the three angels' messages. It rang true for us; it was the picture of Jesus we had both been seeking. It was not just right because it was *factually* right (and it was); it was right because the God who had been whispering to our hearts and teaching us about Himself for years had just pulled back the veil and revealed Himself in undeniable ways.

So when we went to church for the first time, it somehow felt like we had been going there for a very long time. It was familiar because God was in it. It was *His* house, and so it was *our* home. We had not been dreaming when we hoped that such a place existed; we had sensed the eternity that God had placed in our hearts. We had once been far off, as Paul puts it to a Gentile audience who were finding a home among God's people, but now we had been brought near by the blood of Christ.

Every human heart senses that there must be something better, some place where they are meant to be. People live with an uneasy feeling that they are not yet where they are supposed to be. It is crucial for us, as we go about the task of carrying the three angels' messages to "every nation, tribe, tongue, and people" (Revelation 14:6), to remember that we are not inviting them into *our* church. It is theirs. They are not houseguests that we tolerate in our home; it is *their* home.

We are not in the business of trying to convince people that we are right, even though teaching Christ's doctrine is essential. We are in the business of welcoming people home. We are not arguing with people (it never really works); we are showing them where the home they are hoping for can be found.